# Euros and Europeans

Economic and Monetary Union (EMU) is one of the most important developments in modern European politics. Building on two decades of monetary integration it transfers monetary policy, a core function of the modern state, to an independent European Central Bank (ECB) and limits member states' fiscal policy discretion. The ECB insists that growth and employment depend on "flexibilizing" Europe's labor markets through deep reforms of the social policies and employment relations which comprise the "European social model." Member states retain authority over these areas at the heart of national politics, but how will EMU affect the domestic politics of institutional change? Will EMU reinforce deregulation and retrenchment or will it facilitate reforms that maintain the protections against economic insecurity, inequality, and unilateral employer power that the European social model has provided? To address these questions, a transatlantic team of leading experts analyzes the evolving tensions between monetary integration and national social policies.

ANDREW MARTIN is a research affiliate at the Center for European Studies, Harvard University. He is the co-author of *The Brave New World of European Labor* (with George Ross, 1999).

GEORGE ROSS is Morris Hilquit Professor in Labor and Social Thought and Director of the Center for German and European Studies at Brandeis University. His recent books are *The Brave New World of European Labor* (with Andrew Martin, 1999), *Jacques Delors and European Integration* (1995), and *Searching for the New France* (edited with James Hollifield, 1991).

# Euros and Europeans

*Monetary Integration and the European Model of Society*

*Edited by*

Andrew Martin and George Ross

CAMBRIDGE
UNIVERSITY PRESS

PUBLISHED BY THE PRESS SYNDICATE OF THE UNIVERSITY OF CAMBRIDGE
The Pitt Building, Trumpington Street, Cambridge, United Kingdom

CAMBRIDGE UNIVERSITY PRESS
The Edinburgh Building, Cambridge, CB2 2RU, UK
40 West 20th Street, New York, NY 10011–4211, USA
477 Williamstown Road, Port Melbourne, VIC 3207, Australia
Ruiz de Alarcón 13, 28014 Madrid, Spain
Dock House, The Waterfront, Cape Town 8001, South Africa

http://www.cambridge.org

First published 2004

Printed in the United Kingdom at the University Press, Cambridge

*Typeface* Plantin 10/12 pt.     *System* LATEX 2ε   [TB]

*A catalogue record for this book is available from the British Library*

*Library of Congress cataloguing in publication data*
Euros and Europeans : monetary integration and the European model of
society / [edited by] Andrew Martin and George Ross.
   p.   cm.
Includes bibliographical references and index.
ISBN 0-521-83570-4 – ISBN 0-521-54363-0 (pbk.)
1. Euro.   2. Monetary unions – European Union countries.   3. European
Union countries – Social policy.   I. Martin, Andrew, 1929–   II. Ross,
George, 1940–

HG925.E974   2004
332.4′94 – dc22   2003069666

ISBN 0 521 83570 4 hardback
ISBN 0 521 54363 0 paperback

To Anne and Jane

# Contents

# Preface

The culmination of two decades of monetary integration, Economic and Monetary Union (EMU) fundamentally transforms the European political economy. Replacing national currencies with the Euro, EMU shifts monetary policy, the key instrument of macroeconomic policy and a core function of the modern nation state, to the European Central Bank (ECB), the most independent in the world. Although EMU leaves fiscal policy in the hands of the member states, it sharply limits their discretion over its use. In no other policy domain has there been such a centralization of power in a supranational EU institution. By providing increased economic policy autonomy against the forces of globalization, monetary union as such has the potential for enabling Europe to overcome the high unemployment that has increasingly strained the "European social model" since the 1980s. Offsetting this potential, however, EMU institutionalizes a highly restrictive macroeconomic policy regime which subordinates growth and employment to price stability. Unemployment can be reduced consistently with that goal, the ECB insists, only if "rigidities" in Europe's labor markets are eliminated by far-reaching changes in the social policy and employment relations institutions at the heart of the European social model.

The member states retain formal power over those institutions, however. There have been reforms in those institutions in response to problems internal to the national variants of the European social model, as well as pressures from monetary integration. So far, however, the national social models have proved resilient in the face of pressures from the ECB and others for changes making European labor markets as "flexible" as America's, reflecting the widespread commitment of continental and Nordic Europeans to the greater protection against economic insecurity, inequality, and unilateral employer power that the European social model provides. What remains uncertain is how EMU will affect the domestic politics of institutional change over the long run. Will it augment the political resources of domestic actors seeking deregulation and retrenchment, or will it strengthen those endeavoring to improve the efficiency and equity of national social models while preserving high degrees of social protection and labor rights?

Although EMU has not been in existence long enough to answer these questions with any confidence, some insight into its potential effects can be gained from an exploration of the evolving tensions between monetary integration and the politics of change in national social models until now. This is what an interdisciplinary transnational team sets out to do in *Euros and Europeans*.

We want to express our appreciation to the Council for European Studies for a grant enabling the team to come together for two conferences, hosted by the Center for German and European Studies at Brandeis University and the Free University of Brussels, which provided additional support. Andrew Martin is grateful to the German Marshall Fund of the United States for a Fellowship which provided the principal support for his research, and for additional support from the Observatoire Social Européen, Brussels, the Labor Institute of Economic Research, Helsinki, the Institute of Labor and Social Research and Advanced Research on the Europeanization of the Nation-State program, Oslo, as well as for facilities and discussions at the Centre de Sociologie des Organisations, Paris, the Max Planck Institute for the Study of Societies, Cologne, the Wissenschaftszentrum Berlin für Sozialforschung, and the European University Institute, Florence. George Ross would like to thank Toby Harris, Debi Osnowitz, and Jane Jenson for wonderful editorial work and advice, Brandeis University for its support, and Yani Sinanaglou for his help over many years. In addition, both of the editors have benefited greatly from the intellectual stimulation of colleagues at the Center for European Studies, Harvard University. Other sources financed the research of each of the contributors.

In addition to our appreciation to colleagues and conference participants for comments and advice on our own contributions, our main debt of gratitude is to the other contributors to this volume, who wrote and rewrote many drafts in response to our insistent demands. If the volume makes a coherent contribution to understanding the social implications of EMU it is due to their knowledge, creativity, and perseverance.

Belmont and Newton,
September 2003.

# Contributors

JOS DE BEUS, Professor of Political Theory, University of Amsterdam, the Netherlands

VINCENT DELLA SALA, Associate Professor of Political Science, Facoltà di Sociologia, Università di Trento, Italy

JON ERIK DØLVIK, Research Director, Institute of Labor and Social Research (FAFO), Oslo, Norway

KEVIN FEATHERSTONE, Eleftherios Venizelos Professor of Contemporary Greek Studies and Director, Hellenic Observatory, European Institute, Florence; London School of Economics and Political Science, London

MAURIZIO FERRERA, Director, Centre for Comparative Research, Bocconi University, Italy

ANTON HEMERIJCK, Director of the Netherlands Council for Government Policy and Senior Lecturer in the Department of Public Administration, University of Leiden, the Netherlands

ANDREW MARTIN, Research Affiliate, Center for European Studies, Harvard University, US

SOFÍA A. PÉREZ, Associate Professor of Political Science, Boston University, US

PHILIPPE POCHET, Director, Observatoire Social Européen, Brussels, Belgium

GEORGE ROSS, Morris Hilquit Professor in Labor and Social Thought and Director, Center for German and European Studies, Brandeis University; Associate, Center for European Studies, Harvard University, US

ALBERTA M. SBRAGIA, Director, European Union Center and Center for West European Studies and UCIS Research Professor of Political Science, University of Pittsburgh Pittsburgh, US

NICO A. SIEGEL, Lecturer in Social Policy, University of Kent, UK

# 1 Introduction: EMU and the European social model

*Andrew Martin and George Ross*

The political structure of the European economy has been fundamentally transformed by the two decades of monetary integration culminating in Economic and Monetary Union (EMU). Centuries-old national currencies were replaced by the Euro and monetary policy, a core function of the modern state, was transferred to a supranational European Central Bank (ECB). The ECB was endowed with more autonomy from EMU's member states than any other European Union (EU) institution except the European Court of Justice (ECJ) and greater independence than any other central bank in the world. The Stability and Growth Pact (SGP), also applicable to member states remaining outside EMU in addition limited member states' discretion over fiscal policy, their remaining macroeconomic policy instrument.[1] There is no other policy domain where centralization of power in EU institutions has gone so far.

In contrast, the EU's treaty/constitution leaves authority over welfare state and employment relations institutions in member state hands. These institutions largely shape individuals' relation to the economic life of their societies throughout the life course, before, during, and after participation in the labor market. Despite important national differences, these institutions have enough in common in European countries, Britain excepted, to be understood as variants of what Europeans typically refer to as a "European social model." This model is distinguished from the American, or Anglo-Saxon, model by its greater protection against economic insecurity, inequality, and unilateral employer power. Much domestic political conflict and partisan competition is focused on the distributive and normative issues raised by these social models.

These two different institutional arrangements create an EU polity that sharply separates authority over macroeconomic policy from that governing social models. The two domains are highly interdependent,

---

[1] While the 1997 SGP was subsequently incorporated into the Treaty of the European Union (TEU), its operation depends on decisions by the Economic and Financial Council (ECOFIN), comprising member states' finance ministers, which failed to agree on enforcing it against violations by France and Germany (see chapter 3 in this volume).

however. Macroeconomic policy significantly affects the burdens on and resources available to social policy. It also helps shape the distribution of bargaining power among labor market actors. In turn, welfare state and employment relations institutions condition the impact and effectiveness of macroeconomic policy measures.

Throughout the first three postwar decades these two policy domains interacted within national political economies. Issues raised in both were contested in the same political arenas and by broadly similar democratic political constellations. To some extent, policies for each domain mutually reinforced one another, as captured by the term "Keynesian welfare state."[2] Economic growth, helped by government commitments to full employment, provided resources for growth in monetary and social wages, assured demand for increased output, and dampened conflict over distribution. Broad political support for national variants of the European social model flowed from this. Now that power over key macroeconomic policy decisions has been shifted away from the national political arenas in which social model issues are decided, however, the question is whether the macroeconomic foundations of the European social model will be maintained. This is the basic question addressed in this volume.

Expectations that European integration could threaten national social protection and labor market regulation is not new. Indeed it was evident from the very start of what became the EU. Negotiations for the 1957 Rome Treaty succeeded only because France, fearing that the proposed customs union would undermine its forms of social protection, won significant concessions on social and agricultural policy. As it turned out, the customs union and national social models then growing to maturity coexisted fruitfully. When the original Common Market gave way to the single market program in the 1986 Single European Act (SEA), anxiety was renewed. The SEA aimed to remove non-tariff barriers (NTBs) and assure the free movement of "goods, services, capital, and labor." In time, this was meant to transform Europe from separate national economies linked within the Common Market to a genuine single economy. Many feared that the results might undercut national capacities and practices in social policy areas, particularly through "social dumping." Development of the single market thus far has not confirmed these fears.

Any threat that monetary union, the third and biggest step in European integration, might pose does not flow automatically from the single currency and centralization of monetary and exchange rate policies. For European countries, the utility of national monetary instruments was already greatly circumscribed by volatile international financial markets

---

[2] The mutually reinforcing character of policies in the two areas was emphasised in the French *régulation* and similar literatures. See Marglin and Schor (1990).

and, within Europe, the dominance of the German Bundesbank (Buba). Monetary union was an alternative. The incorporation of the separate European economies within a large, relatively closed regional economy with a single currency could provide a degree of insulation from disturbances in the international economy, while management of the currency by a supranational central bank would eliminate Bundesbank power. In principle, therefore, prospects for reducing the high unemployment that Europe had suffered since the 1980s could improve. This could in turn facilitate the reconfiguration of the European social model to preserve high social protection and labor standards, improving their equity and efficiency, and adapting them to new needs.

Whether or not monetary union actually achieves such positive results depends on its specific design and operation. Our analysis suggests that it may not, and that the intergovernmental politics of monetary integration has channeled EMU in a direction that is more likely to threaten the European social model's viability than to facilitate its rejuvenation. Our major reason for claiming this (elaborated in chapter 2 in this volume) is that EMU's dedication to price stability, and the ways in which the ECB is likely to pursue this dedication, will keep EU employment levels lower than those needed to nourish the European model. On the other hand, our analysis also suggests that national variants of the European model have considerable resilience, and that the national politics of social model change may refract the pressures generated by EMU in directions that preserve high degrees of social protection and labor rights. How the tensions between highly centralized macroeconomic policy and decentralized national social model policies play out is contingent on the dynamics of domestic politics, which are likely to feed back into the continuing evolution of monetary union, as demonstrated by intensified controversy over the SGP in 2003. But as also demonstrated by this controversy, conflicting interests of member states can create stalemate and possibly even crisis in the construction of Europe.

These conclusions, cautious and tentative as they are, flow from the exploration of the tensions between monetary integration and national social models in this volume. In this introduction, we first sketch the politics of monetary integration that gave monetary union the form it has. Then we discuss the European social model and the politics of change in its national variants. Finally, we indicate how the interaction of these two streams of politics will be analyzed in the chapters that follow.

## 1    Europe and the politics of monetary integration

From the rubble of the Second World War, the architects of European integration came to believe that binding European nations to one another was the best way to achieve lasting peace.[3] Directly joining European states within a common political structure, such as a "United States of Europe," was unrealistic, however. The strategy that emerged was to pursue common economic projects and build new European institutions to carry them out. This meant that each step in European integration was contingent on a confluence of economic interests, as perceived by governments and key domestic actors.

Monetary integration did not reach the agenda until European institutions had been built around other economic projects. The first application of the economic approach was the European Coal and Steel Community (ECSC) in 1951. The Rome Treaty of 1957, signed by the original ECSC six – France, Germany, Italy, Belgium, the Netherlands, and Luxembourg, then added the European Economic Community (EEC) and Euratom. The institutions that the Rome Treaty established – Council of Ministers, Commission, Parliament (EP), and Court (ECJ) – provided the basic political structures until EMU added the ECB.

The EEC, or Common Market, placed the member states within a customs-free zone for trade in manufactured goods with a common external tariff, special arrangements for agriculture (the Common Agricultural Policy, CAP) plus a few other common policies. The Common Market stimulated trade between member states and more rapid economic growth and modernization in general, helping to carry Western Europe's postwar economic boom to its apogee.[4] Intra-EEC politics in the 1960s, in particular French objections to supranationalization, assured that the Common Market was compatible with national development paths and the large degrees of national autonomy that went with them.

The first important initiative toward monetary integration was the 1970 Werner Report proposing that EMU be achieved in three stages by 1980.[5] Before this proposal could get very far, however, Europe's economic world changed dramatically. Inflation shot up, fueled by American policies around the Vietnam War as well as internal European factors, such as labor militancy, and the American abandonment of the Bretton Woods system in 1971 plunged the European monetary world into confusion.

---

[3] On grand integration theory see Rosamond (2000) and Moravcsik (1998).

[4] "Europe" has had different names. The European Economic Community (EEC) was the Common Market component of the Rome Treaty. The European Communities (EC) was created by a 1960s Treaty uniting the EEC, Euratom, and ECSC under one legal roof. The European Union (EU) began in 1993 with ratification of the Maastricht Treaty on European Union (TEU).

[5] The following draws upon Ludlow (1982); De Grauwe (1994); Henning (1994, 1998); Padoa-Schioppa (1994); Eichengreen (1996); Tsoukalis (1997); Cameron (1998); McNamara (1998); Moravcsik (1998); Dyson and Featherstone (1999); Heisenberg (1999); Verdun (2000); Magnusson and Stråth (2001); Collignon (2002); Jones (2003).

The ensuing economic crisis was aggravated by the first Organization of Petroleum-Exporting Countries (OPEC) oil shock, which was simultaneously contractionary and inflationary. The divergent policy responses of EU members challenged the European Community's fragile equilibrium, making it virtually impossible to decide anything, let alone innovate. Implementing the Werner Report was thus forgotten.

European monetary relationships nevertheless stayed on the agenda because of dangers to EEC and national stability from fluctuating exchange rates. A series of efforts was made to stabilize exchange rates among the increasingly integrated European economies, including a joint float against the dollar, "snakes" linking a varying set of European currencies to each other, and the European Monetary System (EMS), established in 1978. The fundamental difficulty these efforts encountered stemmed from diversity in inflation rates. This produced recurrent conflicts over responsibility for adjusting domestic economic policy to maintain parities between high- and low-inflation countries, most importantly between France and Germany. The German position – usually but not always that of the Bundesbank – repeatedly prevailed. This was crucial in shaping the course of monetary integration and assuring that it would be institutionalized in a form giving primacy to price stability.

The Bundesbank, freed from the obligation to support the D-mark:dollar exchange rate by the collapse of Bretton Woods, declared in 1973 that its monetary policy would henceforth be dedicated to domestic price stability. In fact, low inflation was integral to Germany's highly successful export-based growth strategy but its effectiveness was contingent on exchange rate stability between Germany and its European trading partners. As long as Germany's inflation was lower while nominal exchange rates remained unchanged, Germany's exporters gained competitive advantage from real depreciation of the D-mark. This gave higher-inflation countries a stake in currency arrangements that imposed symmetrical adjustment obligations on both strong and weak currencies, while it gave Germany a stake in resisting such arrangements. Germany's effort at combining internal and external nominal stability within Europe was further complicated by global exchange rate volatility.[6] Germany needed to keep inflation differentials from being so large as to make intra-European exchange rate stability unsustainable. Whenever realignment became irresistible, therefore, Germany typically sought to minimize its

[6] Wide fluctuations in the dollar's value exerted divergent pressures on European currencies, mostly upward on the D-mark and downward on the higher-inflation countries. Besides straining intra-European parities, this resulted in capital inflows that had to be prevented from easing monetary conditions in Germany.

size and make it conditional on the adoption of disinflationary policies in the weak-currency countries.

Establishment of the EMS, the first actual step toward monetary integration, ended up strengthening Germany's capacity to pursue these objectives. EMS originated in a deal struck by Helmut Schmidt, the German Chancellor, and Valéry Giscard d'Estaing, President of France. Schmidt, concerned about economic growth, sought to blunt upward pressures on the D-mark by bringing France, Germany's largest trade partner, back into exchange rate coordination, after France's second exit from the snake. Seizing the opportunity for France to recapture a leading role in Europe, Giscard also welcomed the external support for disinflation that coordination required, provided that the burden of adjustment would be shared, which meant more expansionary policy in Germany. Knowing the Bundesbank's opposition to any arrangements impinging on its freedom of action, Schmidt initially bypassed it. But needing the bank's support, he eventually agreed to technical provisions that "fundamentally altered how the EMS would operate over the coming years" (Henning 1994: 188).[7]

All EC member states belonged to the EMS, but only those who chose to participate were in the Exchange Rate Mechanism (ERM).[8] Exchange rates of ERM members were defined bilaterally with one another, forming a "parity grid" which they were committed to maintain within +/− 2.25 percent.[9] When currencies ran up against these limits, central banks were obliged to intervene. The D-mark was *de facto* at the center of the grid and divergence from the D-mark became the trigger to action, putting pressure on members to converge toward low German inflation rates rather than the higher average of all EC members. Exchange rates could be realigned if actions to support the rates were insufficient, but realignment required the unanimous consent of ERM members. This put Germany, and particularly the Bundesbank, in a position to make measures, typically disinflationary, a condition for allowing a devaluation by the "offending" country. *De facto*, therefore, through EMS the "Bundesbank took control of Europe."[10]

EMS thus perpetuated the asymmetrical distribution of adjustment burdens. Renewed efforts by weak-currency countries to remedy this by

---

[7] Heisenberg concludes that "the German government essentially used a bait-and-switch tactic to get the commitment of France to the system" (1999: 71). Although endorsed by a European Council resolution, the EMS was not formally an EC arrangement. Its rules were embodied in an agreement among EC central banks which were responsible for managing the system (Henning 1994: 189).

[8] Britain stayed out until much later.

[9] A +/−6 percent limit in the case of Italy and new members.

[10] The title of chapter 3 of Riché and Wyplosz (1993).

moving toward EMU were launched after the failure of the French Left experiment with "social democracy in one country" following the election of François Mitterrand in 1981 (see chapter 4 in this volume). The new French administration was initially committed to expansionary policies that challenged EMS and created new Franco-German tensions. By March 1983, facing EMS negotiation over a third devaluation, the French had to choose between pulling out of the ERM to salvage their post-1981 reformism, possibly ending EMS altogether and European integration along with it, or staying in and making its domestic policies consistent with the Bundesbank design for the EMS. Mitterrand made the second choice and the EMS survived. With that choice, France joined the countries switching to a price stability regime, albeit at a high cost for French employment. In time, France's choice would become a strategy to strengthen the franc against the D-mark to reinforce French positions in EMS negotiations.

Having made this decisive "choice for Europe," Mitterrand turned to regenerating European integration, opening the way for the new Jacques Delors-led European Commission that drafted the 1985 White Paper on completing the Single Market by 1992, followed by the SEA, ratified in 1987. The SEA made no provision for macroeconomic management, but the Commission succeeded in inserting vague references about European monetary policy (Article 102a). Moreover, the SEA's commitment to the free movement of capital as well as goods, services, and people entailed the abolition of remaining exchange controls.

EMU officially re-emerged as a result of new Franco-German disagreements. As in the past, these were exacerbated by the disruptive effects of D-mark:dollar movements on intra-European exchange rate stability. After the 1985 Plaza Accord, which reversed the dollar's extreme appreciation, the Bundesbank as usual refused to abandon its strictly German domestic point of view. This led French Finance Minister Edouard Balladur to come out for EMU, an ECB, and a single currency, adding that "the European Monetary System should resist the influence of countries with the most restrictive monetary policies" (Heisenberg 1999: 100). Hans-Dietrich Genscher, Germany's Foreign Minister, welcomed the French initiative, to the Bundesbank's dismay. In 1988, the European Council set up a committee to plan EMU. Chaired by Delors, it consisted of central bankers. This, as well as the pre-existing Committee of Central Bank Governors which later drafted the details, enabled the Bundesbank to press its position that any "future European monetary order . . . is not geared to stability to a lesser extent . . . than . . . at present in the Federal Republic of Germany" (Heisenberg 1999: 106). By insisting on provisions designed to assure that this would not be acceptable to other governments, the Bundesbank anticipated that it could prevent EMU from ever happening.

The Delors committee's Report (submitted in April 1989) incorporated many of the Bundesbank's demands. The German government was divided, with some sharing the Bundesbank's continued opposition to the whole idea. The international context after the fall of the Berlin Wall tipped the balance within the Kohl government, however. In exchange for the French supporting German unification (Mitterrand initially reacted negatively) the Maastricht EMU negotiations were scheduled to begin in the fall of 1990.

The resulting Treaty satisfied most German concerns. It created an EMU with a single European currency managed by a European System of Central Banks (ESCB) consisting of an ECB and member states' central banks.[11] Price stability was defined as the ESCB's "primary objective." The ECSB had also to "support the general economic policies in the Community," including "a high level of employment and social protection," but only insofar as this primary objective was attained (Articles 2 and 105).[12] In addition, the Treaty left it up to the Bank to both define price stability and decide when and how it could support a high level of employment without prejudice to price stability. The degree of restrictiveness of the EMU regime would thus depend mainly on the Bank's interpretation of its mandate, and the Bank was left free to interpret this mandate as it saw fit. Its legal basis in a treaty was changeable only by the member states' unanimous agreement, making it the most independent central bank in the world.[13] In addition, the independence of national central banks was made a condition for national membership in EMU. Neither the ECB nor national central banks were to "seek or take instructions" from any EU bodies or member state governments, which in turn "undertake to respect this principle and not seek to influence . . . the

---

[11] All EU member central banks belong to the European System of Central Banks (ESCB) set up by the Treaty but central banks of non-EMU members (Denmark, Sweden, and the UK) do not participate in the ECB's decision bodies. These are the Executive Board, consisting of the President, Vice-President and four other members, appointed by the "common accord of the the Heads of State or Government" of the EMU member states, and the Governing Council, consisting of the Executive Board and governors of the member state central banks. These comprise the "Eurosystem" as opposed to the ESCB. The Council makes the monetary policy decisions. (ECB 2001e: 9–11).

[12] This is almost exactly the formulation in the Bundesbank's statute. It contrasts starkly with the US Federal Reserve Bank's "dual mandate" to pursue not only price stability but growth and employment as well.

[13] In contrast to a legislative majority, as in the case of other central banks, including the Bundesbank prior to EMU as well as the US Federal Reserve Bank and the Bank of England.

decision-making bodies of the ECB or of the national central banks"
(Article 108).

The ECB's independence was reinforced by what was omitted from
EMU. Unlike other central banks, the ECB was not embedded in an
institutional environment – a *gouvernement économique*, as French governments have sought – within which it shared political responsibility for
macroeconomic policy, and it had no supranational fiscal policy counterpart.[14] Fiscal policy was left in the hands of member states but the SGP
strictly limited their ability to use it to combat recessions. The only formal mechanism concerning member states' fiscal policies was the surveillance procedure by which the Commission and the Council of Economic
and Finance Ministers (ECOFIN) monitored compliance with the SGP
(chapter 3 in this volume). There were no mechanisms for coordinating
the member states' fiscal policies to construct a fiscal stance for Euroland
as a whole, much less for coordinating fiscal policy and monetary policy to
arrive at an optimal policy mix. Thus, while EMU severely constrained
fiscal policy as a macroeconomic policy instrument – even tending to
make fiscal policy pro-cyclical – it made macroeconomic policy for the
eurozone as a whole the exclusive prerogative of an exceptionally powerful
central bank.

There are Euro-level forums where the ECB must or may explain its
decisions and hear criticisms: the EP, Commission, ECOFIN, the smaller
informal Euro Group of EMU member state finance ministers, the Economic and Financial Committee which prepares ECOFIN and Euro
Group meetings, plus the semi-annual Macroeconomic Dialog, where
the ECB, the troika of Euro Group presidents, the two relevant Commission Directorates, and the European-level organizations of employers and unions meet to discuss the economic situation.[15] But with one
exception, none of these bodies has any authority over macroeconomic
policy instruments, in none can binding commitments be made about
any aspect of the policy mix, and in none of these contexts can there be
negotiations over the eurozone policy mix with the ECB, which regards

---

[14] The EU's budget of 1.27 percent of aggregate GDP has little macroeconomic significance.

[15] The ECB president may attend ECOFIN meetings (which include EU member states not
belonging to EMU) and the ECOFIN President and a Commission member may attend
ECB Board meetings, but none has voting rights in each other's decision bodies. The
ECB President or Vice-President is invited to attend the meetings of the Euro Group,
which has no decision-making authority, however. The Euro Group has no formal legal
status. The Macroeconomic Dialog was established by the 1999 Cologne European
Council.

such negotiations as infringements on its independence.[16] The exception is the Euro exchange rate, about which the Council is authorized to take positions by qualified majority vote, subject to consultation with the ECB to assure consistency with price stability.[17] While no central bank, including the ECB, can entirely ignore the political context in which it operates, the ECB enjoys exceptional insulation from political actors subject to democratic accountability (Jabko 2001).

Maastricht, like the Delors Report and Werner Plan, specified a staged transition to EMU. The first stage was deemed already to have begun in 1990 with the liberalization of capital movement prescribed in the SEA. Stage Two would begin in 1994 with the creation of the European Monetary Institute (EMI) to monitor compliance with the five convergence criteria determining eligibility. The criteria were: inflation levels and interest rates close to an average of the three best records in the EU, annual budget deficits lower than 3 percent, cumulative debt less than 60 percent of GDP, and currencies that have been in the ERM "narrow band" for at least two years. EMU would go into effect in Stage Three. It could begin as early as January 1997 if a majority of member states were eligible but in January 1999 no matter how many qualified. Setting a fixed final date for movement to Stage Three was a last-minute victory for the French (backed by the Italians) that might have ensured that EMU actually happened, because passage through the three stages turned out to be very difficult.

Extremely contractionary Bundesbank policies in 1992 to counter inflationary pressures from unification dragged Europe into deep recession and EMS crisis. Potential EMU members suddenly faced much more daunting prospects. The Germans and the Bundesbank then tightened the screws even more, insisting in 1996 on the need for a "stability and growth pact" to continue key convergence criteria beyond the beginning

---

[16] Only ECOFIN has authority to make decisions binding on member states, primarily in the form of legislation within the EU's areas of legal competence. It also adopts the annual Basic Economic Policy Guidelines (BEPGs), embodying recommendations for policy actions to member states, and not the ECB, largely aimed at securing budget discipline and not the coordination of fiscal policy as part of a eurozone macroeconomic policy mix. From the ECB's standpoint, there can be no question of "*ex ante* coordination of macroeconomic policy between other bodies and the ECB" (Issing 2002: 350–351). The Economic and Financial Committee of national, EU, and ECB officials which prepares ECOFIN meetings "consciously refrains from discussing the conduct of monetary policy" (ECB 2000d: 59). This is true of the Commission as well, though not of the EP or Macroeconomic Dialog meetings.

[17] This seems to have no practical significance, especially since the Euro floats against other currencies.

of EMU.[18] Nonetheless, in May 1998 eleven member states qualified and EMU was successfully launched on January 1, 1999.[19]

## 2    The European social model and its national variants

In European debates, the "European social model" (or model of society) refers to the institutional arrangements comprising the welfare state (transfer payments, collective social services, their financing) and the employment relations system (labor law, unions, collective bargaining). The general term "social model" refers to "ideal-types" in the Weberian sense, conceptual abstractions of distinctive and central commonalities derived from a variety of empirical situations. Ideal-types are designed to help social analysis by virtue of their capacity for elucidating the underlying similarities and differences across a range of complex social phenomena.[20]

Social models are conceptualizations of the ways in which different types of societies construct social interdependence – i.e. what citizens owe to one another and how such obligations are created, decided, and organized. Modern market democratic social models – as opposed to those in authoritarian, feudal, or slave societies – distribute obligations among interdependent members differently and unequally located in the division of labor and economically related to each other primarily by market transactions regulated by politically constructed institutions. They combine public policies, market mechanisms, and kinship relations in different ways. In general, they structure individuals' access to resources through income from work and its alternatives, such as transfers and public provision (e.g. education and healthcare), before, during, and after the stages in life when they participate in the labor market. They thereby affect how and to what extent individuals are subjected to and protected from

---

[18] The pact was incorporated into the Amsterdam Treaty in 1997.

[19] The UK and Denmark had opted out at Maastricht, Sweden decided not to join, and Greece did not qualify until 2000. Euro notes and coins were introduced without incident in the first weeks of 2002.

[20] For those unfamiliar with its sociological use, an ideal-type is not a value-laden or utopian statement of what analysts might think desirable. Instead "An ideal type is formed by the one-sided accentuation of one or more points of view and by the synthesis of a great many diffuse, discrete, more or less present and occasionally absent *concrete individual* phenomena, which are arranged according to those one-sidedly emphasised viewpoints into a unified *analytical* construct" (Max Weber, in Coser 1977: 223–224, emphasis in the original). Ideal-types are most often used in the construction of comparative taxonomies. They are abstract and not, strictly speaking, falsifiable. Instead they are "useful" to the degree to which they capture the central elements of the complex phenomena they seek to typify.

typical biographical risks (unemployment, disability, poverty, illness, old age) throughout the life course. These forms of insulation from the vicissitudes of the labor market interact with institutions that organize other markets, such as those for products and capital, to influence the relative bargaining power of employees and employers and forms of work organization. The resulting distribution of income from work and property and the allocation of resources between individual and collective forms of demand is in turn altered by taxation and related mechanisms for tapping the flow of income. Through all these mechanisms, social models decisively shape the structure of social stratification and the ways individuals are socialized and recruited into different social roles.

In the European social model, localized in Western and Northern continental Europe, welfare state and employment relations' institutions have historically been combined in ways that make citizenship, more than markets and/or families, the most significant axis of solidarity. The European model is most pertinently compared with the American – or, more generally, Anglo-American – model (including the UK, Canada, New Zealand, and Australia) that relies much more on markets and individual choice than public institutions and collective choice. The European model has comparatively higher levels of taxes and transfers, extensive legal regulation of labor markets, and more fully institutionalized bargaining between legitimate "social partners." The transfer payments to counter the risks of lost earnings from unemployment, health problems, old age, and other accidents of the life course are more generous (i.e. levels of coverage and replacement rates tend to be higher). Protection against arbitrary managerial power is greater in areas such as hiring and firing and workplace health and safety. Poverty is lower and inequality and insecurity in the face of market forces more limited. These features of the European model reflect the comparatively large role that public decisions reached through democratic processes play in defining obligations of social solidarity, determining terms of employment, supplying alternatives to employment income, and shaping general life chances.

Moving from ideal-type to reality reveals as many variants of the European model as there are Western European countries, each reflecting distinctive historical and political developments. Following Richard Titmuss and, more recently, Gøsta Esping-Andersen, social models can be clustered in terms of their welfare states, identifying the arrangements in the six continental country cases we analyze as "conservative" or "corporatist."[21] Welfare states are only part of a social model, however.

---

[21] Esping-Andersen (1990, 1999); see also the chapters by Daly, Guillén and Alvarez, Kosonen, and Ginsburg in Sykes *et al.* (2001). Modifying Esping-Andersen's "three

Students of employment relations systems, who have not yet developed a similarly accepted typology, have focused particularly on variations in wage-setting structures, contrasting those in which there is coordination across the economy with those in which wage-setting is highly decentralized.[22] Finally, recent work analyzing the "varieties of capitalism" has focused on the interaction and interdependence of different social model components and other institutions, emphasizing complementarities among institutions that jointly support particular "production regimes" (Hall and Soskice 2001).[23] By identifying linkages not only between different social policy and employment relations institutions but also between them and other institutions that support distinctive production regimes, this approach points to a broader range of stakeholders than in most recent analyses of the politics of the worlds of welfare.[24]

These available schemes do not enable us to categorize European social models precisely, but they clarify significant differences and also suggest that as a group they have enough in common to distinguish them from other models. The schemes also stress that the institutional ingredients of broadly similar social models are more or less "tightly coupled" in distinctive ways, providing us with clues to the politics of social model change. A particular institution will have different social effects depending on a wide array of other institutions governing wage-setting, public services, and pensions, and these effects can also be expected to structure the institution's constellation of support.[25] More broadly, the institutional complexes defining social models have identifiable effects

worlds of welfare," the continental cases are often grouped into Bismarckian "conservative" or "corporatist," Nordic "social democratic" or "universalist," and Southern "dual" or "familist" categories, all of which are contrasted with the Anglo-American "liberal" or "residual" category.

[22] The former are often designated as "corporatist" or "neocorporatist" while the latter are designated by some as "pluralist." See chapter 12 in this volume.

[23] Its focus on two paradigmatic "varieties" ("coordinated" and "uncoordinated" market economies) makes it somewhat unwieldy for understanding societies that deviate from these polar types Among our cases, Germany is the paradigm for a "coordinated market economy" but the others diverge widely.

[24] Those stakeholders are seen as a major source of a "status quo bias," adding to path dependence, constitutional factors, and the dynamics of party competition in explaining why national institutional complexes show strong tendencies to persist in the face of pressures for change (Wood 2001). An effort has been made to combine the worlds of welfare and varieties of capitalism approaches in comparing models of "welfare capitalism" in Ebbinghaus and Manow (2001).

[25] To illustrate, strong legal employment protection in Italy, currently an object of intense conflict between the Berlusconi government and unions, gives strong job security to full-time adult, predominantly male, employees, at the expense of youth and women. But in the absence of adequate public provision for childcare and generally available unemployment benefits the families of the advantaged "insider" male breadwinner have a strong stake in his job security, contributing to the persistence of Italy's "familialist" version of the Bismarckian welfare state while also reducing fertility among women choosing to

around which multiple constituencies combine to form coalitions of support. Associated with those functional effects, social models are subject to characteristic vulnerabilities to pressures for change while possible policy responses to such vulnerabilities are limited by the support coalitions (chapter 11 in this volume; Scharpf 2000; Pierson 2001a). From this perspective, the resilience of most variants of the European social model is understandable.

Yet some change has occurred, and more will come. For us, the question is how to explain it. "Globalization," or at least increasing integration into the international economy, has been widely cited as one main cause. The distinctive institutional configurations of social model institutions are then invoked to explain divergent responses to this common challenge, including resistance. In this view, the causes of change in national social models are thus conceived as predominantly exogenous. Such exogenous pressures are undoubtedly at work, especially in Europe where they have been powerfully exerted by monetary integration and EMU. But this view overlooks endogenous causes that may be as important.

The importance of endogenous pressures with respect to welfare states has been forcefully stressed by Paul Pierson, who argues that "fundamental symptoms of declining governmental capacity and mounting budgetary stress would clearly be with us even in the absence of trends associated with globalization." He attributes the "unprecedented budgetary stress" facing welfare states "to . . . 'post-industrial' changes occurring within advanced industrial societies themselves" (Pierson 2001a: 98, 82). Four are at work, Pierson claims. The first is slowdown in productivity and economic growth associated with the shift from manufacturing to services. This makes it increasingly difficult for welfare states to meet demands generated by the second change, the expansion and "maturation" of welfare state commitments.[26] New demographic patterns (mainly population aging) then causes dependency ratios to rise even more and aging increases health expenditures. Finally, changing household structures and increasing female labor force participation shifts the challenges facing welfare states. Smaller households, often with more single parents,

---

participate in the labor market (chapter 6 in this volume). In contrast, strong job security combined with abundant public childcare and generous income maintenance has facilitated high labor market participation in Sweden without a corresponding decline in fertility. However, an equally generous welfare state and a strong workplace presence have evidently led Danish unions to accept very low employment protection, while female labor force participation (and union membership) is also high as in Sweden (Esping-Andersen 1999).

[26] Benefits increase and are extended to cover more risks as the portions of the population becoming eligible for them increases. This is particularly the case for pensions, as more cohorts qualifying for full pensions retire.

create new caring needs for services outside the family that women previously provided without pay. Because the first three changes create financial problems, confronting such new needs implies redistribution from other programs that is likely to be resisted by those who regard such programs as rights.

Pierson's argument illustrates some ways in which endogenous pressure on social models can trigger distributive conflict along new cleavage lines. Similar analyses can be made concerning endogenous pressures on employment relations. Sectoral shifts and accompanying changes in skill demands and work organization, the changing gender composition of the labor force, and, most fundamentally perhaps, the difficulty of reconciling low unemployment with low inflation, all generate pressures for change in the governance of employment relations. These too are pressures that could still arise in the absence of changes in the international economy.[27]

The argument that different types of social models exhibit distinctive vulnerabilities to pressures for change and politically constrained possibilities for policy response applies as much to endogenous as exogenous pressure. It is not clear how far it goes in explaining actual policy, however. There is some truth in Michael Shalev's observation that "Countries cluster on policy because they cluster on politics."[28] Strong and slowly changing cleavage patterns, rooted in evolving deep social structures and organized by parties with their respective ideological orientations in the context of distinct and durable state traditions have been decisive in shaping worlds of welfare and employment relations.[29] Coupled with new constituencies built up around components of social models, these political constellations contribute to the models' persistence (Manow 2001).

However, such political constellations are subject to slow erosion or transformation by long-term tendencies, some related to Pierson's "post-industrial changes" and others not – changing class structures, declining class and confessional identities, and the mediatization of electoral politics. They are also subject to abrupt disturbances. We repeatedly encounter the decisive intervention of unique events like the implosion of the party system in Italy, sudden successes by fringe personalities in realigning electorates around new issues (as recently in the Netherlands,

---

[27] It is well known that some advanced capitalist countries with especially high exposure to the international economy are among those with relatively high union density and highly regulated labor markets, notably the Nordic countries but also Germany. On the importance of the large sectoral shift from industry to services, analogous to but different in some important respects from the shift from agriculture to industry, see Iversen (2001).

[28] Quoted in Pierson (2001b: 429).

[29] On the importance of state traditions in shaping labor movements, see Crouch (1993).

Denmark, and France). Waves of change can sweep across several countries as well, pendulum swings reacting to government failures to cope with common problems like the mid-1990s shift to the center left and the more recent shift to the center right. Governing parties can even lose elections despite policies that seem effective, as the French Socialists learned in 2002. The course of politics, in other words, is highly contingent.

In order to understand actual trajectories of change it is therefore necessary to go beyond the general political logic of countries sharing similar social models. In addition, one has to examine the ways that distinctive vulnerabilities are translated into the political issues around which domestic conflict is structured, how they are linked to other, sometimes unrelated, issues, and how policies are devised and implemented in response to them. These processes are all contingent on political institutions, party systems and structures, the roles played by interest groups, and the sometimes unpredictable dynamics of electoral competition.

To trace the specific trajectories of change in individual national political arenas, however, it is not sufficient to analyze the ways in which the endogenous pressures for change enter into domestic politics. While there would be such endogenous pressures even without globalization or European integration, domestic political conflict over social model issues has nevertheless taken place in the context of changing external environments. It is highly implausible that this context has had no effect on how the politics of social model change plays out. For European countries, the change in the external environment that matters most is European integration. The far-reaching reallocation of policy jurisdictions to European institutions makes Euro-level decisions a direct constraint on national policy options. National trajectories of social model change can be understood only by analyzing how these pressures from the integration process enter member states' domestic politics and there interact with endogenous pressures. This is what we set out to do in *Euros and Europeans*.

## 3    Euros and Europeans

Where does *Euros and Europeans* fit? It belongs to the growing body of research looking at the political effects of EMU and monetary integration on EU national states and national politics.[30] Work in this area focuses on the effects of EMU on the "Europeanization" of national politics. EMU, to cite Kenneth Dyson, "alters the configuration of strategic constraints and opportunities within which actors behave, privileging certain actors and certain courses of action. It also changes the way in which

---

[30] Dyson (2002) has a substantial bibliography. The book itself provides an excellent survey of key issues in Europeanization.

domestic actors define their interests and form their identities" (Dyson 2002: 3). "Europeanization" is an elusive concept, however (Radaelli 2000). It can mean the adoption of European perspectives by national actors (particular elites) as a result of participation in and interaction with Euro-level policies and politics. It can also mean the relative degree of congruence between European and national policy-making levels in different policies areas, hypothesizing that mismatches are likely to lead to national reforms. Yet another angle measures the effect of Euro-political initiatives on national convergence and/or divergence on European norms.

National actor interaction with Euro-level policy and politics clearly can have any number of outcomes. *Euros and Europeans*, by examining complex interactions over time between monetary integration and national variants of the European social model, researches the effects of the single most important and supranational step in European integration on the single most important areas still reserved to national politics. Our inquiry thus confronts some very large issues. First of all, if we are correct in choosing to use the concept of "European social model," "Europeanization," in terms of the relative convergence of Western European welfare state and employment relations toward similar institutional configurations, *pre-dated* monetary integration. Monetary integration posed challenges to the European social model that involved adapting central policy complexes that were already quite Europeanized to new macroeconomic circumstances. Here many possible outcomes existed, whether harmonization or otherwise, or "de-Europeanization" toward a different, perhaps more market-oriented, model of society.

Dyson's remarks about the effects of Euro-politics on the strategic outlooks and capacities of important actors at both European and national levels are very pertinent. Monetary integration impinges on different key actors with different strategies and different resources to pursue them. In response, strategies are bound to change. Some actors will push toward greater Europeanization in terms of "convergence" toward transnational norms. Others will point to greater Europeanization, in the sense of more integration, *tout court*. Still others may experience pressures for change in ways that make them more anti-European. Resource bases of different actors will also change, another way of saying that monetary integration produces winners and losers. All such responses and new resource balances then need to be fitted into an equation to illuminate the present and immediate future.

As our country chapters show, the European social model has proven more resilient in the face of these challenges than many actors and analysts had anticipated. Still, responses to challenge that seek to buttress existing arrangements through reform are not the same thing as stasis. Reforms themselves bring change in both the outlooks and relative strengths of actors. It is important to map the sources of resilience, to be sure, but also to learn about the way reforms change "trend lines." If actors' outlooks and capacities have been altered and reform has occurred, what can we predict about future logics? Finally, by examining national responses to these challenges we are likely to learn something very important about the relative valences of European integration and national politics, and, as a result, the varying limits of Euro-political initiatives to prod national changes.

In our initial consideration of the politics of monetary integration we were led to hypothesize the possibility that transition to EMU and EMU's subsequent operation could threaten the European social model. In particular, the macroeconomic policy regime established by monetary integration and EMU seemed likely to keep unemployment fluctuating around the high levels that Europe has experienced since the 1980s. This in itself would put erosive pressures on the European social model. As Andrew Martin suggests in chapter 2 in this volume, it might do so directly through pressures by the ECB to diminish the protection provided by national social models and endow the euro area with a social model more like that in the US. Indirectly it could also undermine the social model's financial viability by keeping unemployment high, exacerbating conflict over the distribution of new burdens and decreases in benefits, and shifting power from those seeking to preserve labor market security toward those seeking to intensify exposure to market forces.

If present tendencies continue they might not necessarily result in the erosion of the national variants of the European social model, however. In chapter 3 in this volume Alberta M. Sbragia reflects on how Europe's existing and unique multi-tiered political structure affects the formulation and implementation of macroeconomic policy and the implications for social models. National social models in Europe were established well in advance of their inclusion in any currency union, in contrast with the US. They have already shown great staying power in the face of prolonged high unemployment, budgetary strains, and the tight fiscal constraints imposed by Maastricht and the SGP. Indeed, Britain is the only European country where there has been radical social model policy retrenchment, resulting not from monetary integration but a breakdown in the postwar social model in a context where political institutions concentrated political authority. Elsewhere, radical change has proved politically impossible and changes have typically been the adaptation or recalibration of elements of national social models.

We cannot project Europe's EMU future, but we can learn quite a lot about the prospects for the European social model and its national variants by analyzing the interaction of monetary integration and the domestic politics of social model change until now. In part, this is because we can be reasonably certain that despite the centralization of authority over monetary policy in the ECB and regardless of the extent to which other EU bodies reinforce its calls for "structural reforms," authority over policy decisions concerning social models will continue to be vested almost exclusively in member state governments. Whatever impact monetary integration may have had in limiting domestic policy options, and whatever direct pressures the ECB and other EU institutions may now be exerting, governments' responses will be contingent on how these external sources of pressure for change enter the dynamics of domestic politics.

Analytical narratives of monetary integration in six continental country cases detail the empirical core of our volume. In chapters 4 and 5 in this volume, George Ross and Nico A. Siegel discuss monetary integration and domestic politics in France and Germany, respectively, the two leading national actors in monetary integration. Two other large EU member states with less and differently developed social models come next: in chapter 6 Vincent Della Sala analyzes the Italian case while in chapter 7 Sofia A. Pérez reviews Spain. Finally, Jos de Beus and Philippe Pochet consider two key small EU countries, the Netherlands (chapter 8) and Belgium (chapter 9).[31]

After these national narratives come three chapters considering relationships between monetary integration and social model change from a comparative perspective. In chapter 10 Kevin Featherstone focuses on the broad political and institutional implications of monetary integration at national levels. Anton Hemerijck and Maurizio Ferrera in chapter 11 then examine welfare state evolution in the face of monetary integration. In chapter 12 Jon Erik Dølvik does the same for employment relations, with particular emphasis on the responses of trade unions. Finally, chapter 13 summarizes what we have learned from researching and writing *Euros and Europeans*.

---

[31] We will also discuss other cases more briefly in the comparative chapters later in the volume. It is also of interest that all six of our cases have "continental" or "conservative" welfare regimes and corporatist inclinations in employment relations. According to Gøsta Esping-Andersen (1999; Esping-Andersen *et al.* 2002) such "continental" welfare states, built on Bismarckian social insurance practices with male-breadwinner biases, will have the most difficulty in adapting to contemporary economic circumstances.

# 2 The EMU macroeconomic policy regime and the European social model

*Andrew Martin*

Over time, the impact of EMU on the European social model (ESM) is likely to depend most fundamentally on its effects on unemployment. If EMU makes it possible to significantly reduce unemployment, it poses no threat to the ESM. On the contrary, EMU could facilitate its reconfiguration, preserving its high level of social protection and labor rights while adapting it to new needs and improving its equity and efficiency. If EMU instead keeps unemployment high, it threatens the ESM's two main components: the welfare state's financial viability and the trade unions' capacity to bargain over wages and working conditions. Monetary union as such could potentially help Europe reach the reaffirmed goal of full employment.[1] But the EMU macroeconomic policy regime, as the European Central Bank (ECB) interprets it, could make that goal unattainable.

This chapter argues that EMU is likely to keep unemployment at high levels. The argument hinges on two propositions: (1) in order to bring unemployment back down after an extended period of disinflation which has kept growth below its potential and unemployment high, a period of economic growth above its long-run potential – a growth spurt – is necessary, and (2) the EMU macroeconomic policy regime, as interpreted and implemented by the ECB, blocks such a growth spurt. Section 1 describes the policy regime, arguing that the ECB's implementation of it so far and the bank's rationale for doing so indicate an unwillingness to permit the growth spurt needed to significantly reduce unemployment. Its rationale invokes the orthodox view that monetary policy has no long-run effects on growth and employment. However, this view is challenged by an alternative view. Described in section 2, this view rests mainly on an empirical analysis of cases in which disinflation was and was not followed

My thanks for help to Ton Notermans, co-author of early drafts, and to Laurence Ball and Peter Hall for detailed readings and advice as well as to Dean Baker, Iain Begg, Paul De Grauwe, Steinar Holden, Jacques Le Cacheux, Cathie Martin, and participants in several conferences for comments on previous versions. Responsibility for errors of course remains mine.
[1] Presidency Conclusions 2000, Lisbon European Council, March.

by growth spurts during the 1980s and 1990s. Showing that in the long run unemployment was lower without higher inflation where monetary policy permitted growth spurts than where it did not, this analysis casts serious doubt on the ECB's orthodoxy.

# 1    The EMU macroeconomic policy regime

Economic policy regimes are the systematic patterns of policy pursued by official decision-makers over the long run, reflecting basic priorities to which they are committed (Temin 1989: 91–105; Forsyth and Notermans 1997: 39–48; Notermans 2000a: 33–37).[2] Policy regimes shape private economic actors' expectations about the conditions under which they must make their own decisions. As argued in the literature on regimes prioritizing price stability, for example, wage- and price-setters are influenced by the expectation that central banks will not accommodate what the banks regard as inflationary decisions. These expectations are formed not so much by the banks' declared commitment to price stability as by their repeated monetary policy tightening in the face of inflation increases which renders their declarations credible. Equally important from the perspective of unemployment is the influence policy regimes have on the expectations of business investment decision-makers. Their judgments about how much investment in new capacity (additions to the capital stock) and corresponding increases in labor are likely to be profitable hinge on whether the prevailing policy regime leads them to expect sufficient growth in demand to absorb the resulting output growth, given prices that cover costs, including the cost of capital.[3] Employment growth depends heavily on these judgments. Unemployment in turn depends on the relationship between the resulting employment growth rate and the growth rates of productivity and the labor force. Put simply, if investment is insufficient to absorb the growth in the labor force, given productivity growth, unemployment will increase; if the investment is sufficient to generate demand for labor exceeding labor force growth at concurrent productivity growth, unemployment will decrease. Thus, unemployment is crucially affected by the impact of policy regimes on investment

---

[2] "The regime is an abstraction from any single policy decision, it represents the systematic and predictable part of all decisions. It is the thread that runs through the individual choices that governments and central banks have to make. It is visible even though there inevitably . . . [are] some decisions that do not fit the general pattern. These isolated actions have little impact because they represent exceptions to the policy rule, not new policy regimes" (Temin 1989: 91).

[3] The relationship between policy regimes and capital formation is discussed more fully below (pp. 45–48).

decision-makers' expectations of demand growth (Temin 1989: 104; Collignon 2002: 167–170).

In response to rising inflation in the 1970s and 1980s, most governments that had been more or less committed to a full employment regime in the earlier post-Second World War period successively abandoned it in favor of a price stability regime, typically increasing central bank independence to make their commitment credible and thereby reshape other actors' expectations (Notermans 2000a: 166–172). EMU institutionalized this regime shift at the European level, making price stability the "primary goal" to be pursued by the ECB while leaving it to the Bank to define the goal, how to pursue it, and how to reconcile it with the EU's other economic goals (chapter 1 in this volume). How the ECB interprets this mandate is bound to be decisive in shaping investment decision-makers' expectations in the euro zone.

As noted in chapter 1, the ECB is in an extraordinarily powerful position to interpret its mandate as it sees fit. It began by adopting a relatively restrictive definition of price stability as a "year-on-year increase in the Harmonized Index of Consumer Prices (HICP) of the euro area below 2 percent" (ECB 2001e: 38).[4] It subsequently used its discretion in ways that sometimes suggested it was being less restrictive and was pragmatically taking growth and employment into account more than might have been expected. Its actions provide ambiguous evidence for this, however. Initially, the ECB eased policy. In December 1998, it orchestrated a reduction of interest rates by the national central banks to 3 percent, the level at which EMU was to go into effect a month later (ECB 1999a: 8).[5] Then, in response to continued international financial turbulence, it lowered its rate for "main refinancing operations," its principal monetary policy instrument, 50 basis points in March 1999.[6] With tensions eased, the rate went back to 3 percent in November. It was then rapidly increased by another 175 points to 4.75 from February to October 2000, staying there until a small cut of 25 points in May 2001, despite the slowdown in European growth and the sharper slowdown in the US. Despite proliferating calls for earlier and stronger action from public and private

---

[4] The 2 percent upper limit, is regarded as too restrictive by a number of economists including Akerlof *et al.* (2000), Wyplosz (2000), Sinn and Reutter (2001), and De Grauwe (2002). In May 2003, the ECB slightly changed its goal to "close to 2% over the medium term" to "provide a sufficient safety margin against the risks of deflation" (ECB 2003: 5), but with the explicit intent of avoiding inflation much below 2 percent rather than of accepting inflation above 2 percent as implied by a target range of 1–3 percent urged by some.

[5] All data in this and the following paragraphs are from the ECB *Monthly Bulletin.*

[6] Rate changes dated by month they go into effect.

sources,[7] the ECB made no further cuts until a 25 point cut in August, followed by a series of cuts bringing the rate down to 2.0 in June 2003.

The rapid 225 point runup in the rate from November 1999 to October 2000 contrasts sharply with the Fed's 250 point reduction in its key rate over the 14 months up to May 2001. However, the timing as much as the size of the ECB's tightening raises the question of the ECB's willingness to support a growth spurt sufficient to permit unemployment to be significantly reduced. When EMU went into effect in January 1999, the eurozone was experiencing a strong recovery from the deep 1990s recession. The initial recovery from its 1993 trough, when GDP declined 0.8 percent, was interrupted in 1996 but was renewed, reaching a peak annual rate of 3.7 percent in the second quarter of 2000. This brought unemployment down to 8.9 percent from its 1996 level of 11.5 percent. Since its peak, growth slowed sharply, falling to 2.5 percent in 2001 Q1 and continuing to a trough of 0.3 percent in 2002 Q1. The decline in unemployment continued until it leveled out at the still high rate of 8 percent throughout 2001, rising gradually after that. It was precisely in the period of most rapid growth that the ECB's interest rate increase was concentrated, rising by 125 basis points from February to May 2000, and by a further 50 points to 4.75 percent in October. The ECB, like others, evidently underestimated the impact of the American economy's sharp slowdown on Europe when it repeatedly insisted that its effect would be minimal and eurozone growth would decline only to around 3 percent, but to the extent that the considerably greater decline was indeed due to factors internal to the eurozone, the ECB's marked tightening of monetary policy was probably the most important of them.[8]

To the ECB, its sustained tightening in the face of declining growth was required by its self-defined price stability goal. The "headline," or total HICP, inflation rate breached the 2 percent limit in June 2000 and continued rising to 3.4 percent in May 2001. However, the Bank acknowledged that this was the combined result of sharply increased oil prices, aggravated by the Euro's fall against the dollar in which oil prices are denominated, and the livestock epidemics that pushed up meat prices (ECB 2001a: 5–6). These presumably temporary inflationary pressures were

---

[7] For example, the IMF (IMF 2001), Germany's IFO institute (*Financial Times* 2001a), and the *Financial Times* editorial (*Financial Times* 2001b).

[8] The ECB in effect said as much by crediting its interest rate increases with lowering the growth of M3 (ECB 2001b: 5). The contractionary effect of increased interest rates were partially offset by the Euro's depreciation against the dollar. But that itself probably resulted from expectations that the ECB would keep growth lower in the eurozone than the USA, so the ECB was essentially sacrificing domestic demand growth for export demand (reflected in eurozone trade surpluses), a doubtful bargain given the relatively low export share in the eurozone economy as a whole.

essentially the only ones in the eurozone, as reflected in its core, or under-lying, inflation rate, excluding energy and unprocessed food. It remained below the 2 percent threshold until April 2001, having crept up as the oil and meat price spikes worked through the economy. The ECB explained that its policy was pro-actively aimed at averting an increase in inflationary expectations and "second-round" inflationary pressures from efforts to maintain margins and real wages (ECB 2001c: 6). While undoubtedly so, its actions also seemed to reflect a fundamental position that a growth rate exceeding the 2–2.5 percent it views as the economy's long-term trend is not consistent with price stability and therefore cannot be allowed.

However, according to European Commission estimates, a growth rate of 3–3.5 percent would have to be maintained over the medium term in order significantly to reduce Europe's unemployment.[9] That the ECB might permit such a growth spurt was hinted by its Vice-President, Christian Noyer, when he assured the European Parliament in September 1999 that the Bank would "give an economic upturn a chance" (European Parliament 1999). However, its subsequent swift, strong tightening of monetary policy as the growth spurt got under way suggests that it is not ready to give above-trend growth much of a chance. Whatever ECB policy may have contributed to a fall in the eurozone growth rate to the midyear revised estimate of 2–2.5 percent in 2001 (ECB 2001c: 5), the fall was welcomed by the ECB. Otmar Issing, ECB Executive Board member and chief economist, said it would not be "bad news but good news" if the eurozone grew at its long-term trend rate (Issing 2001a).[10] That is, it is good news that the brief growth spurt that brought unemployment down somewhat was aborted. If, as we argue, a sustained growth spurt is necessary to bring unemployment down to pre-disinflation levels, this implies that the ECB has a growth rate target which condemns Europe to continued high unemployment.

Although such a growth target is not part of the Bank's declared strategy, it is implied not only by its actions but also by its rationale for them. Acknowledging that unemployment was "still high" and that further decline requires higher growth, the ECB repeatedly insists that higher

---

[9] Cited in Collignon (2002: 155). A French study estimated that in order to bring French unemployment down from the 1998 level of 12.5 percent to 7.5 percent in five years, a growth rate of 3.6–3.8 percent a year would be necessary, exceeding the long-term potential growth rate by 1.5 percent per year over that period (Blanchard and Fitoussi 1998: 25).

[10] The ECB *Monthly Bulletin* welcomed the 2001 slowdown of growth to its trend rate as reducing inflationary pressures (e.g. ECB 2001b: 5–6). The ECB was already defending its 100 basis point interest rate increase between November 1999 and March 2000, saying that "Rather than nipping economic growth in the bud, such measures" create "the conditions for lasting strong economic growth" (ECB 2000a: 3)

growth can be consistent with price stability only if there is "comprehensive structural reform" to remove market "rigidities." While the rigidities to be removed are in product and financial as well as labor markets (e.g. Issing 2000), "they relate in particular to European labor markets" (ECB 1999a: 2, 31). The ECB described the "far higher" unemployment in the euro area than the US in 1999 as "overwhelmingly structural," attributable to "a host of factors, including structural features of the two labor markets such as wage and non-wage labor costs, employment protection legislation, and the scale and duration of unemployment benefits"(ECB 1999b: 13, 42; 2001a: 6). By making labor markets in Europe more rigid than in the US, such institutional differences reduce the speed with which the European economy adjusts to shocks and limit "the pace at which an economy can grow without fueling inflationary pressures" (ECB 2001e: 15).

To the ECB, then, the unemployment rate associated with that growth pace is the lowest consistent with its definition of price stability – its view of what economists refer to as the equilibrium or non-accelerating inflation rate of unemployment (NAIRU). An attempt to bring unemployment below that rate by exceeding the speed limit without the structural changes in labor markets deemed necessary to increase the potential – i.e. non-inflationary – growth rate would succeed only temporarily. Over the long run, it would only increase inflation, which could be stabilized only by bringing growth back down to its potential and unemployment back up to its equilibrium rate. Accordingly, the ECB's standard response to calls for monetary easing is that monetary policy "cannot substitute for structural reforms" (Otmar Issing, quoted in *Financial Times* 2001c).[11] Central banks can thus do nothing to achieve higher growth and lower unemployment except to maintain price stability; that is the "best monetary policy can do to foster a high rate of growth of output" (Issing *et al.* 2001: 67).[12]

The ECB thereby denies that demand management, particularly monetary policy, has any direct responsibility for growth and employment. Virtually all responsibility is assigned instead to supply-side policies that reform the structure of markets, particularly labor markets, and to those, "governments as well as . . . economic agents on both the business and

---

[11] This is reminiscent of advice to Ramsay MacDonald in July 1930 to maintain the Gold Standard and "sweep away ruthlessly any lingering illusions that a substantial reduction of unemployment figures [was] to be sought in the artificial provision of unemployment" (quoted in Temin 1989: 63).

[12] Similarly, a Bundesbank president stated that "It's not our job to guarantee full employment; we're concerned with stability and price levels." Quoted in Henning (1994: 199, n. 41).

labor sides," who must carry them out (ECB 2001a: 6). The part that differences in macroeconomic policy might have in accounting for the difference in unemployment trends in the US and Europe is virtually ignored. Absolved of any blame for increasing unemployment earlier, macroeconomic policy is also denied credit for reducing it in the late 1990s, even though eurozone nominal short-term interest rates in 1999 were a little over a quarter of what they were at their 1992 peak (OECD 2000b: 244). Without controlling for this huge easing of monetary policy, the bank instead ascribes "a considerable decline in unemployment" in some countries to labor market reforms (ECB 2002: 5).[13] But "structural rigidities remain and these explained the still high levels of unemployment in the euro area in 2000" (Issing 2000; ECB 2001e: 15).

The institutions targeted for change by the ECB comprise a large part of the European social model. Given the ECB's attribution of America's lower unemployment to the institutions making its labor markets much more flexible than European labor markets, its implicit prescription for bringing European unemployment down to recent American levels is to transform the European social model into one more closely approximating the American one.[14] Although the Treaty confines the ECB's formal authority to monetary policy, reserving authority over employment relations and welfare state institutions to the member states, the ECB is strongly positioned to use monetary policy as leverage to bring about the changes in institutions it deems necessary: it sets implementation of those changes as the condition on which it will allow growth and employment to increase. It would not necessarily succeed in bringing about those changes but its control of monetary policy enables it to hold employment hostage to its essentially neoclassical vision of well-functioning markets.

The ECB can claim with some validity that its view of the institutional determinants of equilibrium unemployment and hence the growth rate consistent with price stability reflects a "consensus" among economists (Duisenberg 1997; Issing 2000: 12). Layard, Nickell, and Jackson (1991) provide an authoritative statement of this view and it has been widely propagated by the *OECD Jobs Study* (1994a), its follow-up reports, and a voluminous literature.

---

[13] The Commission, in contrast, reversed the relative weight of macroeconomic and structural factors, saying that "The strong employment performance of recent years . . . has been *due in large part to the favorable macroeconomic conditions*, but labor market developments also strongly suggest a reduction in structural unemployment thanks to reforms and policies to improve the functioning of labor markets implemented over the past decade" (*European Economy* 2001: 72, emphasis added). See chapter 7 in this volume, for the effect of monetary easing in Spain.

[14] A member of the ECB Governing Council told the author (not for attribution) explicitly that Europe could solve its unemployment problems by importing the American labor market.

The consensus is by no means complete, however. An alternative view offers evidence that the primary reason why unemployment has been higher in Europe than in the US since the early 1980s, and higher in some European countries than others, is not that labor markets are more rigid but that macroeconomic policy, especially monetary policy, has been more restrictive, resulting in lower growth in output and employment and hence higher unemployment. It thereby also casts doubt on the theoretical underpinning of the ECB's insistence that monetary policy can have no durable effect on growth and employment. The alternative view does not deny that the structure of labor and other markets interacts with macroeconomic policy to affect the pace at which unemployment can be lowered without accelerating inflation, nor does it deny that changes in Europe's social model are desirable for many reasons apart from any macroeconomic effects they might have. However, it suggests that no amount of change in Europe's social model, including transforming it into one more like the American model, would bring European unemployment down to American levels without a shift to a more expansionary policy regime. With such a regime shift, on the other hand, Europe might well achieve non-inflationary full employment with institutional changes consistent with its social model rather than moving toward the American model and the greater inequality and insecurity inherent in it.

Which of the views is more nearly correct is accordingly central to evaluating the implications of EMU for the ESM. While we cannot pretend to settle the issue, we can show why we find the alternative view more persuasive.

## 2    Explaining unemployment

That differences in macroeconomic policy are a large part of the explanation of variations in unemployment is strongly suggested by a cursory comparison. There is no doubt that the American economy has been much better at providing jobs than the European economy since the 1960s.[15] Over that whole period there has been an upward trend in unemployment in Europe and, despite large fluctuations, virtually no upward trend in the US (figure 2.1). The increasing gap in unemployment rates reflects much higher employment growth in the US, where it has doubled since the 1960s, compared with little more than 10 percent in Europe. Since the working-age population has grown more slowly in Europe than in the US, employment growth could have been somewhat lower without higher unemployment if productivity growth had not

---

[15] "Europe" refers to the fifteen EU members prior to the 2004 enlargement. Data are missing for some countries in earlier years (OECD 1994a: 10–17; ECB 2000b: 58).

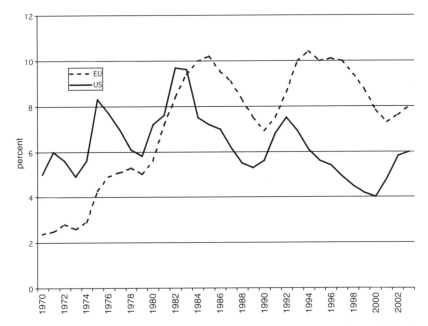

Figure 2.1    Unemployment rates, 1970–2003 (commonly used defini-
tions)
*Source:* OECD *Economic Outlook*
*Note:* German data include former GDR from 1991 on. 2003 estimated
See n. 15.

been higher in Europe. With somewhat higher productivity growth and
employment growth so much lower in Europe, the unemployment rate
increased relative to the US rate despite an essentially stagnant participation rate in Europe. Employment growth was so much higher in the US
that the gap widened despite not only higher US working-age population
growth but also a substantial increase in participation. In short, higher
job growth enabled the American economy to employ a higher share of
a faster-growing working-age population.

Differences in unemployment, employment, and participation rates
such as these between the US and European averages can also be found
within Europe, however. Unemployment varies widely among European
countries: it is lower than in the US in those countries with the lowest
unemployment and higher than in the US in those with the highest
unemployment. There are also large differences between regions within
countries, especially Italy, Germany, and Belgium. Generally speaking, in European countries where unemployment has been relatively

low, employment growth and participation rates have been relatively high, as in the US, although the countries experiencing this combination of trends have varied over time (Røed 2000: 2). Thus, higher job growth has permitted both higher participation and lower unemployment in the US and some European countries than in other European countries.

Comparing just the US and Europe, two features of unemployment differences stand out. First, prior to 1982, unemployment was higher in the US than in Europe. Second, the divergence in unemployment trends was not steady but was concentrated in specific periods. One was in 1975–1979, when unemployment still was higher in the US than Europe. Since the unemployment gap switched in favor of the US in 1982, there were two periods in which the gap widened, 1982–1986 and 1992–1996, after which the increased unemployment in Europe persisted at successively higher levels but without further widening of the gap. What has to be explained then is why the gap widened in those periods and why it persisted in the subsequent periods.

It is hard to believe that markedly contrasting policies coinciding with the increases in the gaps do not have a lot to do with them. In both the US and Europe there were shifts to macroeconomic policy regimes giving higher priority to price stability. In the US, however, price stability was essentially added to the goals of growth and employment, whereas in Europe employment and growth were subordinated to price stability. This contrast is discernible in the patterns of policy pursued by the two main central banks, the American Federal Reserve Bank (Fed) and the German Bundesbank (Buba) which came to set monetary policy for most of Europe (Clarida, Galí, and Gertler. 1998).[16] Both shifted to a pattern of policy in which they acted swiftly and strongly against inflation. However, the Fed subsequently acted as swiftly and strongly against recession as against inflation, exhibiting a "symmetrical reaction function," while the Buba moved less swiftly and strongly against recession than inflation, exhibiting instead an "asymmetrical reaction function" (Clarida and Gertler 1997; Soskice 1998; Dolada, Maria-Dolores, and Naveira 2000). The timing of the shifts also differed, with the Buba making it in 1973 and the Fed in 1979 (Clarida and Gertler 1997; DeLong 1997).[17]

---

[16] Additional sources for the comparisons of the policy mix in the USA and Europe are Henning (1994), Ball (1997, 1999), De Grauwe (1998), Baker and Schmitt (1999), plus the OECD country surveys and semi-annual *Economic Outlook*. Central bank rates from IMF *International Financial Statistics* and the US Federal Reserve Bank website.

[17] Most other European countries made the shift at various times, including Britain in 1979, France in 1983, and Sweden in 1991.

The period between the two shifts was the first in which European unemployment rose sharply relative to the US. The collapse of Bretton Woods under the weight of the "Great Inflation" that diffused from the US to the rest of the OECD freed the Buba to reorient monetary policy to the price stability goal written into its statute (chapter 5 in this volume). This reinforced generally restrictive responses to the further inflationary pressure from OPEC I in 1973, while the US response was more expansionary. The Fed did not react strongly to inflation until OPEC II aggravated it and a new chairman, Paul Volcker, was appointed in 1979. When unemployment rose as steeply in the US as in Europe in the following three years, the Fed's extreme tightening of monetary policy seemed to signal a shift to a regime every bit as restrictive as in Germany. But by 1982 the Fed had reversed itself and moved strongly in an expansionary direction for two years. By the time the Fed turned restrictive again, albeit briefly, highly expansionary fiscal policy had the US economy booming. In contrast, the severe contraction initiated by the Buba and the Thatcher government in 1979 was reinforced by the French U-turn in 1983 so that European macropolicy continued to be restrictive in the early and mid-1980s when the unemployment gap again widened.

Comparisons of policy and performance since the late 1980s are complicated first by the exchange rate gyrations and policy conflicts between US and European governments, which triggered the relaunch of monetary integration (Henning 1998), and then by German unification and the ensuing 1992–1993 EMS crisis. Nevertheless, variations in macroeconomic policy continued to be broadly consistent with variations in the US–Europe unemployment gap. From the mid-1980s to 1992, the macroeconomic policy stances on both sides of the Atlantic were broadly similar, though with different mixes, consistently with a relatively unchanged unemployment gap. Both policy and performance then diverged sharply again, producing by far the largest gap yet. While the Fed continued to reduce interest rates, kept them low between 1991 and 1993, and varied them slightly around a slightly higher level after that, the Buba increased interest rates continuously from 1988 until monetary policy became extremely tight in 1992, only slowly relaxing it thereafter. This combined with the fiscal policy tightening required by the Maastricht deficit criteria to make macroeconomic policy so contractionary as to plunge Europe into the deepest recession of the whole postwar period. The responses to the issues posed by German unification contributed to this disaster in a scenario too complex to describe here.[18] Clearly, though,

---

[18] The impact of the Bundesbank's policy was amplified by the refusal of France and other EMS members to agree to a D-mark revaluation within the EMS Exchange Rate Mechanism, which would presumably have diminished inflationary pressure in Germany, eliciting a less restrictive response by the Bundesbank (Heisenberg 1999: 129–130).

the resulting macroeconomic policy mix drove European unemployment to record levels, while in the US growth sustained by the relaxation of monetary policy made it possible to gradually reduce the Federal deficit without offsetting the expansionary effect of lower interest rates, reducing unemployment to the lowest levels in decades (Blinder and Yellin 2001). In Europe, unemployment finally began falling in 1997 and the gap with the US stopped increasing as recovery took hold. Accelerating growth enabled the EMU entrants to meet the deficit criteria without further fiscal tightening, while monetary policy eased as interest rates converged downwards to the 3.0 rate set for the start of EMU.

Only as US labor markets continued to tighten, with unemployment running at around two-fifths of the Euroland level, did the Fed gradually raise real interest rates to levels above those set by the ECB in an effort to bring the American economy down to a "soft landing" before inflation, running at twice the Euroland rate, began accelerating.[19] But when the American economy turned down, the Fed again displayed its readiness to act decisively in an effort to head off recession by bringing the key Federal funds rate down. The ECB, on the other hand, acted more as the Bundesbank had done and kept monetary policy tight instead of trying to sustain the recovery in the face of the US slowdown, lowering interest rates slightly and very slowly.[20] As in the 1980s, the central banks reacted in contrasting ways that coincided closely with variations in the unemployment gap between Europe and the US in the 1990s.[21]

---

[19] The Fed arguably tightened too slowly, failing to restrain the asset price bubble that burgeoned only to be burst precipitously, and contributed to the bubble by fueling unrealistic expectations (De Grauwe 2003). Serious as it is, asset price inflation is more difficult to curb with the standard instruments of monetary policy (Gramlich 2001).

[20] Over the five years of the ECB's existence, its real interest rate averaged 1.3 percent, 1.9 percentage points higher than the Fed's –0.6 real interest rate, while unemployment in the eurozone averaged 7.9 percent, 2.9 percentage points higher than the US average of 5 percent. In comparing Fed monetary policy favorably to that of the Buba and the ECB, I in no way imply the infallibility sometimes ascribed to Fed Chairman Alan Greenspan, who has exploited his reputation to play a reactionary and illegitimate role in the politics of fiscal policy (see Krugman 2004).

[21] Writing in February 2002, D. Begg et al. (2002a: 38–46) argue plausibly that the ECB acted differently in the eurozone than the Fed did in the US because the fall in output was not as great as in the US, and that the Fed would have acted as the ECB did in response to the same conditions, based on Taylor-type rules or models that tracked both banks' actual reactions to price and output variations quite closely through 2001. However, in a November update they found that, contrary to what they expected, the ECB did not cut interest rates "despite a worsening in the economic outlook," and that even if the bank subsequently did so (which it did) it would be exhibiting the same "slow reaction . . . evident . . . during the summer of 2001 when interest rate cuts also came late." They contrast this with the Fed's action in cutting "interest rates once more by more than 0.5 percentage points" even though "growth forecasts for the US economy during the same period . . . have been revised upwards" while those for the eurozone had been revised downwards (D. Begg et al. 2002b: 4). This suggests that the ECB and Fed do indeed have different reaction functions. (On limits of Taylor rules, see n. 36.)

Stronger evidence that differences in monetary policy largely explain unemployment variations is provided by Laurence Ball (1997, 1999). He shows that a crucial difference in policy is whether it permits or prevents a growth spurt following an increase in unemployment resulting from a disinflationary tightening of policy: if policy permits a growth spurt, unemployment goes back down toward its pre-disinflationary rate; if policy prevents a growth spurt, unemployment persists at around the high rate to which the disinflationary policy raised it. That a period of above-potential growth was needed to bring European unemployment back down to pre-disinflation levels was already argued in the early 1980s by some mainstream economists: "*The economy must grow faster than its sustainable long-run growth rate*" (Layard *et al.* 1984: 465, emphasis in the original). That such growth spurts enabled unemployment to fall after recessions in the US was shown in work by Sichel and Romer and Romer cited by Ball (1999: 192). Comparing monetary policies in North America and Europe, Ball shows that those which permitted or prevented such growth spurts go a long way toward accounting for the different unemployment trends in the two areas. This provides an explanation for the persistence of the successive increases in the US–Europe unemployment gap. Ball's work, recognized by the ECB as a "forceful defense" of an "heterodox viewpoint" (Issing *et al.* 2001: 18), provides the main empirical basis for our argument.

Ball's 1999 paper compares cases in which disinflation is and is not followed by a period of above-potential growth. The potential (or sustainable) growth rate, is understood in the standard way, as the rate at which the economy can grow over the long run without accelerating inflation. The idea is that when the economy is at its potential growth rate, the unemployment rate is sufficient to discourage wage pressures that increase inflation – the so-called equilibrium unemployment rate or non-accelerating inflation rate of unemployment (NAIRU). However, estimated NAIRUs vary over time, posing a puzzle for theories attributing the NAIRU primarily to relatively invariant labor market structures.[22] Ball's analysis suggests a solution: the unemployment rate when the economy is at its potential growth rate depends not primarily on labor market structures but on whether a period of below-potential growth is followed by a period of above-potential growth which brings output back up to its trend level and the corresponding demand for labor.

---

[22] And, to James K. Galbraith, an "embarrassment" to the profession. "When unemployment rises, analysts tend to discover that the demographic characteristics of workers are deteriorating, or that the job–wage and wage–price dynamic has become unstable. And when the unemployment rate drifts down again, those flaws mysteriously disappear and a lower NAIRU is estimated" (Galbraith 1997: 101). See also Akerlof, Dickens, and Perry (2000).

Briefly, the results are as follows. After a period of disinflation that keeps growth lower and unemployment higher than they would have been if growth had remained at its potential rate, a period of growth above that rate brings the level of output up to where it would have been if the period of disinflation had not lowered the growth rate – i.e. output is brought back to its trend level. At that level, unemployment eventually falls to its pre-disinflation rate. Where there is no such growth spurt and growth simply returns to its potential rate at the lower level of output resulting from below-potential growth, unemployment remains higher than it would have been if there had been no below-potential growth. Where there is a growth spurt, it is initially accompanied by an increase in inflation, but it proves temporary. When the growth spurt is over and growth returns to its potential rate at the trend level of output, inflation comes back down to roughly the steady level associated with the potential growth rate. At that stage, inflation is not significantly higher than where there has been no growth spurt and no temporary increase in inflation but where unemployment is therefore higher. Policy that prevents a growth spurt in order to avoid a temporary increase in inflation at the cost of persistently higher unemployment achieves no significantly greater reduction in inflation over the long run than policy that permits a growth spurt and a temporary increase in inflation in order to achieve a greater reduction in unemployment over the long run.

The NAIRU, as conventionally estimated in terms of total unemployment, thus appears to have increased where there was no growth spurt while not increasing where there was one. If it is assumed *a priori* that equilibrium unemployment is determined by labor market structure, something about that structure would have to explain the increase in the NAIRU where it appears to have occurred. Ball's analysis suggests that, on the contrary, the apparent increase in the NAIRU can be accounted for primarily by restrictive policy which keeps unemployment high beyond the point where it has disinflationary effects, and which prevents a growth spurt that brings output back up to its trend level and unemployment back down to its corresponding level, and not primarily by labor market structure.

The clearest evidence for these findings comes from a comparison of monetary policy in the early 1980s in response to recessions brought on to reduce the high inflation of the 1970s in six of the G7 countries, the North American two (NA2) and European four (E4).[23] Central banks in the NA2 shifted rapidly to strongly expansionary policies, cutting "nominal rates sharply whereas" the banks in the E4 "held them steady or raised them slightly." Measured from pre-recession peak to the quarter after

[23] France, Germany, Italy, the UK.

the trough, these contrasting policies produced a cumulative average real interest rate cut of 3.4 percentage points in the NA2 and average rise of 0.2 points in the E4 (Ball 1999: 196). The strong, rapid expansionary policies in the NA2 produced a growth spurt, averaging 5.2 percent annually in the US and 6.2 percent in Canada over two years following the trough, well over their long-run growth trends. In each, the average annual growth rates had settled back to approximately its long-run potential by five years after the pre-recession peak, and unemployment was reduced to below its previous level in the US and nearly its previous level in Canada by eight years. Without an initial growth spurt in the E4, output remained "far below the level implied by its previous trend" over the five post-peak years, and unemployment remained an average of 4.7 percentage points above what it had been at the pre-recession peak eight years afterwards (Ball 1999: 199–200).

Moreover, the E4 did not gain much more disinflation in return for durably higher unemployment than the NA2 did from temporarily higher unemployment. Inflation did initially increase in the NA2 but not in the E4. But by eight years after the pre-recession peak, the disinflation gain within the E4 ranged between less and more than in the NA2, averaging 9.1 percentage points in the E4 and 6.8 percentage points in the NA2. Except in Italy, with the greatest disinflation, most of the disinflation gain had occurred by the fourth year. Thus, the "high unemployment in the E4 eventually stopped putting downward pressure on inflation" (Ball 1999: 201–202). What was apparently accomplished by preventing a growth spurt and prolonging unemployment was only an *increase* in the E4 NAIRUs, as estimated by the OECD, by an average of 2.9 percentage points. In contrast, the growth spurt which brought ouput and unemployment back to trend-predicted levels in the NA2 was accompanied by NAIRU *reductions* averaging 0.9 points (Ball 1999: 202). That the prolongation of disinflation and unemployment buys little more reduction in inflation is confirmed with a larger sample of nineteen countries (Ball 1999: 208).

Similar analyses fail to yield such strong results for the more turbulent 1990s (Ball 1999: 211). However, evidence that variations in demand, policy-induced or not, help explain variations in actual unemployment and the NAIRU between 1985 and 1997 is provided by comparing four OECD "success stories" in which the NAIRU fell significantly with six "failures" in which the NAIRU rose or barely fell. What distinguishes "successes" and "failures" is the presence and absence of demand expansions. Expansions are identified by increases in inflation since such increases should result from expansions that push unemployment below the initial NAIRU. During the years covered, this happened in three of the four successes – the UK, Portugal, and the Netherlands. Ireland was the exception, but it subsequently fit the pattern. While the largest runups in inflation between 1985 and 1997 in the other three averaged 4.5 percent, they averaged 1.8 percent in the failures. Yet the inflation runups were temporary in all the European successes, as in the NA2 in the 1980s, and those with the highest runups had the largest NAIRU fall (Ball 1999: 217–226). They were successes precisely because they could disinflate after the initial runup without arresting declines in the NAIRU, consistently with results for the 1980s.

While details varied, demand expansions in the successes occurred primarily because their economies were overheated by nonmonetary shocks rather than "intentional easings" of monetary policy, producing the temporary inflation runups, but monetary policy contributed to higher growth because it was not tightened until inflation was rising and was eased as soon as inflation stopped rising. Although the failure economies did not become overheated, policy was nevertheless tightened after small inflation runups and kept tight even after inflation was stable or falling and recessions had begun (Ball 1999: 219–220). The conclusion: "Demand expansions played an important role in the success stories, and . . . a lack of similar expansions helps explain the failures." By enabling unemployment to be durably reduced with only a temporary increase in inflation, "demand expansions helped reduce the NAIRU," confirming the results of the NA2-E4 and nineteen country analyses of the 1980s (Ball 1999: 217, 219).

That estimated NAIRUs vary over time and that they track actual unemployment quite closely is widely accepted; it has been shown repeatedly (Richardson *et al.* 2000). What is contested is how to explain it (and whether a time-varying NAIRU retains any policy relevance). Orthodox explanations attributing NAIRU variations over time solely to differences in structural features of the economy, especially labor market institutions, run up against a difficulty. While such structural features might help to explain NAIRU variations across countries, they do not vary over time as rapidly as variations in estimated NAIRUs. What does vary about as rapidly is aggregate demand, to which policy contributes. A plausible counterargument is that even unchanged labor market institutions affect responses to changes in demand. Thus, institutions might turn unemployment increased by a demand contraction into persistent unemployment that cannot be reduced by demand expansion without re-igniting inflation, meaning that the NAIRU has increased. But if after having risen the NAIRU then falls, the difficulty remains. If the institutions that had earlier turned unemployment resulting from demand contraction into persistent unemployment have not changed sufficiently to so sharply reverse the institutions' alleged effect, it is difficult to see why a demand expansion that reduces unemployment can be accompanied by a fall in the NAIRU.[24] Some other mechanism must evidently account for the downward as well as upward effects of demand variations on the NAIRU.

The mechanism Ball suggests hinges on evidence that short- and long-term unemployment, conventionally defined as under and over a year, respectively, have different effects on the downward pressure on wages that keeps inflation from rising: short-term unemployment ($S$) exerts such pressure but long-term unemployment ($L$) does not (Ball: 1999: 227–233, notation mine). Thus, if a contraction that pushes unemployment above the stable inflation rate of $S$ is prolonged, it turns some of the unemployment into $L$, raising total unemployment ($U$) without further reducing inflation, thereby increasing the NAIRU in terms of $U$, even if the stable inflation rate of $S$ has not increased. Similarly, a decrease in $U$ which lowers $L$ without pushing $S$ below its stable inflation rate means that $U$ has decreased without increasing inflation, thus decreasing the NAIRU.

The different effects of $S$ and $L$ are ascribed to employers' preference for job applicants who have been unemployed for the shortest time, placing applicants into queues in order of unemployment duration. The rationale is that hiring long-term unemployed is more costly because they require more training to overcome rusty or obsolete skills or are harder to recruit because they engage in job search less intensively. (Employers may also believe, validly or not, that long unemployment reflects other deficiencies.) Employers go only as far back in the queue as is needed to fill existing vacancies. If vacancies are less than or equal to $S$, only the short-term unemployed compete for jobs; the long-term unemployed have little prospect of employment.

The willingness of employed workers to press for wages that would increase inflation (or increase unemployment if policy blocks it) is described as depending on the prospects for re-employment if a successful wage claim leads to elimination of their jobs. If demand (policy-driven or not) and hence employment stays high enough for vacancies to exceed $S$, the chances of re-employment within a year might be judged good enough to risk a wage claim that might eliminate jobs. If the wage increase does not result in job losses, it feeds increased inflation. When vacancies exceed $S$, then, $S$ is below the stable inflation rate. When $S$ exceeds vacancies,

---

[24] "It is difficult to see how rigidities – a permanent feature of continental European economies for the past 30 years – can suddenly produce a drop in growth rates from more than 3 percent in 1998–2000 to close to zero now. And why did the same rigidities not prevent a European economic boom in the second half of the 1990s?" (De Grauwe, 2003).

however, the prospects of re-employment within a year might be sufficiently lower to make workers unwilling to risk wage increases that could result in job losses. $S$ would then be above the stable inflation rate. When $S$ equals vacancies, however, it is not necessarily at the stable inflation rate. If $S$ continues to equal vacancies, prospects of re-employment within a year might be judged good enough to risk wage claims that could eliminate jobs. $S$ may therefore have to exceed vacancies by some margin that raises the risk of becoming long-term unemployed sufficiently to inhibit such wage claims. But, then, assuming employment growth does not eliminate the margin, some short-term unemployed will not be re-employed within a year, becoming long-term unemployed. Slightly reformulating the argument accordingly, some $L$, making the risk of becoming long-term unemployed sufficiently great to provide enough downward pressure on wages, is necessary, with $U$ exceeding $S$ by the necessary margin of $L$.

This leaves the argument's basic thrust unchanged. Any $L$ beyond the margin of $S$ exceeding vacancies would still not contribute any additional downward pressure on wages. Competition for jobs would still be confined to short-term unemployed, and the $L$ exceeding the necessary margin would still raise the NAIRU by increasing $U$ without further reducing inflation. The same reasoning indicates how the mechanism might work in reverse. When a demand expansion produces a growth spurt, vacancies initially exceed $S$ (plus the margin of $L$), pushing it below its stable inflation rate. Wages therefore rise to retain existing and recruit new employees, fueling the initial inflation increase. Employers no longer able to fill vacancies from the pool of short-term unemployed go further back in the job queue, hiring from among the long-term unemployed, despite any extra recruitment and training costs. $L$ therefore declines, along with the corresponding $U$ (the queue does not shorten as fast as employment rises because those who dropped out of it and others who never entered do so as job prospects brighten, implying that wage pressures do not increase correspondingly either). When the growth spurt ends, growth comes back down to its trend rate, output is at the level at which vacancies no longer exceed $S$, and $U$ exceeds $S$ only by the margin of $L$ needed to keep inflation stable, so that the NAIRU measured in $U$ has come back down. Thus, if the NAIRU rises during a disinflation long enough to increase $L$ beyond the needed margin, it stays high in the absence of a growth spurt and falls if there is one.

Ball presents this suggested explanation as a version of hysteresis theories. The term "hysteresis" originally referred to physical systems displaced by a shock from a previous steady state and which remain in the new state after the shock instead of returning to the previous state. It was applied by Blanchard and Summers (1986) to tendencies for changes in unemployment induced by a demand shock to persist long after the shock in order to explain the persistence of high unemployment in Europe following the 1980s disinflations. In their and most subsequent versions, unemployment increased by a demand contraction is turned into persistent unemployment by various labor market mechanisms, such as the power of employed workers (insiders) to set wages low enough to preserve their jobs but too high to employ the unemployed (outsiders), institutions that diminish employed workers' risks of unemployment and unemployed workers' incentives to seek jobs, and the erosion of skills, search intensity, etc. supposed to result from lengthening unemployment.

In Ball's version, the prolongation of a demand contraction itself rather than such labor market mechanisms makes unemployment persist. The amount of long-term unemployment is the direct effect of macroeconomic, especially monetary, policy decisions determining the size and duration of disinflations. Since there is no further disinflation while unemployment persists the NAIRU measured in $U$ has risen, but this is misleading since the long-term unemployment resulting from the prolonged contraction adds no additional downward pressure on wages, providing that the equilibrium rate of $S$ (or of $S$ plus the margin of $L$) has not increased. That it has not increased is suggested by the ability of a demand expansion to reduce unemployment without a long-run increase in inflation once the growth rate is back to its potential at the trend level of output. Persistent unemployment created by prolonged demand contraction is thus no obstacle to its own reduction by a demand expansion – i.e. hysteresis, understood this way, is reversible. By the same token, if a demand contraction engineered to bring down inflation is quickly counteracted by an expansion, hysteresis can be largely avoided.

Blanchard and Summers suggest the possible reversibility of hysteresis, without explaining why. In Ball's version, a labor market mechanism also plays a role but is not what causes unemployment persistence. The principal mechanism is the employers' practice of filling vacancies from only as far back in job queues as needed. This explains not only why the additional $L$ produced by prolonged contraction provides no additional downward pressure on wages and hence no additional disinflation over the long run, but also why a demand expansion that reduces most $L$ does not relax the downward pressure and thereby increase inflation in the long run. In other words, hysteresis is reversible because "demand expansions reduce the NAIRU in the same way that contractions increase it" (Ball 1999: 211, 228).

Two important issues remain. One concerns the role labor market institutions may have in explaining NAIRU changes. As summarized so far, Ball's argument offers evidence that demand variations have a role in explaining those changes. However, that role's importance cannot be evaluated without controlling for the effects of the labor market institutions which, in the orthodox explanation, determine the NAIRU independently of demand variations.[25] Otherwise the conclusions are as unpersuasive as the claims that labor market reforms explain declining unemployment in the late 1990s which the ECB and others make without controlling for macroeconomic policy easing. Fully aware of this, Ball notes that large residuals remain in the regressions in his 1997 paper showing strong relationships between variations in the size and length of disinflations and changes in the NAIRU in twenty OECD countries.[26] He accordingly investigates the effects labor market institutions might have on the response of unemployment to demand variations. By themselves, none of the institutions identified in the literature is found to have a significant relationship to NAIRU changes except the duration of unemployment benefits, and no labor market variable "explains nearly as much of the rise in the NAIRU as the size and length of disinflation" (Ball 1997: 176). When benefit duration is included in an equation in which it interacts with disinflation size and includes disinflation size, however, the residual is considerably smaller, so "the explanatory power of macropolicy variables increases greatly when we account for interactions with benefit durations."[27] None of the other institutional variables adds to the regressions' explanatory power.[28]

[25] The institutions commonly cited as having negative effects are employment protection, unemployment benefit replacement ratio and duration, union density, bargained or statutory minimum wages, and the tax wedge (between gross and net wages), while degree of wage bargaining coordination and active labor market policy are credited with positive effects. See the summary in Baker, Dean, and Schmitt (2002).

[26] Percentage point changes in the NAIRU are regressed on the size of disinflation measured by the percentage point decrease in inflation over the decade and on the length of disinflation measured by the maximum number of years of continuous disinflation within the decade. The size of the disinflation has an adjusted $R^2$ of 0.37, the length of disinflation (squared) an adjusted $R^2$ of 0.53, and the multiple regression, with both variables, an adjusted $R^2$ of 0.55 (Ball 1997: 172–174). Thus, each "independent variable explains a substantial fraction of the variation in the change in the NAIRU," as do the two variables jointly, though only slightly more than the length of disinflation, making the prolongation of disinflation rather than its size the main explanator.

[27] Change in the NAIRU is regressed on various combinations of interactions of two measures of disinflation, size and length, and duration of unemployment benefits. The interactions of each measure of disinflation with benefits duration yield an adjusted $R^2$ of 0.55 and 0.57, respectively, and when both measures of disinflation are included the adjusted $R^2$ rises to 0.67. An equation including the length of disinflation and the interaction of the size of disinflation with benefit duration yields the highest adjusted $R^2$ of 0.75 (Ball 1997: 177). However, the adjusted $R^2$ of 0.55 when NAIRU changes are regressed on both the size and length of disinflations suggests that demand variation explains substantially more than the labor market variable.

[28] Only coverage of collective bargaining adds to the explanation but only a "little once we control for the interaction between disinflation and benefit duration" (Ball 1997: 178).

Similar conclusions are reached somewhat differently in the 1999 paper. Although the comparison of the NA2 and E4 shows a strong relationship between monetary policies which permitted or prevented growth spurts and the difference in unemployment trends in the two regions during the 1980s, it "cannot separate the roles of [unemployment benefits] and monetary policy" because the NA2 have shorter benefit durations as well as easier monetary policy than three of the E4. However, in the nineteen-country sample testing the results of the G6 analysis there is sufficient independent variation in the institutional and policy variables to "try to disentangle" their roles (Ball 1999: 203–204). When measures of the degree of hysteresis and change in the NAIRU are regressed on measures of monetary policy easing and benefit duration, each variable is found to be significant. The degree of hysteresis is reduced most when regressed on both variables, with maximum easing of monetary policy having a somewhat greater effect than maximum reduction in benefit duration (Ball 1999: 206–207).

While the economic complexities of the 1990s preclude similarly strong results, the narrative comparisons between the "success" cases where unemployment fell substantially and "failures" where they did not suggest conclusions like those for the 1980s. Thus, no consistent relationship is found between economic outcomes and labor market institutions, whether using indicators at a particular period or of changes over time. Although "labor market variables do not change much over time," there were some reforms in institutions such as unemployment benefit duration and replacement rates and employment protection, as well as new incomes policies aimed at curbing wage growth. But reforms occurred in all of the ten cases and incomes policies occurred in both successes and failures, so that "there appears to be little correlation between the extent of reforms and changes in the NAIRU" (Ball 1999: 216–217).[29] Nevertheless, Ball stresses, his results "do *not* refute the view that major labor market reforms would reduce unemployment," while they might "complement demand expansions," politically as well as economically (Ball 1999: 236, emphasis in the original).

There is considerable support for Ball's view of the limited role of labor market institutions relative to demand variations in explaining unemployment despite the contrary view of OECD and academic economists comprising the "consensus" invoked by the ECB. Critics of this orthodox view argue that the econometric evidence for it is much weaker than

---

[29] Other studies of successes similarly assign primacy to demand expansions while finding no consistent relationships between labor market institutions and outcomes, though the countries vary depending on timing and criteria (Fitoussi and Passet 2000; Freysinnet 2000).

the strong claims made for it.[30] A recent survey of six major studies by Baker *et al.* (2002), supplemented by the authors' own analysis, argues that the many regressions in the six studies are "decidedly not robust" to variations in variable specification, time period, and estimation method" (Baker *et al.* 2002: 23). Given the sensitivity of the regressions to "reasonable alterations in the definitions of institutional variables" and other alternative procedures, it is not surprising that the results are inconsistent and sometimes contradictory (with opposite signs), even within the same study, suggesting a wide range of effects from very small to so large as to be implausible, with empirically falsified predictions.[31] At the same time, unemployment benefit duration, alone significant in Ball's analysis, is one of two variables significant in all regressions "most supportive" of the orthodox view in which it appears (Baker *et al.* 2002: 22). The other is the tax wedge which Ball finds not significant (Ball 1997: 176). Incomes policy or wage bargaining coordination, "a step *away* from a Walrasian labor market" (Ball 1999: 214, emphasis in the original), is a variable for which he finds ambiguous evidence but which is significant, with the right sign, in five of the six most supportive regressions and in the authors' own analysis (Baker *et al.* 2002: 22, 26). Their conclusion that there is "Certainly . . . little evidence . . . of the consistency of results which could convincingly underpin sweeping recommendations for labor-market reform" (Baker *et al.* 2002: 26), supports Ball's position.

Summing up, Ball does not hold that demand variations, policy-induced or not, are the whole explanation for unemployment trends over the long run, a position as implausible as the orthodox view that labor market institutions are virtually the whole explanation. Instead, his position is broadly consistent with other work analyzing the interaction of institutions and macroeconomic factors, in which the main issue is not whether both matter but the relative weight to attach to each.[32]

---

[30] "There is no question that current official rhetoric that attributes the rise in the natural rate to labor and goods market rigidities has run far ahead of the evidence" (Blanchard 1997: 186).

[31] A regression in which generosity of unemployment benefits and wage bargaining structures has the most significant relationship to unemployment predicts a difference between early 1990s unemployment rates in Spain and Portugal (which provide "an acid test of any theory of unemployment") of "only 4 percent, in contrast to an actual difference of 12 percent" (Blanchard 1997: 187–188). For the argument that macroeconomic differences, including monetary policy, largely explain the different unemployment rates in the two countries, see Ball (1999: 225–226), Collignon (2002: 167–168), and Pérez (chapter 7 in this volume).

[32] They also disagree on which institutions matter. The main studies are Blanchard and Wolfers (2000), Fitoussi *et al.* (2000), and Bertola, Blau, and Kahn (2001). The latter build on Blanchard and Wolfers (2000) and also refer to Ball's work, but discuss only his 1997 paper. Reanalyzing the data, they conclude that labor market institutions explain

There is also evidence besides that cited by Ball that labor markets operate as postulated in his suggested explanation for NAIRU variations, especially on how increases in labor demand improve the "employability" of workers far back in job queues. Unemployment among those relatively disadvantaged in US labor markets – less educated, nonwhites, and less-skilled women – typically fluctuates more than that of the relatively advantaged – more-educated white males (Hoynes 1999). Thus, as US unemployment moved to long-time lows in the 1990s, employers sought workers in central city black ghettoes, providing training and helping reduce the black–white unemployment gap (Freeman and Rodgers 1999; *New York Times* 1999a, 1999b, 2000). Similarly, as the French economy experienced unprecedented employment growth between September 1997 and September 2000 (over a million jobs), unemployment among the long-term unemployed and those less than twenty-five years old or without secondary school diplomas fell by 4–7 percentage points more than the 20.5 percent average decline. Although women's unemployment declined less than average, it still fell more relative to the 1987–1990 boom period than that of any other of the groups (Pisani-Ferry 2000: 34, 287).[33] While it has been shown that lower skilled workers are "bumped down," and off, job queues in recessions as skilled workers fill vacancies for which they are "overqualified" in many countries, French data and preliminary data for Germany and Sweden show the process is reversed in expansions as more qualified workers move up to jobs for which their skills are more needed and the less qualified move into jobs for which their skills suffice or for which they can be trained (Gautié and Nauze-Fichet 2000; Åberg 2003, 2004).[34]

The 1990s recoveries brought long-term unemployment down, not only in France but elsewhere. A comprehensive survey of long-term unemployment in Europe concludes that it "is not a problem independent of unemployment itself" (Machin and Manning 1999: 3086). During the late 1990s European expansion (before the ECB aborted it), "The share of the labor force . . . unemployed for more than 6 or 12 months has fallen in all the countries that have registered falling aggregate unemployment rates . . . notably (more than 5 percentage points) in Portugal,

---

most of the US–Europe differences (Bertola *et al.* 196–197). However, they fail to address the more fully elaborated argument in the 1999 paper and its emphasis on growth spurts. All three are discussed in Baker *et al.* (2002).

[33] Unemployment of workers over fifty fell much less, only 7.6 percent. Some of the improved employment of the other relatively disadvantaged groups is attributable to lowered costs for hiring the lowest skilled but the overall rise in employment suggests that not much subsidized employment substituted for unsubsidized employment (Pisani-Ferry 2000: 34–35).

[34] On Germany, Wolfgang Scheremet (personal communication).

United Kingdom, Denmark, Netherlands and Norway" (OECD 2000a: 216–217) – i.e. countries with above-average declines in unemployment identified as "successes" by Ball and others. In the eurozone, the share of long-term unemployment in total unemployment fell considerably more than unemployment fell, 3.2 compared with 2.5 percentage points, respectively, during 1997–2000 (ECB 2002: 11, 13). Participation rates also rose, though more modestly.[35] Such evidence certainly confirms Ball's assertion that the long-term unemployed "can be reemployed if demand is sufficiently strong" (Ball 1999: 231), and hence why hysteresis is reversible, and why the NAIRU rose where monetary policy was persistently restrictive but fell where it more quickly turned expansionary. This, in turn, strongly supports our suggestion that the successively larger unemployment gaps between Europe and the US in the 1980s and 1990s result largely from the different reaction functions of the Fed and the Buba.[36]

However, this brings us to the second issue: the direction of causality. Even if differences in central bank reaction functions largely explain unemployment differences, there remains the question of why the reaction functions differ. Differences in labor market institutions could be the answer. If those differences largely determine how low unemployment can be without accelerating inflation, as the ECB insists, that could explain the differences in the banks' reaction functions and therefore the differences in unemployment trends. As a commentator on Ball's (1999) paper suggests, "Countries that experienced large increases in their NAIRUs were induced to pursue less expansionary policy" (Mankiw 1999: 238). Instead of running from monetary policy to the NAIRU, as Ball argues, the direction of causality could therefore be the reverse. This issue was already raised in Blanchard's comments on the (1997)

[35] Hence a sustained reduction in unemployment requires enough employment growth to absorb not only the unemployed at the time unemployment was highest but also those who had left the labor force or did not enter it at that time but are now drawn into it (Pisani-Ferry 2000: 62–68, 179).

[36] Taylor-type rules (see n. 21) may be a misleading basis for comparing central bank reaction functions with respect to unemployment. Such rules model interest rate decisions as a function of gaps between actual and potential output and between actual (or expected, in a year or two) and targeted inflation (Clarida, Galí, and Gertler 1998: 1034). If the difference in central bank reaction functions that matters most for their long-run effects on unemployment is whether they permit or prevent growth spurts, Taylor-type rules may not capture it. To do so they would presumably have to allow for growth spurts in some way, such as an inflation target term that varies over the longer period in which output is brought back up to its trend level. They could also be misleading if the output gap term is too low, as is likely if the output gap is built on estimates of equilibrium unemployment that attribute most of it to labor market structures rather than demand, as the ECB consistently does, or if the inflation target term is too low, as is likely if it is the ECB's target. In both cases, restrictiveness would be understated.

paper. Blanchard suggests an econometric test of the alternative interpretations: "Decompose disinflation as inflation in 1990 minus inflation in 1980, and allow the two inflation terms to enter with separate coefficients. Under Ball's hypothesis that disinflation matters, the two terms should come in with coefficients equal but of opposite sign. Under the alternative . . . only inflation should matter, not how low governments decided to push inflation down at the end of the 1980s." Blanchard concludes that when Ball carried it out his interpretation of the direction of causation was unambiguously confirmed. "It works like a charm: the coefficients are equal and of opposite sign" (Blanchard 1997: 188). Solow agrees (1999: 12).

Ball finds additional evidence in the central banks' own explanations for their actions (Ball 1999: 197–198), suggesting that their actions stemmed from their *beliefs* about the determinants of country NAIRUs, even if the diverse NAIRU changes were actually caused mainly by the banks' own actions. Much has been written on the "political power of economic ideas" (Hall 1989), including the continuity of ideas between the Bundesbank and the ECB (Fitoussi 1995; McNamara 1998; Heisenberg 1999).[37] The contrasting policies of the Fed and the ECB in the late 1990s US boom and the current European recession in recent years are attributed by De Grauwe (2003) to paradoxically similar ideas, which in both cases were wrong, leading to wrong policies. In both cases, "policymakers decided that the economic conditions they observed were driven by structural factors." Claiming that America's "boom was not just some temporary demand upsurge" but resulted from structural changes wrought by the "information technology revolution, promising permanently higher growth rates," the Fed fueled a "classic bubble led by the exaggerated expectations of believers in fairy tales." The ECB, blaming the eurozone's recession on "structural rigidities," especially in labor markets, as we know, "has been slow in stimulating the economy," helping to "sustain the recession by spreading the word that nothing can be done about it for the foreseeable future," making the ideas "self-fulfilling prophecies."

Thus, Ball's argument seems to successfully meet the two issues. If the argument is therefore essentially right, it casts doubt not only on the empirical basis of the ECB's position but also the neutrality of money postulate providing its theoretical basis. That postulate, holding that demand variations caused by monetary policy can have only short-run effects on

[37] Of course, the power of economic ideas has much to do with the power of those who hold them. It also has to do with their changing plausibility in changing contexts. For a subtle analysis of "periodic changes in the ideas informing economic policies," see Notermans (2000a: esp. 37–41).

real activity such as growth and unemployment, which return to their structurally determined levels in the long run and leave only changes in prices, seems untenable in the light of the effects of contrasting central bank policies on output and unemployment which Ball finds over periods of up to ten years. Critiques of the neutrality postulate based on the effects of monetary policy on capital accumulation point the same way.

While Ball's analysis focuses explicitly on how the effects of monetary policy on labor market tightness interact with firms' employment decisions, it implicitly refers to effects on the investment decisions on which the employment decisions depend, and which in aggregate determine the growth in the economy's productive capacity, and hence the rate at which output can grow consistently with stable inflation. Others link monetary policy explicitly to investment decisions. Blanchard argues that it is "now widely accepted" that "real interest rates . . . play an important role in accounting for the natural rate of unemployment." High interest rates help explain "why the natural rate remained high in Europe in the 1980s" because they increase "user cost, which leads to lower capital accumulation, which in turn leads to lower employment." If those interest rates result from "monetary policy – as seems plausible during a period [of] disinflation policies, the creation of the euro, and so on – does this not imply that monetary policy can have long-lasting effects, not only on the deviation of the actual unemployment rate from the natural rate but also on the natural rate itself?" (Blanchard 2000: 297).[38] Citing capital accumulation, too, Benjamin Friedman questions economists' acceptance of the "simplest theory" that monetary policy's real "effects are not long-lasting . . . though the evidence for it is so slight," whereas there are "plenty" of "not simple" theories, "typically focusing on various kinds of either human or physical capital formation, according to which monetary policy plausibly has very long-lasting real effects" (Friedman 1999b: 56–57).[39]

Proposing one such theory, Collignon also starts with the increased cost of capital resulting from high interest rates (2002: 144, 180–185). This makes it necessary to reduce unit labor costs to restore profit margins. Productivity is accordingly raised, but by eliminating labor-intensive units rather than investing in new higher-productivity units, thereby increasing

---

[38] Collignon (1998) answers that question in the affirmative because of monetary policy's effects on capital accumulation. While noting that "this is an important issue, on which there is surprisingly little work," Blanchard cites Ball's 1999 argument as "related, but not identical" (2000: 297–298).

[39] Friedman points out that the growth of human as well as physical capital may be retarded by recessions insofar as they keep young people from entering the labor market, depriving them of job training and experience at a crucial stage in life (personal communication).

unemployment while increasing the capital share.[40] There appears to be an increase in the capital–labor ratio in response to earlier wage pressure, as some have argued, but it is a statistical artefact of scrapping labor-intensive units in response to the increased cost of capital while new investment is simultaneously inhibited.[41] Unless central banks reduce nominal interest rates as inflation declines, the real interest rate stays high (at best) or rises (at worst), leaving the cost of capital high or increasing, inhibiting investment and hence retarding employment growth and keeping unemployment high.[42] Thus, the reduction in the wage share is not followed by an increase in the capital stock because it is not accompanied by a sufficient reduction in real interest rates to reduce the cost of capital.[43] If, however, real interest rates decline enough to reduce the cost of capital, the prospect improves that profits from new investment in productive capacity will exceed returns from alternative (risk-free securities) investments, plus a risk premium. The capital stock and therefore employment increase, provided that demand can be expected to grow sufficiently to absorb the resulting increase in output, and unit labor costs remain consistent with the required profit margins.[44] Whether unemployment decreases or not then depends on whether monetary policy induces sufficient capital accumulation to increase employment more than labor force and productivity growth.

From this perspective, the ECB can only claim that most unemployment is structural and hence intractable to monetary policy over the long run by ignoring monetary policy's lasting impact on capital accumulation, as done in Layard *et al.* (1991), OECD (1994a), and related analyses of relationships between various labor market institutions and unemployment underlying the ECB position which typically assume a constant capital stock. As Rowthorn points out, they make "the problem of job

---

[40] The capital share rose in Europe where interest rates were kept high but did not in the US where they were not kept as high.

[41] See also Rowthorn (1995: 31). Berthold, Fehn, and Thode (1999) argue that the capital–labor ratio increased in France and Germany in response to union power to raise wages.

[42] Monetary policy rather than labor market institutions is thus the source of hysteresis that increases the NAIRU, as in Ball's (1999) account (Collignon 2002: 173–174, 189).

[43] This describes the European situation.

[44] Collignon's model of the relationship between monetary policy and investment is based on the ratio of the expected real rate of profit to the real money market interest rate, known as "Tobin's $q$." From the firm's standpoint, investment projects will be worthwhile only if they are expected to yield at least enough to service the debt at the money market plus risk premium rate – or, in the case of financing out of retained earnings, at least as much as alternative investments. The expected real rate of profit depends on the rate of growth of demand for the output resulting from the investment that is expected over the life of the investment. This in turn depends on the rate of growth of output in the economy as a whole that the macroeconomic policy regime may be expected to sustain.

creation primarily a matter of encouraging more employment on exist-ing capital stock" (1995: 27). While this may hold in the short run, it can hardly be extrapolated over the long run during which capital accu-mulation occurs. If monetary policy has long-run effects on growth and unemployment through its effect on capital accumulation, however, it is not simply its stance at any particular juncture that matters but its *pattern over time* – i.e. the policy regime. Since the growth rate of capital stock is the aggregate result of investment decisions, it must be based on the decision-makers' expectations about the growth in demand for the resulting production. Hence, as argued earlier, their expectations of how macropolicy will affect demand growth as well as costs over the economic life of the investments must enter into their decisions.

As we saw, the ECB's actions and statements suggest that it believes growth cannot be allowed to exceed the 2–2.5 percent long-term trend rate the ECB evidently regards as consistent with stable inflation even if output remains below its trend level. It thus seems to have a growth rate target as well as an inflation target, even though it is not included in its announced strategy. If the ECB does in fact aim at keeping the growth rate from exceeding such a target rate, it is likely to prevent a period of sufficient above-trend growth to lower unemployment to where it would have been if disinflation had not pushed growth below trend – i.e. a growth spurt such as Ball observed in the NA2 and European success stories. The ECB would thus prevent a return to low unemployment just as E4 central banks did in the 1980s. In doing so, the ECB would turn its view of the allowable growth rate into a self-fulfilling prophecy. This would result not only from keeping long-term unemployment, and there-fore the NAIRU, high. It would also result from keeping the growth rate of capital stock too low to decrease unemployment significantly. If the ECB's actions convince investment decision-makers that it will tighten policy if an expansion pushes output growth above its long-run trend rate, as it did in 2000, they will presumably invest in only as much new capacity as will be profitable at the level of demand which the ECB can be expected to allow. This would increase the capital stock only enough to produce output at the level at which growth would be restored to its trend rate in the absence of an above-trend growth spurt, leaving out-put at a level lower than predicted by the pre-disinflation growth trend and unemployment higher than it would be at the higher output level. With capital stock limited to the lower output level, an effort to reduce that unemployment by expanding demand would come up against capac-ity constraints, increasing inflationary pressures. This would apparently confirm the ECB's position that unemployment cannot be lowered by macropolicy without accelerating inflation. However, this would result not from the labor market institutions to which the ECB attributes the "speed limit," but from the ECB's own policy of keeping growth from exceeding its trend rate, thereby keeping the capital stock from growing enough to produce higher output and lower unemployment without higher inflation – i.e. the sustainable growth rate is what it is because the central bank makes it so. As long as the ECB is unwilling to tolerate the temporary increase in inflation that would accompany a growth spurt large and long enough to increase the capital stock sufficiently to permit output to reach its pre-disinflation trend level, unemployment will continue to fluctuate around high levels.

## 3    Conclusion

This chapter argues that the macroeconomic policy regime implemented by the ECB so far is likely to keep unemployment high especially insofar as it precludes a growth spurt sufficient to significantly reduce unemployment. That the ECB is unwilling to permit such a growth spurt is indicated by its actions that contributed to ending the late 1990s European expansion and by the rationale it provides for its actions. Based on the orthodox view that monetary policy has no long-run effects on growth and employment, that rationale permits the ECB to abdicate from any responsibility for unemployment, which it ascribes almost entirely to structural factors, especially "rigidities" in the labor market, which it is up to other actors to remedy. Pending such a remedy, the ECB insists, the best it can do to promote growth and employment – also part of its Treaty mandate – is to maintain price stability, defined as very low inflation.

The proposition that a period of growth above its trend rate – a growth spurt – is needed to reduce unemployment to what it would have been if growth had not been interrupted by a recesssion, policy-induced or not, is the core of an alternative view of the relation between monetary policy and unemployment. This view is based on empirical analysis of variations in unemployment between the US and Europe and within Europe in the 1980s and 1990s. It provides strong evidence that differences in monetary policy largely explain the unemployment variations, without denying that labor market institutions can have some effect on monetary policy's impact. In particular, it shows that unemployment was lower without higher inflation in the long run where monetary policy permitted growth spurts than where it did not. The mechanisms which might account for these results are suggested in the analysis, and I cite additional empirical evidence that seems to confirm the operation of such mechanisms. If the analysis is correct, the proposition that monetary policy can have no long-run effects on growth and employment on which the ECB relies to justify its policies seems untenable. That proposition is also challenged directly in other work on the basis of monetary policy's effects on capital accumulation.

Strong doubt is thus cast on the rationale for the EMU macroeconomic policy regime as implemented by the ECB. However, it is obviously impossible to demonstrate that the ECB view is wrong and the alternative correct within the confines of this short chapter; it may well be impossible in work of any scale, given the vast amount of empirical and theoretical issues involved.[45] All that is attempted here is to show that there is a serious case to be made for the alternative view.

This chapter also concentrates almost entirely on issues of monetary policy at the core of that case. Thus, fiscal policy, the focus of intense current controversy over the Stability and Growth Pact (SGP), verging on an EMU crisis, is virtually ignored.[46] The SGP is certainly an integral part of the EMU macroeconomic policy regime, as the ECB and Commission insist. And in that role, however, as many point out, it has serious flaws (Buti, Eijffinger, and Franco 2003; De Grauwe 2003a).[47] Among its most egregious are its pro-cyclical tendencies and insufficient room for maneuver for countries where the one-size-fits-all monetary policy is particularly restrictive, notably Germany (Mackie and Pepino 2003a, 2003b).

Yet the main problem with the regime is not the SGP but the ECB's policy orientation, from which the SGP controversy deflects attention (*Financial Times* 2003). There are good grounds for prescribing budget balances over the cycle, implying surpluses during expansions as well as deficits during recessions, provided that there is ample scope for automatic (and even discretionary) stabilizers, and also for public investment (in human as well as physical capital), and, in the EMU context, coordination of national fiscal policies to achieve a eurozone fiscal stance consistent with a growth-promoting monetary policy (Pisani-Ferry 2002; I. Begg 2003). EMU is now poorly equipped to meet those conditions. Even as it stands, however, the SGP would pose much less of a problem if the ECB's monetary policy were not so restrictive. By keeping growth too low – cutting off the late 1990s growth spurt and subsequently easing policy too little and too late – the ECB has retarded the growth of revenue as well as adding to social policy burdens, making it much more

---

[45] Citing Pierre Duhem and W. V. O. Quine, Notermans suggests that "it is well-nigh impossible to refute theories by empirical evidence" (2000a: 16).

[46] Also ignored are such fundamental issues as the composition and ecological sustainability of economic growth.

[47] From a political perspective, as Collignon argues, its fundamental flaw is that it is "normatively incoherent with democracy" (Collignon 2004: 5).

difficult than it would otherwise be for governments to meet the SGP's requirements.

If the ECB's policy orientation is indeed wrong and the alternative view more nearly correct, then, there will be no progress to the renewed goal of full employment. Unless there is a shift in the EMU policy regime toward one in which monetary policy takes responsibility for growth and employment as well as price stability, Europe is therefore likely to experience continued high unemployment, posing what is probably the most serious threat to the European social model.

# 3    Shaping a polity in an economic and monetary union: the EU in comparative perspective

*Alberta M. Sbragia*


The system of governance in the EU gives national governments a central role. Brussels has not supplanted nor replaced national capitals, and thus the EU co-exists with powerful national political systems. While governance takes place in Brussels, government takes place in the member states. It is there that electoral accountability, legitimacy, and identity are anchored (Sbragia 2002). Even those who argue that the EU "bears a growing institutional resemblance to the established multi-tiered systems of traditional federal states" accept that national governments "remain extremely powerful" (Pierson and Leibfried 1995: 6).

Federalism has been an attractive referent for scholars precisely because the national governments retain so much power within a system of governance in which an important "center" is nonetheless present (Sbragia 1992b; Rodden 2002). That center is so strong that the EU is no longer simply a sophisticated international organization, but it is weaker than the center found in the decentralized federations of Canada and Switzerland (McKay 2001, 2002; Nicolaidis and Howse 2001; Börzel and Hosli 2002).

Although placing the EU within the universe of federal states certainly presents analytic problems, it does permit useful although not rigorous comparisons. In particular, it highlights features of the process of European integration which might not seem significant if analyzed in isolation.

The issue of policy change is particularly interesting in both the EU and the US. Both systems of governance must cope with a large population, a territorially diverse economy, and the dispersal rather than the centralization of power. Most fundamentally, decision-making is so difficult that scholars find it necessary to explain how policy-making happens at all. In both, major policy change in any single policy area is relatively

I would like to thank Peter Leslie for his exceptionally incisive critique of an earlier version of this chapter as well as my colleague Mark Hallerberg for his generous assistance with this chapter.

51

infrequent; legislation, once adopted, is difficult to modify. The kind of political bargains which are needed to underpin major legislation can be put together only with difficulty (Kingdon 1984; Scharpf 1988; Héritier 1999).

Within this universe of difficult decision-making, the EU's Economic and Monetary Union (EMU) stands out. The Maastricht Treaty and the Stability and Growth Pact (SGP) have carved out a "European space" in which the European institutions are supreme, fundamentally transforming the dynamics of EU decision-making.

All decisions about monetary policy in the Euro zone member states are now taken at the EU level. Frankfurt has indeed replaced the national central banks which previously decided national monetary policy. The European Central Bank (ECB) is the key actor in its policy domain in a way that no other EU institution can claim to be. When compared to other policy areas in which the EU is a key player, the SGP stands out because of the scrutiny given to its implementation. Aimed at ensuring fiscal discipline by requiring that budgets be balanced or in surplus in the medium term while allowing some flexibility in the short term, the SGP brings to bear on national public finances restrictions, monitoring, and scrutiny that are exceptional in their precision and the effort made to enforce them.

Has conflict between central and non-central authorities, in fact been neutralized when it comes to EMU? Does EMU represent one of those policy areas in which the center holds undisputed authority? Is EMU a singular exception to the kind of complicated and consensus-driven political dynamics that are characteristic of policy-making within the EU? This chapter answers each questions with a "no." It argues that EMU is characterized by politics which, while distinct from the kinds of politics found in policy areas governed under the traditional Community method, incorporate national political choice. In fact, some facets of EMU are far more dependent on national collaborators than are many other policy areas.

The existence of a single currency and a powerful and independent central bank would seem at first glance to support the argument that EMU adds very significantly to the prerogatives of the "center," thereby neutralizing national politics and political choice. The power of central banks is recognized in a great deal of literature as having expanded since the early 1980s as the emphasis on price stability has become dominant. Central banks are exemplars of nonmajoritarian institutions which, insulated from electoral pressures, can pursue policies which run counter to the expressed preferences of elected officials (McNamara 2002). Furthermore, it is certainly true that the ECB, unlike the early very decentralized Federal Reserve System (Fed), is a true central bank (Meltzer 2000: 2).

Finally, the impact of EMU is viewed by some scholars as being so profound as to qualify as a cultural shaper of behavior (Dyson 2000: 655).

Yet noncentral actors are extremely important in two aspects of EMU outside of monetary policy-making. As Wessels and Linsenmann argue, "EMU is not a single-rule exercise" (2002: 56). It is important that monetary union was accompanied by a form of (partial) *economic* union in Europe; that fact distinguishes the EU from the US. The Federal Reserve System was created well after both an economic union and a single currency had been established. The embedding of monetary policy-making in a process of *economic* union (however partial) is the key to understanding how the political dynamic between the center and national governments is structured within the EU.

This chapter thus analyzes two aspects of EMU which do not concern monetary policy-making. The first is the framework for public finance which is now emerging in the post-Euro era. Although still evolving at the time of writing (June 2003), it is clear that a great deal of conflict about that framework lies ahead, especially if economic growth remains low in the Union's major economies. The second has to do with labor market reforms which are viewed by the center as essential for the successful functioning of both the economic and monetary union. Comparing both components of EMU with their US counterparts can throw into relief aspects of the European experience which are important to European governance.

## 1    EMU: beyond monetary policy-making to economic policy coordination

EMU is clearly an area of governance in the EU in which a "center" exists: as well as the ECB and the SGP, it includes the European Council (which brings together the Heads of State and Government as well as the Commission President), the Council of Ministers for Economic and Financial Affairs (ECOFIN), and the Commission. Although analysts make the link between the pressure for neo-liberal reforms and the SGP in particular (McKay 2002: 82), the pressure for such reforms has been building since 1993, and although the SGP is an important contributor to such pressure, it is far from acting in isolation. In fact, the arguments for neo-liberal reforms were circulating in key policy-making and political circles, including the OECD, before the SGP was negotiated (Crouch 2002: 286).

Economic Union, while partial and certainly not equal to that found in even federal systems with weak central powers, nonetheless brought with it an ongoing and complex process of institutionalization that goes well beyond the SGP. The coordination of economic policy provides the umbrella under which a complex set of relationships are being created among most of the EU's institutions. Noticeably absent from the list, however, is the Parliament (EP).

The member states, acting within the European Council, ECOFIN, the Economic Policy Committee (EPC) and the Economic and Financial Committee (EFC) which both report to ECOFIN, the ECB, and the Commission are enmeshed in a complex web of proposing, reporting, assessment of implementation, peer review, "naming, praising, and shaming," benchmarking, and attempts at the transfer of "best practice" (European Commission 2002: 41). Civil servants from national finance ministries staff both the EFC and the EPC and ECOFIN plays a crucial role as the gatekeeper by which this policy dialog is transmitted to the European Council. Finance ministries have effectively sidelined COREPER and Foreign Ministries in this policy domain. However, the ECB and the Commission are also represented on both the EPC and the EFC so that the three key sets of actors – civil servants from the member state finance ministries, Commission officials from the Directorate-General for Economic and Financial Affairs, and ECB staff – are in constant interaction.

One of the key principles undergirding the relationship between the member states and the Commission and the ECB is that of "multilateral surveillance." This general concept embraces a whole set of reporting mechanisms which culminate, after approval by the European Council, in the publication by the ECOFIN of the Broad Economic Policy Guidelines (BEPGs). Those guidelines, called for in the Maastricht Treaty (and first produced in 1994), are proposed by the Commission, modified by the EFC and the EPC, finalized by ECOFIN, and given final approval by the European Council (Hallerberg 2002). Both the process of formulating guidelines and assessing how well each member state has implemented them puts the public finances of each national government under unparalleled scrutiny. The BEPGs, published annually, provide the foundation for more specialized documents, reports, and policy dialogs all of which are structured along the lines set by the BEPGs so that some rough consistency is achieved.

Although the BEPGs are not binding on the member states and do not have legal force, they do structure the agenda of analysis, discussion, and argument which characterizes the various processes which feed into the BEPGs (known as the Cardiff, Luxembourg, and Cologne processes). Each of them highlights certain aspects of economic coordination such as the reform of product and capital markets (Cardiff), labor market reform (Luxembourg), and wage bargaining (Cologne).

Furthermore, the "multilateral surveillance" mentioned above begins with the BEPGs, is reinforced by the SGP, and is elaborated still further by the Employment Guidelines (EGs). The EGs, modeled on the BEPGs, and adopted by the Employment and Social Policy Council, focus on issues of employment, job creation, and the functioning of labor markets. Thus, EMU incorporates far more than simply the monetary policy-making carried out by the ECB. As the Commission points out, "in the EU and EMU 'economic policy co-ordination' is used as an umbrella term" (European Commission 2002: 3). EMU provides a wide space for national choice, national politics, and conflict between central and noncentral actors.

The European Council was critical during the 1990s in providing the strategic impetus for the various types of "multilateral surveillance" which these processes represent. In brief, the kind of increasingly institution-alized oversight, discussion, efforts at policy transfer and learning, and shaming by the collectivity of member states of each other are quite strik-ingly innovative when compared with the US and with the processes internal to the member states themselves.

For their part, the Commission, the ECB, and ECOFIN are critical in both public finance and labor market reform, but they play different roles in each. Furthermore, the "center" in the aggregate is far stronger in the area of public finance than in labor market reform, precisely the opposite of the American case.

### Public finance

What is striking from a comparative perspective is that one can now begin to conceptualize something akin to "public sector finance" within the EU whereas that concept is alien in the US. Even though the "center" in eco-nomic policy does not begin to approach the ECB's power in monetary policy, it is nonetheless far more powerful and intrusive in terms of direct oversight and surveillance than is the American Federal government *vis à vis* American state governments. In the US, although the federal budget has an important impact on state and local budgets, the con-cept of "public sector finance," "public sector debt," and "public sector borrowing requirement" are not widely used; the figures discussed in Washington in relation to "government borrowing" are those pertinent to the Federal government and do not include state and local borrowing. The lack of both such a conceptualization and direct regulatory oversight allows the Federal government to downplay the large impact its taxing and spending policies in fact do have on sub-Federal budgets. By contrast, the EU's evolving public finance framework includes central coordination and oversight of national, regional, and local finance combined – expenditure, borrowing, and debt are all conceptualized in terms of national aggregates. Such a process builds on the way public finance has traditionally been treated within many of the member states themselves (Sbragia 1981).

Although the BEPGs are a "soft" form of coordination, they do put pressure on national officials: the BEPGs approved by the Seville European Council in June 2002, for example, offered country-by-country recommendations on budgetary policies. (Council of the European Union 2002b, 10093/02). The SGP, on the other hand, offers a "harder" form of economic coordination. The process is one in which the Commission can, and has, recommended that national governments be officially warned that they risk running a deficit greater than 3 percent of GDP. The ECB, not surprisingly given its commitment to price stability, is a very strong and consistent supporter of the SGP.

The main actors in the area of public finance, however, are the Commission and ECOFIN. Both institutions are key to the issuance of the BEPGs and the monitoring and surveillance which are central to the SGP. Monitoring has in fact been very much in evidence. The Commission and ECOFIN have annually evaluated national multi-annual budgets, and the results have been widely publicized. The report on the implementation of the BEPGs gives a country-by-country evaluation of the state of national finances as well as an assessment of how well budgetary policies have followed the previous guidelines.

The SGP, for its part, also requires "multilateral surveillance" which again leads to widespread discussion of national budgets. This process is a more important one than that associated with the BEPGs, for the SGP has a great deal of visibility and is viewed as far more constraining than the BEPGs. In the SGP process, projected deficits are evaluated, and if the Commission feels that a member state might go beyond a previously agreed-upon deficit target, it can recommend that the member state receive a formal warning. It is up to ECOFIN, voting by qualified majority voting (QMV), to issue the warning. If the Commission cannot garner the necessary votes in ECOFIN, it will seek a compromise.

Nonetheless, the process gives both the Commission and ECOFIN a good deal of influence over national budgetary policies (ECOFIN in general approves the bargains which have been struck in the EFC and EPC). National governments must balance their tax revenue and expenditures in such a way as to satisfy the Commission and especially ECOFIN in order to be able to avoid warnings. If they do permit a deficit larger than 3 percent of GDP, fines between 0.21 and 0.5 percent of GDP can be levied (McKay 2002: 81–82).

*National politics and public finance*

Until 2002, the SGP had been very effective in constraining member states from deficit spending. The threat of exclusion from the Euro zone had been extremely important in disciplining countries such as Italy whose public finances had traditionally entailed very large deficits, and that discipline had been maintained until the economic slowdown contemporaneous with the appearance of the Euro as a physical currency (Sbragia 2001; Radaelli 2002). Since then, however, national ministers have begun to chafe against the stringency of the Commission's interpretation of the SGP. In 2003, finance ministers allowed France and Germany to circumvent the Pact's requirements, a decision challenged by the Commission, which decided in January 2004 to take the finance ministers to the ECJ for violating the procedures called for by the SGP.

The ECB and the Commission first insisted that all EU member states bring their budgets into balance by 2004 (Italy was to balance its budget in 2003 rather than wait for 2004). That position, however, became untenable. As France and Germany began to breach the 3 percent limit in 2002, it became clear that such a balance would be impossible to achieve. The Commission, in September 2002, responded by changing the target date from 2004 to 2006. However, in May 2003, the German Finance Minister, Hans Eichel, announced that Germany could not achieve a balanced budget by 2006 while his French counterpart argued that the Commission no longer insisted on a balanced budget by 2006 (a claim strongly denied by the Economics Commissioner, Pedro Solbes). By the end of June 2003, it was clear that the actual implementation of the SGP would be subject to persistent negotiation and conflict as the big member states struggled with very slow economic growth, a Euro which was strengthening against the dollar, and the promises of tax cuts made by the Berlusconi, Chirac, and Schröder governments.

When Germany and France breached the deficit limit of 3 percent of GDP in 2002, a dynamic developed which threatened the implementation of the SGP. (Portugal, too, breached the limit but it was the big member states' actions which were the real threat to the system of surveillance in place.) The headlines became routine – not only had Germany and France breached the 3 percent deficit limit in 2002 but as of June 2003 they were going to breach it in 2003 and were likely to do so in 2004 as well. (In fact, in April 2003 the German government even began discussions with its state governments about how to share the burden of the possible fines which might be levied if it were to breach the limit in 2004) (Parker and Harnischfeger 2003: 4). Furthermore, it was very likely that in 2004 Italy as well as France and Germany would breach the limit.

Attitudes toward the SGP began to shift in 2002 just as deficits larger than 3 percent of GDP began to emerge. In June 2002, Ecofin struck two compromises which crystallized this shift. France was allowed to bring its budget "close to balance" rather than completely balanced in 2004 while linking the ultimate target to rates of economic growth.

The Italian government had a similar experience. The ECOFIN meeting in June agreed that Italy's budget in 2003 would not need to be balanced but could show a deficit of 0.5 percent of GDP. That concession allowed the Berlusconi government (elected in May 2001) to announce that it would cut corporate and personal income taxes as promised during the electoral campaign. The Commission, however, demanded that Italy change its accounting practices, and when Italy complied, the 2001 deficit shot up to 2.2 percent (its target deficit for 2001 had been 1.1 percent, Kapner 2002: 2). Given the size of the 2001 deficit and the forecasts for 2002 and beyond, the Commission was worried that Italian public finance would be a major concern for the SGP. The Commission was not convinced that the Berlusconi government would cut spending enough to offset the announced tax cuts. The Italian government, however, argued that the structural reforms – particularly in the area of labor market and pension reform – that it was in the process of achieving mattered far more to the overall strength of the Euro in the long term than did slight changes in deficit figures.

In response, Commissioner Solbes demanded that Italy balance its budget in 2004 because of its very high debt burden (110 percent of GDP) and that it have only a 0.5 of GDP deficit in 2003 (as agreed in June). However, at the mid-July ECOFIN meeting, the Italian Finance Minister proposed a 0.8 percent of GDP deficit in 2003 and an 0.3 percent deficit in 2004 (Papitto 2002).

Whereas the Commission had attempted to interpret the SGP literally, finance ministers (supported by the European Council) were willing to interpret it with a greater degree of flexibility. In response, the Commission proposed introducing more flexibility into the Pact, with states with a low debt – GNP ratio and small deficits being allowed to borrow for large infrastructure projects, for example (COM (2002)668 final). However, in March 2003, ECOFIN and the European Council rejected the Commission's proposal (only Ireland supported it) and decided to keep the Pact in its original form (Lynch 2003). Only minor changes would be permitted, and the 3 percent deficit ceiling was maintained (Buti, Eijffinger, and Franco 2003). In January 2004, the Commission's decision to seek a judgment from the ECJ seemed to introduce the possible "judicialization" of the SGP.

*US experience*

The role of the Commission and ECOFIN in overseeing the SGP contrasts with the lack of a "center" in US state and local finance. If a state government (or a municipality) borrows beyond its capacity, it will be punished by the specialized bond market in which sub-national governments borrow, but the Federal government has no responsibility for the financial problem. The jousting between the ECB, the Commission, ECOFIN, the ECJ, and the member states outlined above does not resemble any process in the world of US public finance.

State and local finance in the US converged without Federal interference.[1] After state governments defaulted on their debts in the nineteenth century, the Federal government refused to accept responsibility for repayment. Washington's refusal established its credibility; the notion of "public sector borrowing" did not emerge and is still absent today.

In fact, a wave of popular "revulsion" against the corruption and mismanagement attendant upon public borrowing led to state constitutional restrictions on state borrowing. State government budgets had to be balanced – without any exceptions. The Federal government did not oversee state budgets nor did it check whether the state budget was in fact balanced. Surveillance by public authorities of the type practiced by the Commission and ECOFIN is unknown; surveillance is carried out by market rather than public actors.

Since states regulated their own finances, they set up their own borrowing systems, which differed from that of the Federal government. It was left to private lenders to punish state governments if the latter did not meet their self-imposed restrictions. Ratings agencies in particular assessed whether state governments' budgetary policies were sound so that ultimately it was the market that regulated state government finance (Twentieth Century Fund 1974). In general, the system has worked very well. State operating budgets are widely thought to be reasonably well balanced while the system of state finance allows capital expenditures to be financed by borrowing (Sbragia 1983b, 1996).

*Comparison*

In comparing the two systems, the EU will undoubtedly continue to maintain a relatively strong central presence in the budgetary policies of the member states; the system of public finance in the EU will not become more similar to that of the US unless market actors become more influential. The difference between the EU's current position in the

---

[1] This section is largely taken from Sbragia (1996).

international economy and that of the US in the nineteenth century is so great that it would be difficult for the EU to allow national governments the kind of latitude that Washington allowed state capitals. The moral hazard problem is simply too great. The pressures within the member states to increase deficits in order to fund the welfare state or to cut taxes, however, will underpin a good deal of conflict between Brussels/Frankfurt and the national governments.

Quite possibly the central rules about national budgetary policies will evolve over time so as to require relatively balanced budgets in some areas of national expenditure while allowing deficits in others, such as a distinction between operating and capital budgets. Although some flexibility in the SGP will undoubtedly be introduced in the future, Ecofin must always bear in mind that the ECB might well raise interest rates if it objected to how the SGP was being interpreted. The ECB's monetary policy power gives it a great deal of clout which cannot be ignored as issues of economic policy are contested. On the other hand, the ECB's monetary policy decisions are not determined solely by how the SGP is implemented.

## 2    Labor market reform

The contrast between the power of the "center" in the US and the EU is sharp in the area of labor regulation as well as public finance. In contrast to the area of public finance, however, the US center has been much more powerful than the EU.

### Labor market reform in the EU

Labor market reform has been a leitmotif at the EU level since the publication of the *White Paper on Growth, Competitiveness, and Employment* (European Commission 1993). The European Council, meeting in Copenhagen in June 1993, asked Jacques Delors to produce the paper, submit it to Ecofin so that it could be used in the drawing up of the first BEPGs (which appeared in 1994), and to submit it to the European Council meeting in Brussels in December 1993. The White Paper called for a "new solidarity – between those with work and those without." It recognized

the need for a more efficient labor market and associated policies . . . This means significant changes, but it does not simply mean a deregulation of Europe's labor markets. Rather, it implies an updated, rational and simplified system of regulation and incentives which will promote employment creation, without putting the burden of change on those already in a weak position in the labor market. (Chapter 8: 8.1)

The December 1993 European Council meeting explicitly called on member states to improve "flexibility within enterprises and on the labor market by removing excessive rigidities resulting from regulation as well as through greater mobility." Although the Presidency Conclusions also called for a "high level of social protection," they clearly accepted the White Paper's focus on creating more jobs within the Union by pursuing labor market reforms. Furthermore, it used the BEPGs as a kind of template. The Council set up an action plan which included a monitoring procedure and raised the possibility of guidelines in the area of employment policy.

This approach was developed in a succession of Councils, culminating in the Extraordinary Meeting on Employment in Luxembourg in November 1997. While the Treaty of Amsterdam did not go into force until May 1999, the Luxembourg Summit decided to put the new title on employment introduced in the Treaty into effect immediately. It explicitly used the BEPGs as a template for the formulation of "employment guidelines" and the assessment of the implementation of those guidelines. The Conclusions, while calling for "the required balance between flexibility and security" contained the most detailed and explicit recommendations concerning labor flexibility. More specifically, national governments were asked to consider the use of "more adaptable types of contract" (Presidency Conclusions, November 20–21, 1997: 10) and to review their benefit and training system so the unemployed would have sufficient incentives to seek either training or work.

Thus by 1997, the European Council had slowly come to accept that more flexibility was needed in the labor market and that benefit systems had to be reviewed to ensure that they encouraged employment. The drive for such flexibility was accompanied by concern for the low labor force participation of women and therefore for equal opportunity in the job market. While accepting the need for more flexibility, there was always concern for security as well. The European Council accepted the need for both, a formula re-affirmed at Barcelona in March 2002.

### The ECB and labor markets

The ECB, upon its establishment, added an important new voice in support of those who favored more labor flexibility. While the European Council and the Commission supported "flexibility with security," the ECB clearly emphasized more strongly the "flexibility" side of that equation.

The creation of a powerful and very independent central bank has created a political space in which the ECB (and the Commission) have been able to play a prominent role as policy advocates but not as policy-makers. The success of the new single currency – the Euro – is viewed as linked to a set of policy areas which traditionally have been thought of as rather separate from monetary policy. The ECB is now an advocate for a whole range of policies which do not lie strictly within the field of monetary and exchange rate policy as traditionally understood. Rather the ECB has used its privileged institutional position to advocate and otherwise support ideas and policies which are very much politically contested, of which labor market reform is one of the most politically controversial.

The ECB views labor market policy as central for the success of the Euro, and has been promoting increased flexibility in its reports, testimony by its President, and briefings to national officials.[2] It argues that efficiently functioning labor markets have become especially important now that eurozone governments cannot "use country-specific monetary and exchange rate policies to address asymmetric economic shocks" (ECB 2002: 4). The bank views rigid and inefficient labor markets as limiting the rate of growth consistent with price stability, which is its primary objective (ECB 2002: 4).

The Bank thus supports both labor deregulation and welfare state reforms designed to reduce nonwage labor costs, measures which Crouch characterizes as "the main planks of the neo-liberal approach to labor-market problems" (Crouch 2002: 280). Labor market flexibility, from the ECB's perspective, includes greater wage differentiation, more latitude for employers in allocating work time, shaping unemployment benefits so as to encourage greater labor force participation, and – most controversial of all – a lessening of employment protection. In support of its views, it cites economists who believe that benefit systems in many countries discourage job creation and especially the development of a low-wage labor-intensive services sector.

While the ECB is singularly powerful in setting monetary policy, its power *vis à vis* the state of the labor market is far more circumscribed. The labor market in all eurozone countries has been shaped by many decades of legislation, collective bargaining agreements, and custom. Although significant cross-national differences exist among the labor markets in continental member states, all of them are far more regulated than are

---

[2] See chapter 2 in this volume.

the Anglo-American markets. As Paul Pierson (1994) has pointed out, retrenchment in the welfare state is a very arduous process and politically very costly. The same is true, and perhaps even more so, in the area of labor market regulation. The ECB, for its part, is very poorly equipped to force change in the shape of labor markets. Its instruments – such as the money supply and interest rates – are not suited to such changes. Its "toolkit" in the policy area is rather empty. It can not legislate, veto, nor overturn existing labor market regulations. It is dependent on national governments for the execution of ideas which it advocates and supports. That basic fact underlines the importance of the electoral choices made by voters at the national level. And in fact it is at the national level that we see movements toward the kinds of labor market reforms advocated by the ECB.

### The Commission and ECOFIN

It is not only the ECB, however, that has been a "policy-pusher" (Dyson 2000). The Commission, with its BEPGs and the reporting of the implementation of those guidelines, has also been a supporter of greater labor flexibility. Furthermore, employment policy, which is being formulated using the "open coordination" method codified at the Lisbon European Council in March 2000 which also set new targets for labor force participation, has led the Commission to throw a great deal of support behind recommendations concerning labor flexibility.

Finally, finance ministries and ECOFIN have also joined the chorus asking for a reform of benefit systems and increased flexibility of labor. In March 2002, the EPC published the results of its country examinations which are carried out as a peer review exercise. That evaluation involves a great deal of scrutiny as "almost a week is devoted to non-public sessions in which each country is being examined by another Member State. Shortcomings in structural policies are pinpointed and examples for best practice are identified" (European Commission 2002: 41). In March 2002, the EPC reported that

In a number of Member States temporary employment contracts have become substantially more widespread, contributing to job creation and labor market flexibility. This has especially occurred at the entry level, hence contributing to lower youth unemployment. Very few Member States have addressed dualism in labor markets by reforming *employment protection*. In a few Member States employment protection is being partially replaced by extended access to, and generosity of, unemployment benefits. (Economic Policy Committee 2002: 9, emphasis in the original document)

The ECB, with its responsibility for price stability, the Commission with its responsibility for overseeing economic union as well as employment, and ECOFIN and its related committees such as EPC, have fashioned a powerful alliance in favor of reforming the labor market so as to make it more flexible. Their analysis of labor markets, furthermore, leads them to consider areas of the welfare state such as benefits to the unemployed, the incidence of taxation on the low-skilled, and the existence of "poverty traps" or "inactivity traps." The Commission, finance ministries, and the ECB have linked labor market policy and the welfare state in a way which has eluded many scholars (Wood 2001: 368) but which is central to this volume.

In fact, the linkage made between labor markets and benefit systems by both the ECB and the Commission underlines Pierson's point that "welfare states are not just a Polanyian 'protective reaction' against modern capitalism. They are a fundamental part of modern capitalism" (Pierson 2001a: 5). Thus, the three institutional actors have taken on a role of arguing for policies which challenge the traditional structure of benefit systems, treatment of the unemployed, the often low labor force participation of women and the elderly, and employment protections. Although the welfare state and the direct regulation of labor markets are still very much under national control, the pressure from Brussels/Frankfurt to change the direction of their evolution since the 1960s and the 1970s is very clear and persistent.

The European "social model" is being challenged to become more market-friendly, more conducive to job creation, more capable of integrating women and the elderly in the labor force, and more sensitive to the need to create job opportunities for the low-skilled. At the same time, the argument that the ECB's monetary policy contributes significantly to the problem of unemployment in Europe (see chapter 2 in this volume) is downplayed if not rejected. The position taken by the EU's institutions strengthens those who argue for changing the social model and delegitimizes those who stress the need for a macroeconomic policy stressing economic growth as the best way to create jobs.

### *Labor flexibility vs. the single market program*

This pressure, however, is not being exerted along the lines of the single market program. That initiative involved the adoption of legally binding directives adopted by QMV if necessary, numerous ECJ cases, and very explicit monitoring of the single market's implementation (Egan 2001). By contrast, labor market reforms are being promoted by the "open mode of coordination," which explicitly eschews binding EU legislation. Policy convergence must be driven by national rather than EU legislation and political choices. Unlike the single market program, employment policy is being steered by the Commission, ECOFIN, and the ECB in such a way that it is individual national politicians who must take the lead in carrying out the very painful reforms desired by the Commission and the ECB. The "open method of coordination" fundamentally puts the burden on national politicians working within their own national contexts to legislate while the Community method which created the single market put the burden on the Council of Ministers to pass appropriate legislation (Hodson and Maher 2001).

### National choices and labor market flexibility

The conflict over labor market flexibility is a national conflict which occurs only within a member state rather than within Brussels. It is of tremendous concern to the EU's institutions, but it differs from the conflicts over the single market. In that case, Hooghe and Marks argue that the conflict was one in which neo-liberals wanted economic liberalization controlled at the European level while keeping the regulation of economic activity at the national level. "By resisting the creation of a supranational Euro-polity, neoliberals minimize the capacity for European-wide regulation of economic activity" (Hooghe and Marks 1999: 82). In the case of labor flexibility, however, the EU level can encourage but only national politicians can deliver. The lack of a supranational polity in this case allows those leaders less enthused about labor flexibility to decide which aspects of such flexibility to choose to promote within their own national system.

In fact, if as Peter Hall argues, Andrew Shonfield's classic *Modern Capitalism* (1965) represents a "national policy styles" approach to understanding variety in economic policies, the structure of the conflict over labor flexibility represents a new version of that national style (Hall 1999). Yet, while Shonfield could discuss the organization of economic power without reference to the EU, the conflict over labor flexibility is intimately entangled with the future direction of the EU's political economy. The direction of the EU can be decided at the EU level or alternatively it can be decided by a convergence at the national level. In practice, the results of national conflicts will affect the results of the EU-level struggle.

The ECB and the Commission are in fact trying to reshape the contours of the labor market not by focusing on EU-level initiatives but by bringing pressure on national decision-making. The social partners are being drawn in at the national level far more definitively than at the EU level. We thus find that a political struggle over the nature of labor markets is being influenced by EU institutions but the action is at the national level.

Much of the literature on the "neo-liberal model" focuses on the UK and the US when talking in general terms (King and Wood 1999). Yet, "neo-liberal" views of the labor market have been gaining ground on the continent. It would be much more difficult in 2002 to write that "the neoliberal project is a minority project" than it was in the late 1990s (Hooghe and Marks 1999: 83). Of particular importance was the Spanish case. As Sofía Pérez's chapter 7 in this volume indicates, the Socialists in Spain began the process of deregulating the labor market. After Aznar and the Popular Party came to power in 1996, the pressure to erode employment protection continued, and the Aznar government also began trying to export its model to the rest of the EU.

The Lisbon Summit of 2000 saw the presentation of the Anglo-Spanish Strategy for Sustainable Development. It represented the Aznar government's emphasis on market deregulation and his ideological predisposition to agree with Tony Blair's views on the requirements for a competitive economy (Closa 2001: 26–27; Egurbide 2002). With the commitment of the Aznar government to a variety of changes which began to move the labor market and the system of benefits toward a more neo-liberal model, Tony Blair had found an ally.

"Neo-liberalism" had come in some fashion in one of the continent's large member states. Whereas the Socialists had accompanied deregulatory measures with discussions of "solidarity," Aznar was ideologically more neo-liberal. The opposition to such policies was perhaps most visibly demonstrated by the huge demonstration before the Seville Summit in June 2002. The largest demonstration in eight years mobilized against the Aznar government's plan to place restrictions on employment benefits.

But it was with the election of Italy's Berlusconi government in May 2001 that the issue of labor flexibility began to find real traction on the continent. Employment protection in Italy was extremely rigid while unemployment benefits were relatively modest. That type of balance in fact was not that unusual – that kind of trade-off exists in many systems (Buti, Pench, and Sestito 1998). Within the EU, systems with generous unemployment benefits typically have a lower threshold of employment protection than do systems with very modest unemployment benefits.

The Berlusconi government proposed a substantively minor change in the laws affecting labor which, however, took on a huge symbolic importance.[3] One of the government's advisors who had been instrumental in

---

[3] The Berlusconi government proposed changes to Article 18 of the Italian Labor Code, the Article which the unions argued was the cornerstone of employment protection in Italy.

formulating the proposed changes was assassinated by the Red Brigades and a huge general strike took place in April 2002 (the most extensive in twenty years). The Employers' Confederation, Confindustria, by contrast attacked the government for not moving faster to liberalize markets. In spite of widespread opposition in the left and in the union movement,[4] the government managed, by threatening to exclude the entire union movement and pushing changes to Article 18 through Parliament on its own, to divide the labor movement and isolate the CGIL, Italy's largest union (closely allied with the Communist Party in the pre-1989 era) (Palmerini 2002). The government proposed a bargain – unemployment benefits would be increased and employment protection decreased.

In February 2003, Parliament approved legislation which made the labor market considerably more flexible, and in June 2003, a referendum which would have increased employment protection failed because of a low turnout. Berlusconi, for his part, explicitly announced that he was following Aznar's lead (Palmerini 2002).

Although the Berlusconi government dealt with the issue at the national level, it could claim that the EU supported its efforts. In February 2002, the Council of Ministers (acting on the recommendations of the Commission and the joint opinion of the Employment Committee and the EPC) adopted a set of recommendations on the implementation of Italy's employment policies. Those recommendations were specific: Italy should

Continue to increase labor market flexibility with a view to better combining security with greater adaptability to facilitate access to employment, pursue the implementation of the reform of the pensions system . . . and undertake the planned review of other benefit systems in order to reduce the outflow from the labor market. (Council Recommendation of 18 February 2002, 2002/178/EC; L 60/76)

In a similar vein, the Commission's Report on the Implementation of the 2001 BEPGs concluded that "it is now widely acknowledged that greater wage differentiation is needed to achieve a significant reduction in the unemployment rate in the south" (p. 97).

By contrast, the recommendations for Spain noted that employment under short-term contracts was high and recommended that their use be reduced while part-time work be encouraged (2002/178/EC; L60/74). In fact, many short-term contracts were renegotiated weekly which allowed employers to fire workers without severance pay (*Financial Times*, May 2,

---

[4] The number of strikes in Italy soared during the first five months of 2002. The vast majority of those strikes were called to protest the Berlusconi government's proposals for labor market reform (CNNItalia.it, 28 June 2002).

2002). Clearly, the Spanish labor market was far more flexible than the Italian.

In fact, leaders such as Berlusconi could use the EU to legitimate their positions because the "open method of coordination" leads to guidelines and recommendations which can be used by prime ministers in national debate to legitimate their own positions in the national debate. On the other hand, those leaders who do not want to move in the direction of the recommendations and guidelines do not need to; at the very least they can choose the balance they desire between "flexibility and security." Yet the fact that ECOFIN, the Commission, and the ECB all support greater labor flexibility as do several large member states does mean that national leaders who are less predisposed to such liberalization must engage in the debate.

### *A pro-flexibility coalition*

In 2002, a coalition between the UK, Spain, and Italy began to form which attempted to strengthen the EU's support of the kinds of initiatives they were undertaking. In February 2002, the British and Italian governments signed a joint declaration calling for more flexible labor markets as well as increased liberalization of other markets (particularly energy). In an interview, Berlusconi was clear as as to his role models: "look at Spain – there the economy is growing at 4 percent a year. In Germany it's less than half that" (*Sunday Times*, February 10, 2002). When the Commission put forward a proposal in March 2002 which would have given temporary workers the same pay and holidays (but not social security benefits) as permanent employees, the British and Italian employers' organizations jointly attacked the Commission's proposal in June (Milner 2002). Politically, therefore, the ECB, ECOFIN, and the Commission have found important allies in the UK, Spain, and Italy. All three want to export their model to the rest of the EU.

It is especially noteworthy that this coalition includes Spain and Italy, two countries rarely considered when discussing the differences between the "neo-liberal Anglo-Saxon countries" and the North–Central European countries with their "coordinated" (whether it be centralized or decentralized coordination) market economies. Given the focus of the literature on macroeconomic management on those member states with social market economies in Northern Europe, it is perhaps ironic that neo-liberalism on the continent has been promoted by two large member states which have been of little interest to those concerned with important changes in European capitalism.

By June 2003, however, the Spanish and Italian moves toward a more flexible labor market seemed to be in the mainstream as Germany's Chancellor Schröder incorporated labor market reform in his "Agenda 2010" package. Throughout the first half of 2003, various actors (including the Social Democratic Party, SDP) had accepted the need for changing Germany's social model. In June, the cabinet approved measures designed to increase labor flexibility – unemployment benefits would be cut and job protection loosened Further, other aspects of the social model were under scrutiny, including healthcare and pensions (Simonian 2003: 2). The failure of a month-long strike in the eastern *Länder* by the traditionally powerful engineering union *IG Metall* indicated that the traditional defenders of Germany's social model were unlikely to be able to prevent the government from pursuing the kind of welfare state reforms which the EU institutions had been seeking and which Spain and Italy had already pioneered.

### US labor regulation

The issue of labor regulation in the US involves the regulation of a market rather than its deregulation. It thus represents the reverse of the European debate about labor flexibility. Given space constraints, we can only highlight a key institutional difference between the US and the EU which we argue is critical in understanding how central/noncentral relations are being shaped in the two systems.

The regulation of labor in the US was affected both by courts and the nature of trade unions themselves. Undoubtedly, the strength of the craft unions in the early union movement, unions which typically opposed state or federal intervention and favored obtaining concessions through trade union action, shaped the way adult male laborers were treated by the state. The fact that the state federations, made up of weaker unions, had little representation in the American Federation of Labor (AFL) meant that the trade union movement pursued a strategy beneficial for the craft unions rather than for unskilled and semi-skilled workers (Lescohier and Brandeis 1935: 557; see also Lipset and Marks 2000). Such a strategy tended to focus on trade union action rather than on legislation.

Although the role of the AFL was certainly important, it is noteworthy that in the US, both the national and state judiciary were critical in limiting the definition of public purpose, in using the power to regulate interstate commerce so as to limit the state legislatures in their attempts to construct regulatory regimes, and in limiting the scope of the police power as exercised by legislatures in benefiting labor. The role played by the American judiciary is important in understanding how the market–state relationship evolved in the US. In brief, both the state courts and the Supreme Court for several decades vetoed the exercise of regulatory power at both the Federal and sub-national level. The US common market evolved as it did because the power of business was protected by the courts – the fact that state and federal legislation was overturned by the courts indicates that public opinion (as expressed in legislatures) and majoritarian institutions supported a greater role for governmental intervention than did the nonmajoritarian institutions of the judiciary.

The doctrine of laissez-faire was championed above all by the courts so that they became "the ultimate censors of virtually all forms of social and economic legislation" (Fine 1956: 126). The judiciary was key to creating one of the most important conditions underpinning market-preserving federalism. As Fine concludes:

With large sections of bench and bar thus committed in principle to a policy of laissez faire, it is not surprising that during the period 1865–1901 laissez faire was read into state and federal constitutions and that judicial formulas were devised to limit the scope of state social and economic legislation. Laissez faire might be overthrown in the state legislature, but it was still to have its day in court. In effect, courts set themselves up as the special guardians of the negative state. (Fine 1956: 140)

The state courts, for their part, especially after 1885, restricted the state legislatures from exercising their police powers in such a way as to regulate market activity for the benefit of adult male labor (Fine 1956: 158–162). Using the argument of "liberty of contract," state courts struck down legislation attempting to improve their economic position. Such cases were not sent to the Supreme Court because under the Judiciary Act in place at the time, the Supreme Court heard only appeals of cases which the state courts had decided were constitutional. The state courts thus were veto players during a certain period of time – if they decided a piece of legislation was unconstitutional, there was no recourse. It is noteworthy that before 1896, the Supreme Court ruled on only one type of labor law although state courts (after 1885) had ruled numerous pieces of legislation unconstitutional – being unconstitutional, they simply could not be appealed.

The toll on labor was high. For example, "In the field of hour legislation a number of important state decisions had been rendered before 1896 which left the constitutionality of most kinds of hour laws in serious doubt" (Lescohier and Brandeis 1935: 662). Wage payment laws were also typically struck down: although legislatures prohibited workers from being forced to accept commodities rather than wages, state supreme courts overruled them. Child labor laws and safety and health laws, by contrast, were usually upheld by the state courts (Lescohier and Brandeis 1935: 664–666); in those areas, the exercise of the state's police power was often approved.

Although many state courts overruled legislative efforts, it is the US Supreme Court which stands out as the "veto player" in the area of labor legislation. As Lescohier and Brandeis wrote in 1935:

It is a commonplace that American labor legislation has been shaped in large measure by court decisions . . . the United States Supreme Court has exercised an effective veto power over Congress and the state legislatures. It not only invalidated a number of important laws in this field; the position it might be expected to take determined the context of many others. (1935: 660)

For example, in 1923 the Supreme Court concluded that the minimum wage for women was unconstitutional. That decision shaped future attempts by the states to set minimum wages, affecting the nature of statutes and the willingness to enforce whatever laws might have been passed. The states tried to avoid being taken to court for they feared the outcome (Lescohier and Brandeis 1935: 503–505).[5]

The growth of a relatively unregulated market within the US was not a given. Its gradual dominance in the nineteenth century had a great deal to do with the judiciary which, in the post-Civil War era, struck down the attempts by both the federal and state legislatures to strengthen the power of public power *vis à vis* private power. Here, we find "picket fence federalism" in that the judiciary at both levels worked largely in concert to limit the intervention of public power in many market domains. Whereas the judiciary in the pre-Civil War era had supported an active role for state governments in developing their economies, they opposed the intervention of both the federal and state governments in the economy in the post-Civil War era. Regulation of the market strengthened the court's role as a "veto player" but did not strengthen the power of the center's elected institutions over those of the states. In a similar vein, the state courts, at least for a time, stopped the flow of legislation designed to protect labor. Neither the federal nor the state governments, therefore, can be treated as unitary actors in this sphere. After the introduction of the New Deal Program in the 1930s, the Supreme Court changed its position and labor regulation became permissible at both the state and Federal levels.

---

[5] Organized labor was either indifferent or hostile to the movement for the minimum wage for women and minors. It argued that the minimum wage would threaten union wages and that such a wage would discourage employers from hiring women (Lescohier and Brandeis 1935: 507, 514–515). In a similar vein, many of the craft unions, which had succeeded in obtaining reduced working hours through collective bargaining, opposed the movement for an eight-hour day for men, fearing that it would hurt the union movement (1935: 556).

However, more recently, the Supreme Court has once again shown an inclination to pursue deregulation. Given the overwhelming power of the federal judiciary in this area and the differences between courts and central banks, it is likely that the Supreme Court will be less dependent on finding "allies" than is the ECB. In the field of labor regulation, courts, when they have jurisdiction, may well trump central banks.

## 3    Conclusion

The US experience in the area of both labor market regulation and sub-central finance was very different from that of the EU. First, the Fed was not an actor. Rather, the conflict over labor regulation was judicialized. Instead of being framed as an issue having to do with competitiveness or economic growth, it was viewed as a question of the appropriate nature of state intervention in contractual relations between employers and employees. Secondly, the issue of public finance, for a variety of historical reasons, was compartmentalized and was not viewed as a component of central power. Rather, the states came to regulate themselves with the federal government remaining very detached from the regulation of state and local public finance.

In comparing the EU with the US in the areas of public finance and labor regulation, therefore, one of the most striking differences between the two systems has to do with the role of law and the judiciary. In the US, public finance is regulated by constitutional or statutory law at the state level rather than hierarchical control and supervision by Washington over the state capitals. In the case of labor regulation, it was the judiciary (both state and federal) that consistently determined which areas of labor reform were legally acceptable and thereby shaped the nature of labor regimes until the New Deal.

The EU, however, presents a striking contrast. Labor reform has not been "judicialized," while the decision about whether public finance will in fact be judicialized hangs in the balance at the time of writing (January 2004). The very fact that such a decision will be taken distinguishes the EU's public finance arena from that of the USA.

Prior to January 2004, both labor market reform and public finance had not been addressed by the "Community Method" and its accompanying ECJ jurisdiction. The SGP (although binding and part of the *acquis*) had been viewed by many as a type of agreement somehow different from that represented by directives and therefore not appropriate for litigation. In fact, the decision by the Commission to take finance ministers to the ECJ was highly controversial within the Commission and was approved only by majority vote rather than by consensus. Prior to the decision, the SGP had been dominated by the kind of political dynamic within ECOFIN already discussed in this chapter. In fact, that same type of dynamic was at work in November 2003 when finance ministers decided not to punish France and Germany for not respecting the 3 percent deficit ceiling.

The decision to take the finance ministers to court represented a turning point for the public finance sector. It introduced a new and powerful actor – one whose own credibility could suffer if the affected states were not to comply with a ruling with which they did not agree. Even if the Court were to decide not to intervene, the mere fact that it had been drawn into what had previously been a political rather than judicial matter introduced a degree of uncertainty about its potential role in the future.

The ECJ could in fact overshadow the ECB if it were to intervene. While the Court, if it so chose, could deal directly with the issue brought before it, the ECB would find it much more difficult to do so. Prior to January 2004, the ECB had been viewed as the potential "enforcer" of the Pact through its control over monetary policy which it could use as a weapon to discipline national politicians. The use of monetary policy in such a fashion could not, however, be targeted. National governments playing by the rules would be hurt just as much as those which were not. Furthermore, given the complexities of monetary policy in a global economy with floating exchange rates, it would not be a simple task to give priority to problematic public finances rather than to other issues. The ECJ, by contrast, could rule directly against those governments which were breaching the SGP; its impact in that case would be far more direct and needless to say politically explosive. An intrusion into French and German sovereignty by an adverse ECJ ruling would be a far more direct challenge to those member states than would be the use of monetary policy.

The contrast with the issue of labor flexibility is instructive. That policy area has not been judicialized at all – it has remained firmly within the control of national governments. The ECB, for all its power in the area of monetary policy, cannot create labor flexibility in the way that the state supreme courts and the Supreme Court in the US were able to stop labor regulation. The American courts institutionalized labor flexibility for many decades while in the EU such flexibility is the subject of political rather than judicial activism.

While it is certainly true that it is easier to veto new regulations than to dismantle existing ones, there are also sharp differences between the kind of power exercised by a central bank and a court like the American Supreme Court or the ECJ. A bank has a very strong but narrow domain whereas a court's reach and effectiveness, while certainly tied to political contexts (Conant 2002) can be much more extensive. A bank does not need allies "on the ground" in the field of monetary policy, but it does when it tries to re-shape regulatory patterns such as those found in labor markets. A supreme court, by contrast, can strike down state laws while needing only enough allies to prevent a constitutional amendment which would overturn its decision.

Thus far, the "Open Method of Coordination" (OMC) in the area of labor flexibility has insulated national governments from becoming entangled in the EU's judicial system. In that sense, the issue of labor flexibility contrasts with the new reality of the public finance arena. If national labor market regulatory regimes, politically sensitive as they are, were subject to the jurisdiction of the ECJ and if the Court were to rule that, for example, employment protection had to be cut back – or, alternatively, that such protection had to be maintained even in the face of, say, the Berlusconi government's position in favor – the political ramifications for the process of European integration would be highly unpredictable. It is quite likely that a very significant legitimacy crisis would emerge.

That unpredictability, and the possibility of such a legitimacy crisis, is one of the key reasons underlying the criticism of the Commission's decision to take public finance to the ECJ. Many would argue that given the sensitivities in both areas, and the intrusion into national sovereignty which judicialization would entail, it would be far better for both areas to remain subject to political negotiation and conflict among member governments and the Commission but excluded from the ECJ's jurisdiction.

Until January 2004, the lack in the fields of both public finance and labor market reform of a supranational framework similar to that of, for example the single market or environmental policy, privileged national politics. National leaders were able to choose the balance between the restrictions of the SGP and their own electoral needs and in the same vein were able to choose (within national political constraints) the balance they desired between flexibility and security in the labor market. After January 2004, they still retained that choice in the area of labor market reform but saw it threatened in the public finance arena by the potential intervention of the ECJ.

Regardless of how the Court rules, the very fact that it has been drawn into that policy arena reminds us all once again how fluid the EU policy-making regime still is. The relative power of the ECJ and the ECB in economic governance is not settled, and the type of supranational framework which will characterize such economic governance is still very much in the process of being stitched together. Yet to the extent that the ECJ becomes a potentially important actor, compliance by national governments becomes critically important. While national governments must accept the monetary policy selected by the ECB, they could in fact refuse to comply with an ECJ decision which favored the Commission. The costs would be very high, but it is not an impossible outcome. Thus, in spite of the turning point represented by the decision of January 2004, national politics will still retain their key role in EMU.

# 4    Monetary integration and the French model

*George Ross*

Much of contemporary French history is about defining and maintaining the French version of the European social model in changing economic conditions. By the early 1970s, a solid, if comparatively idiosyncratic, employment relations system balanced weak, politicized, competitive unions and anti-union employers, both reticent about bargaining, with a strong state and legal order. The French welfare state was a Gallic translation of Bismarckian social insurance with "paritary" management, once again backed by a strong state.

In the 1980s, however, French politicians took the lead in consolidating the European Monetary System (EMS), in making it happen, and opening the road to EMU. As the major actors in renewing and changing the shape of European integration, they also were the instigators of new European-level economic constraints that would force reforms to France's employment relations system and welfare state. In the 1980s, when France committed to achieving price stability within EMS, labor market and welfare state changes were largely improvised in the face of a rapidly changing economic environment. In the 1990s EMU "convergence" period old and new leaders partially absorbed these new constraints to conform to the new situation, in large part through significant reforms. French leadership toward EMU thus paralleled developments in French social policy.

The French postwar economy was successful until the 1970s. Growth, state-stimulated and state-centered, then boosted by the coming of the Common Market, was so robust (5.6 percent annually) that in the 1960s, France became the international model of the day, despite chronic inflationary propensities managed by periodic devaluation (Shonfield 1965). French inflation was thus already high when the first oil shock hit in 1973 and after the US ended its commitments to Bretton Woods, Keynesian domestic politics fell under siege.

Domestic politics in the 1970s shaped responses to new economic troubles. In 1972 the big players on the Left, Socialists and Communists, historically almost always at loggerheads, negotiated a radical and economically nationalist program deal that brought them enough new support to threaten electoral victory for the first time since the founding of the Fifth Republic in 1958. Next, the Center-Right, in power since 1958, began to split. Valéry Giscard d'Estaing, who had barely won the 1974 presidential election over Socialist François Mitterrand, appointed Jacques Chirac as Prime Minister. Chirac stimulated the economy, but his policies and personality led to conflict with the President, leading Chirac to resign in 1976. Chirac then re-founded the Gaullist Party as the *Rassemblement pour la République* (RPR), dedicated to restoring Gaullist predominance on the Right and, by implication, to destroying Giscard's Presidency.

Chirac's replacement was Raymond Barre, a liberal economist and former European Commissioner. Growth had dropped, productivity growth had halved, inflation, 4.3 percent on average in the 1960s, had shot up to 10 percent, and unemployment was beyond 5 percent (from below 2 percent in the early 1970s), fueled by crisis and the arrival of France's baby boom on the labor market. Giscard and Barre preferred liberalization and deflation but polls that showed Left and Right each with half the vote indicated that the government would lose power if these preferences were followed. In the meantime, post-Bretton Woods international monetary confusion threatened the common market and common EC policy areas, particularly the Common Agricultural Policy (CAP), at the core of France's position in Europe and French domestic politics (Becker 1998: chapters 3–4).

EC leaders rapidly sought new monetary policy arrangements, eventuating in a deal between Helmut Schmidt and Giscard d'Estaing to found the new EMS (Ludlow 1982; Heisenberg 1999: chapter 3). EMS began as a compromise. Stronger currency members, Germans in the lead, used monetary policy to maintain price stability. Those with weaker currencies, France first off, were prone to cycles of inflation and devaluation. The Germans, at least initially, were unwilling to compromise and this meant that others, like the French, would have to pay the adjustment costs of EMS. Giscard probably hoped that the Germans would impose limited constraints upon French domestic policy while the French worked the intergovernmental politics of EMS to gain more flexibility from the Germans. All of this changed, however, after François Mitterrand won the Presidency in June 1981.

1    **Monetary integration and the last gasp of French Keynesianism**

From 1981 to the 1991 Maastricht Treaty, the French path was determined by the Left's policy failures. Mitterrand brought pledges derived from the 1972 Socialist–Communist common program to re-invigorate France's *dirigiste* model of development. Almost immediately there were new nationalizations, industrial policies and planning, employment relations reforms granting more power to unions and workers, a devolution of powers from center to regional level, redistributive shifts in social protection programs, and Keynesian stimulation including extensive public sector job creation (Favier and Martin-Roland 1990).

This Mitterrand experiment rapidly ran into difficulties (Hall 1987; Muet and Fonteneau 1990). By 1981 the Federal Reserve–Reagan recession had begun to touch Europe while the future of the new EMS was uncertain. The Left was divided about how to manage external constraints, with some anticipating serious international problems from the new domestic policies while others, more voluntarist, were optimistic. The Left's new Keynesianism fueled France's already high inflation while other countries, Germany in particular, pursued price stabilization. The resultant pressures on the franc produced three devaluations within EMS through March 1983 (Cameron 1996). In the spring of 1982, the government, under strong German pressure, turned to austerity. It temporarily de-indexed wage and pension levels from the various *ex post* mechanisms that had kept them rising with the consumer price index, raised interest rates to a peak of 18 percent, imposed controls on currency exports, and put short-term price and wage controls in place (Bauchard 1986: chapter 2).

By winter 1982–1983 it was clear that short-term fixes had not been enough and that basic choices were necessary. Leaving the EMS and floating the franc might have allowed continuity in relative autarky, but carried high risks of failure. Staying in the EMS at the cost of major economic policy changes carried major domestic political dangers for the Left as well. Mitterrand listened to both sides, initially favoring the nationalists (or "Albanians," as they were called), who included some of his closest friends. The "Europeans" counterargued that floating would lower French living standards dramatically, disrupt and perhaps destroy the EMS, and quite possibly end the EC itself. From the beginning of the EC, and in particular since the heady years of 1960s Gaullism, the French had believed that domestic *dirigisme* was compatible with European integration as long as the economy thrived and French diplomacy could prevent Europe from imposing too many constraints. March 1983 was the moment of divorce for these two fundaments of French European policy.

### *Shifting economic and foreign policy: the "Europe option"*

Mitterrand was concerned initially about maintaining his power. The Left's polls were at record low levels: in October 1983 only 38 percent expressed confidence in Mitterrand, a year later only 26 percent (Becker 1998: chapter 3). New legislative elections in the spring of 1986 were already lost. The President thus needed to minimize this loss and maximize his own prospects for re-election in 1988. "Floating" the franc promised turbulence and uncertainty plus major political maneuvering. Cutting losses through austerity would disavow what the French Left stood for, but it seemed less costly. Mitterrand thus decided to negotiate terms for a new devaluation with the Germans. France would stay in the EMS, a striking – perhaps even humiliating – confirmation of German monetary hegemony and an important lesson: if Europe was the only French option, then strengthening French positions relative to Germany in monetary affairs would be essential.

The new period started with a shift toward austerity, budgetary constraint, and market liberalization. It also initiated a new hard-currency monetary policy – later called the *franc fort* policy – to deflate rapidly toward parity with the D-mark, creating recession-deepening high interest rates. Next, the government stopped using the public sector to maintain employment and began a harsh program of restructuring, which under a Right government (1986–1988) turned toward privatization. Surrounding all this was a tornado of talk about rediscovering the firm, the market, good management, best international practices, technological change, and a French Silicon Valley (Bauchard 1986: chapter 4; Favier and Martin-Roland 1990: chapter 3). Mitterrand imposed a ceiling (44 percent) on *prélèvements obligatoires* – the total of taxes and social security contributions as a percentage of GDP. The stock market was reformed, leading to a boom. The share of wages and capital in GDP began to shift against wages for the first time in two decades (from 74 percent in 1981 to 68.5 percent in 1990), and inequalities grew. Inflation dropped from an annual average of 9.6 percent between 1980 and 1985 to 3.5 percent over the next five years (Smith 1998: chapters 7–9).

The 1983 shift was as much diplomatic as economic.[1] The French 1984 EC Presidency resolved the biggest issues underlying "Europessimism," the "British check" problem, and Spanish and Portuguese accession. Jacques Delors was also appointed to the Presidency of the European Commission, effective from January 1985. With Delors in office and the beginnings of greater economic policy convergence among EC members, the French sought to renew European integration. French strategists had good reason to think that France might take the lead in this. The British were too ambivalent about Europe. The Germans could not lead, despite

---

[1] Mitterrand had cultivated the German government before the 1983 shift. His dramatic gesture of support for then-new Chancellor Kohl in a pro-Euro-missile speech to the Bundestag in January 1983 created a friendship that would be pivotal.

their economic power, because of their history. Making European integration the centerpiece of policy might also ensure longevity for the Mitterrand Presidency. Austerity was obviously unpopular, and to succeed politically, Mitterrand needed plausible reasons to justify the post-1983 changes. Belt-tightening could be presented as a means to achieve noble European goals. If all this worked, Mitterrand might have a chance of re-election in 1988.

Delors and his Commissions were central in initiatives to regenerate European integration. The program to complete the single market led immediately to the Single European Act (SEA) expanding EC prerogatives and changing EC decision rules to make "1992" feasible. After SEA ratification in 1988, EC budgeting was reformed and linked to new EU federalism through reconfigured and expanded regional development policies. Delors also managed to insert language favoring new monetary initiatives into the SEA (Quatremer and Klau 1997: 150). The first explicit suggestions for creating an ECB and a single currency then came in 1987 from Edouard Balladur, finance minister of Chirac's 1986–1988 "cohabitation" government, who was exasperated by the Bundesbank following the 1985 Plaza Accord (Quatremer and Klau 1997: 153). Then, at the Hanover European Council in June 1988, Delors became chair of a top-level committee of central bankers to bring forward EMU proposals.[2]

What did French leaders expect from EMU? Given the dangers to the single market from monetary policy divergence, EMU and a single currency made policy sense. They would reduce transaction costs, prod restructuring, and make intra-European factor costs more transparent. Wages would then have to reflect national productivity and budgetary and fiscal polices would have to fit better real economic fundamentals. In international terms, EMU's single currency could, in time, become a rival to the dollar, perhaps limiting American use of dollar diplomacy to shore up its domestic economy at others' expense. EMU, finally, could be a giant step in promoting new European integration. The real French story line on EMU was borrowed from the EMS, however. The French wanted to seize some control over monetary policy from the Bundesbank by constructing a new institutional basis for European monetary policy that would be less harshly biased toward price stability and more growth-friendly.

### The French social model challenged: the EMS period

France began the EMS period with macroeconomic policies that harked back to the post-1945 era and ended with completely different outlooks.

---

[2] EMU had been proposed much earlier in the 1970 Werner Report, itself largely inspired by Raymond Barre, then a French European Commissioner.

"Competitive deflation," designed in part to strengthen French positions in a new, monetarily integrated, EC, brought new liberalism to domestic economic life. Unpleasant results came quickly. Growth dropped to below 2 percent in the 1980s, inflation dropped from 13 percent in 1981 to 3 percent in 1990, and France moved to mass unemployment (France 1997: 15–26). The average period of unemployment rose from eight months in 1975 to between fourteen and sixteen months in the 1980s and 1990s, with numbers for those unemployed longer than one year rising from 16 percent to between 35 and 40 percent after 1983.

*Monetary integration, employment relations, and the labor market*
France, like most Latin European countries, had a competitive pluralist labor movement where divided unions historically fought one another for shares of potential membership and for influence in employment relations institutions and politics. Weakly organized French employers, in turn, distrusted unions, conceding little to them until the later 1960s and then only in the aftermath of May–June 1968. The social partners sought to compensate for organizational weakness through politics, feeding a state-regulated employment relations system based more on legislation and controls than bargaining. The importance of the statutory minimum wage (the SMIC) and public sector wage-setting further reinforced this politicization.

French employment relations had begun changing well before 1981. After peaking in strength in the mid-1960s at 24 percent of the workforce, French unions immolated themselves in competitive pluralism in the 1970s connected to the vicissitudes of the French Left. When the Communist–Socialist *Union de la Gauche* split around the 1978 legislative elections, the *Confédération Générale du Travail* (CGT, indirectly tied to the PCF) and the *Confédération Française Démocratique du Travail* (CFDT) broke their "unity-in-action" alliance that since 1964 had been the backbone of union success (Ross 1982: chapter 10). The CGT veered toward highly politicized militancy while the "recentering" CFDT began a quest for more negotiation. Ensuing conflict brought decline for the CGT, stagnation for the CFDT, and crisis for unionism in general (Labbé 1996). Despite this, unions retained serious capacities for inciting unpredictable strike movements.

In their divided and declining state, French unions were in no position to take advantage of the Mitterrand–Left victory in 1981. The government nonetheless honored its Keynesian pro-labor commitments, but the 1982–1983 policy shift changed their meaning. Employment insecurity made workers more skeptical of unionism and risk averse. Thus in conflict-prone France, the number of strike days dropped from 501,000 in 1980, already low compared to earlier years, to 19,000 in 1991. Union density, 14.5 percent in 1985, dropped toward 9.1 percent, overwhelmingly in the public sector, by the mid-1990s, the lowest of any industrialized country (Mouriaux 1996; ILO 1998: 252). Because of France's statist–legalist employment relations system, however, general coverage of collective bargaining remained close to 90 percent.

In the new context the Left's reforms acquired a different valence. Reducing work time to thirty-nine hours, adding a fifth vacation week, and reducing the retirement age to sixty together kept unemployment levels from rising even more, but also reduced labor force participation and put new strain on employers, pensions, and unemployment compensation funds. The 1982 Auroux Laws created new forms of worker representation in health and safety, "rights of expression," annual obligatory wage negotiations, and a "democratized" public sector. French employers virulently denounced them, but after their implementation the new laws became excellent vehicles for these same employers to promote flexibility, wage lowering, and anti-unionism (Coffineau 1993).

Beginning in 1984, after pulling the plug on rust-belt industries and creating new economic disaster areas in the North and Northeast of the country, the government created special public programs for "conversion poles" to ease the shock. Traditional union bastions in places like state-owned Renault were broken. In early 1986 the Socialists passed a law to promote negotiations on working hours to allow more fluid work scheduling. Next, during 1986–1988 President Mitterrand "cohabited" with a Right government led by Chirac that gutted strong laws from the 1970s limiting firing (in particular the "administrative pre-approval of dismissal") and encouraged temporary employment contracts. Enforcement of labor law weakened during the same years. Strengthened employers experimented with fads like quality circles, just-in-time production, Total Quality Management, and the individualization of labor contracts.

In this storm, France's workforce and labor market changed dramatically. The participation rate stagnated in general, but dropped precipitously among young people under twenty-five and those over fifty-five, leaving the bulk of those still employed between twenty-five and forty-nine. Female participation continued to rise between 1982 and 1990 while male rates declined (from 70.6 percent to 64.8 percent, Gambier and Vernières 1995: 20). Part-time jobs rose from 9.2 percent of the labor force in 1982 to 14.2 percent in 1992. "Precarious" jobs (temporary employment, internships, apprenticeships, and the like) doubled in number between 1982 and 1993 (INSEE 1995: 75). Atypical contracts and working-time schedules – weekends, night shifts, staggered hours – became much less unusual.

In employment policies the Mitterrand governments initially followed policies from the 1970s to reduce labor force size, albeit more decisively (Heller 1997). A new wave of youth employment programs began in 1983 with tripartite agreement on integrating young people into the labor market (Gauvin 1993: 162–169). In 1984 the TUC program (*travail d'utilité collectif* – non-market but "useful" public jobs) began, quickly enrolling 27 percent of those eligible. Next came SIVPs (*stages d'insertion à la vie professionnelle* – temporary "real" jobs in which employers' social insurance contributions and sub-minimum wages were subsidized by government). In 1990 came the CES (*contrat emploi-solidarité*), similar to the TUC. There were new internships, apprenticeships, and training programs, plus more spending on education in general, particularly on new early-childhood programs that facilitated female labor force participation. Effective measures were also taken to push a higher percentage of each age cohort into university and technical training, including a commitment to achieve 80 percent success in baccalaureate exams.[3] Much in this policy mix involved statistical techniques to cap youth unemployment, but a small part was also newly active labor market policy to enhance skills and engender better work habits.

The biggest problem was long-term unemployment. The Left's first major labor market reform lowered the retirement age to sixty. After 1983, the Left also promoted targeted early-retirement schemes for workers in areas and sectors where restructuring hit hardest. A 1982 ordinance also gave workers strong incentives to "pre-retire" or go half-time (often being obliged to do so) at fifty-five, and in some cases even at fifty. After 1986 there was also expansion of training and apprenticeship programs for the long-term unemployed, reflecting new notions of "activation." Employers with more than fifty workers who intended to lay off ten or more within a period of thirty days were enjoined to negotiate "social plans" to maximize prospects for successful re-employment. In all, by the 1990s, France had the lowest average retirement age in the EC, a fact deeply felt in public pension budgets.[4]

Spending on labor market measures rose from 2.3 percent of GDP in 1981 to 3.5 percent in 1988. Passive actions (increased unemployment compensation plus expenditure on early retirements) predominated, rising from 57.6 percent of the total in 1981 to nearly 61 percent by 1988.

---

[3] In 1985 19.3 percent of men and 22.1 percent of the 20–24-year-old cohort were in school. By 2000 the figures were 41.8 percent and 46.2 percent. In 1985 77.7 percent of men and 60 percent of women in this cohort were working. By 2000 the figures were 55.4 percent and 46.9 percent (CERC 2002: 28–30).

[4] By 2000 in the EU only Belgium had a lower employment rate for those aged fifty-five to sixty years old.

Table 4.1 *"Bismarckian" vs. French welfare states*

| System criteria | Bismarckian (German) | French |
|---|---|---|
| Nature of social protection | Social insurance based upon socio-professional status | Social insurance with general scope |
| Management | Decentralized | Decentralized under state control |
| Method of financing | Contributions tied to salaries | Taxes and contributions |
| Service provision | Proportional to salaries and capped | Proportional with social minima |
| Obligations for . . . | Ensured with salaries lower than the cap | Everyone |

The cost of unemployment compensation, a program originally designed to cope with frictional unemployment, rose rapidly – 15 percent in 1985, with the annual growth rate slowing during the upturn of 1988–1989, then rising back to 15 percent again by 1991. Average contribution rates rose commensurately from 3 percent in 1980 to 5.8 percent in 1984 to 6.95 in 1989 (Join-Lambert *et al.* 1997: 463–467).

*A welfare state besieged*   The 1945 decree that instituted the French social security system established "an organization . . . to protect workers and their families against risks of all kinds that might undercut their ability to earn . . . cover their costs of maternity and their family burdens" (Documentation Française 1997: 59). The new system was to be universal, unified in one general plan, and uniform in contributions and benefits. Social protection was insurance-based and financed through payroll taxes on employers and workers. Programs were administered in "paritary" ways by producer and consumer organizations, which meant that the French state, often touted as all-powerful, had at best indirect influence over the broad range of organizational stakeholders that managed the system. The state did stand behind the system to ensure that accounts balanced and budgetary holes were filled, and it assumed responsibility for those ineligible for insurance-based benefits. In the broader scheme of things, the French system was generally "Bismarckian," but with Gallic twists, as table 4.1 shows.

The system took three decades to mature (Palier 2002: chapter 3). Financed on a "pay-as-you-go" basis, it sub-divided into numerous programs grounded in occupationally based insurance funds. The largest of these, the *régime général* (originally to be the only one), covered most private sector workers. Parallel and separate regimes also sprang up for a

Table 4.2 *Growth in spending on social security, 1950–1995*

| Spending on social protection | 1950 | 1960 | 1970 | 1981 | 1990 | 1995 |
|---|---|---|---|---|---|---|
| % of GDP | 10.0 | 13.8 | 19.2 | 26.0 | 27.2 | 29.8 |
| % of gross household income | 16.0 | 19.0 | 15.3 | 35.5 | 40.5 | 42.7 |

*Source:* Documentation Française (1997: 55).

great range of special types of work – farmers, miners, transport workers, civil servants, public utility employees, plus scores of others. Each *régime* covered five types of risk – health, old age, maternity, disability, and death, and each was legally private, belying France's statist reputation. Family policies, daycare, and family allocations, deemed programs of general solidarity, were run separately by state administrations. Additional insurance systems for obligatory complementary pensions and supplementary healthcare expenses also emerged.

Pay-as-you-go meant that revenues were tied to the business cycle, thus involving the state, which had the last word on the levels of payroll taxation and benefit levels, in deficit-plugging, and financial tinkering. As long as full employment existed the system's coverage was quasi-universal (Viossat 1997). Those who did not work for wages – the disabled, single mothers, the indigent – had separate means-tested safety net programs. The financial growth of the system is reflected in table 4.2.

The largest expenditures have always been healthcare and pensions, together 75 percent of the entire "social protection" budget in 2002. The healthcare system (ranked world number 1 by the WHO in 2000) has hovered at around one-third of the total since 1960, although it has doubled as a percentage of GDP, competing with Germany and Sweden for the highest level in Europe. Pensions rose from one-third to around 43 percent of the total from 1960 onwards. Family policy spending, the third big item, financed out of general revenues, has been cut by half (from 30 percent to 15 percent) since 1960, largely reflecting falling birthrates. Spending on employment, with the biggest share being unemployment compensation, jumped from 2 percent to 6.4 percent between 1970 and 1990 (7.2 percent in 1995).

The French health system combines social insurance financing, state control of hospitalization, and "paritary" co-management with traditional "liberal professional" medical organizations. In ambulatory care, patients choose their own physicians, including specialists who, within loose constraints, have been free to recommend treatment. Reimbursement levels are periodically, often painfully, bargained between social security bodies and organizations of medical professionals. These characteristics have created a system prone to financial perversities. "Paritary" management made costs depend on bargaining in which some actors have had interests in offloading costs to third parties, primarily contributors and taxpayers. The state, responsible for hospital costs, half of the total, has used this leverage to control spending.

With explosive progress in medical technology, growing patients' awareness of service availability, population aging, and the corporatist incentives given to the medical profession to expand its income and status, the costs of healthcare have been rising more rapidly than GDP growth from the 1970s on (Wilsford 1991, 1996; Hassenteufel 1997). But by the 1980s the trend had intensified and the share of healthcare in GDP rose from 7.6 percent in 1980 to 9.1 percent in 1991. Revenues came from payroll taxes and when growth stalled and unemployment grew, chronic funding problems worsened. Moreover, in the post-1983 environment the medical bill placed a strain on national resources that, other things equal, made it more difficult to reduce inflation, balance budgets, and create and sustain a strong currency. The EMS period thus inevitably brought more tinkering and scrimping, drawing on a repertory set out in the 1970s. New "plans" raised costs to consumers, enhanced revenues, introduced user fees and deductibles, and established new regulations and cost controls on hospitals every year but one in the 1980s.[5] A new regulation of hospital costs, in the spring of 1983, replaced financing hospital care on a daily-rate basis (with its incentives to overhospitalization) and obliged each hospital to live within an annual budget. Costs continued to climb nonetheless, and when different healthcare professionals felt squeezed, they mobilized in Gallic ways – strikes, publicity campaigns, and demonstrations – usually to considerable effect.

If healthcare provided similar benefits for all contributors, such was not the case for the public pension system which, designed around the principle of intergenerational sharing, fragmented over time into many regimes. All were financed by payroll taxes, but each had its own contribution schedules, eligibility and benefit rules, and range of retirement ages. Because of favorable dependency ratios benefits grew more rapidly than GDP into the 1970s, while old-age poverty, endemic before 1945, became rare. However, as the system matured and with the French living longer and having fewer children, favorable dependency ratios began

---

[5] Co-payments and user fees created inequality. Complementary insurance existed to cover the deductible, defeating the purpose of user fees. Yet one-eighth of those covered by basic programs could not buy this insurance and became second-class healthcare citizens. The astonishing variety of measures in quasi-annual plans is shown in Palier (2002: 406–422).

to disappear precisely when growth and labor force participation levels dropped in the 1980s. Pension dependency ratios were projected to drop by 2015 to a dangerous 1.22: 1. Beyond budget juggling and endless reporting, however, pensions were not reformed in the EMS period. This was largely because early retirement was governments' weapon of choice to keep unemployment figures down. As a result, change was postponed to a future moment when things would be much worse. The French pension system was also clearly a political third rail, to be touched only when causing a domestic crisis would be less costly than avoiding one.

*Big changes?* The end of French Keynesianism began with Mitterrand's 1983 decision, after which policy moved toward accepting much higher levels of unemployment and seeing welfare state programs as spending to be limited rather than as tools for stimulating demand. There were few real reforms either in labor market or welfare state policies, however, undoubtedly for political reasons. There were two big exceptions to this, however, the *Revenu Minimum d'Insertion* (RMI) and the *Contribution Sociale Généralisée* (CSG).

The new situation fostered long-term poverty (Palier 2002: 282–287). The small postwar safety net had worked with full employment, but mass unemployment made it less and less effective. The long-term unemployed faced grim circumstances when benefits were exhausted. Groups with labor market handicaps – immigrants, young people without a first job, single parents, those close to retirement age – faced daunting situations. Beginning in the mid-1980s, "social exclusion" became a concern. Ghettoes exploded, young people took to the streets, celebrities led demonstrations and ran soup kitchens, and social critics advanced new ideas. Mitterrand responded by proposing the RMI in his 1988 Presidential Election manifesto (Becker 1998: part II, chapter 2).

The RMI, passed in December 1988, was a means-tested guaranteed minimum "citizen's income," administered departmentally and tied to commitments to seek "insertion" – usually meaning training or work.[6] The program was a compromise between a guaranteed minimum income and "welfare to work." In time, despite tight eligibility control, the "insertion" parts of the RMI became less important than "revenu," due to the chronic absence of jobs. The RMI opened the door toward a more Beveridgean means-tested social safety net. The RMI's clientele, 500,000 in its first year, grew to 1 million three years later and nearly 2 million by 1997, and its costs rose commensurately.

[6] The provision excluded those under twenty-five covered by other programs and varied with the household situation, but it was significantly lower than the SMIC minimum wage.

Social policy costs in general rose rapidly in the 1970s and 1980s (see table 4.1). Payroll taxation was the prevailing financing mode, but its level put France out of line with European competitors: In 1989, over 80 percent came from payroll taxes, compared to 71 percent for the Germans, a 66.2 percent EC average, and 46 percent for the UK. Moreover, employer contributions were higher in France (49.1 percent in 1994) than in Germany (39.9 percent), and Great Britain (26.1 percent) (Join-Lambert *et al.* 1997: 482). This problem, which affected French competitiveness, may have prompted the second major pre-Maastricht reform, the CSG in December 1990. The CSG was a new flat-rate tax on incomes dedicated to financing social protection, first set at 1.1 percent to finance family policy. The idea of financing social programs from general taxation, broadening the tax base beyond payroll, income, and VAT taxes, began doing on the revenue side what the RMI had done for inclusion. The CSG was justified not for its impact on workers, but because of the general solidarity that citizens owed one another.

## 2    The 1990s: EMU shapes French domestic politics

The 1991 Maastricht Treaty was another turning point. Negotiations made clear that France would not gain much new control over European monetary policy. EMU would be decisively more "monetary" than "economic," the ECB would be committed to price stability, and the Treaty contained only vague language about coordinating macroeconomic policy and promoting growth. Maastricht set out strict convergence criteria for potential EMU members including targets on national budget deficits (3 percent or less), debt levels (60 percent of GDP), interest and inflation levels, and successful participation in EMS. In 1991 France was well placed to meet these targets. Whether this would still be true when final decisions about EMU membership were made – either 1995 or 1998, according to the Treaty – remained to be seen.

French social politics in the 1980s were driven by the consequences of the French Left's policy turn after 1983. Chronically high inflation rates declined rapidly, budgetary practices were tightened, wage growth controlled, deficits and levels of debt lowered, and the franc was "hardened." The biggest cost of this was very high unemployment. Employment relations and welfare state programs were profoundly affected, losing their status as Keynesian demand management tools and becoming "supply-side" costs to be controlled. Pro-active reformism did not really begin until Mitterrand's second term after 1988. The EMU convergence years of the 1990s turned out even more daunting, with unemployment and budgetary constraints becoming much more severe in the mid-1990s than at any point in the 1980s. The SGP of 1996 and its inclusion in the Amsterdam Treaty in 1997 institutionalized harsh austerity well into the future.

### From Mitterrand to Chirac

The June 1992 Danish rejection of Maastricht led Mitterrand to call a French ratification referendum for the following September. The President was worried about the faltering momentum of European integration and also foresaw a referendum redressing an electoral balance that had shifted dramatically rightwards. (Favier and Martin-Roland 1990: 310–332). Initially the polls were favorable (60–40 percent), but over the summer negativity about Maastricht exploded (Cameron 1996). A Center-Left coalition saved the day – barely – for Maastricht.[7] The 51 percent for "yes" allowed the Treaty to go forward, but did little for momentum on European integration and even less for the Left's electoral fortunes.

The Center-Right won a huge majority in the 1993 legislative elections.[8] Jacques Chirac, coalition leader and logical Prime Minister, sought instead to stay above the fray to prepare his 1995 Presidential run. His "friend of thirty years," Edouard Balladur, got the job and quickly faced a difficult economic situation. German post-unification policies had fueled a brief, mildly inflationary European boomlet in 1991–1992, then the Bundesbank overshot its corrections, promoting a brutal recession that deeply affected France. Short-term interest rates went up, growth stopped and unemployment rose to over 12 percent, its highest post-1945 level (Cameron 1996: 353; Heisenberg 1999: 132–134). The EMS also went into convulsions after speculation forced the pound out of the system on Black Wednesday in September 1992. Trouble continued into the summer of 1993, with virtually all ERM currencies, including the franc, fair game for speculators (Heisenberg 1999: chapter 6; Quatremer and Klau 1997: chapter 7). One result was that France fell way off EMU convergence targets.

The post-Maastricht EMU convergence years brought new reformism in employment relations and social policy. The first sign was a negotiated "activation" reform of unemployment insurance in 1992 that created the AUD (*Allocation Unique Dégressive*). Increased unemployment

---

[7] Raymond Barre, Giscard d'Estaing, and other Center-Right leaders joined Socialists barnstorming the country for "yes" votes. Even Jacques Chirac came out personally for a "yes," despite allowing a free vote to RPR supporters.
[8] The RPR and the UDF won 82 percent of the seats, 474 of 577. The Socialist vote in the first round dropped from 34.8 percent in 1988 to 17.4 percent.

insurance (UI) payouts tied to 1980s unemployment plus the growing inappropriateness of a system designed to cope with frictional unemployment that also contained incentives to discourage job searches were behind this. The AUD brought a streamlined UI system closely tied to individual contributions with benefits that decreased over time, ultimately pushing the longer-term unemployed into safety net programs like the RMI. The employers' association (*Conseil National du Patronat Français* – CNPF) and the CFDT union signed the new deal, with the other unions opposed, coinciding with a change to CNPF–CFDT leadership of the UI program (UNEDIC). The CFDT's new posture indicated that there would no longer be a unified union front against major social policy changes (Palier 2002: 216–225).

Reforms continued when Balladur proposed changes to the pension system. The reference period for establishing benefit levels in the "general regime" (the largest social insurance fund) was extended to twenty-five years (from the ten best years), effectively reducing pension levels, while the contribution period was lengthened from thirty-seven-and-a-half to forty years. Pension benefit growth would henceforth be calculated by reference to a price index rather than wage evolution. Further, in response to union desires to lighten the burden on social insurance funds, the reform established a *Fonds de solidarité vieillesse* (FSV) – Fund for Solidarity with the Elderly – to finance those not eligible for social insurance-based benefits, paid for by raising the CSG by 1.3 percent.[9] Both the FSV and CSG financed accentuated shifts toward "solidarity" to replace insurance for the very poor, funded from taxes rather than contributions (Bonoli 1997; Palier 2002).

These reforms, negotiated with the unions (the CFDT signed, while the CGT and others, although not signing, permitted implementation), passed without incident, but created a ticking bomb for subsequent governments. Only the "general regime" (private sector) was changed, broadening existing disparities between other regimes and leaving civil servants and public sector workers in a more privileged position than before. Balladur also passed a five-year employment law that lowered the costs of employing workers near the minimum wage (SMIC) by exempting their employers from social insurance contributions (Join-Lambert *et al.* 1997: 277–278). The five-year law also proposed a sub-minimum wage for young people (the CIP – *contrat d'insertion professionnel*) that Balladur withdrew in the face of very large demonstrations. Balladur also rescued the healthcare budget by raising co-payments.

---

[9] Income from the CSG tripled in three years. Balladur made the new increment of CSG deductible from income taxes, turning it in a regressive direction.

The 1995 Presidential campaign came three short years before entry into EMU and after deep recession had set back efforts to meet the convergence criteria. Scandals and bungling in Mitterrand's last years helped defeat the Socialists, even with a reasonable candidate in Lionel Jospin. Balladur's popularity meant that Chirac first had to defeat his "friend" in the election's first round. Balladur's government had left 12 percent unemployed and growing poverty. Chirac thus campaigned demagogically, promising to heal the "social fracture" through job creation and economic growth. He was also carefully vague about commitment to EMU.[10] To meet the convergence criteria, however, austerity had to be intensified with, in particular, the budget deficit reduced from 5 percent of GDP in 1995 to 3 percent in 1997. The growth and job creation that Chirac advertised in his campaign were thus idle promises unless Chirac wanted to stop EMU altogether.

Chirac fended off Balladur and won the runoff against Jospin. Alain Juppé, the new Prime Minister, who initially did little about Chirac's pledges, announced his Plan for Social Security in November, a sign that the Chirac Presidency was committed to EMU. The Plan, tied directly to the EMU convergence criteria, proposed the most significant reforms to the French welfare state since 1981. It changed long-standing "paritary" procedures so that henceforth appointments would be made directly by "social partners" (unions and other representative organizations) eliminating electoral mechanisms that unions had long used to assess their relative strengths and acquire power, money, and jobs. Under the Plan, parliament, acting on government proposals, would also set general directions and global levels for social security spending. The most explosive provision, however, would extend the Balladur pension reforms (changed reference years, contribution lengthened from thirty-seven-and-a-half to forty years) to civil servants, public sector workers, and other "special" pension regimes.

The plan was a well-crafted set of proposals to reach the 3 percent deficit criterion. Juppé undermined it, however, by preparing it secretly without consulting involved groups and then presenting it in a peremptory, technocratic fashion. The proposals on paritarism challenged key union organizations while those on pensions threatened strategically placed segments of the labor force. This combination united a variety of groups in opposition, including unions that ordinarily disagreed with one another. Some, like the railroad and Paris transport workers, were eager to bring France to a halt by striking, in particular because the

---

[10] At one point, Chirac actually pledged to hold a national referendum on EMU before French entrance, but this was quickly forgotten.

Juppé proposals coincided with a plan for restructuring the railroads. A five-week strike followed that ended only at the 1995 Christmas holidays. The most immediate result of the strike was that Juppé's pension reform proposals were withdrawn.

Most of the other provisions of the Plan were eventually enacted. First was an emergency finance item for a 0.5 percent addition to income tax to continue for thirteen years – the *Contribution au remboursement de la dette sociale* (CRDS) to pay off an accumulated social security debt of $60 billion. Beyond changing the structures of paritarism for healthcare the Plan gave governments new control over the bulk of the total social security budget. The percentage growth of healthcare expenses would be voted by the National Assembly annually after 1996, changing contractual practices of the decentralized *caisses* and establishing tough cost controls backed by penalties. The Plan also raised the CSG to 3.4 percent, 40 percent more than under Balladur, to substitute for portions of employee payroll taxes for health insurance.

Prime Minister and President paid dearly for the Plan episode. Their poll ratings dropped precipitously – by the end of 1996, the Prime Minister was the most unpopular in the history of French polling. The SGP nonetheless made EMU a daily constraint. Before the EMU decision point in 1998 France would undergo brutal budgetary compression, with unemployment rising to 12.8 percent by early 1997, and even slower economic growth than projected (0.9 percent as opposed to 2.2 percent in the first quarter of 1996, partly because of the strikes). Chirac also had to anticipate parliamentary elections scheduled in 1998 that were certain to eliminate most of the huge 1993 Center-Right majority.

With their seats on the line, parts of Chirac's majority began to behave in unruly ways, second-guessing and criticizing the government. In response Chirac called early elections for April 1997. The electorate interpreted the call as presidential cynicism and an early warning that greater austerity was on the way. Socialist leader Lionel Jospin reassured voters and advocated "softening" the approach to EMU. He also proposed an "economic government" to provide macroeconomic policy guidelines for Europe and the ECB, job creation (700,000 new jobs, almost exactly what Chirac had promised in 1995), reducing the work week to thirty-five hours in the interests of job sharing, and an end to privatization. These proposals facilitated alliances on the Left and provided incentives for National Front voters to vote Left in the second round. The result was a defeat for Chirac and his majority. Jospin then became the first Socialist Prime Minister of cohabitation, leading a Left pluralist alliance including Communists and Greens.

*Gallic third ways and beyond*

At the June 1997 Amsterdam European Council, after but two weeks in power, Jospin announced that France wanted an "economic government," revision of the SGP by new commitments to growth and employment, plus the "European Growth Fund" recommended in the Delors Commission's 1993 White Paper. Amsterdam was a bad choice for a showdown, however, since its agenda included finalizing the Amsterdam Treaty. The new Prime Minister thus accepted the EMU arrangements that he had castigated in his campaign. He did win a *quid pro quo*, however, an important new treaty clause on employment policy.[11] Jospin's EU-level goal was to communicate to the French that EMU could be made politically interactive and was not a fixed object, and that it could be influenced by resolute French action. He also wanted to announce that there was not only a French position, but also a Left position, to be defended at European level.

Jospin's choices on EMU placed his domestic policies under constraints similar to those of his predecessors, in particular the 3 percent budget deficit target.[12] The Prime Minister's initial problem was thus to reduce the deficit without betraying promises. He tried to do this with a wave of active reformism designed to demonstrate that despite EMU there existed space for positive domestic policy change (Levy 2000). First steps were directed toward the labor market, with pledges to create 700,000 jobs over five years, particularly for young people. The new youth employment plan proposed targeted and decentralized hiring for "jobs of a third type" with five-year limited contracts that fitted well into contemporary ideas about "activation."[13] The logic behind the plan was tough, however. Without such a measure, no matter what anyone did in the shorter run, there would be insufficient new employment growth to make a difference for young people.

The next initiative was persuading social partners to reduce the legal working week from thirty-nine to thirty-five hours by 2000. The

---

[11] The EU pledges to "promote economic and social progress and a high level of employment." A new Article 109 added that member states and the Community should work toward a "common strategy for employment . . . for promoting a skilled, trained and adaptable workforce and labor markets responsive to economic change" and see employment growth "as a matter of common concern and . . . coordinate their action" (EU 1997; Goetschy and Pochet 2000).

[12] Juppé had reached only 3.7–3.8 percent, leaving Jospin to squeeze more.

[13] Only local authorities and nonprofits could hire. These minimum-wage jobs, subsidized 80 percent by the budget, employed young people for "third-sector" tasks. Examples included youth animators in troubled urban areas and schools, aids for the elderly and the handicapped – meals on wheels and the like – conflict mediators in cities and public transportation systems.

government hoped that unions would bargain work-time flexibility and wage moderation in exchange and that employers might accept the shorter working week, new job creation, new taxation on overtime, and good-faith negotiation in exchange for lower payroll taxes. Despite rhetoric about bargaining, however, the government insisted on making the thirty-five-hour week obligatory through legislation.[14] The laws enjoined social partners to bargain on work-time reduction and created incentives to compliance, mainly through reducing employer contributions to social security on new lower-wage hires.[15]

Action on welfare state issues was less spectacular. In healthcare, this was because the Juppé Plan had already begun far-reaching financing changes. Shifting the funding base for healthcare toward the CSG – which rose to 7.5 percent of income – was yet another step toward universal entitlements away from social insurance principles. The shift did not resolve the perennial problem of balancing the healthcare budget, however. Like its predecessors, Jospin's government had to plug holes and improvise, even though renewed growth between 1997 and 2000 eased constraints. The Left's one important change in healthcare was the *Couverture Maladie Universelle* (CMU, or Universal Illness Coverage) in 1998, enacting a proposal that the Right had earlier made. Existing safety-net programs covered the basic healthcare regime but not the supplementary insurance that covered deductibles and co-payments in ambulatory care. The CMU established a means-tested entitlement to basic and complementary insurance, granting the poor access to the same healthcare coverage as everyone else.

Pension issues were politically dangerous. Jospin, anticipating the 2002 presidential elections and sensitized by Juppé's 1995 disaster, chose to nourish debate with a variety of reports rather than take risks. The 1999 Charpin Report concluded that without decisive action by 2010 France's public pension system would face deep difficulties and recommended an updated Juppé plan that would extend contributions to forty-two-and-a-half years (*de facto* raising the retirement age) and align all regimes with

---

[14] There were precedents. In 1996 the Center-Right had introduced the Robien Law. More modest than the Socialist proposals, it had provided benefits to employers creating jobs, but without legal compulsion.

[15] Eventually there were two laws, in June 1998 and January 2000. The first made the new scheme applicable by January 2000 for firms with more than twenty workers and 2002 for those with fewer. The second, drawing upon experience with the first, specified the ways that bargaining trade-offs and "carrots" to employers would work. The proposals caused the CNPF to implode. Its President had tried to bargain employer cooperation to avoid legislation, failed, then resigned, leaving the door open, as he noted, to "the killers." The new President of the CNPF (immediately renamed MEDEF – *Mouvement des Entreprises de France*) announced that he would use the thirty-five-hour issue to destabilize the government. MEDEF thereafter became the most strident neo-liberal voice in France.

the already reformed general regime (Charpin 1999). The Report was not well received by the Left, and Jospin solicited another report from his own Council of Economic Advisors (the Taddei Report) which stressed instead the need for increased economic growth. A third report from the Economic and Social Council completely disagreed with Charpin. Contradictory arguments thus buried debate in confusion (Concialdi 2000). The government did establish new reserve funds, claiming that public money could push the day of reckoning with pension problems further into the future, by which time demographics and economic circumstances might both have changed.[16]

Jospin's "plural Left" coalition lost power in the 2002 elections. The causes remain in dispute but it is clear that Jospin's own misdirected campaign plus a proliferation of Left candidates (more than a dozen) helped Jean-Marie Le Pen scrape into second place in the runoff with Chirac (who had himself received fewer than 20 percent of the votes in the primary). Le Pen's relative success then led to a massive "Republican," anti-extremist vote for Chirac, setting up a big Center-Right win in the legislative elections that followed. Chirac appoint Jean-Pierre Raffarin, a moderate, as Prime Minister, clearly indicating that ultra-liberal action was no longer on the French agenda. In his first year Raffarin duly played the "insecurity" (i.e. law and order) card, but otherwise hewed closely to the center.

One of Chirac's campaign pledges had been pension reform. Raffarin's major accomplishment was to carry it out with some skill. Juppé's 1995 fiasco provided Raffarin with a field manual of how not to proceed. Passing laws and invoking parliamentary sovereignty, even with a very fresh and large new majority, was not enough to secure success. The "paritary" nature of the French welfare state created innumerable veto groups, implying the need for effective divide-and-rule tactics. And the grèvicultural approaches of most French unions meant that any reformist government had to find ways to keep its plans alive through a barrage of strikes and demonstrations.[17]

The "Fillon Plan," named after the Minister in charge, proposed phasing-in a lengthened contribution period (to forty years, to match the private sector regime) for civil servants and public sector workers by 2008, to be gradually raised to forty-two years by 2020. It also sought to persuade people to work longer through bonus incentives (3 percent

---

[16] This paraphrases Palier (2001: 227–245).

[17] *Grèviculture* literally means "strike farming." It refers to the strategies of unions, among other French organizations to raise stakes to governments by constantly threatening to create protest uprisings. When these strategies worked – as they sometimes did – they could wreak havoc with governmental goals.

more benefit per year to work beyond sixty until sixty-five) and penalties (5 percent per year less than the required number of years). Rules for combining pensions with continued work were also eased. Employers' ability to summarily retire workers were to be limited. The unions claimed that pensioners would end up with 20 percent less because of this and they were undoubtedly close to the truth.

That the reform was eventually adopted was the more important story. Initially almost all of the key unions opposed it and mobilized for one-day strikes almost weekly. The strikes were very successful for a time, and also promisingly militant for opponents of the reform who hoped that enough disruption would cause the government to pull back. Opponents were also encouraged by strike movements among teachers protesting a parallel plan by the Education Ministry to decentralize the management of some teaching personnel.

There was no massive explosion, however. Raffarin stayed the course, the summer vacation approached, and negative sentiments grew about relatively privileged groups defending their privileges. The key to success was governmental shrewdness in bargaining with unions in a divide-and-rule way. Major concessions were granted to the teachers to remove the dangers of contagion between the two movements. Then the government conceded smaller points on pension reform to the CFDT, which then announced its interest in saving the principles of the existing system and withdrew from the mobilizations. Other big unions, particularly the CGT, continued to promote strikes – primarily because public sector workers were the core membership, but the threat of major disorder faded.

*The French social model in the convergence period*   In 1997 French unemployment reached 12.3 percent, its highest postwar point. Monetary integration was central to this. After 1992, Bundesbank policy stopped European growth and wrought havoc for the EMS. Governments aiming for EMU, including the French, faced declining revenues and rising costs just when the convergence criteria required countercyclical spending. Cost-containment had limits, however, and by 1995 the French had to do major budgetary surgery, accompanied by creative accounting, to meet the 1998 deadline. Once this difficult moment was over, however, job-creating growth returned from 1997 to late 2000, bringing unemployment levels down to below 8.8 percent in 2001 (2.3 million). Growth gave way to new stagnation thereafter and unemployment rose again.

In France, the most striking new labor market trend was lowered labor force participation. In the 1980s governments targeted early-retirement programs to keep official unemployment numbers low and the Left, honoring a long-standing pledge, also lowered the retirement age to sixty.

These programs, which ran directly counter to current wisdom about pension finances and workforce development, were more costly in France than anywhere else in Europe. French wage earners stop working at, and often below, age sixty.[18] On the other end of the age continuum, expansion of higher education raised university numbers by 25 percent in the 1990s. France could eventually benefit from a better-qualified labor force and increasing the numbers of younger people in universities softened the youth unemployment problem. In general, however, early retirement and extended schooling accentuated the problems of current and future dependency ratios for taxation, budgeting and social policy spending.

Substantial flexibilization has occurred, facilitated by weak unions, employment insecurity, and incremental legal changes. Part-time and other atypical work has rapidly increased, even if levels remain lower in France than elsewhere. More people are employed under short-term contracts – from 4.7 percent of the labor force in 1985 to 13.8 percent in 2000. These developments have been driven in part by labor law changes codifying new time-limited contracts, which many employers now substitute for probation periods on new long-term hires, interim contracts, plus contracts for temporary and part-time work (CERC 2002: 56–58). In the name of "activation," government-subsidized, often sub-minimum-wage, jobs have been created in the private sector and by youth employment and apprenticeship schemes.

Work sharing, by reducing the work week through the 1996 Robien Law and the Socialist thirty-five-hour campaign, had effects beyond creating several hundred thousand new jobs. In particular, mandated thirty-five-hour negotiations nourished several years of wage moderation. Obligatory bargaining over the forms of working-time reduction also prompted a vast increase in negotiating – firm-level agreements rose from more than 13,000 in 1998 (already double the level of 1990) to over 35,000 in 1999 (Vincent 2002: 326). The bargaining also further diversified what was negotiated. Many firms continue "regular" five-day work schedules, but there are now a variety of individualized contracts, annualized accounts of working hours adjustable for seasonal demand and/or workers' own preferences for structuring their time, four-day weeks, and new forms of compensation such as stock options, and bonuses tied to firm success.[19]

---

[18] Only 10 percent of French men between sixty and sixty-four are still employed, the lowest figure in the EU, and the figure for women is hardly better.

[19] The 2002 elections showed, however, that many lower-income workers bridled at the thirty-five-hour reform because wage restraint in the negotiating period and the loss of relatively lucrative overtime hours meant that work-time reduction had been bought by income losses. The Raffarin government loosened pressure on employers to comply with the thirty-five-hour limit, however, by softening disincentives to use overtime.

Finally, there has been a significant increase in income inequality and wage dispersion and a sharp decline in the share of wages in added value (wiping out relative gains from the 1960s and 1970s). Perhaps the most interesting change in the structure of French wages, however, is that wages in general have gone up less rapidly (1.6 percent in real terms from 1985 to 2000) than welfare state expenditures and other public transfers (1.9 percent over the same period).

Such labor market changes belied the stereotypes of French rigidity. Legal forms of employment have been greatly expanded. Work can be organized in a variety of new ways. Bargaining is more and more decentralized. Wages have been moderated. Labor market policies have a stronger "activation" focus. The shift between industry and services continues apace. In general, those employed have been obliged to be more flexible. Relative productivity has gone up – presently it is higher than in the US. Those unemployed over the longer term, however, have been left behind, presenting a major new social policy challenge.

Monetary integration, broader socioeconomic trends, changing attitudes, and, for France, more liberal outlooks have substantially changed older statist attitudes. Macro-level planning, public enterprises (except "public services," defined *à la française*), and heavy-handed bureaucratic procedures are out. The result has often been reconfigured forms of statism, however. Jospin's remark that French Socialists accepted markets but not a "market society" summarizes French elite views. Anglo–American neo-liberal zealotry is rare.[20] French industry has changed and become more competitive. The job-rich growth in the 1997–2001 upturn indicated that unemployment might be significantly reduced with a return to strong growth. Here the ECB's policies are fundamental. Without more aggressive ECB growth promotion, unemployment will remain very high and low labor force participation will continue.

*Plus ça change . . .* defines high-level French employment relations matters. Several "representative" unions, weak on the ground, speak for wage-earners and retain their legal prerogatives. Even if ideological and organizational repertories have been revised, these unions still compete with one another at all levels, including in the political arena, producing cacophony and uncertainty. The CFDT's eagerness to bargain about reform has nonetheless been a gift to both Left and Right. Oppositional unions, in their turn, continue their mobilizational pyromania to reinforce claims of legitimacy with a dwindling rank-and-file. The strikes of November 1995, part of a long line of explosions sparked by this *grèvicultural* work, were not the last efforts at union mobilization to oppose

---

[20] MEDEF has been its main carrier, but without making great headway.

"the street" to the state with the purpose of frustrating new governmental reform initiatives, as the 2003 movements against pension reform showed.

The French welfare state has faced roughly similar demographic and cost challenges as other continental welfare states, and its responses have been framed by the same budgetary constraints established by the EMU and SGP criteria. General healthcare costs continue to grow slightly faster than GDP, primarily because of changing demographics (Timbeau 2002: 109–110). In response, governments have regularly issued plans, as in the 1980s and earlier (the Durieux Plan in 1991, the Veil Plan in 1993, and the Juppé Plan in 1995), and finance bills (Palier 2002: 406–422) to balance the books with price and user-fee controls, co-payment adjustments, and tough contracts with providers. Designed to reshape French health-consumption habits, these efforts were often ineffective because complementary health insurance covered the changes for most consumers. The biggest changes have been on the revenue side. Following the Juppé Plan, in 1996 and 1997 the CSG was raised to cover most wage-earner payroll taxes on health, simultaneously lowering the cost of labor and promoting consumption with a more than 1 percent increase in purchasing power for wage-earners. The shift also established the CSG as a more significant source of revenues than income taxes and enhanced state control over "paritary" procedures.

The creation of the CMU in 1999 confirmed a second major process of change. The CMU, and its predecessors, the RMI and FSV, were designed to confront the chronic poverty of those left behind – unable to work – in France's new economy. All three broke with Bismarckian insurance tradition, all were means-tested, and all shifted the welfare state toward Bismarckian social insurance for those who were employed and a Beveridgean safety net for those who were not. Unions were willing to support these changes because they lightened the burdens on insurance funds. This change also brought significant new state involvement, however.

The unemployment compensation system also changed significantly. The general European tendency, followed in France's 1992 reforms, has been to make it more difficult to receive compensation and reduce compensation payments systematically to the extent that unemployment periods last longer.[21] These changes are "activating" by creating increasing incentives over time for the unemployed to re-enter the labor market, and they save money. But they also increase the numbers of longer-term unemployed applying for the RMI that, in consequence, has become a

---

[21] The AUD was reconfigured in 1997.

substitute for unemployment compensation and an alternative funding source (shifting from payroll taxes to the CSG).

Pension reform was the remaining open question until 2003. There were small reforms over the years. The 1993 Balladur reforms extended the contribution period for vesting and changed reference years for private sector workers. In 1996 agreement on similar measures adjusted second-tier "complementary" pensions. The Jospin government then created pension "reserve funds" in 1999 and a small "third-tier" program was initiated. The most important pension event in the 1990s was the massive strike over the Juppé Plan in 1995, however. This made France politically gunshy about the reform issue until after the 2002 Presidential and legislative elections. The reform that finally emerged in 2003 unified public and private eligibility requirements and lowered basic public pensions, raising contributions and lowering benefits. The basic public system remains essentially intact, however, as do existing second-tier complementary pension programs. The "third-tier" individual pension funds (*plans d'épargne-retraite*, IRA-type accounts) are a recent innovation that may or may not become significant in the future, however.[22]

## 3    Conclusions

The story of the French Left in power in the 1980s and 1990s was a disaster for social democratic ideas. In 1983 the Left engineered a complete shift in its own, and France's, macroeconomic policy outlooks, re-launched European integration in strongly liberal ways, and promoted monetary integration leading to EMU. 1980s France thus found itself strongly constrained domestically by its own leaders' international choices and actions. In these years, the French "Europe option" eventuating in EMU acted indirectly, but powerfully, to increase austerity and high unemployment and pressure for greater labor market flexibility. Particular policy choices had then to be made in response to new constraints. Political constraints meant that many of these choices were expensive in the short run and compounded medium-term difficulties. Most were also improvised from existing policy repertoires. When there were new problems and a lack of precedents for coping with them policy innovators could advance pet new proposals, as happened with the RMI. Causal "distance" between European changes and French policy

---

[22] The single market enjoins free movement of capital and EMU seeks a reconfiguration of European capital markets. Major changes that could alter the ways in which capital and investment connect in Europe are thus well under way and, among the new products of new European capital markets, "capitalized" pension plans are likely to be at the very top of the list. To this point the French have not seriously bought into the trend.

shifts were greatest in core welfare state areas like healthcare and pensions, where demographics had already accumulated problems and where "paritary" management made proposals for change vulnerable to stakeholder mobilization. The most straightforward example of this is in healthcare, where costs rose rapidly in both the EMS and EMU periods, largely for reasons endogenous to monetary integration. The effects of rising unemployment made the need for finding remedies considerably more urgent. New budgetary constraints in the 1980s due to deflationary policies to support monetary integration lowered employment and growth levels, causing revenue shortfalls.

EMU convergence in the 1990s created new constraints that made constant incremental adjustments inevitable and played a clear role in the larger shift of revenue base away from payroll taxes to the CSG, particularly important for healthcare. Here the correlation between the Juppé plan and the need for rapid action to meet the convergence criteria was obvious. The pension story was more complicated, and perhaps more ironic. Because the French took the lead in the 1980s in promoting monetary integration and because, in the judgment of French leaders, this demanded a dramatic macroeconomic policy shift that would cause greater unemployment, reducing labor market participation, including through energetic early retirement programs, it was necessary to control official unemployment levels. This meant that above and beyond the actual demographic challenges of declining dependency ratios, French governments created higher numbers of pensioners and established expectations among those with jobs that earlier retirement would henceforth be the norm. Policy in the EMS period thus aggravated problems that had to be faced in the EMU period, hence the rolling changes beginning in 1993 and culminating in the 2003 Raffarin reforms.

How has the French social model been evolving during the monetary integration decades? In employment relations, there has been greatly enhanced flexibility. New forms of atypical work have proliferated, there has been more decentralized negotiation, and "activation" is, as elsewhere, a buzzword. Indirectly, one goal of pension reform is to "activate" older workers to work longer both through carrots and sticks, even though the willingness of employers to keep on older (and better-paid) workers remains to be tested. For activation measures to change labor market behaviors, however, there must be jobs for those who have been encouraged to seek them. Otherwise unemployment gets shifted from one group to another. French officials lack the leverage to change the job situation dramatically because such matters are now in the hands of the ECB.

The welfare state story is different. In the monetary integration decades there has been a distinct separation between a set of means-tested "solidarity" programs targeted on the poor – the RMI, FSV, and CMU (to which we should add much of family policy), financed out of general taxation, largely by the new CSG. Both managerial and financial responsibility for these programs has thus been removed from Bismarckian social insurance programs to the state. France now has a dual-track welfare state whose boundaries reproduce those between employed insiders and precariously or un-employed outsiders. The old French welfare state justified itself in terms of universalism, even if this was an exaggeration. Everyone paid in and everyone was entitled to the benefits thereby accrued. The new one has a stronger redistributive component, from the insiders who still pay in to insurance programs and contribute, through taxation, to substantial transfers to outsiders, managed by the state. Should insiders decide that supporting outsiders through transfers was undesirable, a logic lurking in Beveridgean welfare states, they could pressure the state to squeeze the benefits and beneficiaries. Moreover, given the increase in state control in these welfare state areas and in the context of ongoing EMU constraints and low growth, politicians might come to squeeze "solidarity" areas for their own budgetary reasons (Palier 2002: chapters 8–9).

It may turn out that the most important consequences of monetary integration for the French are changing discourses in French domestic politics. In important ways, monetary integration Europe built upon the French Left's past to create a particular French "third way." From 1997 to 2002 the Jospin government, elected because of popular rejection of neo-liberalism, tried to find space for domestic reformism within the broader constraints of monetary integration. There is evidence from the 2002 campaigns that unenthusiastic voters found the Jospin government's programs less than compelling. The campaign appeals of the Center-Right were interesting, however, in part because they were not that different from those of the Left. If the Center-Right promised new reforms – with pension reform high on the list – it also presented itself as better able to protect the French variant of the European social model than the Left. Most significantly, if it proved conservative in its policies, it completely avoided neo-liberal stridency.[23] Time will tell whether such campaign commitments will be honored and much will depend upon the fortunes of the European economy under EMU. The complicated interaction between EMU and the French social model is far from over, but for the time being the French model is alive and well.

---

[23] See Jérôme Jaffré, "La droite sans complexe," in *Le Monde*, July 11, 2003.

# 5  EMU and German welfare capitalism

*Nico A. Siegel*

Germany's social model is a variant of embedded, non-liberal social capitalism that attempts to bridge the gap between efficiency and solidarity
through interdependent socioeconomic and political institutions. These
arrangements have placed Germany in the middle ranks of OECD welfare states, even though labor market regulation is well above average.
Germany's macroeconomic policy institutions, in particular its powerful central bank, have given primacy to price stability (Busch 1995).
The interaction between this corporatist–centrist welfare state and
employment relations system (Schmidt 1998) and "institutionalized
monetarism" (Scharpf 1987; Streeck 1997) has shaped the adjustment
strategies for responding to changing economic conditions. Evaluations
vary. Germany has often been presented as a model "middle way"
between Anglo-Saxon liberal democracies and Nordic social democratic
welfarism (Schmidt 1987, 2001b). For others, Germany's welfare and
social model provides a negative blueprint, full of institutional rigidities,
insider–outsider conflicts in a rigid labor market, and a dense network of
institutional veto points built into institutions, adding up to a *Reformstau*
(gridlock). To these critics German social capitalism, at least since the
mid-1990s, is no longer a successful "diversified (high) quality production regime" (DQP) (Streeck 1997). Some even call Germany "the sick
man of the euro."[1]

This chapter begins with a brief description of the institutions of the
Federal Republic's labor and macroeconomic regimes in most of the
postwar period, showing how they framed adjustment to changing environments between the end of the postwar "economic miracle" and the
exceptional double challenge of German unification and the introduction
of EMU in the 1990s. It then turns to the strains which those challenges

I would like to thank Manfred Schmidt and the editors for comments on earlier versions, and the Institute of Political Science, University of Heidelberg, and the Center for
European Social Policy, University of Bremen, for support on the research on which the
chapter is based.
[1] *Economist*, June 5–11, 1999: 19.

have created, in particular to the question of whether and how strongly German economic policy has been constrained by EMU since 1999. Its main argument is that German national policy-making is much more constrained by European integration in general and EMU in particular today than it was until the mid-1990s. In Germany, monetary integration was not used to work painful adjustment or neo-liberal restructuring, however. Compared to France and Italy, for example, adjustment pressures on German social capitalism generated by EMU were weak until 1997. Ironically, Germany, after having successfully promoted institutionalized monetarism at European level, thereby trans-nationalizing its own price stability regime, nowadays has difficulties conforming to the SGP, failing to meet the 3 percent deficit criterion in 2002 and 2003. The coming of EMU may not have provided German governments with a *vincolo esterno* for major reforms, but it could well be that the political economy subsequently shaped by EMU is reframing the German political process and contributing to reforms that make German welfare capitalism less generous without restructuring the German welfare regime in more sustainable future directions.

## 1    Social capitalism in Germany

The concept of an "enabling state" (Streeck 1997) captures key features of the relationship between the state and encompassing social partners that made *Sozialpartnerschaft* central to Germany's social model. Article 9 of the German Basic Law is interpreted to guarantee collective bargaining autonomy (*Tarifvertragsautonomie*) to employer associations and trade unions. At 29 percent of the labor force in 2000, union membership was in the middle range in Europe.[2] A shrinking majority of German workers are nonetheless covered by collective agreements that set wages at sectoral and regional level, leaving some room for maneuver at firm level. The resulting flexible and densely coordinated system of pattern bargaining has led to comparatively low wage dispersion between sectors, regions, and firms (Jacobi, Keller, and Müller-Jentsch 1998).

Significant aspects of employment relations are nevertheless regulated by the state, in particular a dense set of employment rights for workers. Most important, worker representation in supervisory boards and works councils is legally prescribed, giving workers, at least in medium-sized and large companies, strong co-determination rights at the workplace (*betriebliche Mitbestimmung*). Co-determination was expected to

---

[2] This organizational gross density rate includes pensioners. If pensioners are excluded, the density ratio is near to 22 percent (Ebbinghaus 2002: table 1).

generate higher decision-making costs at plant level, but also to reduce implementation costs, facilitate flexibility in work organization, and foster stakeholder outlooks, especially among qualified workers benefiting from skill upgrading. Incentives to invest in training were reinforced for management and labor by laws giving workers comparatively strong job security.

Important steering capacities were also delegated to associations and para-public institutions where representatives of employers and unions are responsible for decision-making and implementing policies such as social insurance and vocational training. Employment and the welfare state are also linked through benefit structures and their financing, reflecting the Bismarckian social insurance principle that dates from the origins of Germany's welfare state. Workers with full-time employment careers receive comparatively generous transfer payments, with entitlements calculated largely on the basis of wage incomes (the "equivalence principle") and geared to the male-breadwinner model. Deviations from strict equivalence produce significant redistribution, however, such as those going to workers (almost exclusively women) who stay outside the labor market to raise children or care for relatives. As in other continental social insurance systems, benefits are financed largely by payroll taxes, roughly two-thirds of total social budget revenues, with important variations at program level. Total social spending was 32.2 percent of GDP in 2001 and total government outlays 48.3 percent.

Germany's welfare state has often been regarded as the prototype of the conservative, or corporatist welfare regime in the Esping-Andersen taxonomy (Esping-Andersen 1990). Yet the public–private welfare mix contains important Christian democratic, social democratic, and liberal ingredients, and might therefore better be described as a "centrist" welfare state (Schmidt 1998) or "corporatist–centrist" welfare regime (Siegel 2003). This corporatist–centrist welfare regime is the key pillar of what has been described as the "policy of the middle way" (Schmidt 1987).

State-enabled social partnership is a defining characteristic of labor relations and social insurance systems that together comprise the Federal Republic's social model. Social partnership, with its capacity for delegated and decentralized governance, has sustained a cooperative climate that stabilized German social capitalism for decades. Although *Sozialpartnerschaft* did not end labor–management conflict, it mitigated it, while promoting and reflecting a basic consensus about socioeconomic institutions. This mode of governing the labor market was closely coupled with institutions and practices that gave firms access to "patient capital," enabling them to implement product market strategies with longer-term commitments to workers, suppliers, and others needed to carry them out.

According to the "varieties of capitalism" literature, complementarities among these institutional arrangements provided Germany during much of the postwar era with a "comparative institutional advantage" in DQP (Streeck 1997). Germany has thus been characterized as a paradigmatic case of a "coordinated market economy" (CME), coordinated at industry or "meso-level" rather than centrally coordinated, like Sweden until the 1980s (Soskice 1999).

A decisive element of central coordination was provided by an exceptionally powerful, independent central bank. While the legislation establishing the Bundesbank in 1957 made the preservation of the external and internal stability of the currency its major responsibility (§ 3, *Bundesbankgesetz*), it was also required to support the general economic policy of the Federal government (§ 12), as long as this support did not collide with its primary obligation to secure the value of the currency. Since the bank's turn to a monetarist paradigm in 1973 the Bundesbank has viewed price stability as its primary goal. If governments viewed the central bank's council policy as excessively restrictive, offsetting it by fiscal policy was made difficult by the bank's power over monetary policy. To this were added the obstacles to discretionary countercyclical fiscal policy created by the intergovernmental interweaving in German federalism (*Politikverflechtung*). The complex distributions of taxing and spending authority between the Federal and state governments and between the Federal government and social insurance funds made the political coordination required for a coherent macroeconomic policy extremely difficult (Scharpf 1987). The imbalance between a coherent veto player committed to price stability and competing actors dispersed in a federalist polity who had to be well coordinated to promote a full employment policy helped to give price stability *de facto* priority in the Federal Republic. During the "golden age" of almost continuous rapid economic growth from the early 1950s (with the exception of 1966–1967) until the first oil price shock in 1973, the predominance of price stability was not as problematic for employment performance as it became in the later era of reduced output and employment growth. When the "dream of ever-lasting prosperity" (Lutz 1984) abruptly ended in 1973–1974, the "performance gap" between price stability and employment growth widened.

The Bundesbank was typically in a position to set the parameters within which other key actors operated. Along with the Federal and state governments, these also included the wage-bargaining parties, whom the bank could influence by credibly threatening to tighten policy if settlements it regarded as inflationary were reached. Through its signaling, the bank served as a central anchor for the coordination of sectoral bargaining (Hall and Franzese, Jr. 1998). While formal concertation at the macro level was the exception, informal consultation – among government representatives and peak organizations of unions and employers – was a key characteristic feature of Germany's "negotiational democracy" (Lehmbruch 1997). The strategic choices of the main collective actors in Germany's DQP production regime were thus decisively conditioned by a macroeconomic policy regime in which the Bundesbank and Germany's federal system gave priority to price and fiscal stability. This institutionalized monetarism was incorporated into the German political economy well before Europe embarked on the road to EMU. Rather than being a consequence, it provided the model for transition to EMU, transferred to the European level through German bargaining power and coalition-building capacity.

*Beyond the "golden age": slow growth and smooth consolidation, 1973–1989*

When the Bundesbank adopted money supply targeting in 1973 it consecrated the institutionalization of monetarism in response to international and domestic developments that fundamentally changed the environment in which the German economic miracle had flourished. The global inflationary surge of the late 1960s, the collapse of the Bretton Woods system, and the first OPEC oil price shock (1973) made it much more difficult to reconcile price stability, employment growth, and a favorable exchange rate for German exports. SPD Finance Minister Karl Schiller had been able to do so by introducing macro-level concertation in response to the 1967 recession that was followed by rapid recovery. Schiller's Keynesianism, which seemed to be a successful innovation – codified in the 1967 Stabilization and Growth Act – combined fiscal stimulus, union wage restraint, and easier monetary policy. It ended, along with his role, in 1972 when the Bundesbank successfully resisted Schiller's call to again revalue the D-mark by temporarily floating, as in 1971, to cool an inflationary boom. The bank, and industry, preferred exchange controls over revaluation to blunt the expansionary effect of dollar inflows without impairing export competitiveness. The definitive abandonment of Bretton Woods in March 1973 eliminated the bank's obligation to buy dollars and shortly thereafter, Germany and eight other countries[3] agreed to a joint float of their currencies against the dollar and other currencies within the narrow band of the "Snake."[4] The Snake itself marked the beginning of monetary integration largely based on German terms (Dyson and Featherstone 1999).

[3] France, Benelux, Denmark, Norway, Sweden and, *de facto*, Austria (Scharpf 1987: 162–163).
[4] As Henning (1994) and Notermans (2001a) argue, within the Snake German exporters had the advantage of real undervaluation relative to Snake members with higher inflation.

1975 was a watershed year (Hassel and Schulten 1998). Beginning in 1974 the German model went into its first severe economic crisis since the "economic miracle" had been launched in the wake of the Korean War. Unemployment rose from an average of 273,000 in 1973 to 1,074,000 in 1975. Inflation, though still lower than in most OECD democracies, neared 7.0 percent in 1973 and 1974. Restrictive budget laws were passed under a new SPD Chancellor and former Finance Minister, Helmut Schmidt, who later on became prominent as crisis manager for the German model (Markovits 1982). The Bundesbank, which had already doubled the discount rate from 3.5 in September 1972 to 7.0 in June 1973, kept money tight after OPEC I gave inflation a large new jolt, neutralizing the government's effort to replace demand siphoned off by OPEC by fiscal expansion. The unions won excessive wage increases for 1974, to which the bank responded by announcing explicit money growth targets, effective in 1975, to tie monetary growth to the potential growth rate. If demands on GDP exceeded the money supply, the bank would not accommodate them by increasing the money supply and thereby fueling inflation. Germany's severest postwar recession, with almost no GDP growth in 1974 and a decline of 1.6 percent in 1975 and a quadrupling of unemployment between 1973 and 1975, gave the bank's declaration credibility. The monetarist signaling game central to German macroeconomic policy was thus established (Scharpf 1987).

The social democratic–liberal coalition's fiscal policy stance fluctuated, first providing a large stimulus in 1975, then switching to consolidation measures to reduce the resulting deficits. SPD losses in the 1976 election and international pressure on Germany to be the "locomotive" to pull the world out of stagnation culminating in the 1978 Bonn Summit led the weakened coalition to renewed stimulus. Union wage demands remained moderate. The Bundesbank rewarded government and unions by easing money, at first even accommodating the fiscal fueling of the locomotive. The train was quickly derailed by OPEC II in 1979 and harsh monetary tightening in the US and Britain. In contrast to Sweden, the Bundesbank did not devalue to maintain employment within a Keynesian coordination game, but matched the tightening to resist downward pressure on the D-mark which it saw as threatening inflation. Between March and November 1979, the Bundesbank had already raised discount rates in three steps from 3 up to 6 percent, eventually reaching 7.5 percent. The Bundesbank then did not change its monetary course for more than two years (until August 1982), creating dissent between the Federal government and the Central Bank Council. The lesson that the Federal government had to learn was that the Bundesbank stuck to its legal obligation first to guarantee price stability and if at all, only then, to take into consideration the government's general economic policy course.

International constraints on German policy, especially American brandishing of the "dollar weapon," had already prompted renewed European monetary integration.[5] Although France, which had left and rejoined the Snake twice, had different reasons for replacing it than Germany, its President Giscard d'Estaing and Chancellor Schmidt (secretly at first) formulated a proposal for a more inclusive European Monetary System (EMS) in 1978.[6] The Bundesbank succeeded in shaping the form and subsequent operation of the EMS to meet its own aims (Dyson and Featherstone 1999; Heisenberg 1999). While insufficient to insulate Germany from dollar volatility, EMS gave the bank indirectly effective control over intra-European exchange rates and macroeconomic policy without constraining its management of the German economy, including resistance to depreciation in the early 1980s.

After the breakdown of the social–liberal coalition in the fall of 1982 and the success of the new Center-Right coalition in the 1983 general elections, countercyclical demand management lost any remaining attraction as a powerful economic policy idea (Hall 1989) within the Federal cabinet. By 1982, conflicts between the SPD and FDP over how much to cut budget deficits in the wake of the recession contributed to the end of their coalition. The FDP then switched its support to the CDU, paving the way for a Center-Right coalition under Helmut Kohl. While there were instances of differences between the Bundesbank and the government in the Kohl era, none was serious prior to unification. Until then, the Kohl government's fiscal policy was contractionary or neutral except for a brief expansionary moment in 1988 with the bank's encouragement (Henning 1994: 213, 216).

The new government's commitment to budget consolidation was demonstrated by austerity packages in 1982–1983 that included expenditure cuts and increased co-payments by social insurance beneficiaries (Siegel 2002), encouraging the Bundesbank to ease monetary policy. The government's consolidation packages were not a dramatic shift, however. In both 1975 and 1981, its social–liberal predecessor had cut benefits and increased social security contributions. While the CDU–FDP coalition pursued consolidation more vigorously, it differed less in its incremental fiscal policy squeeze than in being less willing to use fiscal policy to

[5] "The reckless conduct of the United States with respect to monetary policy . . . had painful effects. We knew that the national European economies individually were not in a position to arm themselves sufficiently against the turbulences of the world" was Schmidt's 1990 recollection of initiating EMS, in Henning (1998: 558).
[6] Britain stayed out until joining the ERM in 1990, only to be forced out in 1992.

expand demand to the limited extent that its predecessor did. The *Wende* was therefore not accompanied by a sharp policy turn like those occurring in the US and Britain (Zohlnhöfer 2001). There were significant changes in fiscal, employment, and social policy, yet consensus on German social capitalism remained basically intact.

Even the moderate deregulation of the labor market in the 1985 Employment Promotion Act and the limited restriction of strikes in the revision of paragraph 116 of the *Arbeitsförderungsgesetz* were not a frontal attack on the basic pillars of the German social model. The unions protested intensely against these measures, and the government used paragraph 116 to support employers in a long and bitter strike in 1985 by the largest union, *IG Metall*, for a thirty-five-hour work-week. Nevertheless, the climate of social partnership at company level was restored, and the employment relations system still appeared "capable of combining macro-rigidity and micro-flexibility" (Visser and Ruysseveldt 1996: 160). Rather than battling over the German social model, major actors relied on its core institutions of social partnership and social insurance to negotiate adjustment to the relatively restrictive macroeconomic regime, greater international competition, and increased structural unemployment (Siegel 2002, chapter 9).

One important adjustment strategy was to reduce labor supply, mainly through early retirement.[7] Germany's economy continued to be exceptionally dependent on internationally exposed industries relying on DQP to succeed in markets for specialized, high-quality products. To meet increasing competition, companies concentrated investment in capital-intensive product innovation and improvement plus complementary training for highly skilled core workers. Cuts in labor costs for other workers maintained margins by limiting new hires and laying off workers judged less productive. Older workers became the prime target because seniority entitled them to higher wages and more generous social rights than younger workers and because they were deemed less capable of skill upgrading. The problem for employers was how to do this without falling foul of the unions and the dense structure of protective labor law. With less leeway for labor force rationalization than employers in Anglo-Saxon "liberal market economies," German employers had to do it through negotiation with unions and government officials.

Through its provisions for early retirement, the social insurance system facilitated a consensual solution. The 1972 pension reform already allowed those with at least thirty-five years of contributions to retire two

---

[7] *IG Metall*'s goal of a thirty-five-hour week can also be subsumed under the heading of labor supply-limiting strategies.

years before the legal age of sixty-five without any reduction in benefits. Court decisions made disability pensions easier to get by requiring consideration of labor market conditions in determining "inability to work." Those unemployed for a year at age sixty became entitled to a pension. Large companies brought the age down to fifty-nine and younger by paying the difference between unemployment benefits and final net wages until entitlement to pensions (Manow and Seils 1999). Employers thus got their wage bill reduced, unions won what they considered an earned social right for older members and workers in general, and were convinced to open jobs for younger members, while the government could claim credit for a popular extension of social rights and also avoid the direct, short-term budgetary consequences of doing so.[8]

This three-way positive sum outcome reinforced widespread conviction that the German model could be adjusted to a more challenging international environment by incremental, system-immanent, and even system-stabilizing measures that reconciled consolidation, modernization, and high degrees of social protection. "Smooth consolidation" (Offe 1991) seemed to continue throughout the 1980s, culminating in wide agreement among the social partners and political parties on a major pension reform in 1989. The adaptability of German welfare capitalism seemed once more confirmed. However, the policy of early retirement could offer only a short-dated positive sum solution to keep (official) unemployment within acceptable limits.

Under the surface of consensual adaptation lurked persistent problems and potentially troublesome long-run trends. The government's gain from the early-retirement strategy was contingent on making social insurance funds bear the lion's share of costs. While the funds were financed mainly by employer and employee contributions, the Federal government had to cover shortfalls between the unemployment funds' income and benefit obligations and accept mounting contributions to the public pension scheme. The government kept deficits down by repeatedly raising contribution rates, since growing early retirement increased spending obligations in pension and unemployment insurance. This, along with economic recovery from 1984 on, facilitated consolidation. The general government budget deficit went from 3.3 percent of GDP in 1982 to a small surplus of 0.3 in 1989. Furthermore, the share of social expenditure as a percentage of GDP declined from 32.9 percent in 1982 to 30.1 percent in 1989, indicating consolidation success on the expenditure side. However, social security contributions as a percentage of total

---

[8] However, due to the mixed financing structure of the German public pension scheme and unemployment insurance and assistance, indirect and "lagged" costs for the central government were a nonintended side-effect of the early retirement schemes.

gross wages (up to the assessment threshold) were even higher in 1989 (36.0 percent) than during the recession of 1982 (34.0 percent).

Success in shifting costs to the social insurance funds meant an increase in employers' labor costs and a decrease in employees' net/gross wage ratio. The employment effects of the strategy were problematic. Declining labor force participation by older workers was an obvious mark of the strategy's success. The rate for men aged fifty-five to sixty-four fell from 83 to 49 percent between 1962 and 1995 (OECD 1996: 187–189), feeding a worsening dependency ratio. Moreover, the strategy inhibited employment growth by raising nonwage costs. At the low end of the skill distribution, nonwage costs kept gross wages too high relative to the correspondingly low level of productivity, particularly in the services where low-productivity jobs were most likely to be located. This, plus wage floors set in collective agreements and court decisions requiring net wages to exceed social assistance benefits, was important in explaining why Germany has had a relatively undeveloped private service sector, at least in official terms and neglecting Germany's comparatively large shadow economy. Germany's highly competitive industry still had the highest share of employment, although declining, while the share of service sector employment was the lowest among OECD countries (OECD 1998). Fiscal austerity precluded Nordic strategies of enlarging public service sector employment to offset declining industrial employment (Jochem 1998). Comparatively low wage dispersion plus the low share of (predominantly private) service sector employment were viewed as evidence that low-wage service employment was being priced out of the market (Siegel and Jochem 2000; Scharpf 2001). Moreover, despite the labor supply reduction strategy and accelerated growth at the end of the 1980s, unemployment had declined by less than two percentage points from its 1985 postwar peak.[9]

While social-democratic and centrist observers argued for modest reforms to bring down unemployment, economists focused on unemployment to urge deeper structural reforms than the center-right coalition contemplated. While welcoming the Kohl government's combination of budget consolidation and tax cuts, employer associations and the Council of Economic Experts shared the economists' complaint that the Federal Republic lagged behind the US and UK in privatization and labor market deregulation. This, they argued, placed Germany at a disadvantage as a location for investment (the *Standortdebatte*). Consensus was flawed even

---

[9] According to EUROSTAT data, unemployment declined from 7.2 in 1985 to 5.6 in 1989, according to OECD figures (national definitions) from 8.0 to 6.9, and according to the more broad unemployment definition of the German Ministry for Labor and Social Affairs unemployment from 9.3 (1985) to 7.9 (1989).

on the surface, therefore. Nevertheless, most major actors remained confident that smooth consolidation would adapt German welfare capitalism to the challenges confronting of the future as it had in the past. However, easy consolidation ceased to be an available option in the face of the challenge of two epochal events: German unification and the advent of EMU.

## 2    From euphoria to problem overload: the double challenge, 1990–1998

The process of creating EMU was well under way when the Berlin Wall unexpectedly fell in November 1989. Unification, rather than EMU, would have the most severe consequences for the German social model. Only as the immediate transition to EMU approached (1996–1998) did its requirements begin to cause difficulties for German policy-makers, particularly for a Finance Minister who had to struggle to keep the deficit below the 3 percent criterion. By 2003 the ECB's monetary stance and the SGP, on which Germany itself had insisted, were constraining German fiscal policy and generating additional pressure on the red–green coalition government to reform social policy and labor market regulation. Even then, EMU was far from determining the strategic choices of the Federal government.

### Unification and EMU negotiations

When France, supported by Italy, renewed movement toward monetary union in late 1987, Germany's Foreign Minister, Hans-Dietrich Genscher, seized the opportunity to give them powerful support as a way to advance political union. Chancellor Kohl, as committed to European integration as Genscher, then took a series of initiatives crucial to making EMU happen. Genscher led a "security coalition," anchored in the Foreign Ministry and Chancellery's foreign policy division, that saw EMU as "centrally about binding Germany into Europe," while an "ordo-liberal coalition," comprising the "Bundesbank, the Economics and Finance Ministries, and academic economists" held that "EMU would inflict more damage than benefit if it were not constructed as a 'stability community'" (Dyson and Featherstone 1999: 261–262). Kohl, and for that matter Genscher, shared both views, but the "ordo-liberals" were much more dubious about EMU, seeking to delay it until their conditions could be met, which some expected might never happen. Kohl's political achievement was overcoming that resistance, sometimes using "his role in the

European Council to present *faits accomplis* to German negotiators wedded to ordo-liberal ideas" (Dyson and Featherstone 1999: 263).

If the ordo-liberals could not block EMU, however, they did succeed in incorporating their ideas into its design. The key was the Bundesbank's bargaining power in both European and domestic arenas. Coopted into the negotiations from the Delors Committee on, the Bundesbank could mobilize opposition to the single currency project if it did not meet the conditions that the Bank set out. This was possible despite the big parties' solidly pro-European programs because key political and economic elites were skeptical about EMU. As in previous steps of monetary integration, German participation was acceptable to the Bundesbank and Finance Ministry only if it did not reduce the advantages of Germany's institutionalized price stability regime (Busch 1995).

More monetary integration was not needed to get the stability that EMS already provided, and whatever critics of smooth consolidation foresaw, they did not view European institutions, and certainly not the transfer of monetary policy to a European central bank, as a *vincolo esterno* for achieving the domestic changes they believed necessary to reconfigure German welfare capitalism. In fact, prior to EMU, and in contrast to France under EMS, monetary integration had no discernible impact on the German social model. Public opinion was also skeptical about EMU, and Germans widely opposed losing the symbolically potent D-mark, even though the public generally supported Germany's integration into Europe. Yet in *Länder* elections, politicians who tried to exploit attachment to the D-mark were attacked by party leaders. As a result, EMU never became a major issue in *Bundestag* elections.

Before the design of EMU was completed and its establishment assured German unification intervened, and it may be that this unforeseen event altered the German stakes sufficiently to tip the domestic political balance in EMU's favor. Scholars strongly disagree over whether German support for EMU in 1990–1991 was an exchange with other governments for supporting unification, especially the French.[10] But at the Strasbourg European Council in December 1989, Kohl agreed to an early date for the Intergovernmental Conference (IGC) on EMU that France sought, without the commitment to a parallel IGC to advance political integration that Germany had made as a core condition for EMU. Also against the German "economist" blueprint for monetary integration, fixed time schedules were accepted for the final stage of EMU, reflecting a "monetarist" approach.

---

[10] For a more detailed discussion compare Moravcsik (1998: chapter 6) and Dyson and Featherstone (1999: 363–369).

*Unification and its consequences: promises vs. reality*

Unification was not expected to create fundamental difficulties for the basic institutions of German capitalism, although relatively early on and during the 1990 elections a number of politicians and economists warned of the costs of integrating the ruined GDR's command economy. The Chancellor in particular painted the economic prospects of a reunited Germany in glowing colors. In his successful 1990 election campaign, Kohl promised that incorporation of the former GDR into the West German model would bring "flourishing landscapes." Initially, unification was implemented in a way that stimulated a demand boom. Eventually, the reality proved starkly different.

The Kohl government managed German unification under great time and expectation pressures. Most former GDR citizens clearly indicated that they wanted to participate in what they regarded as a prosperous society offering opportunities unprecedented in the former GDR (Grosser 1998). The Kohl government responded by putting unification on a fast track, as defined in a treaty with the expiring GDR government that brought the more or less complete export of the basic socioeconomic and political institutions of the Federal Republic to the East. Wealth transfer also accompanied the policy of "institutional transfer" (Lehmbruch 1991), consisting of a 1:1 conversion of up to 4,000 East German marks for D-marks and the conversion of wages, salaries, and pensions at the same ratio. Thus within five years the average pension level in the former GDR rose from 40.3 percent of the level in the old *Länder* upto 85.4 in 1997 (BMAS 1999: 159, table 124). The trade unions, moving eastward, pressed for fast equalization of wages and working conditions (Schroeder 1996).

This drive to equalize living standards could not be sustained, however. The Eastern European markets of the former GDR were rapidly disintegrating, while poor infrastructure and low productivity left Eastern companies without the conditions for successful participation into the DQP regime into which they were pushed (Czada 1998). By 1997, average productivity in the East had only reached 60 percent of the level in the West, approximately as high as in Spain and nearer to Portugal and Greece than to the West German *Länder* (German Council of Economic Experts 1998: table 73). Low productivity combined with German monetary union and rapid wage and benefit equalization put many companies in the new *Länder* at a severe competitive disadvantages. In an effort to prop up the Eastern economy and start a rapid, self-sustaining catch-up process, the government supplemented the sudden increase in Eastern purchasing power with special state loans, investment incentives in the form of tax breaks and subsidies, targeted labor market policy, and other transfers. The strong fiscal stimulus provided by this "involuntary unification Keynesianism" (von Beyme 1994) fueled a boom that for a year or two kept Germany from slipping into the recession beginning in most OECD countries in the early 1990s.

The Bundesbank contributed to the end of the unification boom by a tightening of monetary policy. Leading representatives of the Bank had warned that it would do so if the government implemented the generous conversion rate, which it (and many other economic experts) had strongly criticized, along with the government's promise not to raise taxes (Henning 1994: 221). These decisions, the growing public sector deficit that flowed from them, and high wage settlements in 1991 and 1992 prompted the bank to raise discount rates from 6.5 in February 1991 to an historical peak of 8.75 in July 1992 (Deutsche Bundesbank 1992). Reinforcing international downturn, Germany plunged into a recession marked by a real GDP decline of 1.2 percent in 1993. While growth was only negative in the West (−2 percent), output growth in the former GDR was far lower and the catch-up process slower than the government had expected. De-industrialization in the uncompetitive industrial sector of the new *Länder* brought large job losses. Within two years, roughly 1.1 (out of 7.3) million jobs were lost, no less than 800,000 in the manufacturing sector. Unemployment rates in the East increased by 5.3 percentage points to an average of 15.8 percent in 1993 (BMAS 1999). Massive transfers from the West kept demand in the East from collapsing, however. In the same year, social security expenditure peaked at 66.8 percent of GDP in the East, a level unprecedented in the history of democratic nation states. Hence, by 1993, the dream of a rapid self-sustaining catch-up process in the new *Länder* was over and fiscal problems had dramatically increased.

While growth recovered in 1994, it fell back below 2 percent for the next two years and remained below the OECD average for five years in a row to 1997. German unemployment rose to a postwar peak of 10 percent in 1997, and the level was nearly double on average in the Eastern *Länder*. German "normality" returned only in inflation rates. Although they were significantly higher than in the 1980s in 1992–1993, depriving Germany of its top rank in price stability, weak domestic demand and relatively moderate wage agreements from 1993 on brought inflation back down (Hassel and Schulten 1998).

After the brief episode of involuntary Keynesianism, therefore, the monetarist game was re-established, but after unification the conditions under which it was played had fundamentally changed. With high unemployment and low output growth in the new *Länder* driving annual net West–East transfer payments up to roughly 4–5 percent of GDP in 1997

(Deutsche Bundesbank 1996), Germany became increasingly trapped in a self-made fiscal straitjacket. Since taxes had already been increased to finance unification (e.g. introduction of a "solidarity tax," increases in mineral and insurance taxes), despite Kohl's 1990 election promise, further increases were not an option after 1993. Big expenditure cuts would have posed further electoral risks for the government, however. The remaining alternative was to finance much of the increased social policy expenditures by raising social security contributions. But increased contributions had already been combined with expenditure cuts to close the budget gap in the 1980s. In the 1990s, the colossal costs of unification hampered effective expenditure cuts to reduce the deficit. The result was that the sum of payroll taxes for health, pension, and unemployment insurance rose from 36 percent in 1989 to 42.1 percent of gross wages in 1998 (inclusive of long-term care insurance introduced in 1995).[11] This only aggravated the perverse effects of using the social insurance system to achieve the "smooth consolidation" that had already been observable in the 1980s, intensifying the "vicious cycle of high wage costs, dismissal of less productive workers, and increases in social security contributions" (Hemerijck, Manow, and van Kersbergen 2000).

In the mid-1990s, the Kohl government was left with no alternative to continued high deficits except cutbacks in entitlements and/or eligibility in welfare state programs. By this time high deficits were excluded not only by the deeply ingrained tradition of fiscal discipline and Bundesbank insistence, but also by the requirements of transition to EMU. Unless Germany could reduce its budget deficit to 3 percent of GDP, it would not meet the convergence criteria on which it had itself strenuously insisted and which it had reinforced by the 1997 SGP that Finance Minister Theo Waigel had adamantly demanded. For Kohl, a "key animateur behind the project," and for whom EMU and German unification were "two coins of the same model" (Dyson 1998: 38), German failure to qualify for EMU, bringing with it the almost inevitable collapse of the entire project, was unthinkable. Therefore, although monetary integration had not been used earlier as a means of overcoming domestic resistance to change, the government now invoked the convergence criteria as an external commitment requiring fiscal discipline.

In contrast with the 1980s, however, "re-consolidation" in the 1990s was anything but smooth. German welfare capitalism confronted fundamental challenges while different majorities in the upper and lower houses and further eroding consensus among social partners left the government without the political conditions to achieve the structural reforms that

---

[11] This excludes employer wage costs for the public occupational injuries and diseases insurance as well as for sickness pay so nonwage costs are actually higher.

might have durably reduced adjustment pressure on the German model. The savings measures the government was able to implement involved the largest cutbacks in social policy in the Federal Republic's history (Siegel 2002, chapter 9), stimulating intense controversy that contributed not only to the breakdown of the first attempt for a social pact, the Alliance for Jobs in 1996 (Bispinck 1997), but also to the loss of popular support that defeated the coalition in the 1998 general election (Zohlnhöfer 2001). The coalition nonetheless succeeded, just barely, in guaranteeing Germany's entry into EMU. The tasks of completing the transition and learning to live in Euroland now fell to the SPD–green coalition led by Gerhard Schröder.

## 3    Between continuity and change: EMU and the red–green coalition, 1998–2002

For the first time in the history of the Federal Republic, the September 1998 elections brought a complete government turnover at Federal level rather than a change of coalition partners as in 1966, 1969, or 1982. The first red–green government was headed by Gerhard Schröder, reputed to be a "pragmatic modernizer" and a purely power-oriented politician with rather weak commitment to the SPD party organization. Until his spectacular resignation in March 1999, the chairman of the SPD was Oskar Lafontaine, who was Finance Minister in the first Schröder cabinet. Lafontaine represented the traditional wing of the SPD and pushed for new Keynesian demand management at and beyond the national level. He thus tried to build a coalition to press the ECB for a more expansionary monetary policy, joining with his French counterpart Strauss-Kahn in an effort to remedy what both saw as a major EMU design flaw, the absence of a political legitimized counterweight to the ECB.

During its first weeks, the red–green coalition promoted a number of social policy reforms that seemed to indicate that the government would follow the traditional social-democratic path of expanding social rights and labor protection. The new government (temporarily) abolished the so-called "demographic factor," a main issue of conflict in the 1997 pension reform that had aimed at making public pension insurance more sustainable by a gradual reduction in the net replacement ratio. Together with additional measures to expand social policy generosity, legislation for part-time workers and the so-called "spurious" self-employed resulted in an increase of labor market protection. Temporarily, at least, it seemed as if deregulation and fiscal consolidation had been removed from the reform agenda.

Most of this honeymoon activism did not reflect a coherent paradigm shift (Hall 1993) at either domestic or European level, however. First of all, with its expansive social legislation the government sought to fulfill its election pledges and to meet the demands of the party's left wing and unions. Far more important for the red–green coalition was that the government's senior partner was internally split between "traditionalists" and "modernizers" (Egle and Henkes 2003; Siegel 2003).[12] During and after the elections a superficial compromise had been reached resulting in the "double leadership" of Schröder and Lafontaine.[13] Lafontaine's energetic agitation for a paradigm shift in economic policy clashed with the reform leanings of mainstream economic policy advisers and experts on social and labor market policy in Germany and abroad (Siegel and Jochem 2000). At the same time, however, it echoed traditional union and SPD positions and joined increasing criticism of the asymmetric supranationalization of policy authority within the EMU. Compared to Schröder, a pragmatic conflict manager, Lafontaine proposed a policy course based on hard-nosed ideological assumptions. While Britain's yellow press presented Lafontaine as the "most dangerous man in Europe," his political style and policy goals attracted widespread criticism elsewhere. Given the long-standing personal and policy tensions between the Chancellor and his Finance Minister it was thus not surprising that Lafontaine resigned in March 1999. The unprecedented radical style of his resignation as leader of the SPD was noticed, however. "Escapism" à la Lafontaine was criticized almost unanimously within the SPD and was the big media event during the coalition's first six months.

Lafontaine's resignation ended populist quasi-Keynesianism in the government, but for Germany's EU partners it had one major and lasting consequence. In contrast to the Kohl government, the new coalition tried to establish more institutionalized patterns of coordination in social policy and employment policy (Ostheim 2003: 353). The Kohl government had been an important veto player in EU networks when more or less formal techniques of coordinating national social and employment policies were put on the European agenda. During the German presidency during the first half of 1999 the red–green government took a different path with regard to an intensified European coordination of economic policy.[14]

[12] Egle and Henkes (2003), in a detailed chapter on the programmatic debate within the SPD, offer a more differentiated picture of the different party and parliamentary factions, their relative weight within the party and the cabinet and the ambiguous 1998 party manifesto labeled "Innovation and Justice" (*Innovation und Gerechtigkeit*).
[13] Furthermore, Walter Riester, of *IG Metall*, became Minister of Social Affairs and Work.
[14] Though EU issues were not central in the 1998 elections, it is noteworthy that the coalition treaty of SPD and Bündnis 90/Die Grünen included the goal to actively promote a coordinated European economic, fiscal, and social policy (Ostheim 2003).

However, as in other domains, during its first term the government's EU policy was marked by inconsistencies. The Chancellor's initiatives and declarations reflected harsh critiques of EU policies, and in the case of the End-of-Life-Vehicles directive, Schröder pushed his green Minister of Environmental Affairs to violate procedural rules within EU networks to secure powerful economic interests in Germany. Above all, however, Joschka Fischer, the Foreign Minister, was a central player in European and international affairs.

Following a rather volatile survey-based agenda-setting strategy, Schröder focused mainly on popular domestic issues that seemed more important for winning popular support than EU or international issues. This changed markedly during the 2002 election campaign with the issue of taking an active part in the war on Iraq. By stressing the government's international independence he sought to compensate for losses in support in other policy domains. European politics were not *per se* a major issue during the 2002 election campaign. Yet Schröder more than once used the term "national interest" to announce positions that promised electoral profits: the German government should neither subordinate its foreign policy to a hegemonic partner like the US, nor accept overly restrictive European constraints, particularly with regard to the possible punishment of Germany's failure to keep its deficit within the 3 percent margin.

Hans Eichel, the former Hessian prime minister, was Lafontaine's successor as Finance Minister in 1999 and brought the Keynesian intermezzo to an end. Eichel was personally convinced that fiscal consolidation, though electorally risky and likely to be painful, was an imperative that had to be managed successfully, not just a necessary evil dictated by EMU. He thus returned to a consolidation course in fiscal policy, with partial success in 1999 and 2000.[15] The government's economic policy problems were temporarily eased by the economic recovery under way when it came to power, however. Renewed growth in Europe was facilitated by an initial Euro area interest rate that amounted to a loosening of monetary policy for the area. The ECB then reinforced this when it responded to international financial turbulence by reducing the rate by half a percentage point in March 1999. Slow recovery of GDP growth in Germany, close to 2 percent in 1998 and 1999, then accelerated to 2.9 percent in 2000, continuing a slow decrease in unemployment to 7.8 percent. Growth combined with earlier budget consolidation resulted in

---

[15] Universal Mobile Telecommunications System (UMTS) licenses were auctioned off in 2000 for a total sum of almost €51 billion (99 billion DM), which decisively paved the way for the budget surplus during the same fiscal year.

a decline in the net borrowing requirement and even a surplus of 1.1 percent of GDP.

The economic boomlet aggravated tendencies toward nondecision-making in social and employment policy, however, and contributed to further delay in structural reforms, labor market policies in particular. The second German employment pact, the *Alliance for Jobs, Training and Competitiveness* was initiated and backed by the government, in contrast to the first social and employment pact in 1996. Yet the results indicated that consensus among the government, unions, and employers about necessary reforms did not exist. As a core project of the Chancellor, the Alliance talks became one of the government's most disappointing projects. There were a few policy changes decided in the Alliance, but no major reforms got through the macro-concertation process. On several occasions unions and employers threatened to quit. It became clear that the absence of a common crisis perception was an important barrier to success. The most important issue of failure was about whether or not wage issues should be included in the talks. Solving insider–outsider problems built into the German labor market and amplified by Bismarckian financing in social policy was another problem. There was more than one reason for failure, which some observers came to call it the "alliance for *stillstand*" (gridlock) (Streeck and Heinze 1999). The segmentation of policy authority within Germany's welfare capitalism and federalism was one big impediment. Another was the government's inconsistency in economic and social policy-making, in particular its multiple policy reversals. Unions, for their part, insisted on delegated policy responsibility as in the wage-setting process: in particular, the representatives of *IG Metall* and of *verdi*, the new service sector union, were influential informal veto players, building a powerful coalition with the left wing of the SPD Bundestag faction. As a result, the Alliance achieved little from 1999 through the second half of 2001. The government's reforming energy returned in 2002 under the shadow of economic crisis and coming elections. Tripartite macro-concertation did not play an important role in this return, however.[16]

Changing external conditions and domestic policy failure had contributed to the abrupt end of the intermezzo of recovery for an economy bedeviled by structural problems and with the second lowest average growth rate of all EU member states between 1992 and 2000. In the wake of a slowdown in the US, a mini-oil shock, and September 11,

---

[16] Most prominent in this respect was the so called "Hartz Commission" and its much-debated report, initiated in the wake of a scandal within the Federal Employment Office (*Bundesanstalt für Arbeit*).

German growth slowed even more than in other European countries. The ECB helped the slowdown by tightening monetary policy by 2.25 percentage points from November 1999 to October 2000. German growth fell sharply, to 0.6 and 0.4 percent in 2001 and 2002, respectively, and turned to actual decline in the first quarter of 2003, presaging recession or stagnation, while some observers even feared the onset of deflation. Because Germany's inflation rate was among the lowest in the Euro area, the ECB's rate hike resulted in higher real interest rates than in most of Euroland, an illustration of the effect of the one-size-fits all monetary policy punishing countries with lower inflation.[17] Finally, because of Germany's dependence on exports outside the Euro area, the Euro's rapid appreciation raised its effective real exchange rate more than for other large Euroland countries (Mackie and Pepino 2003a, 2003b).

The drop in economic growth and its consequence, increasing unemployment, pushed Germany's budget back into high deficits. At 2.8 percent of GDP, the borrowing requirement was already close to the limit defined in the SGP in 2001, then breached it in 2002 and again in 2003. The originator of the Pact was thus subjected to the Pact's disciplinary procedures of warnings and demands for deficit reduction. Whereas in 2002 and the first months of 2003 the German government tried to consolidate budgets to keep within the Pact's boundaries, in June 2003 it presented a staged tax reform that included tax reductions. For the first time since the existence of the SGP a German government hazarded the consequences of a failure to keep within the 3 percent criterion because tax reforms would generate an even higher deficit in the short run. Four years after the introduction of the Euro and in the shadow of EU punishment for excessive deficits, EMU had become a somewhat more important external constraint for the largest EU country. Despite increased restrictions, it still was not a decisive determinant in national policy-making.

## 4    Conclusion: new irony in German history?

As the German model entered the new millennium its future was much less secure than it had seemed on the eve of unification. Although EMU had contributed to the "Europeanization" of German policy-making, the transfer of authority through supranationalization was and still is highly variable in different policy areas. Yet the bastions of national sovereignty – the welfare state and labor relations – are now at least partly affected by

---

[17] As Mackie and Pepino (2003a) have calculated, the ECB rate was 167 basis points higher for Germany in the last quarter of 2002 than appropriate according to the standard Taylor rule, while it was lower than it should be by 88, 149, and 366 basis points in France, Italy, and Spain, respectively.

EU regulations, new forms of monitoring, and "soft law" coordination. It is a difficult task, however, to assess the specific and precise effects that EMU could ultimately have on the basic pillars of Germany's social capitalism because international, European, and domestic challenges are simultaneously pressuring German capitalism. Each of their impacts have, in strict analytical terms, to be isolated to arrive at robust conclusions about their specific impact on the German model. Together they have eroded the autonomy of national policy-makers to a perceivable degree, even though the intensity and longevity of this erosion remains an open question.

From a comparative perspective what seems most remarkable and to be emphasized is that the political economy of the German social model was shaped by institutionalized monetarism long before European monetary integration was relaunched in the 1980s. German monetarism has therefore been more or less a constant since the mid-1970s, excepting a few years (1978–1980, 1990–1991). Thus for the Federal Republic, European monetary integration has not been associated with a *paradigmatic* shift in the macroeconomic policy regime as it had in countries with "softer" currencies and a less alert guardian of the currency than the Bundesbank. Germany has experienced EMU not as pressure for a monetarist turn but as a trans-nationalization of the German price stability paradigm as favored by the Finance Ministry, the Bundesbank, and principally by the then Chancellor, and as institutionalized on a European level by the finance ministers and central bankers who designed EMU implementation. The promise of a trans-nationalized price stability regime paved the way for the final German "yes" to the single currency project which throughout the 1990s was not backed by a broad majority of the German electorate but was based on a rather broad and stable consensus among *political* elites.

The puzzle of why German negotiators agreed to EMU is only partly solved by speculating about the implicit "coupling" of German unification and European integration around Maastricht. That the German "yes" was stabilized in the 1990s despite severe domestic criticism and strong voter skepticism can be understood only by considering Kohl's and his party's general pro-European stance and a broad, quasi-functionalist consensus among German party elites that monetary union was the next step to deepen European integration. An even more important factor was the power of finance ministries, central bankers, and Bundesbank representatives who negotiated the details of EMU architecture. Ironically, however, the success of German negotiators in making monetary integration into a stability-oriented regime has turned out to be Janus-like, returning to haunt them when the bills for unification came due. Although the primary causes were and still are rooted in domestic policy legacies, Germany, for the first time in the history of European integration, was deeply affected after 1996 by the constraints of EMU on fiscal policy. The 3 percent deficit criterion could be met only through savings measures and the proceeds of privatization.

Socioeconomic regimes embedded in political–institutional configurations have a tendency to stabilize and "freeze" as long as a robust majority of key actors regards them as superior institutional frameworks when compared to the alternatives. A precondition for altering existing policy patterns is that these actors come to share a perception of crisis, triggering reforms that may, in turn, result in major, "paradigmatic" policy change based on policy learning[18] (Hall 1993). Major reforms initiated by these actors, channeled through national institutions, and then legitimized by national democratic processes and discourses, oblige other domestic actors and institutions to take them into account to understand processes and outcomes. EMU may have framed the reform corridor of the German social model, but this does not imply that it was a major, "independent," exogenous factor determining the initiation, direction, and scope of consequent reforms. Nevertheless, EMU can be judged to be an important indirect, "systemic" source of reform pressure on the German model. The SGP in particular has narrowed the room for fiscal maneuver in a way that has spilled over into social policy-making. The relationship between EMU and national social models can thus be specified as *indirect*, working via reduced degrees of freedom in fiscal policy making.

The struggle to fulfill the EMU convergence criteria had already provided evidence that EMU defined a new corridor for national policymakers by the later 1990s. The success and failure of the red–green coalition at keeping budgets within Pact boundaries nonetheless demonstrated that domestic factors still generated the major challenges and the sources of direction and energy for responding to them. Recent tax reforms indicate that even the German government, until then at least officially trying to keep to the 3 percent deficit criterion, was willing to risk endangering the Pact to overcome economic stagnation. During the post-Maastricht years many in Germany feared that other EU countries would threaten a stable European currency, while others feared that the Pact was a dangerous straitjacket prohibiting reforms that might jeopardize nearly balanced budgets. At time of writing, many observers were seeing France and Germany as the more or less willing gravedigger coalition of the Pact.

---

[18] Major policy reforms are referred to as "third-order changes" by Hall (1993), fundamental changes due to a paradigm shift among those with the power to push through policy changes that result in path deviation.

Independent of whether this is the case, thirteen years after German unification high structural unemployment, the consequence of an aging society, soaring public deficits, increased debt service, below-average economic and employment growth, above-average wage costs and social expenditures, mediocre investment in education and research, and increased price competition in international markets have generated tremendously increased pressure for reform but only diffuse crisis perception. This could become the common basis for problem-solving and a definition of "common interest," thereby triggering reform-induced recovery. Or, if perceptions of crisis among key collective actors remain divided, it may not prevent Germany from proceeding onto a dead-end road for German social capitalism.

After the re-election of the red–green coalition in 2002, tripartite macro-concertation was completely removed from the government's agenda. Instead, the government returned – as in the case of the "Hartz Commission" – to reform commissions at sectoral level, particularly in pension and health policy. Together with the so-called "Agenda 2010," which defined the government's medium-term program for structural reforms and the consolidation of public finances, plus efforts for health reform in summer 2003, the suggested measures again pointed more to the immense pressure on basic institutions of the German model than to sustainable reform paths into the future. Meanwhile, intra-union dissent and a dramatic crisis of the programmatically split *IG Metall* signaled that key pillars of Germany's social partnership had eroded to a degree that alarmed advocates of social capitalism. On the other hand, these processes of institutional erosion were welcomed by those devoted to "free-market principles" who seek to dismantle social capitalism altogether. If successful, they can claim to be the gravediggers of the German variety of welfare capitalism.

## 6    Maastricht to modernization: EMU and the Italian social state

*Vincent Della Sala*

In few EU member states was the tension between EMU and commitment to the ESM so apparent as in Italy in the 1990s. It was a decade of political and policy upheaval that shaped, and was affected by, the EMU process. Moreover, EMU was the catalyst and the basis for a debate about modernization in Italy that left few areas of economic and social life untouched. It will be argued that the *vincolo esterno* (external constraint) of monetary integration has been instrumental to bringing about changes to the basic economic, social, and political structures of the postwar order (Dyson and Featherstone 1996). It would be wrong to assume that the political and economic elites were passive, benignly accepting European dictates that might undermine their position. A constellation of social and political forces looked to use monetary integration for profoundly different reasons and objectives. For some of the forces on the left, but not exclusively, it was a means to dismantle entrenched political and economic oligarchies of the postwar constitutional order. Some of those vested interests sought to manage the requirements of the external constraints to hold on to their position. There were other political forces that looked to monetary integration as a way of bringing about some form of institutional change, be it economic or constitutional. Yet, they all framed the debate about EMU and its attendant policies as one about "modernization." A consequence of the coming together of these different interests is the seemingly paradoxical situation in which the neo-corporatist settlement that became part of the governance of the macroeconomic policy agenda emphasized control of inflation, retrenchment of the welfare state, flexibility in labor markets, and economic liberalization (Martin 1997).

The discussion will be divided into two main sections. Section 1 will provide a very brief examination of Italy's macroeconomic and labor

The author would like to thank Sergio Fabbrini and Rianne Mahon for their helpful comments.

policy prior to the Maastricht agreement. It will argue that the regimes may be described by the term the "social state," which represented a consensual approach to social and distributive conflict. Section 2 argues that EMU was the basis for a discussion about "modernization" that led to a major restructuring of the social state.

## 1    Creating the social state

The Italian term, *"stato sociale"* (social state), has been used to describe a consensual approach to regulating social conflict by using the instruments and processes of both macroeconomic and labor regimes to deliver benefits to particular groups and interests. The social state, especially in the 1970s and 1980s, was used to minimize conflict and competition among social forces. It was the Italian version of the postwar compromise and was characterized by a macroeconomic regime that essentially emphasized growth over price stability, and a labor regime that sought to reduce distributive conflict by tempering the effects of a market economy.

### *The macroeconomic policy regime*

Italy's postwar economic history can be divided into three major periods, each with its own distinctive phases: recovery and growth in the 1950s and 1960s; inflation and growing public debt in the 1970s and 1980s; and transformation in the 1990s in the wake of the commitments assumed with the Maastricht treaty (Targetti 1998: 1037). The first runs through the 1950s and to the late 1960s with the "Hot Autumn" in 1969. It began in the immediate postwar years with a liberal phase, led by the Treasury and the Bank of Italy, in which exchange controls were lifted, imports eased, a firm grip imposed on government spending, and the money supply kept tight (Salvati 1984). Between this dominant liberalism and a Left that saw Keynesian economic management as providing too little governance of the economy, there was little political support for a mixed economy in this period. The moderate growth of this earlier period was replaced by the economic boom of the 1950s fueled largely by internal demand stimulated, in part, by public spending on housing and infrastructure. Labor shortages began to appear by the early 1960s, along with pressures for wage increases. There was no formal commitment to full employment targets in this period. This was partly due to the large migration of workers from the south to the industrial north that masked the structural bases of southern unemployment and defused the political and social tension it might have caused. Trade liberalization was consistent with Italy's fledgling macroeconomic regime that was based on internal demand and a growing export economy.

The 1970s and the 1980s have been described as the period of inflation and uncontrollable public finances. Public debt and deficit levels doubled in the 1970s, and the lira was subject to seemingly constant devaluation. Italy was caught in a vicious circle of rising prices, devaluation, growing public debt levels financed largely through domestic savings, and rising unemployment. The growing fragmentation of governing coalitions facilitated the use of very permeable and porous decision-making structures to distribute benefits to specific interests. Export-based industries could find short-term relief from rising labor and borrowing costs through a devalued lira; this also put off major restructuring until the 1980s and 1990s. Organized labor could count on indexation to protect wages, and it had little interest in changing the structure of the welfare state, which as shown below, emphasized rewards for unionized workers.

There were a few attempts in the 1980s to change the course of macroeconomic policy. An important development was the "divorce" of the Bank of Italy from the Treasury in 1981 to create an independent central bank (Epstein and Schor 1989). This was partly a response to entry into the EMS three years earlier. While it would take over a decade for Italy to enter into the narrow bands of the ERM, and the lira would be devalued on numerous occasions, the EMS ensured that fighting inflation could not be ignored as a policy concern. Governments throughout the decade, especially the Craxi governments, had set out price stability and control of public finances as primary objectives, but budgetary targets were rarely met. The figures in table 6A.1 (p. 149) reveal that deficits averaged about 10 percent for the decade, and the debt grew from just below 60 percent to over 110 in 1991. The obstacle remained that there were few political incentives, with many institutional outlets for sectional interests to affect policy outcomes, to think of a more long-term strategy to impose financial discipline and address questions of restructuring the welfare state.

### The social model

It is hard to find an Italian Bismarck or Beveridge, nor is there some blueprint that provides a comprehensive and coherent vision of the institutions to govern the labor regime. The Italian welfare state evolved during the course of the first three decades of the Republic in a haphazard way, often in response to pressing political and social tensions. The immediate postwar reconstruction took place with weak civil society institutions so that mass political parties became the principal agents for mediating social and political demands. They divided into three political "families": the Christian Democrats (DC), the Communist Party (PCI) and its ally until 1956, the Socialists (PSI), and the secular parties. The three also dominated the trade unions, making it difficult in the 1950s and 1960s for a labor regime to develop that was not closely tied to the dynamics of party competition (Regini and Regalia 1998). The social state was constructed partly as a way of accommodating interests and social forces that would otherwise have been politically excluded. This was part of a broader political settlement that gave Italy many of the features of a consensual democracy (Fabbrini 1994). The deep social and political division between the secular Left (and permanent exclusion of the PCI from governing coalition), and the Catholic world meant that consensual mechanisms were sought to guarantee social peace.

In the 1950s and early 1960s, during the period of strong economic growth, low unemployment, and internal migration, industrial relations assumed a minor role in Italian political and social life (Baglioni 1998: 31). Governments remained fairly distant from collective bargaining in the 1950s, and there were no social pacts whereby labor and capital agreed on incomes policy with governments providing guarantees on macroeconomic or social policy targets. A steady supply of labor migrating from the South to the rapidly industrialising North, relatively poorly organized trade unions, and the fear that social unrest might undermine the fledgling democratic order marginalized the politics of social models. The situation began to change dramatically in the 1960s. As the decade progressed, tighter labor markets and increasing trade union autonomy and organization led to growing conflict in industrial relations (Bordogna and Provasi 1998). The turning point is often identified as the "Hot Autumn" of 1969, when worker and student unrest expressed an emergent civil society that was able to take some distance from the political parties. It ushered in a period of great worker militancy and social tension, and marked the entry of trade unions as important mediators of social and political demands.

Although many would lament the decline of the Keynesian welfare state in later decades, the Italian version as it emerged in the late 1960s and 1970s lacked many of its essential features (Ferrera 1996). It was based on the social and economic demands of the industrial northwest, with its high rates of unionization, relatively low levels of unemployment and strong consumer demand. The result was that there was very little concerted effort to pursue positive strategies to ensure full employment. Trade unions were able to extend wage indexation against inflation so that workers, mostly in large industry, had quarterly adjustments to protect their wages. In the case of wages, labor was able to move to national wage settlements in the late 1960s that did away with differentiated pay scales that reflected regional or local labor markets (Ferrera and Gualmini 1999).

The welfare state directed benefits at very particular groups. Pensions were extended so that benefits could be collected after thirty-five years of contributions, regardless of age. Moreover, a fragmented pension system was created piecemeal with at least seventeen different funds for specific groups, ranging from shopkeepers to journalists. There were few positive labor market strategies, and Italy continued to be among the OECD countries that spent the least on training and skills development for workers (Negrelli 1997: 47). Little was done to help families and the growing number of women entering the labor market in the 1970s. More importantly, the evolution of the welfare state reflected the attempt to assure social peace through consensual politics. Social tensions were resolved with haphazard policy decisions that provided benefits for political groups close to the major political parties (Maestri 1987). The welfare state expansion in the late 1960s was just as much about accommodating a wide range of political interests as it was about redistribution of wealth or dealing with market failure.

There are few areas in the 1970s that better illustrate this attempt and the contradictory and often confused nature of the Italian welfare state than healthcare. The national healthcare system (SSN) was established in 1978 with great expectations that have proven to be largely unfulfilled. Inspired by the British National Health Service (NHS), it sought to establish a comprehensive and universal system that would make healthcare a social right. The reform sought to pursue a number of aims that reflected pressures at the time to make institutions, including those that provided social services, more democratic and accessible. The SSN was to be the first major initiative that would involve the newly formed regional governments. The central government would provide the funding through general revenue, a broad national healthcare plan, and national standards, and the regions would organize the delivery of healthcare. This would be done around local health authorities (USL) that were supposed to be vehicles for citizen participation in the delivery of healthcare. The coordination between the national, regional, and local governments did not develop structures and institutions to be effective. More importantly, the central state provided the funding for a healthcare system where spending was diffused and scattered, with little control over outcomes.

The figures for industrial conflict indicate that the 1970s continued to be a turbulent decade for labor relations. It was compounded by a wave of left- and right-wing terrorism that struck at the heart of the state, and by the economic crisis in the wake of the first oil shock that raised fear of widespread social conflict that might spill outside of party control. Despite growing pressure from some employer groups and the Bank of Italy to have an incomes policy to rein in wages, and pressure on trade union leadership to minimize social tension, there were few concrete attempts to create the forms of concertation found in some northern European countries (Regini and Regalia 1998: 471–473). The PCI put pressure on those within its ranks in the labor movement to accept wage moderation, and the broad-based government made it easier for the major confederations to support austerity packages and to curb wage demands (Golden 1988: chapter 3). Meanwhile governments' strengthened labor legislation that provided greater job security, and made firing workers harder and more expensive for employers.

A number of factors inhibited the emergence of a structured and institutionalized approach to regulating industrial relations. The most apparent obstacle was the fragmentation within the trade union movement that mirrored that within the party system. The CGIL (close to the PCI, with some PSI representation), the CISL (DC) and the UIL (PSI) had put some distance between themselves and the parties, but the links between the two remained strong. Tensions between the parties continued to spill over into relations among trade unions (Regini and Regalia 1998: 471). In addition, the growing militancy of the union membership meant that the leadership had to remain sensitive to some of its very active members who wanted industrial action to challenge the ruling parties. Another possible obstacle was the fact that the Italian state did not have the capacity to produce outcomes enabling the leading social partners to count on full employment in exchange for wage restraint. There was no clear center of decision-making within constitutional and political structures, so there were no guarantees that government representatives in negotiations could deliver on any agreement.

Things changed in the first half of the 1980s, albeit temporarily. There were serious attempts to reach tripartite agreements to address inflation, which had reached double figures. Employers and governments sought a revision of wage indexation (the "*scala mobile*") and to introduce greater flexibility for hiring and firing workers. What distinguished these efforts was that the government was willing to use public finances to get the social partners to adopt an incomes policy to curb inflation. Workers were offered protection against fiscal drag and increased family allowances, while employers were given tax breaks for their employer contributions to social programs (Regini 1984). There were a number of factors that made a tripartite agreement possible in 1983. Entry into the EMS did make it more difficult to ignore the need for price stability, and employers were able to push the government to make it a policy objective. Moreover, the beginning of the decade was a difficult one for organized labor as it was affected by tensions between the major parties of the Left and by the aftermath of a failed strike at Fiat in 1980. As Miriam Golden argues, cooperation within organized labor among the major confederations, and with employers, became necessary to maintain some credibility with their members and may have added impetus to the attempt at some form of concertation (Golden 1988: 79).

The tripartite experience of the early 1980s was short-lived, as attempts to renew the annual agreement in 1984 were unsuccessful. The unity within organized labor broke down as political tensions that were causing strains on the Left made it difficult for the confederations to find common ground. The government, led by Craxi, sought to introduce changes to wage indexation. The Communist Party and the CGIL led a referendum in 1984 to preserve the *scala mobile*, while the CISL and the UIL remained more faithful to the line pursued by their political allies in government. In addition, the Craxi and subsequent governments during the decade found it difficult to use public finances to produce agreements among the social partners. There was little confidence among the social partners, especially employers, that governments could use public finances in the tripartite agreements without causing further damage. Nor could governments or employers promise employment growth in return for wage restraint as industrial restructuring was well under way by the middle of the decade, and it was more than likely that it would continue to produce job losses rather than gains (Regini and Regalia 1997: 213).

The second half of the 1980s continued to be a difficult time for organized labor. Membership among the active labor force continued to decline, and relations among the three large confederations remained strained in the wake of the referendum on wage indexation. By 1990 union membership had fallen to 6.15 million, from 7.37 million in 1980. Moreover, a growing percentage of members were pensioners and not active members of the labor force. This was reflected in the drop of percentage of the labor force that was unionized from 48.6 percent in 1980 to 38.6 ten years later (Regini and Regalia: 1996: 8). Moreover, "autonomous" unions called "Cobas" (*Comitati di base*) challenged the confederations' role as representatives of labor. They were willing to defy national collective bargaining agreements and to engage in industrial action, especially in the public sector such as the railways.

In the 1980s questions also began to appear about some of the basic structures of the social model as it emerged from the 1970s. The dualism of labor markets, with deep structural unemployment problems in the South, became more apparent; and began to create arguments for greater flexibility in work contracts. This included minor reforms to make part-time employment more accessible in 1984, and positive labor market strategies to promote youth entrepreneurship in 1986. However, employers continued to argue that the main obstacles to flexible labor markets, such as national wages and centralised employment offices that were pivotal in hiring workers, remained in place (Ferrera and Gualmini 1999: chapter 3). Questions also began to emerge about the ability to sustain some of the social policy commitments that had been made in the 1970s, especially in the area of pensions. Demographic pressures and the generous reforms of the 1960s and 1970s were pushing payments in Italy well beyond the EU average. By 1994, Italian old-age pensions totalled 12.8 percent of GDP, while the average for the 12 EU members was 8.95 (Commissione Onofri 1997: 37). Of more immediate concern to governments was the contribution made by various levels and parts of government to cover deficits between pension payments and contributions, which reached 4.73 percent of GDP in 1994 (Vitali and Visaggio 1996: 180). Again, small steps were taken in the 1980s with respect to tightening requirements for disability pensions; and an ineffective attempt was made to introduce some targeting of pension benefits.

## 2    From Maastricht to modernization

### The macroeconomic policy regime

Essentially the same governing coalition that was in power in the 1980s and had been unable to rein in public finances agreed to bring them under control within seven years. It is open to speculation why the government agreed to a set of criteria that it realistically could not achieve; but, more importantly, it implied a fundamental shift in its governing priorities. One argument might be that only an "external constraint" could allow governments to bring into line internal social and political forces that had the most to lose from the pressures of economic and monetary union. Asking trade unions to make wage concessions or changes to the welfare state stood little chance of success if they were presented as a response to abstract pressures from global financial markets. However, a concrete objective such as being at the "heart" of Europe presented all political forces with the difficult choice of being seen as rejecting Italy's European role in the name of sectional benefits. The external constraint helped create an "advocacy coalition" around those seeking institutional reform and economic liberalization (Ferrera and Gualmini 1999: chapter 4). Moreover, it created an opportunity to neutralize the opposition of those who had the most to lose from both greater integration and a restructuring of the welfare state.

Whatever the government's motives, it did not take very long for the consequences to be felt in the governing of the economy. The currency crisis that hit the ERM in the summer months leading to the French referendum on the Maastricht treaty in 1992 forced the lira out of the mechanism. The devaluation that ensued led to an export boom that was to last for the first half of the decade. It also led to fears of inflation spiraling out of control, with the attendant consequences for monetary, incomes, and budgetary policies. There certainly was a sense, beginning in the frenetic autumn months of 1992, that the governing of the economy required drastic actions if public finances and inflation were to be brought under control.

The period after September 1992 was characterized not simply by an impressive cut in the size of the deficit and debt, but perhaps more importantly, by fundamental changes in how government spent (Reviglio 1998). By any measure, the changes to Italian public finances in the period from 1992–1998 were impressive. Governments, regardless of their political stripe, introduced changes that amounted to a cumulative reduction of deficits of over €200 billion; two-thirds of this through cuts in spending, the rest through tax increases, and only a small amount through privatization (Camera dei Deputati 1998a). A large portion of the cuts were in general administration of government departments, including a freeze on hiring in the public sector for much of the decade. It also included about 20,000 billion lire (approximately €10 billion) in cuts to healthcare, a slight decrease in spending on education (roughly about 0.2 percent of GDP in 1993) and a virtual halt to capital spending after 1993 (Reviglio 1998: chapter 4). The budgetary measures produced the immediate effect of gaining entry into the single currency in May 1998. An interesting note is that in this period, three budgets were presented by governments of "technicians" (Amato in 1992, Ciampi in 1993, and Dini in 1996) – that is, governments composed of nonelected officials chosen largely for their technical expertise and not on the basis of political or representative criteria. This was not simply a function of a political crisis but the result of a political strategy to present governance as increasingly a technical, and not political, exercise. Politics is presented as competition about sectional claims in porous decision-making institutions, while "good governance" is seen as a neutral apolitical exercise that is best left to technical experts. This is especially in the case of Ciampi and Dini, who came from the Bank of Italy. Moreover, there has been an ongoing trend to insulate the budgetary process from social demands (Della Sala 1997). Claiming that governance is a technical exercise is a political exercise in itself; but it was an effective strategy in the wake of the political and financial crises of the early 1990s.

More importantly, the quest to achieve the convergence criteria for public finances led to a "hollowing out" of state authority in a number of areas of macroeconomic and social policy. First, a series of structural changes were introduced to the financing of some important areas – in terms of both the amount of money spent and of political salience – of social policy such as pensions and healthcare. For instance, in the case of healthcare, downloading in the form of a shift from conditional to block grants has meant that decisions such as choosing between hospital beds or childcare spaces are made by regional governments and not the central state. The regions are encouraged to promote new arrangements between private and public sector healthcare providers as well as to have "clients" (not citizens or patients) pay a larger share of their healthcare costs through user fees (Camera dei Deputati 1997: 77).

It is in the area of privatization that we can find more evidence of a changing role for the state in economic and social life. While there is a tendency to underestimate the extent to which privatization took place in Italy in the 1980s, there was a noticeable shift in the decade that followed in the terms of discourse about how to deal with state assets (Cassese 1994). Whereas the 1970s saw the Treasury collect a not insignificant amount of funds by selling equity in some of its holdings, this was done almost by stealth and without grand policy statements about a change in the role of the state. Privatization in the era of convergence criteria has brought about a change in more than just the scale of the firms turned over to the private sector. We begin to see forceful arguments from all sides of the political spectrum for the selling of state assets as part of a broader strategy to promote competitiveness and entrepreneurship. Important banks and insurance companies were sold off in the 1990s, along with Telecom Italia.

The election of the center-right government led by Silvio Berlusconi in May 2001 did not lead to any immediate changes in macroeconomic policy. Election campaign promises of tax cuts were slowly implemented in the first two years of the government's mandate. A sluggish economy and warnings from the Commission about violating the terms of the constraints of the SGP were not been enough to induce the government to abandon its plans to implement further cuts. There was not much industry left to privatize by the time the center-right returned to government but it has generated funds by selling property and the securitization of assets from art to lottery sales. Revenues lost through tax cuts were partly recovered through one-off measures such as light fines for back taxes owed and for capital illegally taken out of the country.

### Employment relations: rediscovering concertation?

On July 23, 1993, the government led by Carlo Azeglio Ciampi, the former Governor of the Bank of Italy, signed a tripartite agreement with the three major confederations and the largest employer organizations. It was seen as giving Italy its first formal incomes policy, along with a structure that would continue tripartite negotiations on a wide range of policy issues. The agreement called for an end to wage indexation and for wage increases that would be in line with the inflation rate projected in the government's annual budgetary forecasts. It also allowed for two levels of bargaining, with four-year national agreements covering a wide range of issues and allowing for salary increases on a biannual basis. Bargaining could also take place at the firm level to decide issues such as compensation for productivity gains and for worker participation in firms' decision-making. The agreement meant a formal commitment by the social partners to curb wages in an attempt to tackle inflation. The pact also opened the way for the introduction of temporary work as part of a broader commitment to introduce greater flexibility to labor markets.

Despite government statements that the pact aimed at growth and employment, there were few concrete proposals in the agreement that labor could point to as a trade-off for making concessions on wages. Commitments were made to education and training, and to restructuring employment agencies to give greater room for public–private partnerships (PPPs) at the regional level. However, there was no discussion about using public finances as a way of inducing labor to accept an agreement in which it accepted wage moderation and few concrete steps to stimulate growth. The commitment given to meeting the convergence criteria precluded any macroeconomic choices that would have been out of step with a priority to tight monetary policy and price stability. What government did provide was a formal role for the social partners, with two meetings each year, to take part in deliberations on macroeconomic policy. Given that the requirements of monetary integration established the parameters for the central elements of monetary and budgetary policies, the formal role for the social partners seemed like a minor concession.

The question that remains, then, is why is it that at precisely the time when organized labor seemed to be in a period of great difficulty was it possible to arrive at a social pact that offered wage moderation but little in return. There are a number of factors that led to the agreement. First, it should be noted that the 1993 pact was the culmination of a process to abolish wage indexation that began in 1990 and to curb wages as part of a broader attempt to put price stability at the center of government policy. The Amato government in 1992 was able to negotiate an agreement to suspend collective bargaining for a year, and to set wage increases in line with inflation targets of 3.2 percent in 1993, 2.5 in 1994, and 2 percent in 1995 (Negrelli 1997: 51). The trade union leadership, especially Bruno Trentin at the head of the CGIL, was heavily criticized by parts of the rank and file, but this did not prevent the continuation of the tripartite negotiations and the subsequent 1993 agreement.

Second, it is hard to understand the emergence of concertation in the 1990s without some reference to the political and social ferment of the first half of the decade. The period between 1992 and 1996 was a turbulent one with a major corruption scandal, three national elections, the collapse of all of the major parties of the postwar period, and the emergence of new political forces such as the Northern League and Forza Italia. These transformations were to have important consequences for the political and policy-making capacity of the government. Michele Salvati has argued that the political crisis weakened the political class, and led it to look for support from the social partners that also were going through a difficult period (Salvati 1995).

The upheaval also provided an opportunity to strengthen the executive and may have enhanced capacity for the government to affect political and policy outcomes. Governments in the 1990s also benefited from a process that had begun in the early 1980s with the Spadolini governments – that is, there had been a gradual strengthening of the executive, and in particular, the Prime Minister's political and constitutional position (Hine and Finocchi 1991). This included changes to parliamentary procedures that made it easier for government legislation to come on to the parliamentary agenda, and harder for factions within the governing coalition to defeat government proposals. More importantly, a referendum in April 1993 voted to end the system of proportional representation and open the way for a more majoritarian electoral law. While the entire political class faced a crisis of legitimacy and credibility, the executive, particularly the Prime Minister's office and the Treasury, were able to seize the initiative. This was due partly to the presence of "technicians" in government and to some of the institutional changes of the previous decades, but also to the external constraints of European integration that favored the executive over other constitutional structures.

A third factor that facilitated the social pact was the position of the social partners. Salvati is right to point out that employers and organized labor were weakened at the beginning of the 1990s. Many of the large industrial and financial groups were implicated directly or implicitly in the scandal that brought down the political class. Italian capitalism had been characterized as a cosy "gentlemen's club" (the Italian term is, "*il salotto buono*") that created close links between the private sector and state-held firms, mediated almost always through Italy's only merchant bank for most of the postwar era, Mediobanca. The single market and monetary integration were adding to the challenges that threatened to undermine the protected position of these firms. The devaluation of the lira following the withdrawal from the ERM in 1992 did provide some short-term help for Italian industry; the benefits were greater for small and medium-sized firms (SMEs) than large industry. This reflected and contributed to a gradual shift within Italian capitalism, away from large private sector industrial groups, usually family-held and run, such as FIAT and Pirelli, and based in the northwest, to a more diffused model, both territorially and with respect to concentration of ownership and market penetration (Barca, Ferri, and Pesarei 1998).

The major trade unions faced similar challenges to their position, especially as declining membership combined with growing challenges from autonomous unions that took little direction from the central confederations. There were moves to create unity among the major confederations, with an agreement on representation at the firm level in 1991 (Negrelli 1997: 49). The crisis of the parties also affected the credibility of the trade unions as they were seen as part of the political architecture of the First Republic. So, in addition to the pressures faced by all trade unions in the face of monetary integration, Italian organized labor had to address internal challenges and one of political legitimacy. However, for both employers and trade unions, the political crisis opened up opportunities. The political parties were, especially in the 1992–1994 period, in a state of collapse, as was their occupation of civil society and the party state. The social partners suddenly became important intermediaries through which the state could dialog with civil society at a time when significant changes in the relationship between the two were taking place. Monetary integration provided a useful context in which the social partners could take measures that would allow them to gain, or regain, some measure of influence on policy outcomes, and to present this as part of an effort to ensure Italy's participation in the single currency. Given the severe crisis of legitimacy of Italian institutions and the political class, there was little political cost to being part of a process that was presented as being imposed from Europe. Employers and organized labor could gain a formal role in macroeconomic policy-making, and, at the same time, claim a role in bringing Italy into the heart of Europe.

In the aftermath of the 1993 agreement, then, discussion of reforming the welfare state centered on pensions. Negotiations began between the Ciampi government and the social partners, but the government lasted only a few months past the July 1993 agreement. The 1994 election, the first fought under the new electoral system, resulted in a center-right government led by Silvio Berlusconi. Confindustria, the largest employer organization, and the Berlusconi government agreed on the need to take on pension reform in a drastic, rapid fashion in September 1994, even if it meant going ahead without the consent of trade unions or consultation. The contentious substantive issues revolved around the reform of the "seniority" pensions – that is, pensions paid when workers had thirty-five years' contributions, regardless of age – and the timetable to gradually increase the eligibility age even when workers had thirty-five' years' contributions. The trade unions responded immediately to the government plan and Berlusconi was forced to back down in the face of popular pressure.

Organized labor supported a series of reforms in May 1995 presented by the Dini government, which succeeded Berlusconi, that were not that far removed from what they had opposed only a few months earlier. They largely centered on gradually increasing the age and contribution period requirement for seniority pensions. This time, it was Confindustria that refused to agree with the changes, arguing that they did not go far enough and had not solved the structural problems in the pension system. It was clear that any discussion about changing the structures of the welfare state would involve a considerable role for the social partners, even if there might be instances of agreements that did not have the support of both labor and employers.

Labour market policies have had to deal with fragmentation and diversity across the territory. There are conditions of full employment and labor shortages in parts of central Italy and the northeast while unemployment rates across the south hovered over 20 percent in the 1990s. Increasingly throughout the decade, the problem became redefined, using the language found in the 1994 OECD *Jobs Study* (OECD 1994a), from one of demand to one of supply in the labor market (Brunetta and Turatto 1996). "Flexibility" became the word around which the social partners and governments began to address the question of employment growth and firm competitiveness (Boeri 1997). There were at least three areas where it was applied. First, there were calls for a more flexible wage structure so that wages could more closely reflect supply and demand of local or regional labor markets rather than be based on national contracts. Second, flexibility was applied to entry and exit from employment. Labor costs were particularly onerous, employers argued, for temporary or part-time work (Carini 1999: 1). Employers and many economists also pointed to labor legislation that made it difficult for employers to fire workers as reason not to assume more employees. Flexibility, then, implied lower labor costs, more incentives to hire and greater ease and lower costs in firing workers in economic downturns. Third, flexibility was used as an argument to change the welfare state so as to provide more "incentives" for workers to seek work as well as to emphasize active labor market strategies such as training, employment agencies, and facilitating different patterns of work.

Wide acceptance of these diagnoses made it possible for the Prodi government and the social partners to sign the "*Patto per il lavoro*" ("The Jobs Pact") in September 1996, with the necessary legislation approved in January 1997. The central feature of the legislation was to introduce and regulate the use of temporary workers, including the possibility for private sector agencies that hire and assign temporary workers, such as Kelly Services or Manpower, to be established. Prior to the legislation, it was difficult and costly for firms to hire temporary workers at peak periods or to replace an employee that would be off the job for a short period of time. Finally, the legislation addressed training and education, with apprenticeship programs put in place along with more powers given to regional governments over agencies to recruit and train workers.

The 1996 agreement set the tone for the negotiations to renew the incomes pact of 1993 that began in the second half of 1998. In the midst of a period of great tension within the center-left governing coalition, with Communist Foundation threatening and then leaving the government over what it saw as neo-liberal macroeconomic policy, Treasury Minister Ciampi issued a call in August 1998 for a new social pact (Camera dei Deputati 1996: 39–43). Ciampi began with the assumption that the incomes agreement of 1993 would remain in place, but that a more deliberate effort needed to be made for growth and employment. He called upon employers to increase their investments in return for a commitment from the government to increase flexibility in labor markets (Sisto 1998: 21). On December 22, 1998 the *Patto sociale per lo sviluppo e l'occupazione* (Social Pact for Development and Employment) was signed. The D'Alema government claimed that the explicit commitment to jobs and growth set the 1998 pact apart from that reached by the Ciampi government. However, while it states that employment growth is an objective, there are few specific targets and no shift away from looking to supply-side measures in labor markets. Most of the measures in the Development Pact were directed to the supply side of the labor market and emphasized flexibility: cuts in employer contributions, tax incentives for research, a commitment to present a "master plan" for education and training, and various schemes for apprenticeships and training programs.

The 1998 Development Pact might be seen as an indication that it was, if not the century, at least the decade for concertation (Pérez 1998). However, it is clear that it has become a means of trying to forge a consensus for changes in the social state in the 1990s. Bringing public finances under control, price stability and the macroeconomic changes brought by monetary integration would have been difficult to achieve without the consent of social partners. A social pact based on tri-partite bargaining over incomes policy seems simple compared to the much more complex process involving a wide range of interests to address the thornier issues of labor markets with less government regulation, and questions related to social programs (Pesole 1997: 3). Moreover, it is likely to be harder to re-create the "shared commitment" among social partners over changes to labor market and to the welfare state that characterized the consensus on macroeconomic policy, and monetary integration, in the 1990s; especially without any prospect of a significant change in employment trends.

The tensions became apparent with the return of the center-right in 2001. Trade union unity was forged around opposition to the government's attempt to reform Article 18 of the 1970 Workers' Statute, which made it hard to hire and fire workers. The changes that would have given employees right of first recall after being made redundant were met with popular, and ultimately successful, resistance that culminated in one of the largest demonstrations in recent Italian history in April 2002. Yet, a few months later UIL and CISL signed the *Patto per l'Italia* with the government and employers; it made a commitment to introduce more flexibility in labor markets by facilitating atypical work contracts. These reforms were said to be aimed at youth and women, groups that would help raise Italy's relatively low labor market participation rates. CGIL assumed a much more militant opposition to the government on a number of fronts. In June 2003, it supported a referendum to extend Article 18 protection to firms with fewer than fifteen employees. It isolated itself not only from the other trade unions but also from most of the center-left. The referendum motion was defeated as less than a quarter of eligible voters (at least 50 percent are needed to validate a referendum result) bothered to vote. UIL and CISL have also agreed to work with employers on competitiveness strategies while CGIL has opposed any measure seen to decrease protection for workers in labor markets.

*Restructuring the welfare state*

The center-left governments after the 1996 elections, led first by Romano Prodi and then by PDS leader Massimo D'Alema after October 1998, made a deliberate effort to use tripartite negotiations to restructure the welfare state. A committee of experts from a wide range of areas, known as the Onofri Committee, was created almost immediately in 1996 by Prodi to examine social programs. Its mandate was to examine the "compatibility" of social spending with macroeconomic objectives. Implicitly, its concern was ensuring that social spending could remain under control, given the parameters of monetary integration, and that social programs would contribute to a more active labor market along the lines set out in the 1994 OECD *Jobs Study* (OECD 1994a). Social spending in Italy, at 25 percent of GDP, was not out of line with other EU countries, but it was the nature of that spending that set it apart. Over 60 percent of spending in 1994 was dedicated to pensions and survivors' benefits, against an average of 45 percent for the rest of Europe. On the other hand, less than 1 percent was spent on employment services, and only 2.3 percent went to unemployment (Commissione Onofri 1997: 3–6). The Committee, using language very similar to that of the EU Commission, concluded that active labor market policies needed to be given a central place in social spending. This would ensure that the social state would be transformed from being based on "passive" social programs to social spending that was "more active" and would increase "opportunity and promote change" (Commissione Onofri 1997: 18) The Committee claimed that monetary integration provided an opportunity for Italy to become more "European" not simply by being part of the single currency and bringing its public finances under control. It also created an opportunity to dislodge the "protected" interests of the existing social state, and to re-direct resources towards areas that would produce more "positive" welfare measures. The Onofri Committee produced few concrete results but it was the basis for a renewed discussion about reforming the welfare state in 1997 and 1998.

*Pension reform*    There have been a number of substantive issues that have characterized the debate about reforming pensions which has been a central element in the restructuring of the welfare state in the 1990s. A number of issues related to pensions were placed on the agenda, almost all of them emerging out of a concern for the present and future costs of pensions. The combination of demographic pressures and generous benefits led to estimates of pensions as a percentage of GDP as high as 25 percent in 2020 and 35 percent in 2040, though there was also a lower estimate of 23.3 percent in 2040 (Cazzola 1995: 13; Onofri 1998: 7).

The Amato government began the process in the wake of the currency crisis in September 1992 by raising the retirement age for old-age pensions for men to sixty-five (from sixty) and to sixty (from fifty-five) for women by the year 2000. In addition, the minimum number of years that contributions were made was raised from sixteen to twenty. But the Amato government did little to address the issue of the seniority pensions other than block them for a year. The most notable feature of the 1995 changes was the raising of the number of years of contributions necessary for the seniority pensions from thirty-five to forty by 2008. The gradual increases between 1996 and 2008 would mean that the age at which workers could collect seniority pensions would increase from fifty-two to fifty-seven. For workers entering into the labor force, the seniority pensions would no longer be available.

One feature of the 1995 reforms that is often overlooked but is no less important than the changes to eligibility requirements for the seniority pensions was the change in the criteria determining benefits. Pension benefits will no longer be determined primarily by increases in wage levels but by a closer fit with contributions paid during a working life. Increases will be determined by changes in GDP rather than industrial salary increases. This does not mean that Italy has moved from a pay-as-you-go pension to a fully funded regime; but it does mean that increases can be kept under control and can match more closely revenues paid into the system. The change in benefit structure, perhaps even more than that to eligibility requirements for the seniority pensions, has been seen as one of the primary factors that reversed the projected cost of pensions in the 2040s (Ministero del Tesoro 1998: 14–15). Another change in 1995 was to begin to harmonize the fragmented regime of at least seventeen different funds, each with its own premium and benefit schemes.

If we look closely at the debate over the seniority pensions in the period since 1995, it is just as much a debate about modernization of the welfare state as it is about future costs. D'Alema, in a speech in Naples emphasized that future restructuring of the welfare state did not center on cuts to spending but a re-allocation of priorities (Luzi 1999: 4). It was not a coincidence that he chose to make his remarks in the largest city in southern Italy. Nor was it a coincidence that he made his remarks about the need to further reform pensions – that is, to look to ways to accelerate the dismantling of seniority pensions – in the same speech in which he spoke of investment and entrepreneurship in the South. What emerges is a constant theme throughout the discourse of the center-left governments' period in power and which continued with the Berlusconi government after 2001. The passive, privileged position of particular interests that had benefited from the previous regime was an obstacle to the adjustment of groups and regions to the new competitive environment of EMU. The terms of the debate about pensions were broadened to arguments about how pensions increased labor costs, and therefore diverted Italian savings away from investment in industry and into financial instruments (Camera dei Deputati 1999: 588–593). In this way, pensions were an obstacle to competitiveness of Italian firms, and a cause for high unemployment rates. Clearly, the debate had moved well beyond simply the question of financial sustainability of the pension regime.

These themes were picked up by the Berlusconi government and a much more aggressive Confindustria after 2001. However, the experience of 1994 was not lost on Berlusconi and his government trod softly on the issue of pensions. He was also constrained by the position of one of his coalition allies, the Northern League, on the question of seniority pensions: the large majority of these are paid to workers in the north, the site of the Northern League's electorate. By July 2003, divisions were becoming more apparent within the government ranks between those who did not want to touch pensions in a significant way and those, largely but not exclusively in Forza Italia, who wanted to introduce changes such as raising the age for eligibility. The trade unions were relatively compact on resisting any major changes, although the CISL and the UIL were willing to negotiate with employers while the CGIL was not. Berlusconi looked to use the Italian Presidency of the EU Council to push for a pensions "Maastricht." This would establish European rules and criteria for pension reform; it also would have deflected blame away from national governments. The proposal did not gain widespread support as the Italian Presidency began.

*Healthcare*    It was in the context of a healthcare system that seemed to have failed to deliver on its promises that the debate on its reform took place in the 1990s. The issue was not so much the total amount that was spent on healthcare, as Italy was in line with other EU countries (roughly between 8 and 9 percent of GDP). More importantly, the level of public sector spending on healthcare dropped steadily in the 1990s from 6.38 percent of GDP in 1992 to 5.27 percent in 1997 (Camera dei Deputati 1998a: 27–29). The share of private sector spending rose steadily in the decade so that over a quarter of healthcare spending was through private funds, mostly private insurance. As we will see, part of this spending included fees for prescription drugs; but it also included the purchase of medical services offered by the SSN. The issue, then, was not the amount of public money spent on healthcare – although an aging population raised concern about future costs – as much as how money was spent, by whom, and for what.

These were the issues behind the reforms introduced by the Amato government in 1992. As with the case of the pensions and budget cuts, the currency crisis of September 1992 created a space to introduce major changes in the name of ensuring entry into EMU. Annabella Corcione argues that the changes were part of a process of convergence of health-care systems in the EU whose objectives are rationalization, containing costs and of greater responsibility to "customers" and service providers (Corcione 1997: 147). The 1992 reform, then, introduced a form of "managed competition" with the USL transformed into Local Health Companies (*Azienda Sanitaria Locale*, ASL) which would operate like private sector firms purchasing from competitive suppliers. Unlike the USL, which were overtly political, the ASL were seen as "modern" management structures with contracts based on private company law for its directors. Moreover, the reform gave greater powers to the regions over determining tariffs to be set for specific services. This was part of a broader objective of making the regions primarily responsible for healthcare. Regions had to provide healthcare plans, along with detailed plans about quantity and quality of services, and to monitor the performance of the ASLs. They were also given greater discretionary powers with fiscal changes. The introduction of a corporate tax to be collected at the regional level also eliminated healthcare contributions by employers. It was up to the regions to make decisions about whether or not to divert the funds from general revenues to health (Collicelli 1998: 59). The "rationalization" of the healthcare system, then, involved creating a competitive environment not only within the sector but also between regions.

The move away from a healthcare system that emphasized social rights to one with greater weight on "rationalization" and "modernization" was also illustrated by what has come to be known as "co-participation" (Ferrera 1995). This essentially means user fees for some services and prescription drugs, but it can also include greater scope for privately funded healthcare. The case of charges for prescription drugs is particularly illustrative of the change in emphasis. They were introduced with the 1993 budget and brought in 4,200 billion lire (roughly €2 billion) in 1993. There was a great deal of political resistance and charges were not collected in 1994 but brought in 1,108 billion lire (about €600 million) in 1995. The figures were minimal compared to the amount spent on healthcare in general (close to 150,000 billion lire), so the issue was not just one of money (Camera dei Deputati 1998a: 28). It was more likely that some policy-makers felt it important to establish the principle of "co-participation" of users in the funding of healthcare. Moreover, there was an explicit connection made between" co-participation" and changing behavior and perception of healthcare, and lowering its overall cost.

## 3    Conclusion: EMU and political modernization

There can be little doubt that monetary integration served as a catalyst for a change in the governing of the Italian economy. It provided the external shock or constraint to a political system that was petrified, and had entrenched economic and political oligarchies. It is clear why the Bank of Italy, and the Treasury, would welcome monetary integration, and not simply for ideological reasons. Monetary integration provided an opportunity to regain some of the decision-making levers of macroeconomic policy and to decrease the influence of social demands on porous, permeable state structures. It is not so apparent why political parties and social partners provided so little resistance to a process that threatened to undermine a regime in which they had a vested interest.

What is of particular interest is the support expressed by the major parties of the left, such as the PDS, and parts of organized labor not simply for monetary integration but some of its attendant policies such as economic liberalization, privatization, a tight money supply, and budgetary austerity. Given the state of Italian public finances at the start of the 1990s and the demands of the convergence criteria, it was easy to make a case for adopting market-based policies to liberalize the economy. For the PDS, intent on creating or enhancing its image as a responsible party of government in the tradition of European social democracy, the crusade to join the single currency provided goals upon which to focus and mobilize support. Opposition to fiscal austerity and even changes to the welfare state was muted, all in the name of the "sacrifices" that needed to be made for Italy to get its finances in order, and assume its rightful place at the heart of Europe. The PDS, beginning with the Ciampi government, essentially adopted the line that there was no alternative to the neo-liberal turn.

However, there are indications that the programmatic shift of the PDS and the Left was shaped not simply by a strategy for economic change, but for social and political transformation as well. For the PDS, and the Ulivo (the center-left coalition), meeting the convergence criteria was a sign of not just the modernization of the Italian economy but of its politics and society as well. The center-left, especially in government, has pursued a broad strategy that tries to project the image of a new Left that breaks with the past. It presents itself as a political force that seeks to bring transparency, efficiency, and accountability to all areas of public life, and to make this the basis of a more participatory democracy. Public finances were presented as the vehicle through which First Republic party elites could use the state to generate support from specific parts of the electorate. Tackling the debt and deficit was not just an exercise to meet the Maastricht criteria but also to dislodge an economic and political oligarchy.

Monetary integration, then, was a way to introduce changes as part of a process of political modernization and democratization. Compared to the secret deals of the First Republic, done not even in boardrooms but in more obscure settings, equity markets were presented as democratic arenas that were accessible and transparent, operating according to rules that were fair and equal for all. Privatization and pension funds became a means of democratizing the economy and taking power away from the private interests and party factions that continued to occupy state holdings (Camera dei Deputati 1994: 468; Cofferati 1999: 13). The same argument is made with respect to restructuring the welfare state. A more "efficient" welfare state is seen to be more transparent, and outside the control of vested interests, and accountable to representative institutions and not party elites.

It was not only the social and political forces looking for change that saw an opportunity in monetary integration. As we saw in the case of concertation in the 1990s, some looked to ways in which to manage the pressures of change to maintain their position, which often was in decline (Romano 1997: 1). This was the case with the "gentlemen's club" of Italian economic and financial power. The protected privilege of both private and public sector firms was less and less tenable, but the history of the 1990s had been one of attempts to maintain control of important firms. The explosion in the number of participants in the concertation process from the major social partners to over thirty in 1998 was also an indication that many organized interests had identified a process of change as a way of maintaining their position.

Italians have remained among the most supportive of monetary and European integration despite the extensive changes that have been carried out in their name. The widely shared objective to be at the "heart" of Europe led to the seemingly paradoxical outcome of the emergence of concertation to moderate wages and restructure the social state, without a commitment to employment. Despite the lack of any concrete evidence, the wages agreement of 1993 was hailed by all sides as an essential step that brought inflation under control, and began the process that led to tighter control over public finances and eventually to entry into the Euro.

Trade unions could claim to have played a role in changing the course of budgetary politics because the 1993 agreement did give them a formal role in tripartite discussions on the drafting of budgets and economic programs (Lerner 1997: 1). When employment and growth became more prominent issues on the political agenda after entry into the single currency, even organized labor accepted that solutions would focus on the supply side of labor markets. This included a discussion of ways in which the social state could be reformed so as to create more "flexibility" in the supply of labor.

The paradox may be explained by conventional TINA ("There is no alternative") arguments. Changes in regulation and technology have created global financial markets and eased trade, so there is little room to deviate from policies that do not give primacy to markets to regulate economic and social life. Once Italian governments had made these European commitments, there were external constraints that led all political and social actors to look for ways to work within the boundaries set by those constraints. Trade unions and parties of the Left could claim that there was no alternative but to change the social state and labor markets, and that they were acting responsibly to ensure that Italy remained part of the European project. However, when these same forces found themselves out of power, the policies, instruments and commitments they put in place stood in the way of their opposition to the government. The terrain and terms of political discourse had shifted; the players may change but the game essentially remains the same.

The argument of the external constraint is a compelling one, but it only partly explains the paradox of consensus around changes to the social state without a commitment to employment. Monetary integration created opportunities and incentives whose result was that there were few left who had an overriding interest and the capacity to resist change. Organized labor faced internal challenges with declining membership in the 1980s and from autonomous unions. Concertation allowed them to assume a central political and policy-making role at a time when they seemed to be in crisis; and they could make concessions and claim that they were in the name of a commitment to Europe. Employers had little to lose by the changes and everything to gain as moves to transform the social state were all in the direction of less state intervention, and greater flexibility for employers over labor markets. Italian governments supported monetary integration because it created opportunities to strengthen the executive at the expense of other centers of political and social power. However, dismantling the social state without an alternative project to hold together a highly fragmented society with an economy characterized by dualism is fraught with risk.

# Appendix

Table 6A.1 *Public debt and deficit, 1970–2002*
*(percentage of GDP)*

|      | Public deficit | Public debt |
|------|---------------|-------------|
| 1970 | 3.7  | 38.0  |
| 1975 | 11.6 | 57.6  |
| 1980 | 8.5  | 57.7  |
| 1981 | 11.4 | 59.9  |
| 1982 | 11.3 | 64.9  |
| 1983 | 10.6 | 70.0  |
| 1984 | 11.6 | 75.2  |
| 1985 | 12.6 | 82.3  |
| 1986 | 11.6 | 86.3  |
| 1987 | 11.0 | 90.5  |
| 1988 | 10.7 | 92.6  |
| 1989 | 9.9  | 95.6  |
| 1990 | 10.9 | 97.8  |
| 1991 | 10.2 | 101.4 |
| 1992 | 9.5  | 108.0 |
| 1993 | 9.6  | 117.3 |
| 1994 | 9.0  | 121.4 |
| 1995 | 7.5  | 122.9 |
| 1996 | 6.7  | 122.7 |
| 1997 | 2.7  | 121.6 |
| 1998 | 2.7  | 116.8 |
| 1999 | 1.8  | 114.5 |
| 2000 | 1.5  | 110.5 |
| 2001 | 1.1  | 107.5 |
| 2002[a] | 1.3 | 107.8 |

*Note:* [a] European Commission estimates
*Source:* Data collected from annual reports to Parliament by the Treasury and Budget ministries; and from data presented by the Governor of the Bank of Italy, Antonio Fazio, to the Interministerial Committee on Economic Planning in: Banca d'Italia, *Bollettino Economico*, 25 (Rome, October 1995: 152–155), Ministero del Tesoro, *Documento di Programmazione Economico-Finanziario, 1999–2002* (Rome, 1998).

# 7 Constraint or motor? Monetary integration and the construction of a social model in Spain

*Sofía A. Pérez*

Spain's inclusion in 1999 among the first wave of countries participating in the eurozone defied the predictions of many observers who just a few years earlier would have deemed such an outcome improbable. A late entrant into the European Community (EC), the country had been plagued by higher than average inflation and by levels of unemployment that well exceeded those of the rest of the European Union (EU). Its system of labor market regulation, a legacy of a *dirigiste* past, was seen to be overly protectionist and rigid (particularly concerning layoffs) and hence, a major obstacle to successful labor market adjustment. Its system of social provision, on the other hand, was still under construction when the move toward monetary union was initiated and fell short of other EU states on many dimensions. Given this labor regime, many feared that the adoption of a currency reflecting conditions in the rest of Europe would cause a sharp loss of competitiveness, with dire consequences for employment. That, in turn, might force a radical deregulation of the labor market, ending any prospect of achieving a truly "European" social model in Spain.

This chapter traces Spain's path to EMU and its implications for the country's evolving systems of social protection and industrial relations. After reviewing the basic characteristics of the Spanish social system, it examines why the Spanish government decided to pursue participation in the first wave of EMU at the end of 1998. Early EMU participation, I suggest, represented the culmination of a long-running project by reformers within the Spanish economic policy-making elite to put the country on a course of economic orthodoxy.[1] This choice in favor of orthodoxy, initiated under the centrist governments of the democratic transition period yet pursued more assertively by the Socialist governments

---

[1] I will use the term "orthodoxy" here in a broad sense, to imply policies aimed at fiscal consolidation and price stability along with institutional reforms aimed at facilitating these macroeconomic objectives.

of 1982–1996, had important repercussions for the course of social relations after the transition to democracy. It constrained the development of the Spanish welfare state and produced a serious deterioration of relations between the government and the labor unions at the end of the 1980s. It also carried serious costs in terms of Spain's employment performance; costs that rose to particularly high levels following the 1992–1993 crisis in the European Monetary System (EMS). Early EMU participation came to be seen by government officials as the payoff that would not only justify the austerity measures implemented in the immediate run-up to EMU, but also vindicate the social costs incurred during the two previous decades of adjustment policies. Anything short of it would have represented an enormous defeat for the policy community that had dominated Spanish economic policy in the 1980s and 1990s. This explains the length to which the Spanish government was willing to go in the mid-1990s to meet the Maastricht convergence criteria.

The chapter then analyzes the impact this decision has had on Spain's system of industrial relations and social regulation. Contrary to expectations, the move to monetary union at the end of the 1990s was accompanied by an affirmation of the role of collective bargaining in the economy, by a return to bi- and tri-partite social pact-making, and by a general easing of tension in the social arena. Several factors, I suggest, explain this development. The first is the negative experiences that both social actors and public officials had in the late 1980s and early 1990s, when a reliance on decentralized bargaining contributed to a resurgence of inflation and a new rise in unemployment. The second is the fact that the policy course pursued by the European Central Bank (ECB) at the end of the 1990s has been looser than that which would have been pursued by an independent Spanish monetary authority. This has had two important consequences. The first was a rapid and significant improvement in Spanish employment levels. The second was that, in the absence of a national monetary policy geared at controlling domestic labor costs, both employers and the government became more dependent on the unions to maintain competitiveness and avoid inflation. The unions, meanwhile, have become more sensitive to the connection between relative labor costs and competitiveness now that exchange rate adjustments have been permanently ruled out.

There has thus been a certain convergence of positions among unions and employers that started during the runup to EMU, and collective bargaining is coming to be seen increasingly as a *de facto* substitute for a national monetary policy. However, as I will point out, these developments have been contingent on the specific economic context in which the move to the Euro has taken place: one in which the Spanish economy grew at a faster rate than the economies of the EU's core countries. Moreover, while, at least in its initial stage, EMU seems to be contributing to a consolidation of the collective bargaining system in Spain, it is likely to have a more ambiguous effect on the evolution of the Spanish welfare state, which will be constrained by the Stability and Growth Pact (SGP) and by the increased need to control nonwage labor costs under a monetary union.

## 1    The Spanish social model *ex ante*

Kept from participating in the process of European integration during the authoritarian regime of General Franco (1939–1975), Spain joined the EC just as the Single European Market (SEM) was being launched in 1986. Spain's system of social regulation at the time was one that had developed in the absence of democratic political contestation up until the first democratic elections of 1977 and was still in the midst of a major transition. Defying easy categorization, the system's two principal features were (1) a paternalistic, highly codified system of labor market regulation that offered some protection to workers but limited the role of collective bargaining, and (2) a rudimentary system of social provision that fell short of European standards in some ways yet was seen as overly generous in others. These paradoxical legacies of the Franco era produced an intense tension in the post-Franco period; one between social demands for higher levels of social provision and protection and the desire of policy-makers to set the country on a course of economic orthodoxy.

The legal base for industrial relations in the new Spanish democracy was set in a 1977 strike law and in the 1980 Workers' Statute, which attributed concrete rights of workplace representation and association to workers. By rendering labor market regulation a matter of legislative design, the Workers' Statute democratized the system while simultaneously opening the legal door to the flexibilization of employment relationships in Spain. Such flexibilization was a major objective of post-Franco elites who viewed the employment framework that had developed under the Franco regime (under which dismissals were outlawed) as a major impediment to economic adjustment. However, in practice, the Statute, which was negotiated with the parties of the Left at a time when the centrist coalition's parliamentary control was weakening, left intact many of the features of the system of industrial relations inherited from the old regime. Most notable among these were the restriction on dismissals and a system of bureaucratic ordinances (*ordenanzas laborales*) that prescribed many aspects of work organization and employment practice. The latter had the effect of limiting the role of collective bargaining to wage-setting. Yet, they were regarded by the unions as ground to be defended, setting the stage for a series of confrontations with post-Franco governments intent on labor market liberalization.[2]

While the system of labor market regulation was being transformed from a highly bureaucratized one to a more liberalized design, the Spanish welfare state was also undergoing major changes. Starting with mandatory retirement insurance for private sector employees in 1919 and the creation of a state pension system for public employees in 1926, social provision in Spain developed (as elsewhere on the Continent) based on principles of social insurance rather than citizenship. Early in the twentieth century, this led to a plethora of government-mandated insurance programs and complementary pension funds. Under Franco, the system was generalized through the Social Security Act of 1963, which created a general pension regime to cover all workers up to a certain income level. A second Social Security law of 1972 further loosened eligibility criteria and indexed pensions to cost of living and wage growth. Nonetheless, the Franco regime continued to differentiate pensions by introducing special funds next to the general social security scheme, "generating a jungle of special treatments and privileges for sectors and categories that were either politically close to [it] or enjoyed the support of a particularly strong trade union" (Boldrin, Jimenez-Martin, and Peracchi 1997: 10). Meanwhile, no noncontributory pension system was in place and other forms of income maintenance (including unemployment pay) were extremely limited. The system thus "covered only two thirds of the population, and it hardly functioned as a guarantee of adequate income maintenance" (Esping-Andersen 1984: 121).

An expansion of social provision became one of the principal demands of the Left during the transition to democracy. The Constitution of 1978 established the principle of universal social rights and was followed by a number of reforms aimed at filling the gaps in the existing system. These included the establishment in 1978 of the National Employment Institute (to administer unemployment insurance and active labor market programs), the creation of a universal healthcare system in 1986, and two further reforms of the contributory pension system in 1977 and 1985. The latter sought to reduce the differences in old-age and disability

---

[2] The first such confrontation took place in 1984, when Felipe González's Socialist government legalized temporary work contracts; a measure accepted by the Socialist labor confederation (UGT) but rejected by the Communist confederation (CCOO). This partial liberalization led to a sharp dualization of the labor market between workers benefiting from traditional (i.e. indefinite) work contracts (and the protection of high dismissal costs) and those hired under the new modality, who could be fired at the end of six months at virtually no cost.

pensions created by the "special funds" introduced by the Franco regime. Yet they also tightened the eligibility requirements for disability and retirement pensions, which were deemed overly generous as labor participation rates began to increase and more people began to qualify for a pension. As in the case of labor market reform, the post-Franco reform of the welfare system thus entailed both an expansion of rights and efforts to limit what were seen as excessive entitlements in certain cases.[3]

Indeed, while the governments of the transition period did much to harmonize benefits, expand income support, and in some cases (as in healthcare) move to universal coverage, the process of democratic welfare reform was hampered almost from the beginning by those same governments' commitment to rein in the growth of public spending. Following the electoral victory of the Spanish Socialist Party (PSOE) in 1982, the burden of this commitment was placed increasingly on the social side of the budget. Thus, while the share of social expenditures in the Spanish budget experienced a significant increase under the centrist governments of the immediate transition period, it subsequently began a steady decline, so that, by the end of the PSOE's second term in office, the Spanish budget had "slipped back to its Francoist structure." (Esping-Andersen 1984: 121). The system of social provision with which Spain joined the EC in 1986 thus still fell short of European standards of social provision in important ways. Two of these were the absence of a noncontributory pension system (introduced only in 1990 and then providing only a marginal rate of benefits) and a very low rate of unemployment pay coverage (less than 50 percent of the unemployed received benefits in 1986). This, along with the continuing efforts to deregulate the labor market, created a climate of protracted confrontation between the government and the unions as Spain approached the process of European monetary integration.

## 2    The puzzle of Spanish participation in EMU

Although the Spanish government was an enthusiastic signatory to the Maastricht Treaty, Spain's inclusion among the first wave of euro zone participants remained doubtful in the eyes of many foreign observers for much of the 1990s (e.g. *Financial Times*, October 21, 1996: 19). Early Spanish participation in 1999 conflicted with the German Bundesbank's preference for a hard-core eurozone that would, at least initially, exclude

---

[3] The years of contribution required for a retirement pension were raised from eight to fifteen, and the computational base was changed from the average of the last two years prior to retirement to eight years, significantly lowering replacement rates (Boldrin, Jimenez-Martin, and Peracchi: 11–12). As Espina (1996: 192) points out, such adjustments are typical of pay-as-you-go schemes as they mature.

the EU's soft-currency Mediterranean periphery, and it is sometimes explained as a second-order consequence of the eventual German decision to back Italy's participation. Paradoxically, however, Spain had come closer to meeting the Maastricht convergence criteria by the end of 1997 than not just Italy, but also Belgium and Germany. It deviated only modestly from the 60 percent of GDP public debt criterion and had a public deficit that, at 2.9 percent, was below that of both Germany and France. It thus could not have been excluded from the eurozone without raising serious questions about the entire selection process.

Spain's compliance with the Maastricht criteria by the end of 1997, however, itself presents an interesting question, for it was the result of a macroeconomic policy that imposed a higher cost in terms of employment than that of any other EU member state. When in September 1992 the Exchange Rate Mechanism (ERM) of the European Monetary System (EMS) fell into crisis, the Spanish government chose not to follow its British and Italian counterparts out of the system, and set out to keep the peseta in the ERM by eschewing the kind of monetary easing required to halt the deteriorating economic situation. The result was a fast rise in unemployment (already at 17 percent in 1992) by a further 7 percent over 1993. This led to a sharp rise in unemployment outlays and a serious deterioration of public finances (the deficit peaked at over 6 percent of GDP in 1995). Yet the PSOE government remained unwavering in its determination to implement a convergence program that would allow Spain to participate in EMU from the start. It seemed willing, as one foreign observer put it, to "scorch the earth it treads on" (*Financial Times*, April 2, 1993), implementing cuts in primary expenditures that prevented a timely recovery, and, without a doubt, contributed to the party's electoral defeat in 1996. Given such sharp social and political costs, it may well be asked why the Spanish government did not follow the British example of opting for an early exit from the ERM in 1992 and a more flexible timetable for participation in EMU.

The answer to these questions is to be found in the relationship that EMU held to the economic policy course followed by Spanish governments since the transition to democracy in 1977. What set Spain's economic policy apart from that of the other two recent democracies in Southern Europe (Greece and Portugal) was the extent to which post-Franco governments gave priority to the achievement of price stability. Spanish governments were by far the most effective in limiting the twin phenomena of inflation and rising budget deficits that resulted during the regime transitions of all three countries, bringing inflation from 30 percent in 1977 to 15 percent in 1978, and a low of 4.8 percent in 1988, while limiting the budget deficit to no more than 6 percent throughout the period (compared to rates well above these in the other two countries). The flip-side, however, was the far worse performance of the Spanish labor market, which saw unemployment rise from 5 percent in 1976 to 22 percent in 1985, and remain above 16 percent through the end of the 1980s, before rising again dramatically to another peak of almost 25 percent in early 1994.[4]

The orthodox tendency in Spanish economic policy in the decades prior to EMU, however, was not just a matter of degree. It reflected a particular understanding of the country's economic trajectory that became pervasive in Spanish economic policy-making circles early in the transition, according to which a key problem in Spain's economic development had been the absence of monetary discipline. The emergence of this view among policy-makers can be traced to a group of reformist economists in the Research Service of the Bank of Spain who opposed the *dirigiste* policies of the Franco regime's planning authority and who stepped into key policy-making roles during the transition of 1976–1978 (Pérez, 1997). As leading academic authorities and mentors of a generation of younger economists who were to occupy important positions under subsequent elected governments, these reformers were able to establish a leading voice for the central bank in economic policy-making from an early point in the new democracy.

After the first democratic elections of 1977, the reformers (represented in the new centrist government of Alfonso Suárez by the finance minister, Enrique Fuentes Quintana) pursued a two-pronged strategy to control the wage–price spiral that took hold at the end of the Franco regime. On one hand, they set out to alter the institutional bases of economic policy so as to allow the central bank greater control over monetary aggregates by dismantling the *dirigiste* regulation of the financial system introduced under Franco. On the other, Fuentes Quintana set in motion a negotiated incomes policy process with the so-called "Moncloa Pacts" of October 1977, which linked wage growth to an expected inflation target for the following year. The Moncloa Pacts were followed by a series of global wage pacts between the new employers' confederation (the CEOE) and the Socialist labor confederation (UGT), as well as, in some cases, the Communist CCOO (Royo 2000).

The negotiated incomes policy initiated in 1977 was critical to the successful disinflation record of post-transition governments in Spain. However, following the Socialist electoral victory of 1982, the process came under severe strain. Under the leadership of a young finance

---

[4] Although the causes of Spanish unemployment were complex, the monetary policy pursued in the 1980s was a key contributing factor (Blanchard *et al.* 1995: 11–12).

minister (Miguel Boyer) drawn from the Bank of Spain, the first González government imposed an unprecedented austerity program that allowed it to accelerate the disinflation initiated under the UCD (from 14 percent in 1982 to a low of 4.8 percent in 1988) while cutting the public deficit from 5.7 percent in 1982 to a low of 2.6 percent in 1989. The price of these achievements was a sharp new rise in the unemployment rate, which rose to 22 percent in 1985 and declined only partially during the economic boom that Spain experienced after it joined the EC in 1986. This experience of persistently high unemployment in the face of strong wage moderation would eventually undermine the unions' willingness to compromise, and with it the negotiated incomes policy process.

During its first term in office, the Socialist government's economic program was supported by two agreements that covered wages for three out of the four years of the period 1983–1986 (the exception was 1984). The first of these pacts, covering wages for 1983, was signed by both the UGT and the CCOO, who sought to lend support to an economic program of the Left. The following year, however, the CCOO refused to sign a second pact, the "Acuerdo Económico y Social" (AES) of 1984, protesting the severity of the PSOE's austerity program and the fact that the new agreement, reached between the CEOE and the UGT, supported the government's plan to legalize fixed-term contracts with very low levels of social protection. Nevertheless, as agreements reached by any representative union in Spain are extended to all workers, the 1984 pact served to limit wage growth through the end of the Socialist first term.

Although the UGT maintained its support for the government's program until the 1986 election, the balance of the first Socialist legislature (negative real wage growth and a loss of 700,000 more jobs) was extremely disappointing to the confederation's leadership. The record in the labor market was compounded by the government's failure to expand the welfare state. While the PSOE significantly increased total levels of public revenues and spending in the 1980s, it also shifted the expenditure balance away from public transfers and consumption and toward public investment. The share of the budget devoted to social wage expenditures (comprising social security transfers, social services, and health services) thus decreased steadily during the 1980s (Esping-Andersen 1994). To the UGT, the most offensive aspect of these budget priorities was the government's unwillingness to fulfill a promise made during the 1984 AES negotiations to expand unemployment coverage to at least 48 percent of the unemployed by 1986. This led the confederation to seek compensation for its past sacrifices in a new round of tripartite negotiations following the PSOE's second electoral victory, in which it demanded a real wage increase of 2 percent for 1987 and a new commitment to expand unemployment coverage. The government, however, refused to accommodate these demands and further aggravated the conflict by insisting on a 3 percent inflation assumption for 1988 even as a 5 percent assumption for 1987 was already being overshot (Gillespie 1990; Pérez 2000a).

The government's uncompromising positions on wages and social spending ultimately set it on a collision course with the UGT. After dragging on for almost a year, the negotiations for a 1987 wage deal collapsed, and this was followed by a series of confrontations over pensions and unemployment pay that came to a head when the government decided not to allocate any part of a windfall surplus in its current receipts in 1988 to increase unemployment coverage. Shortly thereafter, the finance minister, Carlos Solchaga, vetoed an agreement between the UGT and the Labor and Public Administrations ministers to compensate pensioners and public servants for a larger than expected rise in inflation and to extend collective bargaining rights to public servants (Astudillo Ruiz 1998: 346–348). This led the confederation's leader, Nicolas Redondo, to conclude that a global wage agreement could no longer be reached (see Zaragoza 1988; Maravall 1993: 119). In late 1988, the UGT accordingly joined the CCOO in a general strike against the government, initiating a unity-in-action strategy to achieve greater real wage growth in the collective bargaining process.

While the PSOE stance in the 1986–1988 negotiations with the unions contradicted the logic of "political exchange" (see Pizzorno 1978), it was consistent with the view (put forward by the central bank) that the problem of unemployment in Spain was essentially one of excessive labor costs. Persuaded by this view, the first two PSOE finance ministers, Boyer and Solchaga, effectively opposed attempts to address the unemployment problem through income-support measures, opting instead for an aggressive approach to fiscal consolidation and public investment (Boix 1998). Their commitment to this strategy of "supply-side socialism" prevented the government from responding to the UGT's cooperation with the kind of flexibility that would have been needed to sustain the incomes policy process in the late 1980s. Moreover, by the mid-1980s, Solchaga and other members of the government's economic team had become convinced that the central negotiation of wage agreements carried more disadvantages than advantages for their program (Maravall, 1993: 118; Astudillo 1998: 185, 251–255) and that greater wage restraint might be achieved through a tough monetary policy in a less centralized bargaining context.

It is in this context that the decisions leading up to Spain's early participation in EMU came about. After the breakdown of negotiations for a new global wage deal in 1987, the Bank of Spain (still formally subordinated

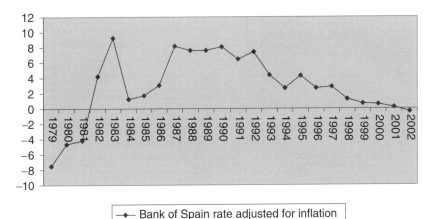

Figure 7.1   Monetary policy, 1979–2002
*Source:* IMF, *International Financial Statistics*; Bank of Spain Rate adjusted by CPI.
*Note:* Figures for 1999 onwards reflect the ECB rate, adjusted by the Spanish CPI.

to the government) began to raise interest rates more aggressively so as to pre-empt inflationary wage settlements (see figure 7.1). It also set out to turn the peseta into a "strong" currency by keeping it within a narrow band of the ERM's central parities. This strategy, officials believed, would serve to impose disinflation by placing pressure on wage-bargainers in place of the defunct incomes policy process (Bank of Spain 1988, 102–103; OECD 1988). Yet it proved ineffectual in braking an upsurge in inflation at the end of the 1980s, leading the government into a pro-longed test of wills with the unions in which EMU participation came to be seen increasingly as an indispensable outcome. Although real wage growth remained moderate (below productivity growth) through 1988, the unions took on a considerably more aggressive bargaining stance thereafter. The government responded by advancing the peseta's move into the ERM (originally scheduled for 1990) to July 1989. Neither the move into the ERM nor the interest rate hikes that preceded it, how-ever, were effective in cutting inflation, which remained stubbornly above 6 percent up until the currency crisis of 1992.

The government's showdown with the unions subjected the Spanish economy to a set of highly pernicious dynamics at the end of the 1980s and early 1990s (Pérez 1999, 2000a). Spain's high interest rate differ-ential with the rest of the ERM encouraged speculative capital inflows that undermined the central bank's ability to control liquidity. It also led the peseta to appreciate dramatically (by almost 30 percent in both nominal and real terms) from 1987 through the end of 1991, in spite of a sharply deteriorating current account over the same period. High interest rates and the loss of international competitiveness encouraged a shift of resources away from sectors exposed to foreign competition and towards sheltered sectors that were less affected by the currency's rise and better able to pass on the cost of high interest rates into prices, producing infla-tion "stickiness" in the face of a tight monetary policy (see OECD 1992: 22, 67; 1994b: 73). The more the government raised interest rates to put pressure on the unions in wage negotiations, the more it encouraged the sectoral shift of resources that made the Spanish economy more, rather than less, inflation-prone.

These contradictions in the government's economic strategy eventu-ally led it to seek a new incomes policy agreement with the unions. After coming under pressure from other ERM governments, who were unable to cut interest rates because of the strength of the peseta, and from the IMF, which warned that monetary policy measures alone would not allow Spain to meet the Maastricht inflation criterion, the government in 1991 proposed a new three-year wage deal that would have tied wages to pro-ductivity growth. The two labor confederations, however, refused the deal. The two sides soon returned to their hostile stances when the gov-ernment, in what was widely perceived as a punitive move, imposed sig-nificant new restrictions on unemployment pay in the spring of 1992.

In the midst of this climate of renewed confrontation, the Spanish gov-ernment had to face the ERM 1992 crisis. The highly overvalued peseta became, along with the Italian lira and the British pound, one of the prime targets of currency speculators on the eve of the French referendum on Maastricht and had to be devalued three times between September 1992 and May 1993. Yet, unlike the British and Italian governments, Span-ish authorities decided to keep the currency in the system in the Fall of 1992 by maintaining high interest rates. The sharp rise in unemployment that followed led the government and unions to attempt a new round of negotiations after the 1993 elections, in which the PSOE for the first time failed to gain an absolute majority. Yet, this second attempt to restore a negotiated incomes policy process also floundered when the government insisted on tying the wage deal (which would have involved a real wage reduction for 1993) to a radical program of labor market reform.[5]

After the collapse of the 1993 negotiations, the government unilat-erally imposed its labor market reform, abolishing all remaining labor

---

[5] These negotiations were also complicated by the PSOE's need to secure the support of the Catalan and Basque nationalist parties, who sought tax concessions for their regions as well as further business incentives and social spending cuts (Fraile 1999).

ordinances in 1994 and leaving it up to employers to cover the deregulated aspects of employment practice (which included such items as wage
scales and the distribution of working hours) through collective bargaining. This move, which the unions at the time believed would lead to a
deregulatory spiral, brought relations between the latter and the government to an all-time low and ended all efforts to seek a negotiated solution
to the economic crisis. Thereafter, the last González government pro-
ceeded unwaveringly to implement its Maastricht convergence programs
with large budget cuts and a markedly restrictive monetary policy in 1994
and 1995. By the time of the PSOE's electoral defeat in 1996, Spain thus
had come closer to meeting the fiscal and monetary convergence criteria
set out at Maastricht than many of its EU partners. It was easy for the
conservative government that took office that year to complete the job by
1997.

Yet, in the end, Spain was able to meet the EMU convergence criteria
with ease, the costs in terms of employment incurred in the process surpassed those of any other member state. Although the monetary easing
that took place as Spanish interest rates were brought down to those of the
EU's core economies from 1996 to 1999 eventually marked the beginning
of an economic recovery, unemployment remained above 20 percent for
a full five years. Given this extraordinarily difficult situation, the Socialist
government's determination to be on board for the first wave of EMU
baffled many foreign observers, who regarded Spain's unemployment
levels as a sign that the country would do best by initially opting out.

However, seen in the light of the policy choices made by the PSOE in
the early 1980s and of the government's long-running stand-off with the
unions, the unwavering path toward participation in EMU appears a less
puzzling choice. The economic logic that had instructed those earlier
choices centered on the notion that the main problem of the Spanish
economy lay in the control of labor costs and that the only way to control
these costs would be through an independent monetary policy. Having
chosen to forgo the incomes policy route in the late 1980s, the PSOE
government, however, had found that its attempt to impose wage restraint
in a decentralized bargaining context by a tight monetary policy proved
ineffectual in a world of rising cross-border capital flows. Unable to reestablish an incomes policy process on its own terms in the early 1990s, it
looked to monetary integration with Europe as an alternative way to create
the monetary context that would serve to control wages at home. EMU
membership was needed, moreover, to vindicate the high unemployment
costs incurred in the PSOE's effort to achieve macroeconomic stability.
Thus, in the 1990s monetary union became both an alternative means
for securing the orthodox monetary environment that the Socialists had

set out to achieve, and the crowning achievement on which the PSOE would stake its political fortunes.

## 3    Monetary union, welfare reform, and collective bargaining

In this section, I consider the consequences of the Spanish government's EMU strategy for two aspects of Spain's "social model": social provision and the evolution of collective bargaining. The precise relationship between the move to EMU and these variables is difficult to establish because the goal of EMU participation was used in the 1990s to justify policy objectives (such as fiscal consolidation and a rapid pace of disinflation) that Spanish governments were determined to pursue independently of the change in currency regime. Nonetheless, we can make a number of observations about the manner in which these aspects of social regulation have evolved in Spain that may shed light on the broader debate about the likely impact of monetary union on social regulation in Europe.

The first such observation concerns the overall macroeconomic impact of the move to a single currency at the beginning of 1999. Whereas in the mid-1990s the Maastricht convergence requirements led Spanish authorities to impose austerity in the midst of an acute recession, the reduction in interest rates required for the final move to the single currency during 1996–1998 (see figure 7.1) and the monetary policy pursued by the ECB thereafter brought a degree of monetary easing far greater than the Spanish economy had been allowed to experience for almost two decades. The result was fast economic growth and an unprecedented recovery in the Spanish labor market at the end of the decade, with unemployment falling from 22 percent in 1996 to 14.5 percent in the first half of 2000. This recovery in the labor market, in turn, facilitated an unexpectedly rapid decline in the public deficit, from 5 percent of GDP in 1996 to 1 percent in 1999, as unemployment outlays fell and tax revenues (including payroll taxes) rose. Thus, while the requirements of macroeconomic convergence exacerbated a vicious circle of rising unemployment and public deficits in the mid-1990s, the actual move to EMU set off a virtuous cycle of declining unemployment and declining public deficits in Spain. Given the Spanish monetary authority's hawkish stance in the past, this virtuous cycle might well have been cut short had the Bank of Spain still been setting interest rates for the Spanish economy.

While the monetary easing that phase 3 brought about provided a long overdue stimulus to the Spanish economy, developments in the area of social spending seem to fit more closely with the expectation that EMU would entail a restrictive policy regime. The rapid fiscal deficit reduction accompanying Spain's recovery might have been expected to lead Spanish officials to resume the process of convergence toward European levels of social provision initiated during the democratic transition. However, there has been very limited change in the area of social provision in Spain. The conservative government used the new fiscal leeway instead to cut personal and corporate taxes and to advance the SGP objective of achieving a balanced budget by 2001 (one year earlier than proposed in the Stability Plan that Spain sent to Brussels) by way of further primary budget expenditure cuts (*El Pais*: July 5, 2000). Despite the fact that Spain still had considerably higher unemployment than other EU countries (14.5 percent in early 2000), it also continued to devote a lower proportion of resources (21.6 percent of GDP) to social transfers in its state budget for 2000 than almost any other country in the EU[6] (European Commission 2000).

More specifically, little progress has been made in addressing two widely acknowledged shortcomings of the Spanish system of social provision. The first is a low unemployment pay coverage rate. Although the income replacement rate offered by Spanish unemployment insurance is relatively high for the first year, a large proportion of unemployed exhaust their benefits. While the proportion of unemployed receiving benefits rose at the end of the 1980s (to 67 percent in 1992), new eligibility requirements instituted by the PSOE in 1992 and 1993 reduced it again, so that only 50 percent were covered in 1999. The second major shortcoming is the low level of minimum (or noncontributory) pensions. The noncontributory pensions received by almost 800,000 pensioners in 1999 stood at less than 60 percent of the minimum wage, which itself, at €413, represented a mere 36.7 percent of the average national wage (*EIRO Online*, January 1998; and September 1999).[7] Agreements between the conservative government and the unions in that year produced a few improvements in these areas: a 5 percent rise in minimal pensions (3 points above expected inflation) and a six-month extension of minimum unemployment coverage for those over forty-five years of age with children. On the whole these changes have been extremely modest; the extension of unemployment pay in 2000, for instance, cost just 0.1 percent of GDP (OECD 2000b: 6), reflecting the government's reluctance to increase any entitlements that might conflict with the SGP in the future.

Rather than commit budgetary resources to approach EU social spending averages, the conservative government's social strategy consisted of promoting employment through targeted cuts in social contributions;

---

[6] Only Ireland, with a far lower rate of unemployment, devoted a lower share.
[7] A further 2 million pensioners received pensions that fell below the poverty line.

again, at a minimal budgetary cost of 0.3 percent of GDP in 1998 and 1999 (OECD 2000b: 58). The Socialist opposition found it difficult to make a political issue of this strategy, given the PSOE's own tough approach to fiscal consolidation during the runup to EMU. The SGP, in any case, makes it difficult for any political party seriously aspiring to form a government in Spain to raise the issue of increased social spending.

Spain's move toward EMU was also accompanied by an effort to reform the contributory, pay-as-you-go, old-age pension system, which as elsewhere in Europe faces the prospect of a severe imbalance between contributions and outlays due to demographic changes in coming decades. In the Spanish case, this imbalance is expected to occur later than in other EU member states but to be all the more extreme because of the dramatic decline in the Spanish birthrate during the decades of high unemployment. It is also complicated by the fact that the old-age pension system, which was expanded to include most workers in the 1960s and early 1970s, set a very low threshold (eight years of contributions) to entitle workers to a pension. The low threshold was necessary to allow the first generations covered by the system to receive pensions and was consistent with a situation where most labor force participants were male breadwinners who were life-long contributors. But it led to a rapid expansion of pension claims once labor participation patterns changed in the 1980s and 1990s (Espina 1996; Boldrin, Jimenez-Martin, and Peracchi 1997).

As noted earlier, changes to the contributory pension system that served to lower statutory replacement rates began to be implemented in 1985. A more thorough review of the long-term feasibility of the system, however, was initiated only during the runup to EMU. The principal development, in this regard, was the 1995 Toledo Pact, signed by the PSOE government and all the major political parties, which spelled out guidelines for reform of the old-age pension system. The centerpiece of this pact was an agreement to maintain the public and universal character of the system but to keep the share of GDP devoted to it steady at 9 percent of GDP. The pact was followed by an agreement between the government, employers, and unions in 1996 which increased the years over which the base of a pension was calculated from the last eight to the last fifteen years (a measure calculated to reduce expected pension outlays by 5 percent over the following years) and segregated the funding sources so that social contributions would be used solely to finance contributory pensions, while other elements of the Social Security system (including noncontributory pensions) would be funded entirely from the general budget. At the same time, the government agreed to devote the entire surplus of the contributory system (beginning in the year 2000) to the creation of a reserve fund (a measure favored by the unions but bitterly opposed by employers who wanted the money devoted to social contributions cuts).[8] A further agreement, signed by employers and the CCOO in 2001, increased some noncontributory pensions, facilitated early retirement, offered social contribution subsidies for women returning to work after maternity, and reaffirmed the government's commitment to guarantee the reserve fund although extending the period during which the funding of the system would be segregated to twelve years. The latter condition was rejected by the UGT, which viewed the long timetable as a threat to the system's financial stability (*EIRO Online*, June 2001).

Although the 1996 and 2001 agreements represented only partial steps toward the ultimate goal of balancing contributions and pensions in Spain (the Toledo Pact was extended in 2003, *EIRO Online*, November 2003), they nonetheless illustrate the kind of social compromises EMU may foster. By segregating the funding sources of the system and moving to a partially funded system, the government and unions have sought to guarantee the survival of the public contributory pension system. By putting a ceiling on the overall expenditures of the system, on the other hand, the government is responding to the need to restrict nonwage labor costs in order to maintain competitiveness within the eurozone. This places the future burden of adjustment on noncontributory pensions and services (e.g. healthcare), which can no longer be financed from social contributions and are therefore more likely to be affected by the limitations the SGP imposes. Although the 1996 and 2001 agreements included some measures to maintain the "solidarity of the system" (increases in widows' and orphans' pensions, and a commitment to maintain the purchasing power of these, and other, pensions), it is likely that noncontributory payments and services would be the first to be affected if Spain were to be threatened by the Excessive Deficit procedure in a downturn. This represents a serious prospect in Spain where these pensions still fall far short of EU standards.

One striking feature of the Spanish process of pension reform has been the seemingly high degree of social consensus surrounding it. The Toledo Pact and the subsequent agreements were reached without any of the bitter confrontations that accompanied pension reform efforts in Italy and France. The 2001 agreement suffered a partial setback when the UGT refused to sign it, but the confederation's stance was viewed largely

---

[8] Spanish employers carried a higher share of social contributions in relation to workers than employers in any other EU state, although the absolute level of employer contributions was not out of line with EU levels.

as a political statement of support for the new leadership of the PSOE and partially also a response to a more contentious debate on labor market reform (see below) rather than a serious rift on the pensions issue. Even the employers, who refused to sign the 1996 agreement have, for the most part, continued to support the general principle of maintaining the public pension system. Part of the reason for this apparent consensus is that all parties have become more aware of the need to limit nonwage labor costs in order to remain competitive under monetary union.

A relatively high degree of consensus also characterized developments in collective bargaining during the runup to and immediate aftermath of EMU. Just a year after the 1996 agreement on pension reform, the unions and employers signed a landmark pact on labor market reform and collective bargaining. The centerpiece of this three-part social pact (the April Agreements) was the unions' acceptance of reduced dismissal costs on new permanent contracts, a measure intended to address the sharp dualism between permanent and fixed-term employment. This acceptance removed what had been one of the principal stumbling blocks in tri-partite negotiations over the previous decade, a major breakthrough. Moreover, the agreement on dismissal costs was accompanied by an agreement to cover regulatory vacuums left by the 1994 abolition of the labor ordinances in those sectors or provinces lacking collective bargaining agents (organized employer associations), and by an agreement to restructure collective bargaining. The first put to rest the unions' fear that employers would use the 1994 labor market reform to embark on a deregulatory spiral. Yet the latter, while receiving the least publicity, is the part of the 1997 pact that may be most telling about the likely evolution of labor relations in Spain under EMU.

The 1997 "Agreement on Collective Bargaining" committed the CEOE and the labor confederations to the goal of "rationalizing the structure of collective bargaining . . . so as to mitigate its existing degree of atomization," and to seek an adequate level of "articulation" in bargaining by expanding the role of national sectoral bargains (CEOE 1997). This represented the first serious effort by the employers and unions to put order in the haphazard structure of bargaining that had emerged during the political regime transition and under which most workers were covered by agreements at the provincial–sectoral level. In promoting the role of national sectoral bargains, the agreement appeared to go in the opposite direction of that apparently sought by Spanish law-makers, who had attached a provision to the 1994 labor market reform that allowed lower-level bargains to override virtually any aspect of higher-level bargains. Indeed, as one employer representative explained, it was precisely the fear of the decentralizing potential of this change in the law that had inspired the CEOE to seek a re-centralization of bargaining by way of an agreement with the unions.[9]

Indeed, the effort to re-centralize bargaining in the period leading up to EMU is not unique to Spain (see Pérez 2002). The Spanish agreement of 1997 bore a striking resemblance to the agreement on collective bargaining reform reached between the Italian government, employers, and unions in 1993. As in the Italian case, the Spanish agreement for the first time attributed distinct roles to different levels of bargaining, with the purpose of achieving a higher degree of coordination throughout the economy. Moreover, the particular division of labor stipulated in the two cases is also very similar. In both cases, the principal thrust of the agreement is to have national sectoral bargains set framework conditions for lower-level bargaining units (in particular, as regards wages), while leaving open the possibility that particular items (such as pay scales and productivity bonuses) be determined by lower bargaining units (see *ABC*, September 4, 1997; CEOE 1997; see Regini and Regalia 1997a). The goal of both agreements is to achieve a balance between coordination to maintain price competitiveness and flexibility to encourage productivity improvements.

However, unlike the Italian agreement, the 1997 agreement in Spain did not mandate such changes. This was made impossible by the organizational nature of the CEOE (whose base organizations have a high degree of autonomy from the central organization) and by the political tension between national sectoral and regional, cross-sectoral organizations within both the employer and labor confederations. This difference in the legal nature of the Spanish agreement has meant that actual change in the structure of bargaining has been slower in coming than in Italy. Since it was signed, sectoral agreements implementing the changes sought in the 1997 agreement have been reached in only a few sectors. Yet, they have been important nonetheless. A 1998 agreement to rationalise the structure of collective bargaining in the metal-working sector, which had no tradition of national-level bargaining in Spain, alone affected close to a million blue-collar workers, that is 11 percent of the total number of workers covered by collective bargaining (*EIRR*, May 1998). And another agreement reached in 1999 in the chemical sector (one of the few with a long history of national sectoral bargaining) broke new ground by requiring companies to disclose information on employment contracts to the "most representative" unions (*EIRO Online*, May 1999). This provision, which set a new standard of information sharing in Spain, also strengthened the power of the two main labor confederations at the expense of

[9] Author interview with CEOE official, Madrid, October 1998.

minority unions and thereby reinforced the degree of bargaining centralization in that sector.

Moreover, while a rapid, mandated implementation of the bargaining structure set out in the 1997 agreement has not been possible in
Spain, there has been a serious effort to re-centralize bargaining by other
means.[10] Although, as pointed out above, the 1994 reform seemed to
encourage a decentralization of bargaining by allowing lower-level bargains to override higher-level ones, the actual trend in collective bargaining since the implementation of the law has been in an opposite direction.
While the number of agreements reached at the firm level increased from
2,642 in 1993 to 3,618 in 2001, the proportion of workers covered by
these agreements decreased from 14 to 11 percent. The most significant
shift in the structure of bargaining has been rather from the provincial–
sectoral level (at which most workers still are covered) in favor of new
sectoral agreements at the regional and national levels. The coverage of
the latter rose from 24 percent of workers in 1993 to 33 percent in 2001
(CES 1998; Ministerio de Trabajo 2003). This upward shift in the territorial structure of bargaining has been accompanied by a gradual process of
consolidation in the extremely large number of sectoral divisions around
which collective bargaining is organized in Spain.[11] And in the spring of
2002, the two labor confederations agreed to a new global wage pact with
the government and employers, thus restarting the overarching incomes
policy process in which they had refused to engage during the 1990s.[12]

Lastly, there has also been a notable degree of change in the content
of collective bargains, which in the past used to focus on little more than
wages and pensions. This is partly due to the abolition of the remaining
labor ordinances, which has forced unions and employers to address a
larger number of items through the collective bargaining round. In the
immediate aftermath of the 1994 reform, many collective bargains simply
took the old labor ordinance standards as their reference. By the end of
the decade, however, a significant number of bargains at the firm and the
national sectoral level had begun to include a wider range of items. These

---

[10] This effort dates back to a landmark agreement in the construction sector in 1991, and
intensified following the 1994 labor market reform (interview with Manuel Garnacho
(UGT), November 1998).

[11] The national sectoral agreements in the metal and chemical sectors, for example, now
cover a number of formerly separate sectors.

[12] There is evidence that even prior to these developments, the confederations exercised
cross-sectoral coordination in wage bargaining. Following the 1997 pact on dismissal
costs, for instance, there was a concerted moderation of wage demands made in the
bargaining round (*EIRR*, December 1997, February 1998; *El Pais*, August 4, 1998).
And, following the shift to a single currency, wage settlements in Spain produced the
lowest average real wage increases in the eurozone for 1999, despite an inflation-adjusted
growth rate of almost 4 percent (*EIRO Online*, February 2000).

include changes in the distribution of work-hours and occupational classifications, increased use of nonseniority-based wage supplements, functional and geographic mobility, and, increasingly, employment-related commitments on the part of employers in return for overall wage restraint (CES 1999). This deepening of the role of collective bargaining reflects a growing tendency by both employers and unions to regard the process as a tool to boost productivity and competitiveness; a tendency that appears to have been reinforced by the new context of EMU.

## 4    Monetary union and social regulation in Spain: some concluding thoughts

This chapter's review of recent developments in Spain suggests that the impact of monetary union on social regulation in the EU's peripheral economies is likely to run in at least two directions. On one hand, the SGP implies that any significant expansion of social outlays can be financed only through increased tax revenue. Yet the heightened importance of relative labor costs under EMU is making both employers and unions more sensitive to the need to limit social contributions (hence the move to general taxation in financing social outlays across several European states), and there are other, political and economic, constraints on the upward revision of income and corporate tax rates in the lower-income countries. This suggests a future of fiscal constraints on the evolution of the welfare state and the possibility that the upward convergence of welfare provision in the poorer member states toward European averages may be impeded. The only way out of this dilemma is through fast growth in the periphery countries, but this may itself be hampered if the ECB maintains its anti-inflationary bias.

On the other hand, the move to EMU has reinforced a return to national social bargaining to address both welfare state and labor market reforms, and to efforts to re-centralize and deepen the role of collective bargaining in the economy. These developments in the area of industrial relations suggest that, while the SGP may, other things being equal, limit the role of the public sector in the promotion of social welfare, the move to monetary union may boost the role of social bargaining institutions. Without recourse to an independent monetary policy or to significant fiscal policy changes, governments, employers, and unions may well come to see such institutions as an alternative mechanism to coordinate their responses to economic challenges.

To be sure, some of the impetus behind the Spanish social pacts of the 1990s came from the short-term need to meet the Maastricht convergence deadline. Another contributing factor involved the political motivations of the Partido Popular (PP), which after taking office in 1996 seized on the social dialog process as a means to demonstrate that the Right could govern Spain while maintaining social consensus. Its support of the pacts between the unions and employers, and its own unilateral pacts with the unions even when opposed by the CEOE, allowed the Aznar government to draw a contrast between its own approach to labor market reform and the more confrontational stance toward the unions taken by the PSOE. The PP (and the social dialog process) also benefited from the final runup to EMU, because the monetary easing that this move implied for Spain stimulated a remarkable recovery in the job market at the end of the 1990s.

These factors were all of a conjunctural nature, as illustrated by the fact that following the 2000 election, in which the PP won a second term with an absolute majority, it embarked on a less compromising stance, seeking to impose a new reform of the collective bargaining system in 2001, and, in fact, imposing tougher unemployment pay eligibility rules in 2002. However, there are other reasons to believe that the social pacts of the second half of the 1990s marked the beginning of a more fundamental transformation in Spanish industrial relations. One of these is the 1994 labor market reform (imposed unilaterally by the PSOE) which forced the unions and employers to negotiate on a wider range of issues, facilitating the emergence of positive trade-offs such as that between internal labor market flexibility, wage restraint, and employment-related clauses, that can be observed in the content of recent collective bargains (CES 1998). Such trade-offs, indeed, have become a central objective of the unions, which, following changes in their leadership in the early 1990s, adopted a strategy of exchanging wage restraint for specific employment-related commitments in the bargaining round.

Another factor contributing to the institutionalization of a social dialog in Spain, and to the effort to recentralize collective bargaining in particular, is to be found in the changing preferences of Spanish employers. The consensus reached in the 1997 agreements on promoting the role of national sectoral bargains was a direct result of the experience that employers had had during the decade prior to the agreements, when (following the collapse of national wage talks) bargaining was pursued in a highly atomized manner. As described above, the attempt by the PSOE government to impose wage restraint through a tough monetary stance in this decentralized bargaining context failed, as sheltered sectors (which were able to pass on the cost of higher interest rates) took the lead in setting nominal wage increases. Employers' inability to restrain wage growth during this period led the CEOE leadership to favor an upward consolidation of the underlying bargaining structure as a way to respond to the challenge of remaining competitive under EMU (Pérez 2000a). And, when in 2001 economists within the PP attempted to impose a reorganization of bargaining that might have resulted in greater decentralization, it was the CEOE's opposition that led the government to shelve the plan.

To be sure, important obstacles remain to the creation of a more centralized and articulated bargaining structure in Spain (foremost among them, the national employers' association's own limited authority over its regional affiliates). Coordination in wage bargaining has been recovered mostly thanks to the labor confederations' agreement to trade wage restraint for employment commitments at various levels of bargaining. However, there are reasons to believe that the move to monetary union will further encourage the process of centralization in wage bargaining and of national pact-making initiated in the 1990s, as reflected by the unions' willingness to reach new, overall wage agreements in 2002 and 2003.

First, the shift to EMU implies a *de facto* de-centralization of wage bargaining in relation to the conduct of monetary policy, presenting a new challenge of coordination between these two variables for governments and economic actors in all EU member states (see Iversen 1998a). As the experience of 1999–2002 illustrates, inflation rates in the eurozone can differ substantially and the ECB cannot target developments in each country. This means that employers and governments in countries with higher than average growth will be more dependent than ever on the collaboration of labor unions to maintain national price competitiveness. This new need for cooperation is likely to reinforce the effort to consolidate bargaining at the national or national–sectoral levels, as the theoretical alternative for solving the coordination problem – that of moving to EU-level wage bargaining – faces many obstacles and, in any case, would be less useful in addressing the problem of differential inflation rates (see Pérez, 2002). Secondly, EMU may also reinforce the effort to centralize bargaining at the national level by highlighting the connection between labor costs, competitiveness, and employment in the eyes of labor unions, leading them to behave more like partners in "national competitiveness alliances" (*EIRO Online*, July 1999). Such a new sensitivity to the issue of competitiveness was palpable in the remarkable moderation of wage growth in Spain in 1999–2002.

These observations on the likely evolution of Spain's social and collective bargaining systems resonate with Dølvik's proposition (chapter 12 in this volume) that the EU is likely to develop a two-level bargaining system under EMU. Yet they also qualify that proposition in the sense that different member states are likely to participate in the two levels (EU-wide coordination and national-level coordination) to differing degrees. More specifically, while unions in the core eurozone states may rely on common negotiating guidelines and thus come to constitute a negotiating block that the ECB may target, unions in the peripheral states are likely to eschew any such move. The national level of negotiation (whether in the form of framework wage pacts or sectoral bargaining with, possibly, a pattern-setting sector) may thus become the mechanism whereby governments and social actors in these countries adjust to the equilibrium achieved between the ECB and wage negotiators in the core countries. However, it should be noted that the ability of wage-bargainers in the periphery to solve the coordination problem created by the shift to a single monetary authority in this way is contingent on the specific macroeconomic challenge at hand. While national-level bargaining might allow eurozone periphery bargainers to compensate for an overly lax monetary policy directed at the core, it will not serve to compensate for the opposite scenario: a policy that is overly restrictive for peripheral economies in the case of a serious downturn. This is one of the scenarios in which the current design of EMU, with its restrictions on the countercyclical use of fiscal policy (which, unlike wage bargaining, can be used to boost demand in the face of an overly restrictive monetary policy), is likely to prove inadequate.

The impact of EMU on the Spanish social model thus may well be double-sided. The combination of a new constraint on public spending via the SGP and the intensified concern with relative labor costs (and hence social contributions) is likely to work as an indirect constraint on the ability of Spanish governments to move Spanish standards of social provision up to EU averages, at least to the extent that improving such standards is a question of outlays. On the other hand, the absence of a national monetary policy capacity has taken the sting of an exceedingly activist monetary policy, aimed at reining in wage demands, out of Spanish industrial relations. It has also made the government and employers more dependent on cooperation from the unions to maintain price competitiveness. Given Spain's long-running problem of unemployment, the unions themselves have become more sensitive to the issue of relative labor costs now that exchange rate adjustments have been ruled out. In this latter sense, EMU has reinforced a renewed reliance on social bargaining in both the area of wage-setting (where there has been a return to overarching wage agreements in 2002 and again in 2003) and welfare reform. There have been exceptions to this rule (notably the PP's unilateral imposition of new unemployment rules in 2002 and the UGT's refusal to sign a new pension accord in 2003), suggesting that the preference for consensual decision-making on the part of different actors is still subject to electoral calculations. Yet, even in such cases, protracted social confrontations have been avoided.

The risk in the long term will come from the way in which the ECB's decisions match conditions in the Spanish economy. As long as interest rates aimed at the eurozone's core are laxer than those that might have been set by the Spanish monetary authority, rapid growth will alleviate the external constraint on social outlays and social bargaining will remain useful in addressing the issue of price competitiveness. However, in the event of an asymmetric shock that produces a sharper downturn in Spain than occurs in the eurozone's core, policies aimed at that core may stall Spanish growth, requiring a disproportionate adjustment in social outlays and undermining the recovery in the Spanish labor market.

# 8     The Netherlands: monetary integration and the *Polder* model

*Jos de Beus*

The Netherlands is an exemplar of peaceful nationhood, democratic stability, and commercial prosperity. It has followed a small-state development strategy of export-led growth, partnership among government, capital, and labor, a mixed economy, and pragmatic crisis management (Katzenstein 1985). Since 1945, it has withstood major changes such as decolonization, the emancipation of citizens and households, European unification, immigration, and the globalization of markets and communications. Beginning in the mid-1970s, however, the Netherlands came to be seen as a model of European sclerosis. Exploitation of natural gas drove up domestic producer costs through currency appreciation and there was rapid expansion of social security and public transfer expenditures (Ellman 1984a, 1984b, 1986). Unemployment rose to 11 percent by 1983 and stayed high for the entire decade.

Since the mid-1990s, however, the *Polder* model has been praised far and wide because of a complete turnaround created by wage restraint, welfare state reform, and seamless entry to monetary union. Unemployment was 2.8 percent in 2000, employment having risen by more than 2.5 million people between 1983 and 2000 (more than 25 percent in labor-years) (Wolfson 2001: 209).[1] There was price stability, a trade surplus, and moderate wage and income inequality, relative to both the Dutch past and to other Western countries today. Indeed, the Dutch record of economic growth, declining unemployment and inflation in the 1990s approached the outstanding performance of the American economy, while public policy remained broadly in line with embedded liberalism – that is, public coverage of the basic risks of an open economy and ongoing internationalization (UNDP 2001).

This chapter shows that the postwar labor regime of the Netherlands shifted to the *Polder* model in incremental ways. Wage restraint remained

---

[1] There is still a gap between male and female labor force participation, high rates of labor disability, protracted unemployment of immigrants, and segregation of immigrant communities, but such things do not undermine the scope of the "Dutch miracle."

a crucial goal, but the setting and design of wage restraint in the 1980s and 1990s differed from the collectivist, centralist experience of the late 1940s and 1950s. Moreover, the Dutch U-turn was prodded more by a domestic crisis beginning in the 1970s than exogenous pressures from Europeanization. Monetary integration and the effort to meet the EMU convergence criteria were significant, but the trajectory of welfare state reconfiguration had already been set domestically. The product, a reconfigured Dutch regime, remains a European model, marked by consensus among elites, labor market regulation, and the broad guarantee of social security (Hooghe and Marks 2001: 119–142).

## 1    The Dutch labor regime from pacification to *Polder* model

According to most participants and observers, the Dutch postwar labor regime worked until the late 1960s (Knoester 1989). The 1930s had been marked by liberal orthodoxy and confusion about remedies for depression. Reconstruction and consolidation after May 1945 led to state intervention and national bargaining for balanced industrial development, an arrangement largely taken for granted by the major parties, the business community, trade unions, top civil servants, experts, and public opinion. In fiscal and monetary policy, the government and the central bank became jointly responsible for expansion and stabilizing the business cycle. The so-called "structural budget policy" required the government to counter insufficient private spending by creating a budget deficit whose size was determined by an equation with two variables, the structural savings surplus and the current account surplus of the balance of payments (determined by considerations about the fixed exchange rate of the guilder and the financing of development aid). The government could determine its future budgetary space by calculating the long-term growth of the economy, a progression factor (i.e. the elasticity of tax revenues at unchanged tariffs with respect to national income), and the structural budget deficit. The space could be used for increased public expenditure, tax reduction, or a combination of the two. The government could exceed the budgetary space in case of slack (compensated by a correspondingly increased tax burden) or use it only partially in case of strain.

Monetary policy aimed first to stabilize purchasing power and the exchange rate by controlling liquidity. The Dutch central bank acted as an independent public agency in consultation with the Ministry of Finance, with both sharing a moderate Keynesianism that sought appropriate financial conditions for the economy rather than monetary action to control outputs, employment, and prices (De Wolff and Driehuis 1980: 53). Wage policy focused on low wage and labor costs, with annual adaptation of the wage level to rising living costs, the compression of wage differences, and gradual loosening of central control by linking wage increases to rising labor productivity in different sectors. After the mid-1960s, the central government accepted inflation-indexed wage increases and wage-leadership (from the metal industry and Philips) constrained by price control and regular interventions in collective labor contracts (Windmuller and De Galan 1977, I: 51–91).

The postwar period brought the incremental buildup of a national welfare state that by the 1950s encompassed unemployment insurance, old-age pensions, and assistance to widows and orphans. In the 1960s, it extended to family allowances, social assistance for the poor, compensation for special medical expenses, and benefits for disabled workers. The replacement rates for sick, unemployed, and disabled workers were high (80 percent of last earned income) and completed in rounds of wage bargaining, which provided an additional 20 percent. After 1969, the legal minimal wage and minimal flat-rate benefits in national schemes of social assistance and security (such as pensions) were linked, while all gross benefits, as well as gross salaries of civil servants, were annually adjusted to the average national change in contractually determined wages (Roebroek 1993: 159–182).

The main domains of public policy have been tightly connected. Promotion of exports – important for job creation and always vulnerable (Scharpf 2002a: 109–110) – required a balanced mix of instruments and measures to avoid overshooting exchange and interest rates, public overspending, catch-up increases in wages and private consumption, and excessive public burdening and regulation of the exposed sector. Policymakers have always understood new legislation as quasi-constitutional, such as the Bank Law (1948), the Extraordinary Decree on Industrial Relations (1945), and the General Old Age Pensions Act (1957) (plus quasi-legal documents such as the Social and Economic Council's Advice on the goals of economic policy, 1951). Institutions facilitated deliberation and bargaining as well as collection of data and planning: the Foundation of Labor (1945), the Social and Economic Council (1951), the Central Planning Bureau (1945), and the Social Insurance Council (1953). Representation was based on group membership and oriented toward consensus. Procedures and rituals of representation became imperative for the large political parties (including Catholics, social democrats, and conservatives), associated employers and employees, multinationals and small firms, the ministries of Finance, Economic Affairs, and Social Affairs, and experts in applied social science.

This regime, which shifted, almost by stealth, from economic recovery, political harmony, and administrative centralization (1945–1959) to expansion, contestation, and liberalization (1959–1973), was in place on the eve of the great welfare state crisis that followed the two oil shocks of the 1970s and depression in 1981 and 1982. The crisis combined economic deterioration, growing ineffectiveness of public policy, divisions and confusion about reform, and a general loss of legitimacy (Braun 1988; Van Zanden 1997). The growth rate dropped from 4.7 percent in 1973 to 1.7 percent in 1983, unemployment increased from 2.2 to 11 percent (an average of 4.8 percent), and inflation slowly declined, from 8 to 2.7 percent (an average of 6.6 percent): 60 percent of the unemployed were out of work for more than a year. Gross private investment shrank, interest rates rose, and the budget deficit, taxes and social insurance premiums grew. The labor cost share in the market sector increased from 84 to 93 percent, indicating declining profitability. The number of inactive citizens and social expenditures increased rapidly and constantly. This was all clearly related to the collapse of world trade, but it also demonstrated a decline in the adaptability of Dutch institutions and practices at both firm and governmental levels.

Conventional remedies either did not help, or made things worse. In 1974 and 1975, the center-left Den Uyl cabinet introduced an expansionary countercyclical program to boost private consumption that failed to address structural problems. Long-term prospects for growth – the core of structural budget policy – were overestimated and misunderstood. Public expenditure and revenues were out of control. The Dutch central bank continued to follow the German Bundesbank, and revaluation of the guilder in 1973 followed revaluation of the German D-mark. This helped, but it could not prevent the ongoing appreciation of the guilder and decline of national competitiveness. Furthermore, monetary authorities were lax when national liquidity rose sharply after 1973 and firms (through diversification) and families (through housing) ran up debt induced by negative real interest rates.

National associations of labor and capital clashed over reforms to introduce industrial democracy and abolish automatic compensation for inflation, often leading governments, themselves the largest employers, to intervene to contain rising wage and salary costs. None of this stopped the relentless reorganization of Dutch business through bankruptcies, industrial decline, and massive dismissals amid growing animosity and immobility between and within unions, employers' associations, and political parties (Hemerijck 1992: 289–346). Governments were reluctant to retrench in social policy to reverse the decrease in labor force participation, increased dependence on social benefits (so-called "inactives"), or the strong interplay between these trends through rising costs of hiring personnel and the rising benefits of leisure. The ratio between inactive and active Dutch workers rose from 49.7 percent in 1973 to 81.3 percent in 1983, with the highest ratio of 83.4 in 1984.

The obvious need for reform sparked proposals for industrial planning, coercive redistribution of labor-time, market deregulation, public sector job plans, and a residual welfare state, all widely discussed by politicians, civil servants, and economists. No proposal acquired solid support, nor did any stimulate consistent innovation in public policy. After 1979, the central bank did turn to monetarism and restrictive policies within the "Snake" arrangement and the European Monetary System (EMS) (after 1979), embracing the West German model and making structural rather than cyclical unemployment the focus. Its presidents (Zijlstra, Duisenberg) saw battling inflation as the priority and wanted politicians to slash budgets and taxes and trade union leaders to moderate wage demands. Many economists and politicians, establishment and left alike, pointed to the negative impact of rising effective exchange rates and real interest rates on competitiveness, export, investment, output, and employment. The central bank defended its policies by emphasizing bilateral relations with Germany, rather than an ideology of "anti-inflationary" and "anti-deficit" radicalism (Sen 1999: 138–142). The bank's form of realism prevailed (Van Ewijk *et al.* 1980; Van Zanden and Griffiths 1989: 53–57).

The crisis led to a loss of system legitimacy. Relations between major players deteriorated, less because of open confrontations than from hidden cost-shifting and avoidance. Actors were willing to postpone coordination and blow up the complex linkages between fiscal, monetary, wage, and social policies. No player could then act on the basis of credible threats and strong capabilities. The government wanted to interfere unilaterally and strip expensive public obligations in the budget. Employers wanted to disengage and rely on their new bargaining power in a slack labor market. Unions wanted to protect workers' rights, the social wage, civil servant privileges, and institutional prerogatives, even at the expense of workers in the exposed sector. An elite rhetoric of exit, oscillation, and the experience of mass insecurity thus undermined the trust of clients and constituencies in welfare statism and corporatist industrialism.

The new *Polder* model is very different. Monetary policy is delegated to the European Central Bank (ECB). Fiscal policy aims at lower equilibrium levels of public expenditure and revenue as well as a budget surplus within Stability and Growth Pact (SGP) limits. Wage policy (without price control) requires sectoral bargaining and voluntary agreements between national associations with or without the state as third party.

Social policy aims to separate public and private responsibility for social risks and to link labor market integration with an active labor market policy that was missing in the postwar regime (Rein and Freeman 1989; Therborn 1989; De Beus and Van Kersbergen 1994).

The numbers about recovery, boom, and overheating in the Dutch economy since 1983 are well known and fiercely discussed. Yet "regime shift" is surprisingly hard to identify. Some question the very existence of a regime, for example:

Although the Dutch experience in the past fifteen years harbours a positive sum solution to the problem of the modernization of the welfare state, it does not add up to a model that can serve as a policy example for others to follow, like the Swedish model notoriously did for academics, journalists and policy makers in the 1970s. There has not at any point of time been a grand design, master plan or major political exchange from which subsequent policies have followed. (Visser and Hemerijck 1997: 184)

Others suggest that the Netherlands is the best case of continental European convergence toward neo-liberalism and Anglo-American capitalism, pointing to growing numbers of self-employed, increasing shareholder power in leading corporations, more flexible jobs (12 percent in 1996), and the rising Gini (10 percent) and Theil coefficients (38 percent) of income inequality and full-time wage inequality between 1983 and 1990 (Van Witteloostuijn 1999; Phelps 2000; De Beer 2001: 219, 248). Still others draw attention to the coalition cabinets of conservatives, liberals, and social democrats after 1994 and connect them to Third Way politics, a new marriage of efficiency and justice, as practiced by Prime Minister Wim Kok (Sassoon 1997: 742; Giddens 1998: 112–123; Hombach 1998: 129–153). Private enterprise has begun to flourish and the Netherlands was ranked number four in the 2000 World Economic Forum report on global competitiveness. In 2001, the *Economist* Intelligence Unit concluded that the Netherlands was the world's leading facilitator of private investment in its "political climate, financial potential, export policy and the attitude towards foreign investment." Furthermore, income and wage inequalities were frozen in the 1990s, while poverty was contained (Goodin *et al.* 1999: 152–186). Finally, some remark on the intermediate character of Dutch macroeconomic policy, redistribution, and industrial relations, arguing that the Netherlands mixes the outcomes of nationally coordinated and liberal market economies (Esping-Andersen 1990: 50, 1996: 86, n. 13, 1999: 86–87, 166; Crouch 1993: 263, 1996: 372; Garrett 1998: 19; Kitschelt *et al.* 1999: 434–435).

The new model features consensual decision-making about basic institutional and policy change, particularly with respect to market-making in the public sphere ranging from internal pricing in government and semi-public services to full-scale privatization of public utility services (Van der Ploeg 1998; Delsen 2000; Labohm and Wijnker 2000). Leaders consult, anticipate each other's actions, and bargain together, reaching agreement through ingenious procedures and informal networks that permit constant discussion. Consensus starts with common definitions of central problems such as "welfare without work," helping vulnerable workers into social security, and promoting access for long-term social security clients into the labor market (Visser and Hemerijck 1997: 136; Hemerijck and Schludi 2000: 159). The model also involves pragmatic application of a mix of liberal and communitarian principles. Government promotes the deregulation of older markets – longer opening hours for shops, for example – and the regulation of newer markets through the privatization of television, hospitals, trains, and buses, for example. New competition must offer least-cost or win–win solutions to social problems, however, and also respect Dutch notions of citizenship of decency, the rule of law, and social responsibility. Government and national associations of capital and labor all are supervised by independent agencies such as the Board of Social Insurance Supervision, the Dutch Competition Authority, and the Independent Post and Telecommunication Authority. There has also been internal reorganization of the public sector by reduced and innovative public spending.

In 1994, the government reformulated its structural budgetary policy for four-year periods. This has entailed forecasting long-run economic growth, limiting growth in public spending, public modesty on taxation (level, structure, and rates), new decision rules on windfalls – unanticipated public savings may finance extra outlays, but unexpected revenue must be used for reducing public debt and taxes and for bad luck. Unpredicted deficits must be matched by budget cuts while analogous revenue losses may engender temporary deficit increases. (*Miljoenennota* 1995: 11–13, 1999: 11–13).[2] Adequate predictions promote a balance between private and public goods. Timely retrenchment and tax changes create space for the fiscal promotion of employment, private spending, and targeted public spending.

The *Polder* model further requires regular renegotiation of wage restraint and moderate wage differentiation to ease tensions between external competitiveness and internal cohesion. Wage restraint is meant to restore profitability, substitute labor for other productive factors, and enhance foreign demand for Dutch products. It should also promote

---

[2] The *Miljoenennota* is the annual document of the Dutch central government on public finance and the state of the economy.

employment of the unskilled in distributive, personal, and social services in both market and public sectors (Kloosterman and Elfring 1991), and it facilitates control of the government payroll and the statutory link between wages in the market sector and social security benefits. There are also a number of new ways to reduce unemployment. They include part-time jobs in the service sector, special jobs in the public sector (32 hours at a maximum of 120 percent of the hourly minimum wage), employability programs, legal protection of flexible labor, temporary relaxation of the minimum wage, working without the loss of social benefits, special tax and social insurance rebates for employers who hire long-term unemployed workers, low-skilled, and partly disabled citizens, differentiation of premiums so that firms with relatively more dismissed employees or more dismissed older and disabled employees pay relatively more, guided transition from subsidized public sector work to regular work in the private sector, and a special civil service for urban renewal.

All of the large political parties are jointly responsible for the success and failure of common initiatives, enhancing the continuity of public policies and public–private arrangements beyond four-year parliamentary terms. Initiatives tend to include organized interests and exclude shock therapies. All actors demonstrate an *a priori* commitment to fixed rules: the central bank through monetary union with Germany after 1983 and convergence towards EMU membership, the central government through strict four-year agreements among incumbent political parties and control of the parliamentary majority by the cabinet, and employers' associations and trade unions through the 1982 Wassenaar Agreement. (Wassenaar is a small town near The Hague where the main employers' association and the main union met in the autumn of 1982 to strike a deal on wage restraint.)

The term "regime shift" captures a number of changes. All three leading actors have increased capacity and authority by disengaging themselves from the postwar regime. The government has focused on the retrenchment of transfer expenditure, control of public finance, new strategies of public management and delegation (including of social policy), and active labor market policy. The central bank has a restrictive monetary policy and accepted the leadership first of the Bundesbank and then the ECB. The organizations of capital and labor have made bilateral agreements about wage restraint (1982), labor-time reduction (1993), and flexibilization (1996, 1999). Each actor survived and increased independence by ceding some margin to free ride and hurt others. In many ways change in the various domains of public policies implies liberalization and a sharper division of public, corporate, and personal responsibilities. Yet Dutch neoliberalism has been marked by

Table 8.1 *Public expenditure for passive and active labor market programs, the Netherlands, 1985–1998 (% of GDP)*

|  | Active measures | | | | Passive measures | | | | Total | | | |
|---|---|---|---|---|---|---|---|---|---|---|---|---|
|  | 1985 | 1990 | 1995 | 1998 | 1985 | 1990 | 1995 | 1998 | 1985 | 1990 | 1995 | 1998 |
| NL | 1.09 | 1.04 | 1.06 | 1.76 | 3.24 | 3.30 | 3.06 | 3.14 | 4.33 | 3.34 | 4.12 | 4.90 |
| BEL | 1.23 | 1.17 | 1.40 | 1.29 | 3.43 | 2.65 | 2.76 | 2.67 | 4.66 | 3.83 | 4.16 | 3.96 |
| GER | 0.81 | 1.02 | 1.33 | 1.27 | 1.41 | 1.16 | 2.14 | 2.29 | 2.23 | 2.18 | 3.47 | 3.56 |
| US | 0.30 | 0.25 | 0.20 | 0.18 | 0.61 | 0.60 | 0.35 | 0.25 | 0.90 | 0.85 | 0.55 | 0.43 |

*Notes*:
BEL = Belgium          NL = Netherlands      US = United States.
GER = Germany
*Source*: Delsen (2000: 43).

consensual management – that is, a shared effort to reach consensus about liberal views and schemes, to define a shared response to globalization and European integration and control the liberalization of bureaucratic and corporatist arrangements (Van der Veen and Trommel 1999). Perhaps the best illustration of constraint on the new economic freedom is active labor market policy (see table 8.1).

Many elements from the postwar regime remain, however. The welfare state is now less generous and permissive but its basic structure is untouched. It provides education, housing, healthcare, personal transport, community work and arts, and broad social security, such as citizen insurance, employees' insurance, and social assistance for the poor. The Netherlands ranks high among EU members in welfare spending, maximal net benefits for the poor, replacement rates in workers' insurances, old-age pension guarantees (basic pay-as-you-go public pensions at 45 percent, obligatory supplementary pensions of 30 percent, voluntary private pensions of 25 percent), the ratio of minimum benefits to wages, and a minimum benefit of 0.8 times the average wage (Becker 1999; SCP 2000).

Dutch labor market structures have been equally resilient. Legal monopolies have granted representation of national associations of capital and labor since 1927. Since 1937, unorganized employers and employees have been legally obligated to accept collective agreements between official national associations. Despite union density of only 29 percent (the organization rate of employers is 65 percent, which includes multiple memberships), wage-bargaining coverage is 83 percent in the private sector, mostly through industry agreements, and 100 percent in the public. The most important changes have been decentralization and de-concentration, caused by the decreasing influence of company agreements by Dutch multinationals, the old wage leaders. The postwar preventive dismissal test, which requires employers to obtain a license from the Ministry of Social Affairs, in particular the Regional Directorate of Labor Provision, before firing a worker, is still in effect, although loosened and frequently bypassed by civil labor law suits. The growth in flexible jobs has been limited, from 5 percent in 1970 to 11 percent in 1998 (De Beer 2001: 46). The most important change has been the growth of part-time jobs, from 12 percent in 1970 to 26 percent in 1998, and the related doubling of the female participation rate from 30 percent to 60 percent in 2000. The Netherlands may very well be the first part-time economy with one-and-a-half jobs per household (Visser 1999). The transformation of the Dutch economy is thus less than total, and connections between it and both Bretton Woods and EMU are evident in "moderation in wage claims, a social compact atmosphere, and a powerful central bank with *rentier* interests at heart" (Maddison 1991: 187).

## 2        Explaining the "velvet transformation"

Given the difficult circumstances of the 1980s and 1990s, how did elites manage the move from "Dutch disease" to "Dutch miracle" (NRC *Handelsblad*, February 5, 1994; Metze 1999)? The Netherlands is an old consensus democracy marked by multi-party government and corporatist power sharing. Elites have needed to be creative in the face of welfare state crisis and cut-throat international competition. Such creativity depends on leadership, the mandate of voters and civil society, mutual trust, and goodwill. More specifically, it depends on containing the forces of exit, parasitic behavior, short-term interests, radicalism, and alienation. None of the big compromises – on fiscal and monetary policy, wage moderation, and social policy – was either effortless or cozy. In fiscal matters, party rivalry was deep. In monetary policy, disagreement emerged between the national political leadership and the financial establishment. In wage policy, the conflict was between capital and labor. Finally, problems in social policy caused a deep crisis at the heart of Dutch society.

Fiscal policy reform was predicated on recognizing the end of Keynesianism by the center-left cabinet of Den Uyl (1973–1977), immobile crisis management by the center-right and center-left Van Agt cabinets (1977–1982), neo-liberalism (Lubbers 1982–1986, 1986–1989), and the third way (Lubbers 1989–1994 and the Kok lib–lab cabinets 1994–2002). The VVD conservatives set the agenda on issues such as abuse of social entitlements and welfare state overload but they lacked sufficient support to pursue a Thatcherite program. Alternatives to Keynesianism were then constructed by the Christian democrats (CDA) and the social democrats (PvdA), the two centrist popular parties and architects of the original Keynesian interventionist state.

In summer 1978, the CDA decided to keep the budget deficit under 5 percent with a major budget cut of 9.5 billion guilders. Two-thirds of this was reducing social benefits and salaries but the CDA wanted to preserve the links between private wages, public salaries, and social benefits. To do so the government had to rely on cooperation from the unions, indecisive about wage restraint and conditional in support for retrenchment. Divisions emerged between public and private sector unions, socialist and confessional unions, radicals willing to strike, and realists willing to talk. Employers strongly favored wage and budget cuts, but they rejected government intervention, even through a temporary freeze. The Christian democrats faced gridlock in the Social and Economic Council and the Foundation of Labor, the evasion of partial wage measures, low commitment from spending departments, and weakness in the Ministry of Finance. In this context most retrenchment plans were window-dressing, corporatist exchange was blocked, and the economy headed for depression. Between 1978 and 1982, the number of bankruptcies rose from 1,047 to 3,487.

The PvdA's moment came in the autumn of 1981, despite a loss of nine seats in the 1981 general elections. Its Keynesian leader, Den Uyl, oscillated between renunciation *à la* Callaghan and Mitterrandist support of demand management, ultimately settling for partial imitation of the German industrial policy model while ruling out devaluation and a return to a postwar incomes policy. Den Uyl struck a deal with the Christian democrats and social liberals (D66) on moderate retrenchment, public sector job creation, and reforms in social policy. A delay in sickness benefits plus a 20 percent wage reduction were to finance a major employment program. Yet conflict between the unions and Den Uyl, then "superminister" of social affairs and employment, led to the fall of the second Van Agt government and inaugurated a phase in which the PvdA could preserve its unity and support only by opposing other parties' recovery policies.

Simultaneous economic decline and political immobility, the victory of the VVD in 1982, the CDA's appointment of Ruud Lubbers – economist, captain of industry, and seasoned politician – and changes of heart among experts, civil servants and industrialists all converged on a retreat by the state from bureaucratic and corporatist systems. Fiscal policy in the 1980s was then reoriented toward controlling and reducing current public deficits through freezes, cuts, and limits to public sector entitlements. According to center-right politicians, such a policy would indirectly encourage the recovery of private enterprise through reduced interest rates and labor costs. Hindsight suggests that Lubbers' no-nonsense approach had slow and contradictory successes. The deficit remained high until 1996, partly because of the 1991–1993 recession and sluggish domestic growth. Real interest rates remained high until 1998, largely because of restrictive monetary policy and a hard guilder. Unemployment remained high until 1998, despite renewed profitability of Dutch firms after 1990.

These limitations failed to jeopardize the neo-liberal party compromise, which survived a great, yet ineffective strike of public sector unions in 1983 and the elections of 1986 and 1989. After 1982, supporters of the four middle parties made thrift the primary prerequisite of economic policy while the social democrats demanded restoration of the linkage between minimal wages, benefits, and national wage development. Lubbers' third cabinet introduced a new norm: linkage would henceforth depend on the volume of benefit claims in relation to employment, measured by the so-called "inactive/active ratio." When the ratio exceeded a reference value of 82.8, the government could suspend the linkage, which it did in 1993, 1994, and the first half of 1995. This, together with first steps toward an active labor market policy for long-term and young unemployed, stopped income polarization but did not reverse retrenchment. For example, Lubbers' first and second administrations tried to cut 16.5 billion by lowering benefit rates, while Lubbers' third administration and Kok's first tried to cut 20 billion through privatization (SCP 1998: 431, 435).

More changes in fiscal policy came with the new structural policy in 1994, SGP limits on excessive budget deficits, and the reform of taxation on capital in 2000 (De Beus 2001a and 2001b: 9–14). These developments were again based on party consensus beyond left and right, opposition and government. Although parties disagreed about balance between provision of public goods, tax reduction, and public debt, they agreed on the primacy of European convergence and domestic equilibrium in the long run and about preventing disequilibrium between public squalor and private wealth, whether domestic or Europe-wide. This became the Third Way compromise after 1998. After years of stagnating public spending (1995–1998), outlays for security, infrastructure, the environment, education, and care began to rise after 1998, while outlays related to social security and interest burdens continued to decrease.

The pattern of monetary policy reform meant ever-closer monetary union with Germany. The Dutch central bank argued early that promoting Dutch–German trade, breaking the wage–price spiral, and maintaining a hard guilder implied a steady restrictive policy under the leadership of the Bundesbank, together with loss of price competitiveness and high interest rates in the short run. After March 1983, the *gulden* was pegged to the D-mark and although the Dutch Bank retained some freedom on the short-term lending rates, it no longer had an independent exchange rate policy. Henceforth Dutch and German bankers, diplomats, and politicians would work together for a specific monetary framework for the European single market involving strict convergence, tight surveillance of budgetary discipline, and full independence for an ECB. The process caused some irritation. For example, Lubbers expressed concern about a lack of reciprocity in German views about central bank autonomy and unification and its impact on Dutch interest rates (Dyson and Featherstone 1999: 767; Szász 1999: 203). Dutch and German policy-makers stuck to the argument that EMU would solve problems of overvalued Northern currencies and competitive devaluations in the South and that any large currency panic would lead to flight into the mark and the guilder, diminishing the competitiveness of German and Dutch firms. The Dutch and the Germans therefore both saw European exchange rate stability as an advantage (Connolly 1995; Moravscik 1998).

The central bank and Finance Ministry were criticized for underspending and creating unemployment by unions, left parties, and movements of the unemployed (Visser and Wijnhoven 1989: 86–98). In March 1983, Lubbers and Minister of Social Affairs De Koning, both Christian democratic leaders, pushed through a 2 percent devaluation against the mark to boost exports and employment. The financial markets, however, punished them by demanding high-risk premiums for several years and the government soon conceded its mistake. Comparable devaluations in the future were ruled out and governments henceforth conformed to central bank efforts to synchronize Dutch and German money market rates. Occasional tensions arose between the cabinet and the Dutch Bank, but lower interest rates, the lucky combination of a fixed exchange rate between guilder and mark and falling wage costs (implicit competitive devaluation) silenced the critics (Soskice 1989: 79; Custers and Van Gils 1997; Szász 1999: 197–212). In its dealings with the Bundesbank the Dutch Bank gained greater leverage through its bargaining with the cabinet and its contacts with unions, reinforced as prominent unions and social democrats came to endorse the new institutional prerogatives. Ruling out devaluation could force governments and unions to moderate their claims, but modern Dutch monetary authorities were expected to give up aggressive monetarism in exchange. The Netherlands thus became the first nation to accept the D-mark as an external anchor

(Notermans 2000a: 167, 173, 181; see De Beus 2001a on the U-turn of Dutch social democrats with respect to restrictive monetary policy).

Wage policy reform has involved sustained wage restraint, labor-time redistribution, and flexibilization on the basis of a bi-lateral agreement between capital and labor. Initially, employers sought to abolish dismissal control, statutory minimum wages, and legally binding collective labor contracts while unions sought uniform labor-time reduction and legal control of pension fund investment. Both sides managed to overcome such class struggle positions, however. They first agreed to autonomous wage bargaining in the public sector (between the government as employer and public sector unions) and to reduced taxes and social charges to promote the hiring of low-skilled workers. Next, they discovered the advantages of part-time work and "flexicurity" – special legal rights for temporary employees. Third, they agreed that cooperation in a context of growing investment and employment would strengthen their common defense of corporatist power in reforms of social security, labor exchanges, and subsidized jobs in the public sector. Many 1990s reform plans implied strengthening central government and private insurance and weakening corporatist organizations (Hemerijck, Unger, and Visser 2000: 209–230). Dutch employers nonetheless preferred the predictable costs of bi-lateral order, harmony, and muddling-through to uncertainties of multiple contracting, polarization, and exploitation of labor through individualized industrial relations. Unions, for their part, preferred industrial peace and joint responsibility at national level to resisting the logic of shareholder value and mobilizing unorganized workers.

Social policy reform has been an incremental process, beginning with spending limits and deteriorating social entitlements and moving to financial incentives for empowerment and constrained labor market integration. Change has encompassed disability and sickness law, protection of the unemployed, social assistance, pensions, and the legal competence of municipal authorities, corporatist boards, national civil service, independent agencies of inspection, and private insurance corporations (Teulings, Van der Veen, and Trommel 1997; Trommel and Van der Veen 1998). Reform has been slow, in particular because it has lacked legitimacy and effectiveness, and it still triggers controversy. Among the striking political features of reform have been the initiating role of national government and the responsive, restrained role of national associations of capital and labor; the lack of strong social movements of the unemployed and other outsiders; and the veto power of voters and public opinion concerning social justice. In 1994, for example, the Christian democrats lost twenty seats when they proposed major cuts in pensions, while the social democrats lost twelve seats for having proposed cuts in labor disability benefits. Policy-makers thus learned to avoid draconian interference while negotiators in bi-partite corporatism tried to protect their constituencies by compensating for sudden, extreme losses of income. For example, collective agreements between labor and capital cover 80 percent of social security earlier provided by the state. Politicians are also willing to tolerate the high transition costs involved in corporatist deliberation and protracted public debate when all possibilities of nondecision have been exhausted. Classical corporatism has itself been reformed and now encompasses planning for the medical, legal, budgetary, and organizational aspects of the significant increase in labor force participation that has been programmed. It also reflects growing belief in market mechanisms, acknowledging private risks for employers, budgetary incentives for authorities and officials, competition and cooperation between collective workers' insurance funds and commercial insurance companies, and personal responsibility for the risks of living in a globalizing service economy.

Why has transformation of the Dutch regime occurred in comparative political and social stability? Why have Dutch workers, civil servants, and social policy clients accepted sacrifice and austerity for so long, until improved macroeconomic performance and a virtuous cycle of social policy began in the second half of the 1990s? Answering these questions using a rational-choice perspective requires introducing a great deal of elasticity. One factor is the lack of market power of labor under the threat of mass dismissal. Another is that new part-time jobs for women may compensate for husbands' loss of income. Institutional factors include the loss of credibility of Keynesians in ministries, commissions, and universities, a desire to preserve formal representation, and the learning capacities and courage of union leaders (Visser and Hemerijck 1997: 109–113). The political culture of the Netherlands, which requires countervailing consensus when faced with difficult problems, is certainly part of the answer. It works when actors with blocking power are divided and feasible solutions advantageous to powerful interests require binding compromise, and when all bargaining parties feel jointly responsible for the success and/or failure of urgent common initiatives.

Stagnation from 1973 to 1983 undermined the world market share of Dutch firms, high Dutch living standards, and the standing of Dutch governments among EU member states. Major disagreements and disorientation among political parties, departments, social partners, and economists tempted actors such as spending departments, political parties, and professional associations to dysfunctional strategies of free riding, blocking, and blaming. Governments threatened to control prices and incomes. Business threatened to accelerate lean production practices and move production abroad. Unions threatened to stretch out bargaining and strikes to defend old social rights. Continuing crisis, in particular the soft expulsion of non-profitable employees through disability, and the continued prospect of regression after initial success (for instance, the growth of long-term unemployment after each peak in the business cycle) promoted a climate for Pareto-efficient, nation-wide deals. There were pacts between governing parties, social partners, and coalition cabinets and these partners about wage restraint, redistribution of labor-time, reform of social insurance, labor market policy, tax reduction and reform, ecological self-regulation, public–private partnerships, and more. In the process, the Dutch state regained its capacity for control and political elites regained capacities for representation that had been gravely damaged by mass unemployment. The rise of part-time labor participation buttressed the authority of trade unions and employers' associations and enhanced their stakes in co-management. No party could then remain credible by shifting blame for failure or claiming sole authorship of success (De Beus 2001a). In these ways, domestic consensus over the terms of Western neo-liberalism and global capitalism led to renewed international success for the Dutch economy.

## 3    Monetary integration in an old European state

Before and after the Maastricht European Council in December 1991, most members of the Dutch government were unaware of the meaning and impact of EMU (Rehwinkel and Nekkers 1994: 116; Szász 1999: 171). The first phase of monetary integration (1987–1992) was a matter for closed circles in Dutch diplomacy and elite society, and the attitudes of high-ranking politicians, civil servants, bankers, and captains of industry – such as Dekker of Philips – were positive throughout. And even though the French–German EMU initiative animated by Delors promoted an important new round of European integration, the Netherlands had in fact already ceded sovereignty in monetary policy. Moreover, the guilder was not a symbol of national identity and most people cared little about the secondary role of the Dutch central bank or the formal influence and prestige Dutch bankers might gain in a new ECB. Monetary integration was appealing for security reasons – post-Westphalian multilateralism being a better guard against foreign occupation than Westphalian power balancing, and because of potential new prosperity: Dutch producers would gain from trade, and workers and consumers would enjoy rising income and welfare. In 1995, the middle of the convergence process, nearly half of Dutch foreign trade was with Belgium, Germany, and France while nearly 70 percent of it was with the EU (EU-15).

The Dutch shared a deterministic view of European monetary integration. The structural convergence of European market economies would lead to closer cooperation among monetary authorities. The Dutch view of political integration was voluntaristic, however: political union needed to be based on federal arrangements and understandings. The successful completion of the "1992" project and German unification seemed only to confirm the appropriateness of these views. Wheeling and dealing about the Delors committee's proposals had produced a compromise that precluded the "monetarist" approach of countries with trade deficits by forcing convergence, creating central bank independence, and establishing excessive deficit procedures. The "economist" approach to convergence as precondition to policy coordination reflected the views of countries with trade surpluses, like the Netherlands (Szász 1988; Verdun 1990). Dutch consensus further reflected a new Dutch–German understanding that Keynesianism was a fallacy and that a mix of supply-side policies was called for (McNamara 1998; Notermans 2000a). The Dutch hoped that Stage Two would spark the formation of a vanguard around Germany, reviving the days of Dutch prominence in the European Economic Community (EEC).

Two worries remained, however. Could the Dutch continue to broker the mighty triangle of France, Germany, and Great Britain? Given its deep welfare state crisis and the rapidity of monetary integration, could the Netherlands put its own house in order in time? The answer to the first question came on "Black Monday" in September 1991, when the Dutch presidency's draft of EMU was widely rejected (Dyson and Featherstone 1999: 438–439, 656–659, 759–764). This led to the decline of federalist enthusiasm in the main political parties and to an alliance with policy-makers in Germany during the end of the Kohl Christian Democrat era and the beginning of the Schröder period. Rejection also fed aversion to grand designs, Dutch self-interest in institutional reform, and endorsement of competitive methods of Europeanization in well-defined areas like employment policy via the open coordination method.

Whether the Dutch economy and regime were strong enough to absorb globalization and Europeanization also remained unclear. Geelhoed, secretary general of the Ministry of Economic Affairs, warned that EMU membership would be unlikely without a major reduction of labor costs, a shift from public transfers to public investments in infrastructure, workfare, and reduction and reform of the tax system (Geelhoed 1991a, 1991b, 1992). Vos, economist of the Industriebond FNV and main author of a report on trade unionism beyond borders, argued that monetary union would weaken labor's domestic identification with wage restraint and strengthen its willingness to coordinate wage demands at European branch level (Vos 1991). Eventually, the Central Planning

Bureau (CPB), a public agency that has played an important role in economic policy since its founding by Tinbergen, decided to recover lost ground. Global turbulence after 1989 made its econometric forecasts about the effects of new policies increasingly messy and the bureau combined institutional and quantitative information to compare three scenarios of global–European–Dutch development from 1990 to 2015 (CPB 1992; SCP 1994: 162–166):

- One scenario, "global shift," described the rise of American and Asian free market economies and new Eurosclerosis. Dutch social policy would expand out of control, with no limits to sickness and disability claims. Labor market policies would feed rising unemployment and massive immigration. Relations between social benefits and wages – including minimum and average wages – would be frozen but real wage restraint would be missing. The labor market would be polarized between a core of well-protected, well-educated native men and a marginal segment of the unskilled, immigrants, the partially disabled, and women.

- A second scenario, "balanced growth," described robust growth based on technological revolution, ecological norms and taxes, sustainable energy, and simultaneous, market-based recovery around the world through improved education and infrastructure in the US, market opening in Japan, and deregulation of markets in Europe. The Netherlands would introduce a residual welfare state marked by sober wage-related social benefits, low individualized basic income, elimination of the statutory minimum wage, flexible and individualized pensions, and controlled costs for medical care. The labor market would become pluriform. Asset-rich workers would choose between traditional full-time jobs and employability in new arrangements, freelance included. The asset-poor would find low-paid, flexible work with the prospect of upward mobility in the service sector.

- A final scenario, called "European renaissance," described the rise of world-wide conglomerates, strategic trade policies, American decline, economic coordination and monetary union in Europe, and effective reform of social policy. The Netherlands would move to an active labor market policy, moderate austerity in social security, public insurance against the risks of illness and old age, and expanded social rights for partners in family households. An integrated labor market would become the bastion of the new employee: flexible, employable, generalist, and willing to share paid work and work in the family and local community. The long-term impact on aggregate demand, purchasing power, employment, the natural environment, and public finance in the Netherlands would be best in a "balanced growth" scenario, worst in a "global shift," and intermediate in a "European renaissance."

Elite debate over these scenarios during recession revealed that most participants were pessimistic about the resilience of the Dutch welfare state and its corporatist policy legacy, the adaptive capacity of European economies facing the Asian challenge, and the sense of urgency among Dutch voters (Kremers 1993). Most discussants sought to prevent "global shift" by breaking with the past, with the break itself being more important than the choice between clean and dirty methods of reconstruction. The choice between "European renaissance" and "balanced growth" was widely conceived as a left–right cleavage. "European renaissance" would mean the triumph of Delors–Rhenish capitalism, social democracy, and left-wing Christian democracy, whereas "balanced growth" would mean neoliberalism, Anglo-American capitalism, liberal parties, and right-wing Christian democracy. Most agreed that policymakers faced a menu that contained neither a free lunch nor a typical Dutch recipe. The term "*Polder* model" simply did not exist in the first phase of monetary unification, nor were *Polder* institutionalists waiting in the wings.

While a small number of insiders worried about the implications of Dutch support for EMU and envisaged abolishing the postwar labor regime, most Dutch politicians and voters welcomed the Treaty of Maastricht. The special law to ratify of the Treaty (December 17, 1992) contained two constraints. The first required that drafts of all binding decisions be presented to the Dutch houses of parliament after they were made public and before the European Council had agreed on them. The second required the approval of both houses of parliament before the government could issue an opinion about which member states could enter EMU Stage Three. The government was thus committed to democratic accountability and to hard-core membership of EMU without manipulating the convergence criteria.

The convergence phase of monetary integration (1992–1998) is a story of a break that never came. One part is the gradual recovery of Dutch profits, competitiveness, output, and employment. Another is the growing credibility and feasibility of institutional and policy reforms. The final part involves de-politicizing the project of monetary integration in which the Dutch did not see themselves as either big winners or losers. Given the steady benefits of European trade and the sunk costs of labor cost control, retrenchment, and sovereignty transfer, big gains and losses could be expected only with exceptional changes in the business cycle, the regional growth path, and international comparative advantage (Bakker 1996: 46, 61–62, 160–175; compare Gros and Thygesen 1998: 303). For Dutch firms, the expected costs of transition to EMU would amount to 5 billion guilders, whereas the expected benefits of price transparency, larger outlets, and lower interest rates would amount to 6.5 billion. The Dutch Bank estimated a long-run net gain of 2.5 percent of Dutch GDP (Prast and Stokman 1997). Public opinion about EMU was not passionately for or against, generally uninformed, and equally divided between supporters and opponents (*NRC Handelsblad*, June 18, 1996, April 25, 1998; Saris 1997).

Political parties, employers' associations, and unions had no big disagreements over the principle and process of monetary integration. Partisan consensus included Christian democrats, social democrats, conservatives, liberal democrats, and Greens while opposition was limited to small Christian and socialist parties. During 1997 conservative leader Bolkestein suggested that in certain circumstances the Dutch might have to opt out of a group that included Italy, with its "book-keeping tricks," at the risk of an appreciating guilder and a currency crisis (*NRC Handelsblad*, February 11, 1997). In the same year, the Greens demanded postponement, fearing that forced convergence would generate recession and polarization. Neither disturbed the government's course, nor were these issues prominent in April 1998 when an overwhelming majority of members of parliament accepted the inclusion of eleven members in EMU. Although 40 percent of the public had growing doubts about the unity and effectiveness of European monetary policy, such skepticism was never mobilized by managers, representatives of small firms, workers, or trade union leaders in the sheltered sector (Bakker 1996: 135–136), nor did it lead to reappraisal among old parties, the rise of new parties, or a referendum and petition movement.

The public had experienced the installation of a neo-liberal regime in the early 1980s as the real U-turn, but the single market and monetary union were not presented or perceived as sideshows. Still, the architects of international public policy (like the powerful civil servants Brouwer, Geelhoed, Maas, and Zalm) successfully maintained continuity by establishing a number of policy routines. Coalition governments could expect covenants that ensured retrenchment, the convergence criteria could function as authoritative guidelines for fiscal policy – from 1993 onward, the government's annual budgetary document contained a special table on Dutch progress – and crisis in the domestic reorganization of finances or European market-making would stay disconnected from daily politics. Neo-liberal recovery would proceed with or without monetary union, while Stage Two of monetary integration would include only member states that had put their houses in order without foreign help. Dutch elites favoring the SGP never referred publicly to EMU either as an external anchor or as a scapegoat, nor did they sympathize with elites elsewhere that did so.

Lofty idealism played a small role. Dutch elites could avoid pre-commitment and blame-shifting because postwar generations accepted market enlargement and adaptation to turbulent environments, rejected shock therapy but supported an embedded liberalism balancing break-throughs and compensation for losers. In the Netherlands, as elsewhere in Europe, the union movement lost leverage in its stance of accommodation, and new wage bargaining under restrictive monetary policy has been relatively harmonious. The exposed sector has remained ambivalent to pursuit of a strong guilder and wage restraint and actors accepted loss of control over internal monetary policy in the 1970s through manipulation of the money supply and surrender of sovereignty in external monetary policy, in the 1980s through manipulation of interest and exchange rates. There was no militant confrontation between bankers and unionists and no exchange of threats between the central bank and union leadership, nor did the central bank or the government frequently assert their supremacy.

The game in The Hague was cooperative and distant from the public. Trade unions accepted external equilibrium and price stability and the central bank's autonomy from government, capital, and labor. As Van der Ploeg explained,

The strength of the guilder is as much due to the wage moderation pursued by the trade unions, and supported by the social policies of government and firms, as by the discipline of the Dutch central bank. Monetary expansion, and the depreciation of the currency that goes with it, is considered a sneaky way to fool the unions. Politicians from the left to the right argue that this induces a wage–price spiral without a sustained increase in jobs. The strength of the guilder and a low inflation rate requires the government to strike a bargain with the unions to moderate wages. (Van der Ploeg 1998: 84)

Dutch moderation on monetary union resulted in reappraisal of policy competition between member states and strengthened the Dutch state.

The new economic wisdom asserted that EMU provided a framework for monetary and competition policy in which national governments and representative associations in national civil society sought high productivity, standards of education, a fiscal base that is insensitive to globalization, control of wage–price spirals, space for autonomous expansive policies, reorganization of vulnerable branches, sectors, and regions, and containment of overdevelopment of the state, through excessive subsidies, and the market, through congestion in the new European space of infrastructure and transport. Social democrats joined the chorus either because they hoped that harmonization of minimal standards of social security and industrial order would be the next step in the European politics of economic policy or because they believed in the dynamic efficiency of social policy (Department of Social Affairs and Employment 1997a,

1997b; Emerson 1998: 38–43). The new conventional wisdom suggested that the *Polder* model was the right mix of Anglo-American and Rhenish capitalism and would improve the Dutch competitive edge (Geelhoed 1993, 1994).

Since 1998, the process has been marked by new prudence and administrative intelligence. The second Kok coalition of social democrats, conservatives, and liberal democrats attained a balanced budget but has had new problems with mass vacancies and inflationary wage drift. New plans have included labor cost reduction for special categories of the unemployed, new markets for Dutch corporations, tax reform, protection of basic pensions, public infrastructure in the new service economy (including the port of Rotterdam and Schiphol airport) and the old industrial economy (basic metals, bulk chemistry, oil-refinery, paper, agriculture), new spending in information and communication technology beyond the European average, extra spending in education, care, and police, and flexibilization of public expenditure. European goals have included reducing net EU contributions, implementing the "best practices" in employment policy, controlling labor immigration, and eliminating the "democratic deficit" without diminishing the ECB's autonomy.

Although some EU member states see integration as an external constraint and a way of usurping sovereignty either because of weak political commitment or limited support for implementation of European regulations and guidelines, the Netherlands has had few problems of costly adaptation. The exception has been labor inactivity closely related to the issue of uncontrolled transfers, a problem that is neither unique in Europe nor an obstacle to modernization of the economy. The Netherlands has also had few problems of indirect implementation, in which a member state uses European integration as an extended opportunity and instrument of national reform to eliminate perennial domestic problems that cannot be solved without jeopardizing political stability and authority. One recurrent tension in the Dutch model has been the clash between wage restraint and pursuit of a strong currency. Wage restraint has helped Dutch export prices to rise less than those of competitors, even if appreciation of the guilder meant that price competitiveness did not improve in the 1990s. Table 8.2 shows both tendencies, the competitive advantage of wage restraint until 1996 (Leering 1998) and that appreciation largely dissipated this advantage. The problem is as old as the strategy of export promotion by wage restraint. Although it recognized the problem, the central bank stated that the long-run costs of devaluation (higher risk premiums, higher import prices) would be worse than those of appreciation. In the 1990s tension between wage restraint and the strong guilder faded, however, as authorities first refused to devalue and, later, could not revalue because of EMU convergence, in all implicitly promoting real

Table 8.2 *Price competitiveness of Dutch exports, 1986–1996 (mutations in %)*

|        | 1986–1989 | 1989–1992 | 1993 | 1994 | 1995 | 1996 |
|--------|-----------|-----------|------|------|------|------|
| CPNL   | −2.1      | 0.5       | −0.7 | −1.1 | 0.8  | 0.8  |
| EXPNL  | −1.2      | −0.3      | −2.8 | 0.8  | 1.0  | 1.0  |
| EXPC   | 2.8       | 1.6       | −1.4 | 3.0  | 5.8  | 0.2  |
| ERG    | 4.6       | 1.9       | 1.6  | 1.3  | 6.8  | −1.8 |
| EXPC*  | −1.8      | −0.3      | −3.0 | 1.7  | −1.0 | 2.0  |
| PCNL   | −0.6      | 0.0       | −0.2 | 0.9  | −2.0 | 1.0  |

*Notes:*
CPNL  = Cost price Dutch export (guilders)
EXPNL = Export price Dutch export (guilders)
EXPC  = Export price export competitors (national currencies)
ERG   = Effective rate guilder with respect to competitors
EXPC* = Export price competitors (guilders)
PCNL  = Price competitiveness position the Netherlands (− = deterioration).
*Source*: Leering (1998: 99).

devaluation, at least with regard to Germany. The Dutch thus pursued a local optimum while discouraging explicit competitive devaluations of others and retaining the option of implicit competitive devaluation. The official argument was, of course, different. The Bank considered revaluation and an interest rate increase to control an overheated economy, yet refrained from such deflationary measures under Bundesbank pressure to prevent a wave of currency relinkages (De Nederlandsche Bank 1999). Finally, the tension disappears completely in a stable EMU.

Although some member states remain ambivalent about European integration, as well-tried economic policies become ineffective and new methods are still experimental, the Netherlands seems unconcerned about disorderly conversion. The Dutch cartel paradise, for example, has been smoothly eliminated. In fiscal policy, the government manages a budget relatively sensitive to fluctuations of national output, with an elasticity coefficient of 0.80 in 1970–1996, surpassed only by Sweden (Houben 1997; Dornbusch *et al.* 1998). Recessions can still generate maximum budget deficits of 2.8 percent, but since 1999 the government has tried to solve this by consolidating the surplus and creating conditions for its preservation after the 2002 elections. A relaxed attitude about future conversion is also evident in the tactics of unions. Rhetorically, they welcome the Doorn talks about European intra-industry wage bargaining but, practically, they ignore it and reject German union campaigning against wage-dumping and wage restraint (Schuit 1999).

The *Polder* model, despite all of its subtle complexity, is not always successful. In 2001 the Dutch economy, along with others in the eurozone, came to a recessionary standstill. Growth forecasts of 2 percent for 2002, 2003, and 2004 turned out to be mistaken, unemployment began to rise again (more than 5 percent in 2003, more than 6 percent in the forecast for 2004) while the inflation rate decreased only gradually, from 4.5 percent in 2001, and 3.5 in 2002 to 2.25 in 2003. In fact, the Dutch relative advantage in wage cost control and price competitiveness had been disappearing since 1996. As the privatization of railways, telecommunications, electricity, and workers' insurance failed, public opinion soured, bringing a mood that resembled that of the mid-1960s (*Economist*, May 4, 2002). In the May 2002 elections all the incumbent parties lost, while the Christian democrat opposition and a new right-wing populist movement triumphed. Aversions to continued lib–lab governance of multicultural society, the public sector and European integration turned out to be surprisingly popular. An entire year since these elections was wasted as far as economic policy was concerned because of government instability, incompetence of the populist party leadership, new general elections, and protracted cabinet formation talks. The new government installed in June 2003 is a coalition of Christian democrats and liberal parties. Its central message is economic recovery based on wage restraint, deregulation, and budget cuts within European rules and restrictions.

How can the Dutch sustain the spirit of moderation and cost sharing after seven years of success and boom? Classical tools – interest rate and tax cuts – seem blunt. Following the myth of Wassenaar, many insist that new agreements between government and civil society are needed. Others have reopened debates about the flaws of consensual economic policy, such as increasing decision costs and contested shares of foreign and domestic investment, the negative relation between wage restraint and the Schumpeterian pattern of technological innovation and productivity growth, wage-drift and domestic inflationary pressure, and reflections about alleged labor cost rivalry between rich countries and emergent poor countries at the expense of the latter (Fase and Tieman 2001). In fact, a number of factors have contributed to these new dilemmas. Most important has been decline of world trade and recession in the large European economies. Another is overheating in the second half of the 1990s, particularly evident in the nonaccelerating inflation rate of employment (NAIRU) and the nonaccelerating inflation rate of capacity utilization (NAIRCU) (De Nederlandsche Bank 2000). Others are the housing market and stock market bubble in the second half of the 1990s, fueled by generous tax relief for mortgage interest as well as pro-cyclical tax cuts and tax reforms, and the excessive rise of CEO salaries, both absolute and relative to the modal Dutch employees. Yet another issue factor is a tight labor market due to lagging female labor force participation, massive disability, skill deficiencies of second-generation immigrants, restrictions on immigration, and illegal work.

Dutch commitment to reducing public debt and enforcing active labor market policy seems unbroken. Europe provides few incentives here, however (Visser 2002). While the market-opening struggles for "1992" and for early entry into EMU reinforced domestic priorities, neither the SGP nor the open method of coordination offer enough options for the Dutch to address new issues such as integrating immigrants, congestion, urban crime, mismanagement in public services, and the lack of power of independent authorities, particularly in the anti-trust area.

## 4    Conclusions: transferring the Dutch case?

Many have argued that there are universal lessons in the Dutch case (Freeman 1998; Teulings and Hartog 1998; Lijphart 1999; Ferrera, Hemerijck, and Rhodes 2000; Wilensky 2002), pointing to the soft trade-off between efficiency and equity, the inclusion of weakly organized groups in the politics of adjustment to internationalization, and the role of learning and linkage in the reform of distinct policy domains. Dutch social pacts have become a particular focal point of international discourse (Bout *et al.* 1999; Fajertag and Pochet 2000).

European transferability of the *Polder* model, however, raises some questions. For example, wage restraint distorts aggregate consumption in large semi-closed economies such as Germany, France, and Italy, and to protect net income policy-makers need to be able to lower tax levels without jeopardizing public provisions. Dutch success is partly based on fierce competition, including fiscal competition. Member states that abandon instruments such as nationalization and subsidization of "infants, champions, and lame ducks," may have to fall back on special deals to attract foreign firms. According to a survey in 1998, Dutch fiscal legislation became both defensive and offensive under the pressure of market globalization:

- Income tax rates were lowered at the end of the 1980s. The revision, amounting to 5 billion guilders, benefited the highest-income groups disproportionately, an effect justified by referring to similar revisions abroad.
- Since 1997, big shareholders have paid a 25 percent tax rate on dividends (previously 60 percent) and on profits from the selling of shares (previously 25 percent). This measure was taken to preempt fiscal emigration to Belgium.

- Taxation on wealth was lowered from 0.8 percent to 0.7 percent, including invested corporate wealth at the end of the 1980s.
- Company taxes were lowered from 43 to 35 percent at the end of the 1980s.
- A number of tax havens have included exemption from regular rates for foreign business plants in the Netherlands and for rich Western immigrants.
- A special fiscal agency was established to inform potential foreign investors about subsidies, exemptions, and rulings (in particular so-called "concern finance," the untaxed internal banking of multinationals).

Government white papers on tax reform in 1997 and 1999 proposed further reduction of the corporate tax burden, arguing that fiscal competition was inevitable:

Asset-liability analysis of the present Dutch fiscal system bears out . . . that reform should focus on wage and income taxes and people's insurance premiums. The Dutch fiscal regime is generally globally competitive, although capital and wealth taxation should be regarded as weak points. It is crucially important to maintain competitiveness in the future and to solve bottlenecks.[3]

The consequences of this approach are increasing taxation on consumption and labor (including high labor income wedges) and a hollowing out of the income tax base (selective tax expenditures). Table 8.3 provides the general picture of tax ratio development. Dutch experts conclude that the Netherlands is turning into a tax paradise (De Kam 1998a, 1998b), but the government nonetheless tends to discuss the future in terms of a Prisoners' Dilemma Game and it claims to be willing to endorse supranational coercion to ban similar fiscal privileges in all member states. Anticipating harsh measures of the European Commission, Secretaries of Fiscal Affairs Vermeend and Bos advocated Dutch initiatives on fiscal harmonization in 2001. The chairman of the largest employers' association, Blankert, disagreed, arguing that small states like the Netherlands should not even consider suicidal first steps toward harmonization. Again in 2001, a committee of industrialists, chaired by Van Rooy, a former secretary of international trade, suggested a 5 percent reduction of company taxation.

Wage restraint seems part and parcel of Dutch *Wirtschaftsgesinnung* (economic morality). Here the cultural factor seems inescapable. Moderation is a token of public responsibility (*burgerzin*). In times of need, leaders can even become popular by advocating moderation and

---

[3] "Belastingen in de 21ste eeuw. Een Verkenning," Tweede Kamer der Staten-Generaal, The Hague, 1997–1998, 25810, no. 2, p. 4.

Table 8.3 *Dutch tax ratios, 1970–1995*

|  | 1970 | 1980 | 1990 | 1995 |
|---|---|---|---|---|
| **Europe (EEC)** | | | | |
| Tax on consumption | 15.2 | 13.5 | 13.9 | 14.1 |
| Tax on labor | 28.7 | 36.7 | 40.9 | 44.5 |
| Tax on residual factor income | 27.7 | 39.7 | 36.8 | 37.6 |
| **The Netherlands** | | | | |
| Tax on consumption | 13.5 | 13.8 | 4.9 | 15.2 |
| Tax on labor | 34.2 | 45.4 | 49.7 | 48.8 |
| Tax on residual factor income | 34.6 | 39.2 | 30.8 | 34.7 |

*Source*: De Kam (1998a: 17).

referring to old rituals of atonement – citing an embarrassment of riches and marking stagflation and pollution as sins, and more recent success stories of postwar reconstruction. Other countries may imitate the Dutch social pact, but they cannot readily import the Dutch culture of consumption.

The fit among the European social mode, EMU, and consensual economic democracy in the Netherlands thus appears to be both thick and thin. It is thick between easy convergence (EMU membership) and the official government view of European monetary order and policy, evident in the stability pact view of the Dutch and the Germans under Chancellor Kohl. Also thick is the connection between contemporary Dutch social liberalism and reorganized capitalism in the Netherlands with European protection and promotion of flourishing diverse "continental" welfare states (Scharpf 1999). The Dutch experience does appear to negate Streeck's prediction about monetary unification as an institutionalization of liberal order with a minimal state (Streeck 1996: 302). There are much thinner connections, however. The ambiguity of defensive and offensive policy competition by the Dutch state is one. The lack of commitment to a modicum of EMU deepening, such as a reconstructed European budget beyond 1.27 percent and a stabilization fund, remains equally tenuous. In general, the Netherlands case illustrates the jointness of European monetary and social policies. Without monetary coordination and discipline by the few, welfare states become ineffective, without employment and social citizenship of the many, monetary authorities become illegitimate.

# 9    Belgium: monetary integration and precarious federalism

*Philippe Pochet*

Monetary integration has long played a central but complicated part in Belgian politics. Exchange rates and their stability are important: the country depends on transformation of intermediate goods, and its industry exports approximately two-fifths of its output to neighboring countries (France, Germany, and the Netherlands). Belgium thus had a high stake in the first wave of EMU – to have failed would have meant pressures on its currency, inflationary tendencies, high interest rates, and increased unemployment – all with political costs. As a founding member of the European Community (EC), Belgium has been one of the strongest supporters of political integration, with an electorate which is one of the most pro-EU among the member states. Failure to qualify for EMU at its inception would have therefore discredited Belgium's claim to more European (federal) integration. Failure might also have undermined a source of national cohesion, as Europe, and the constraints imposed by monetary integration, have counterbalanced long-standing regional divisions. European monetary integration and its effect on the Belgian labor regime are thus tightly connected with Belgian political integration and national identity.

Belgium is divided into three regions: Dutch-speaking and largely Catholic Flanders, Francophone and largely secular Wallonia, and the bilingual capital region, Brussels. Cultural differences have coincided with changing economic conditions. Wallonia was the more prosperous region in the early postwar period but its old industries have suffered continuing decline. The newer industries and services of Flanders have generated economic growth, increasing the gap between regions, and making Flanders a net contributor and Wallonia a net recipient of government financial flows. Economic disparities contribute to a Flemish separatism, which at its extreme seeks an independent state, and give

Research carried out with the support of the National Institute of Working Life (Stockholm). The comments of various people and in particular those of Luc Denayer, Ivo Maes, and Pierre Reman were very useful for a deeper understanding of Belgian society. As usual, all remaining errors are my own.

Wallonia a stake in preserving an integrated Belgium. Although linguistically defined political identities have been constitutionally accommodated through a federal structure, the danger of national break-up remains.

One major reason is that partisan ideological divisions have increasingly coincided with cultural and economic divisions. Belgian politics has been dominated by three political "families" – Christian Democrats, Socialists, and Liberals – organized nationally and cutting across linguistic and regional lines. The parties have been linked to societal organizations, notably the Socialist and Christian labor movements, so that when leaders reached compromises on policy, they could count on support that blurred regional divisions and led to considerable political stability. But growing economic divergence and the accompanying intensification of regional identities has undermined the national character of the parties. The political landscape has become progressively more fragmented with the emergence of two Green Parties (Ecolo for the French-speaking and Agalev for the Flemish part) and an anti-immigrant Flemish nationalist party (Vlaamse Blok). The party system thus no longer mitigates the regional and cultural divisions that increasingly threaten Belgium's political cohesion. Political fragmentation also makes managing the economy more difficult. In this context, the real and symbolic constraints flowing from commitment to Europe, and especially monetary union, have provided an alternative basis for legitimating economic policies and blunting the tendencies toward political disintegration.

Given the conviction that Belgium's interdependence with its neighbors, especially Germany and France, makes stability in exchange rates essential and rules out devaluation, the central macroeconomic problem has been the need to match rising prices and labor costs with exchange rates. To achieve stability governments have supported steps toward monetary integration. For example, after being forced to devalue in 1982 in the wake of the second oil shock, policy-makers sought stability by tying the Belgian franc to the D-mark, making Belgium an early member of the *de facto* monetary union, along with the Netherlands and Austria. The Belgian franc was formally linked to the D-mark in 1990, and Belgian authorities insisted on maintaining the link (as did the French) when the ERM crisis in 1993 widened the margins of fluctuation and led some countries out of the ERM. Belgium thus remained committed to fulfilling the criteria for entering EMU.

Since 1982 Belgium has effectively denied itself use of exchange rates to adjust to macroeconomic divergence and has had to rely on adjustment through labor costs, burdening both components of Belgium's labor regime, the collective bargaining system, which sets wages, and the welfare state which determines nonwage labor costs. Both have proved resistant to the changes needed to meet the demands of Belgium's hard-currency policy. Changes in the welfare state threaten national cohesion in a period of growing regional division while the need to overcome these difficulties has become ever more urgent. Exchange rate stability and, even more, participation in EMU, have provided external constraint plus powerful resources for overcoming difficulties. Yet it has been a prolonged process. The social compromises of other national labor regimes that tied their currencies to the D-mark began to be renegotiated in the 1980s in response to the *de facto* monetary union; it took Belgium until December 1999 to arrive at a social pact that some liken to the 1982 Wassenaar Agreement, the turning point for the Netherlands.[1]

## 1    From postwar Social Pact to EMU

The Belgian labor regime was largely defined by a Social Pact nego-tiated in 1944. Never formally ratified by unions and employers, it is nonetheless considered the basis of the Belgian social contract (Pasture 1993). Under the Pact, trade unions accepted the market economy and employers' rights to run companies as they saw fit. Employers accepted unions as the representatives of employees at the company, sectoral, and national levels. Within this framework, parties to the Pact undertook to share the profits of growth "fairly" between capital and labor. Finally, the Pact proclaimed the freedom to negotiate wages without government intervention.

Historically, Belgian society has been divided into so-called "pillars" (Christian, Socialist, and to a lesser extent Liberal). Trade unions reflect these fault lines: the CSC/ACV (Federation of Christian Trade Unions) for the Christian pillar, the FGTB/ABVV (General Federation of Belgian Workers) for the Socialist pillar, and the CGLSB/ACLVB for the Liberals. The first two dominate the trade union landscape but with different geo-graphical densities: the CSC/ACV is dominant in Flanders, while the Socialist union has its strongholds in Wallonia. Nevertheless, the unions have retained integrated national structures along with strong regional organizations. The collective bargaining system is structured around industrial sectors, although in practice automatic indexing of wages to prices is a powerful centralizing factor (in the 1990s, almost 60 percent of wage increases were due to indexing, which also affects minimum ben-efit levels). Unions' struggle to maintain this automatic indexing system

---

[1] See Van Ruysseveldt and Visser (1996: 205), for a comparison between Belgium and the Netherlands during the period 1980–1997.

has had a dual logic: it helps ensure wage solidarity between the stronger and weaker sectors while at the same time promoting solidarity between those who are working and those who benefit from welfare state programs (pensions, social aid, unemployment benefits, etc.).

Bi-partite consultative bodies, which were not established until the early 1950s, include a Central Economic Council and a National Employment Council at federal level, along with works councils and health and safety committees at company level (building on Joint Committees set up before 1939).[2] The Pact took concrete form with a productivity agreement signed in 1954 in which unions accepted the introduction of new technologies and the resulting need for intersectoral mobility. For their part, employers agreed to use productivity gains to improve standards of living and extend the social security system (Denayer 1996). Productivity began to grow during the late 1950s and accelerated into the 1960s (Cassiers, De Villé, and Sollar 1994). The indexing of wages to prices forged solidarity between sectors and prevented inflation from affecting wage bargaining.

The 1944 Social Pact helped lay the historical and sociopolitical foundations of a coherent social security system in Belgium. Built on the principles of social insurance and solidarity, the Belgian system owed less to the influence of Beveridge than that of Bismarck. Three separate social security schemes cover the three major categories of workers: wage-earners, the self-employed, and public employees. Safety-net social assistance schemes were set up on the fringes of the social security system, but they have always been considered of secondary importance to social security. Social benefits are financed by employers' contributions and by state subsidies and specific levies on incomes (Arcq and Chatelain 1994). Decision-making is shared between the government and representatives of the social partners who manage the system. Mutual insurance funds, trade unions, and employers' organizations are the main bodies.

The 1960s and early 1970s were the Belgian "golden age," replete with considerable investment (particularly American), high growth, rising productivity, and widespread wage increases. These trends were strongest in Flanders, while Wallonia was beginning its industrial decline. The recession and oil crisis of 1972–1973 ended the good years, however. Wages rose sharply and multi-industry bargaining ceased in 1975. Furthermore, as Michel and Denayer (1997: 57) have pointed out, fluctuating exchange rates and the rising cost of raw materials complicated domestic distributional debates with extra-national concerns. The end of the 1970s was

---

[2] These institutions did not prevent very violent disputes during the 1950s (Luyten 1995).

a period of profound political instability as well, as regional tensions increased dramatically, challenging political structures without leading to a stable model of federalism.

### From the 1982 devaluation to the 1990 link to the D-mark

After the second oil crisis and the resulting loss of competitiveness, the government devalued in 1982 (−8.5 percent) and adopted a number of accompanying measures. The governing Christians and Liberals also reaffirmed their commitment to monetary stability. Later, in 1988, Socialist involvement in the coalition government depended on this commitment. The Christian trade union leadership also imposed this commitment on its rank-and-file (CSC/ACV). The FGTB/ABVV was much more critical, however, even as it acknowledged the need for a stable currency. The 1980s thus mark the beginning of the union movement's attempts to internalize the constraints and consequences of a strong currency in a system of fixed exchange rates and increasing commercial openness and internationalization, both reinforced by European integration. The Single European Act (SEA) in 1986 progressively opened new sectors like insurance, banking, and then telecommunications to competition. Moreover, greater capital mobility together with a lack of common taxation rules further limited the scope for national policy.

During the first half of the 1980s, the Christian/Liberal coalition, ideologically dominated by Flemish neo-liberals, worked to reduce the public deficit, moderate wages, and refinance and restructure the social security system. Although devaluation brought imported inflation under control (mainly because of a wage freeze), it also led to a greater increase in interest rates than in other D-mark zone countries (approximately 5 percent more than in Germany). Because of the size of the national debt, the chief consequence was further debt growth, with interest payments peaking at 11.7 percent of GDP in 1986 (Cassier, De Villé, and Sollar 1994). In this context the social partners could not resume the multi-industry dialog that had been cut short in 1975.[3] Furthermore, the government sought to encourage bargaining at the company level through employment incentives.

The Liberal/Christian Democrat majority remained in office after the 1985 elections, but the Christian Social component gained the upper

---

[3] With the exception of a multi-industry agreement in 1981, negotiations did not resume until 1986. No complete breach occurred, however, as shown by the important agreement on technology in 1983 at the National Employment Council (Pasture 1996).

hand and gradually relaxed certain neo-liberal approaches (budget cuts, wage control, cuts in social security). After freezing one wage increase indexed to inflation (at 2 percent) in 1986, the government decided to adopt a more gradual approach to reducing the public deficit, and multi-industry bargaining resumed, resulting in the resumption of automatic wage indexing and bargaining among sectoral labor market organizations (Blaise 1986). During the second half of the 1980s revived growth generated some optimism about the possibilities of confronting the public deficit and employment, illustrated by the decision to abandon the aggregation of incomes in calculating household taxation. Competitiveness, which had become a concern at the end of the 1970s, rose to the top of the agenda in 1982, when the government proposed to align wage increases with those in seven competitor countries. The failure of bargaining led to the Competitiveness Norm of April 1983, which allowed government intervention in the case of wage drift (Arcq 1991). The Act was then ignored when emergency measures were adopted to freeze wages, including inflation indexing.

The Socialists, whose electoral slogan was the "return of the heart," won the December 1987 elections,[4] but institutional problems – the creation of the Brussels region and the regionalization of new competencies more generally, plus the new budget – meant that a new center-left Christian Social/Socialist government coalition was difficult to form. The Socialists agreed to draft a new competitiveness act that contained criteria beyond wage costs (Michel 1994), and in 1989 the new *"loi de sauvegarde de la compétitivité du pays"* (Law safeguarding the nation's competitive position) established five criteria for a systematic comparison with Belgium's main economic partners numbering either five (France, Germany, the Netherlands, the UK, and Italy) or seven (including Japan and the US). The five criteria determining competitiveness – export share, trends in wages, finance, energy costs, and changes in structural determinants (research and development expenditure, company investment) – deemed competitiveness threatened when exports plus at least one other criterion fell behind. Documented loss of competitiveness could then trigger *ex post* corrections. The five criteria shaped the debates of the 1990s. The negative impact of the 1982 devaluation, with high interest rates and the associated loss of credibility, produced broad consensus in 1990 to peg the Belgian franc to the D-mark. The Act thus also sought to reinforce the credibility of monetary policy and help reduce interest rates and the burden of debt (Denayer 1996).

---

[4] One aspect was indexing of minimum social benefits in line with a prosperity index.

## 2    Entering EMU

Until June 1999, the 1990s were dominated by a stable coalition between the Christian Social party and the Socialists under Prime Minister Jean-Luc Dehaene. To be in the first wave of EMU the Maastricht criteria stipulated that public debt had to be below 60 percent of GDP or "has declined substantially and continuously and reached a level close to reference value." The Belgian debt was more than 130 percent of GDP, and, according to calculations by the Federal Planning Bureau, might at best be reduced to 60 percent by 2015. Leaders therefore concluded that scrupulous compliance with the other Maastricht criteria, particularly the 3 percent limit on the public deficit, was imperative.

Until 1993, wage increases could be freely negotiated within the limits of the Competitiveness Act, which mandated corrective mechanisms following a defined loss in competitiveness. The rationale underlying this was that actors would anticipate negative consequences and adjust behavior accordingly. Thus from 1989 to 1993, the social partners on the basis of the Central Economic Council's report evaluated whether the Belgian economy had lost competitiveness. Opinions were sometimes divided, sometimes unanimous, but an emerging consensus on the shortcomings of statistical and technical apparatus made the Central Economic Council the key institution for technical analysis and shared diagnosis of policy problems (Arcq and Pochet 2000; Denayer and Tollet 2002). Employers' and workers' representatives disagreed on the very nature of the concept of "competitiveness." For employers, competitiveness referred mainly to wages, and they sought to make the exercise an appeal for wage moderation. The unions, particularly the FGTB/ABVV, claimed that competitiveness should be measured more structurally, based on such factors as training, infrastructure, and industrial strategy. The government largely shared the employers' perspectives, however, according to which (para-) fiscal measures and wage costs were the only variables that a small, open, financially integrated economy could control in the short term (Löwenthal 1994: 418).

The turning point came in 1993, when the deficit jumped to 7 percent. For the first time the social partners were unanimous in identifying a loss of competitiveness as defined in the Act. With an economic environment comparable to the early 1980s – monetary disruption, a large public deficit, wage drift, and a social security deficit – the parties all agreed that Belgium should be among the first to enter EMU. Because the risk of exclusion might fuel separatist tendencies, the government could rally sufficient domestic support to impose a pro-cyclical reduction in the public deficit and control the system of wage formation. Yet the first application of the Competitiveness Act, in 1993, made clear a lack of consensus concerning the method for evaluating competitiveness that severely limited its effectiveness. So, too, did the lack of a shared diagnosis. Recognizing the need for a revision of the Act, the social partners began strategic deliberations about the internal coordination required to maintain automatic wage indexing within monetary union. Under EMU, wage bargaining has to consider three different economic parameters. First, the integration of macroeconomic variables into wage bargaining meant taking into account that automatic indexing would leave little room for *ex post* maneuvers. Next, national bargaining would have to be restructured to ensure that total wage increases (multi-enterprise, sectoral, and local) were in line with those in neighboring countries. Finally, any deals would have to leave room for job creation.

The government proposed to update the 1944 Social Pact, an idea initiated by the unions. The process forced the government to think about an ambitious program of creating jobs, promoting competitiveness, and reforming social security. The task of exploring possibilities for this so-called Global Plan was entrusted to a group of senior civil servants. The Global Plan was prepared quickly from July to November 1993 during the Belgian Presidency of the EU (Arcq 1993). The Presidency itself began with monetary turbulence, resulting in a widening of the EMS fluctuation margins (15 percent), and ended with the adoption of the White Paper on Growth, Competitiveness and Employment (CEC 1993), and the European agenda spilled over into domestic bargaining. Considerable tension arose between the FGTB/ABVV and CSC/ACV, and inside their ranks between central and sectoral organizations and between regions and subregions. Disagreements between the unions and political parties involved reassessment of links between the Christian Flemish wing of the trade unions (ACV) and the dominant Christian Flemish party (CVP). Several strikes and large demonstrations occurred in November and December 1993, including the first general strike since 1930.

The government did not change course, however, instead insisting upon a Global Plan with a wage freeze (with the exception of indexing) for 1995–1996, a changed reference for price indexing (with removal of gasoline and tobacco), and a series of less important measures to reduce labor costs. Finally a multi-industry agreement was signed, covering 1994–1996 and reiterating the independence of the social partners (Blaise and Beaupain 1995). Unlike the Netherlands, where a temporary wage freeze was implemented early in 1993, Belgium took longer to adapt its wage policy. Having failed to get a new Social Pact, however, the government was forced to impose authoritative measures (Hemerijck, van der Meer, and Visser 2000), made stiffer by the fact that automatic indexing rules prevented real wage reductions. Only in 1998 were the social partners able to resume a substantive dialog.

When the electorate returned the government coalition to office in 1995, reflecting limited support for trade union protest, the ruling political parties interpreted the victory as support for their policies, accelerated reform of the Competitiveness Act, and began discussions concerning margins for maneuver within a single currency. In 1994, the Central Economic Council report again announced a 6 percent loss of competitiveness. Although the unions disputed the figures, they also recognized that devaluation could no longer compensate for this loss. Furthermore, because of automatic wage indexing and widespread wage restraint in Europe, correcting wage slippage would take several years. Preventive action was therefore essential.

Dialog resumed in 1995 but quickly stopped when the parties disagreed about trading job creation for reducing social security contributions. Union demands for representation in small and medium-sized enterprises (SMEs with fewer than fifty employees) were also rejected. When the Germans began their discussions on a Social Pact (*Bündnis für Arbeit*) in 1996, the government tried to rekindle the dialog, but quickly failed again. An eventual Agreement was rejected by the FGTB/ABVV unions (whose president did not really defend it) and was backed by only 52 percent of the votes at the General Council of the CSC/ACV. In response, government adopted a "Contract for the Future" and created an advisory body – the Higher Council for Employment – measures that the trade unions interpreted as ways to reduce their influence over employment policy traditionally channeled through the National Labor Council.

Revised in 1996, the Competitiveness Act focused mainly on wage costs and on Belgium's three main commercial partners (Germany, France, the Netherlands). It adopted a precautionary approach, stipulating that multi-industry bargaining should take place every two years on the basis of the Central Economic Council's technical report to determine the maximum wage increase which had to include at least automatic wage indexing and pay-scale increases (based on seniority, etc.). The negotiated wage margin was to be a maximum figure including increases at all levels (multi-industry, sectoral, and company) to be integrated into the two-year multi-industry agreement (signed by October 31), which was to include not only the margin for wages but also measures for job creation. Should agreement not be reached, the government could impose a decision before the end of the year. On the basis of the maximum wage margin, sectors and companies should negotiate collective agreements on wage trends and jobs, by March 31 and May 31, respectively

(Lamas 1997). During the first year (1997), trade unions and employers disagreed and the government finally set the wage increase ceiling at 6.1 percent, broken down into estimated inflation (2 × 1.8 percent = 3.6 percent) and a remaining margin of 2.5 percent, from which pay-scale increases were to be deducted (0.75–1 percent). Consequently, over two years slightly more than 1 percent could be subject to bargaining at sectoral and company levels, part of which needed, in theory, to be used for job creation.

The new law did not address domestic productivity. Instead, it created a clear disjunction between national parameters of productivity growth and the chosen wage policy which determined wages by averaging the wage increase forecast in the three neighboring countries. The government reasoned that "to safeguard jobs, it is necessary to avoid ensuring competitiveness by increasing productivity to the detriment of jobs" (quoted by Lamas 1997). The new Act also introduced a preventive approach, necessitating improvement in Belgium's notoriously weak statistical tools. In addition, by imposing a maximum rate of increase that encompassed healthy sectors, the law imposed an extremely restrictive legal framework. Furthermore, an overall reduction in working-time (without loss of wages) was made almost impossible because of the reference criterion of wage costs per working-hour.

In the second round of wage bargaining, for 1999–2000, the government intended to reduce social security contributions by €12.7 billion over six years to bring them into line with contributions in Belgium's three main commercial partners. The "wage norm" was to have a differential impact in Flanders than in Wallonia, because some Flemish subregions had nearly full employment, creating labor shortages in certain sectors or for specific skills and employers wanted to allow higher wage increases to keep skilled staff, while some employers in Wallonia believed that wage moderation beyond the "norm" might be used as a means of restoring industrial competitiveness. Although the unions refused to consider regional wage differences, they welcomed the idea of giving sectors greater scope for bargaining.

Agreement over the need for more flexibility in interpreting the wage norm produced a complex compromise. Future reductions in social security contributions would depend either on compliance with the wage norm or on creation of extra jobs and provision of more training. In other words, firms and sectors that awarded wage increases higher than the norm and provided training but also created jobs would not be penalized under the Competitiveness Act. Training (like wages and social security contributions) was to be systematically compared with Belgium's three main commercial partners and over six years, spending on training was to increase from 1.2 to 1.9 percent of total expenditure on wages. To be effective, such a procedure required the compilation of accurate sectoral data, a task delegated the Central Economic Council and the National Employment Council. The lack of appropriate data has rendered these provisions more theoretical than practical.

The two union Confederations and the FEB/VBO (the main employers' association at federal level) approved this agreement by very large majorities. As Pierre Reman (1999) explained, "the terms of the compromise have been profoundly altered: the discussions are less concerned with the problem of redistribution and more with the conditions of growth and job creation," which is a remarkable change in the government's position. In the 1960s, the government facilitated agreements negotiated autonomously by the social partners. During the 1980s and 1990s, efforts to reduce the public debt and ensure stability of wages, competitiveness, and social security, made the government the "framer" of bargaining, determining – and often narrowing – the scope for negotiation. The government guaranteed the rules of the game, which were often set at European level. At the end of the 1990s the agreements tended to redistribute the roles of the players. The social partners were trying to recover some autonomy (albeit under strict supervision), and the government was promoting agreement by using the room for maneuver left by a faster-than-expected reduction of the public debt (Fajertag and Pochet 2000).

Some consider the 1999 agreement to be a Belgian equivalent of the Dutch Wassenaar Agreement (see chapter 8 in this volume). It deals with a range of key issues: wage increase and global wage cost through the lowering of the social security burden and the reform of the minimum wage. It addresses the question of employment (job creation linked to wage moderation) and vocational training. Most of those interviewed on the subject highlight the role of the European employment guidelines in the widening of the scope of issues negotiated at a national level. The agreement for 2001–2002 continues in this direction, indicating that dialog between the social partners has resumed and can again deliver agreement based on an interprofessional framework. The unions have sought the suppression of the law on competitiveness with the wage norm more indicative than imperative (partly because of recent growth of employment), while policy-makers tend again to consider domestic determinants such as national productivity growth or wage share of GDP in the assessment of Belgian competitiveness. In other words, systematic comparison with neighboring countries is waning in favor of a more balanced approach including both external and internal factors. The economic conjuncture began to change dramatically in 2002, however, as growth dropped to 1 percent and unemployment rose again. Public finances were kept under control, however, in this context and after very difficult and tense discussions the social partners struck a deal for 2003–2004 which set an indicative wage norm for those two years.

## 3    The search for a new compromise

Why has it taken so long to sign a new Social Pact in Belgium? One hypothesis is that Belgian productivity gains are distributed across sectors differently from its neighbors and differentially influence actors' preferences concerning trade-offs between wages and jobs. The structure of Belgian unions, which gives more power to declining sectors, is also important. In addition, the common preference of the two unions for automatic indexing of wages to price increases, seen as a way to guarantee social security, has narrowed options. The country's linguistic, political, and regional divisions have also been an obstacle to rapid adaptation because any change in the social model has had to be evaluated according to regional criteria (i.e. whether French- or Dutch-speakers stand to gain more). This is a process that impedes rapid mutual learning and shared understanding. Given these factors, Europe – and therefore EMU – has been a means for overcoming the tendencies toward national disintegration. Yet political actors have also had to reconfigure the Belgian model to make it compatible with EMU rules. What is most striking, finally, is that a small group of people has attempted to preserve and reconfigure the Belgian model under the new EMU rules for price stability. The Economic Central Council was the main institution where this attempt took place.

### From productivity to competitiveness

Belgium has been trying to redesign its "social compromise" around the concept of competitiveness (De Ville 1994) since the early 1980s. As the constraints associated with a fixed exchange rate and EMU have become clearer, the failure of unions to internalize wage norms has produced greater government intervention. The first problem in this process is that definitions of "competitiveness" have often been restricted to wages alone, leading to a trajectory of reducing wage costs without a program for job creation, industrial strategy, and environmental reconfiguration. Budget restrictions have often affected long-term growth by limiting expenditures for education, research and development (R&D), and infrastructure. This has been accentuated because these policies have progressively been devolved to regions and communities, undercutting the capacity for federal coordination. Finally, the growing weakness of Belgian capitalism is also related to the lack of strategic vision about Belgium's role in the world economy. Adjustment to new rules of competition has been a passive process, therefore, focusing on wages, with automatic wage indexing necessitating precautionary action and very strict control over the existing room for maneuver. The difficulty of compromise based on competitiveness has thus been caused primarily by the absence of a trade-off between wage moderation and employment. Further, Belgium's indebtedness has diminished the space for greasing the wheels of bargaining while the bargaining agenda has simultaneously included reduction of the public deficit, wage moderation, and reform of the social security system.[5]

Analyzing productivity gains reveals some Belgian peculiarities. According to the Federal Planning Bureau (Bossier *et al.* 1998):

Since the first oil crisis, the growth of real added value and productivity has been substantially higher than in other countries in industrial sectors, and considerably lower than in other countries in market services. Labor costs have tended to grow more rapidly in Belgium than elsewhere in all sectors of activity. This has been over-compensated for, in industry, by productivity gains higher than in other countries, whereas the reverse has been noted in market services.

Although total productivity gains for all sectors have been around 2 percent, the difference between industrial and service sectors, particularly market services, has been huge. The trend decreased between 1987 and 1994, but the ratio remained 1:2 between gains in industry and in the service sector. The difference is even greater if one excludes construction and focuses on energy and manufacturing industry. Comparison with neighbors reveals more differences: "In other European countries the gap between the manufacturing sector and the entire enterprise sector in both labor and total productivity growth was usually no more than 0.5–1.0 percent. In Belgium the difference was 2.0–2.5 percent" (Englander and Mittelstät, cited by Cassiers, De Villé, and Sollars, 1994). The aggregate Belgian figures show similar general trends (around 2 percent), but productivity gains in energy are more than double those in neighboring countries, and those in manufacturing industry are between 1.3 and 2.7 percentage points higher.

The pattern of job losses and gains since the 1970s is clear, however. During the 1970s, the industrial sector lost the most jobs while the service sector, particularly nonmarket services (administration) had a net gain. From 1980 to 1987, job cuts were still happening in the industrial sector,

---

[5] By contrast, the Netherlands was able to deal with these dimensions in a sequential way (Visser and Hemerijck 1997).

while most new jobs were in market services. From 1987 onwards, far fewer jobs were lost in the industrial sector and they were offset by new jobs in market services. At the same time government and the various levels of the civil service reduced staffs. The net result was less job creation in the service sector than in neighboring countries.

*Employment, wage increases, and the coordination of wage bargaining*    Organizational and geographical asymmetries between social partners have played an important role in employment and wage bargaining. The CSC/ACV is relatively centralized and predominantly Flemish (two-thirds of its members). The FGTB/ABVV has a more equal regional balance, but the central union organization has less clout. There is no hierarchical link between the FEB/VBO and the regional organizations. The Flemish employers' organization (VEV) is increasingly dominant, reflecting the economic development of that region. This asymmetry compounds the difficulty of reaching a compromise. Finally, some sectors, such as metalworking, include very different industries, making common positions difficult to achieve.

The industrial unions, which for historic reasons have great influence, have been faithful to the earlier productivity-related compromise. Their reasoning is that there is little likelihood of creating jobs in the export sector where at best they might prevent losses. Furthermore, most large firms are foreign multinationals, and the unions doubt their ability to make commitments to job creation.[6] The white-collar workers represented by the (French-speaking) CNE and (Dutch-speaking) LBC on the Christian side, and by the SETCA/BBTK on the Socialist side, have tried to reconstruct the social compromise around the reduction of working-time (generally without loss of pay). Yet they have lacked the support of blue-collar unions, with different negotiating margins, especially in high-growth sectors (for example, in the chemicals industry or energy sector) where large wage increases can be achieved. Political support has also been weak. For example, in 2000, the Employment Ministry attempted to place the reduction of working-time on the political agenda but rapidly failed for lack of support from the liberal parties. And technically speaking, the new Competitiveness Act has prevented the reduction of working-time without loss of pay. Employers' organizations also impede change. Three federations (metalworking, chemicals, and banking employers) dominated the debate within the FEB. None of these sectors can embark on job

---

[6] This was confirmed by the Renault case (1997), where large concessions to Renault did not prevent the abrupt shutdown of a suburban Brussels plant during a rough economic moment for the French parent company.

creation (and none wishes to do so) and for various reasons they are all opposed to reducing working-time.

As Michel and Denayer (1997: 67) explained: "Faced with these two specifically Belgian components – a wage structure still dominated by productivity gains in the industrial sector, and low employment growth – the social partners and the government are trying to modify the social compromise and particularly the methods of wage formation." This attempt applies EMU constraints as a lever to forge a consensus by drawing conclusions from statistics (systematic comparison with neighboring countries and an exchange of arguments backed by technical reports). This kind of "top-down" approach has been opposed by union rank-and-file who seek another type of compromise. The word "competitiveness" as an engine for a new Pact has increased the distance between the "elite" and the rest of the population, however, and the central problem is legitimating the competitiveness policy to make it appear as an instrument for promoting employment (Michel 1994: 77). Discussions have been held by the unions on possible room for maneuver within EMU. Officials responsible for economic and monetary matters within the research department of the CSC/ACV (Michel 1994; Dock 1996) have written on the renewal of the social-democratic compromise by, for example, using the Calmfors and Driffill (1988) model, which sees centralization of collective bargaining and coordination of different levels as effective means of ensuring job creation and solidarity.

Although the multi-industry agreement for 1999–2000 adopted an indicative rather than imperative wage policy, it stipulated that sectors and companies must comply with the norm adopted (5.9 percent increase over two years) and also tested the internalization of constraints associated with the single currency and coordination across levels of bargaining. The signature of this agreement just before the general election not only carried political significance but also provided a way to reinforce the federal level and send a strong warning to those who desired to regionalize collective bargaining and social security (Reman 1999). The agreement for 2001–2002 was even more indicative of the wage norm and had a much more global framework, to be filled in at regional level (training) or discussed at the National Labor Council. After 2000, wage increases became more pronounced (see table 9.2) and the technical report of the Central Economic Council indicated some loss of competitiveness. The new multi-industry agreement for 2003–2004 was very difficult to reach and contained no innovative provisions. It was agreed that the maximum increase (indicative norm) should be 5.4 percent over two years and that there should be some moderation in 2003. In a more difficult economic situation a few months before the general election of June 2003, the social partners mainly tried to keep things going.

Since the 1980s threats of government intervention have encouraged the social partners to accept wage moderation, but the rainbow coalition (Liberal, Socialist, and Green) elected in 1999 has tried to claim political credit for growth and job creation. This agenda has interfered with that of the social partners, both because the new Socialist leadership is less in tune with the trade union movement and because the government has been more unstable, with each party seeking victory in media battles.

### Budget deficits and social security

Belgian support for the system of social security is traditionally high, but this has not prevented discussions – unsuccessful to this point – about devolving parts of it, mainly healthcare, to the regions. The scope of social aid is limited as well: the safety-net system is supposed to cover almost all citizens, but fewer than 90,000 people depend on it, compared to 400,000 in the Netherlands and 2 million in France. EMU has not brought new limits to the system, however, and the changes have mainly been incremental.

The bulk of deficit reduction was achieved in two periods, from 1982 to 1987 and from 1993 to 1996. It is commonly held that the budget squeezes of the early 1980s focused mainly on public investment, whereas restructuring in the 1990s targeted social security, healthcare, and pensions because "the least painful ways of achieving savings had been largely exhausted" (Mommen 1994: 213). In an analysis of debate during the preparation of the 1997 budget, Pakaslahti (1997) thus classified Belgium as one of the countries where EMU and social security were clearly linked. As table 9.1 indicates, however, the latest figures show quite a different picture (OECD 1996). The deficit fell from 13.1 percent of GDP in 1982, the year prior to budget restructuring, to 7.6 percent in 1987. From 1993 to 1995, the deficit fell from 7.1 percent to 4.4 percent of GDP, a 2.7 percentage point decrease. The scale of the adjustments made in the early 1980s affected government investment and consumption and also social security. These adjustments were particularly important because interest rates increased by nearly 3 percent. Excluding interest, expenditure decreased by nearly 7 percent, with a 1.6 percent increase in revenue, or a ratio of 1:4.

In the 1990s, the second adjustment period when the issue was the Maastricht criteria, effort was mainly directed to reducing interest rates and expenditure growth, involving measures that were much less painful. Excluding interest rate reduction, table 9.1 shows no other significant

Table 9.1 *Measures to reduce the public deficit in Belgium: changes in percentage of GDP, 1982–1987 and 1993–1995*

| | Direct taxes | Indirect taxes | Other | Total revenue | Social transfers | Consumption | Investment | Interest | Other | Total expenditure |
|---|---|---|---|---|---|---|---|---|---|---|
| 1982–1987 | 0.4 | −0.1 | 1.3 | 1.6 | −1.0 | −2.3 | −1.7 | 2.8 | −1.8 | −4.0 |
| 1993–1995 | 1.6 | 0.2 | −0.6 | 1.2 | 0.1 | 0.2 | −0.1 | −1.5 | −0.3 | −1.4 |

*Source:* OECD (1996).

cuts in spending. Nevertheless, over the whole period (1982–1996), public investment decreased from 3.9 percent to 1.3 percent of GDP. Falling administrative expenditures also contributed to the deterioration in public services (Koene 1997). These figures do not reflect budget adjustments in 1996 and 1997, which brought the deficit down to less than 3 percent,[7] but they do show that social security did not undergo any major cuts in the 1990s. The European Commission's figures (CEC 1998: 15) also show no break in rising social security expenditures, which were just under 4 percent in the periods 1990–1993 and 1993–1995. This trend was unlike that in most other European countries, where 1993–1995 brought lower increases in spending and, in some cases, absolute reductions in expenditures.

Belgians, however, understood things differently, perhaps, as Meulders (1994) has remarked about the 1994 Global Plan, because of the

government's "dual and ambiguous" language. On the one hand, the government loudly and clearly affirmed its attachment to the Belgian social security system and its long-term survival. On the other, it continued to erode services, targeting the unemployed, pensioners and those receiving healthcare.

Thus even if the cuts may have been more symbolic than effective in budget terms, they left their mark. Together with proposals such as reducing governmental contribution to the safety net in some districts, they have contributed to the public's impression of a direct link between EMU and deteriorating social conditions. For example, in the draft legislation the government linked reduced safety-net social aid to Belgium's entry into EMU (Antoons and Pochet 1998). Yet apart from targeting one category of the unemployed (cohabiting partners), social security cuts have aimed at reducing expenditure growth to the level of GDP growth and the ratio

[7] During these two years, however, the budget adjustments were relatively balanced and proportionally smaller (*Année sociale* 1997, 1998).

of social expenditure to GDP has remained stable. The "commotion" over social security may also have been designed to impress the capital markets and push down interest premiums.[8] Whatever the causes, forecasts indicate that a social security surplus should increasingly contribute to reducing the public deficit (Bossier *et al.*, 1998).

The government's approach to restructuring public finances has focused mainly on pensions, with efforts to comply with Maastricht linked to protecting future funding (OECD 2003). In the words of the Higher Finance Council, "Consideration of the future demographic impact of population ageing is an additional and decisive element in favor of the policy of structural debt-reduction decided and accelerated by the Belgian government" (Delvaux 1996).[9] The issue was settled discreetly in 1997 by dissociating the indexing of pensions from average wage increases. The new formula linked the minimum state pension to the minimum wage, indexing only the portion above the minimum. Moreover, new measures will progressively raise the retirement age for women to sixty-five, the same as for men, and extend coverage for those with "atypical" work contracts (Festjens 1997). By limiting growth in pension costs, these new provisions are aimed at resolving long-term funding problems. According to the Planning Bureau, until 2050, "It should be noted that despite the budgetary cost, (new) scope for bargaining appears every year throughout the whole of the projected period. In the reference scenario, the fall in interest costs induced by debt-reduction is indeed higher than the budgetary cost of ageing and is sufficient to finance it" (1998: 49).

Another important choice has been whether to raise the replacement ceiling (maximum pension rate) thereby safeguarding its "insurance" function, or to adapt the lower ceiling partially to the prosperity index, a more egalitarian measure, a long-term perspective making benefits payable on a flat-rate basis. With EMU as a pretext, the reform has had little publicity and has not yet been the subject of public debate. The new governmental policy is to pursue a modest catch-up process for low pensions. The effects are anticipated only in the very long term, the replacement rate for the average public pension was 34.2 in 1987, 29.9 in 2000, and should decrease to 23.3 in 2050 (Englert *et al.*, 2002).

From the early 1990s, debate has focused upon alternative funding for social security, an issue which has strong "community" – i.e. Flemish/Francophone – connotations. The question is whether to distinguish

---

[8] Iversen (1998b) states that "the purpose of the reforms since 1982 in Denmark was not just to reestablish a balanced budget, but also to signal to the capital markets that fiscal and social policies were now subjugated to the requirements of restrictive monetary policies."

[9] This deal was reaffirmed in the Belgian convergence program where it was clearly indicated that debt reduction would serve to finance the increased public pension burden.

Table 9.2 *Wage increases in the private sector, 1996–2002*

|  | 1996 (%) | 1997 (%) | 1998 (%) | 1999 (%) | 2000 (%) | 2001 (%) | 2002 (%) |
|---|---|---|---|---|---|---|---|
| Total agreed wage increase | 1.7 | 1.7 | 1.9 | 1.6 | 2.8 | 3.2 | 3.8 |
| of which indexing | 1.7 | 1.5 | 1.2 | 1.1 | 1.5 | 2.5 | 2.4 |
| Employer funding to social security | −0.1 | 0.1 | 0.2 | −0.4 | −0.6 | −0.3 | −0.1 |
| Wage drift | −0.1 | 0.9 | −1.1 | 2.6 | −0.2 | −0.1 | 0.1 |
| Total wage increase | 1.5 | 2.7 | 1.0 | 3.7 | 2.0 | 2.8 | 3.8 |

*Source:* CEC (2002: 8).

between insurance covered by employee and employer contributions from universal protection like healthcare by using new forms of funding. For any change with large regional implications, however, national debate has been impossible. Because the Flemish are now, on average, richer than Francophones, for example, taxation on income would have a differential effect on the two linguistic groups. Ironically, each side of the debate uses Europe to justify its position. Flemish proponents of federalizing social insurance note that the Commission has adopted subsidiarity as its guiding principle. Similarly, Walloon voices use Europe to bolster their argument that a decision to split the national system will be a terrible waste of effort once Europe requires revisions in member state insurance (Huygebaert, quoted by Kurzer 1997: 48).

Consensus exists about the negative effects of placing the entire burden of social security funding on labor, and Belgian politicians and social partners seek a degree of European-level fiscal harmonization, hoping to resolve the question with tax harmonization on capital (see below). In the meantime, because comparison with the three neighboring countries showed that social security contributions were around 2 percent higher in Belgium, employers' contributions are being cut by 108 billion francs ($3 billion) over five years.[10] In Belgium, this decision affects the future balance of the social security system, but to date, no other way to compensate for the cut for employers has been found.

Table 9.2 summarizes recent trends. Automatic wage indexing is a very important part of the total wage increase. Since 1996 cumulative reduction in employer funding for social security has been slightly more

---

[10] Data showing that nonwage costs have been reduced more in the neighboring countries than in Belgium illustrate the risk of using competitive social pacts to achieve real devaluation (Pochet and Fajertag 2000).

than 1 percent of total wage cost. This is not insignificant, but it has not substantially changed the wage increase trend.

Current debate about rendering the social protection system more "active" makes no links with EMU. The Flemish socialist Minister of Social Affairs and Pensions, F. Vandenbroucke supports an activation strategy in line with the new European strategy against poverty and social exclusion and the Luxembourg employment strategy (Vandenbroucke 1999). Vandenbroucke was also very active at the European level in introducing the "Open Method of Coordination" (OMC) in the pension field (Jenson and Pochet 2002) where he advocated that pensions should not be only considered under fiscal sustainability but also from within a social perspective (Pochet 2003)

### Exerting influence at the European level

In Belgium, EMU has thus often been used as a pretext for decisions that could not be reached by domestic social forces alone – as a *vincolo esterno*, in other words. Proposed European measures have in the main coincided with measures adopted domestically, for example, the Maastricht Treaty's 3 percent deficit criterion was also the rate chosen in 1990 by the Higher Finance Council to stop the snowballing of public debt. In addition, the balanced budget objective contained in the Stability and Growth Pact (SGP) coincided with the 1996 rapid debt reduction (involving a primary budget surplus of at least 6 percent) adopted by the Belgian government.

The EU has had a broader impact than on monetary policy alone, however. The Luxembourg guidelines have helped modify Belgian policies on employment, for example, both on increasing the employment rate and in reducing early retirement schemes, although some argued that this was at the expense of the national social model (Jadot 2000). Resorting to Europe makes it possible to externalize constraints and to impose coordination, or at least a trade-off, across various levels of power. Because of the European Employment Strategy, for instance, Belgian regional authorities for the first time accepted a structured dialog under the auspices of the Federal government, even though education and training policies remain decentralized. Finally, systematic comparison with the average performance of neighboring countries (France, Germany, and the Netherlands) helps avoid a national debate, which could rapidly degenerate into "community" conflict.

Nevertheless, the effects of Europe on Belgian policy have not only been a top-down process. This is because European priorities coincided with some domestic priorities, mainly supported by Flemish political parties supportive of a Belgian Third Way around the idea of a Active Welfare

State. More important is the fact that other people who were much more critical about both the employment strategy and the Active Welfare State have tried to modify the European guidelines. The minister in charge of Employment succeeded in imposing the idea of quality at work to balance the previous quantitative European approach (for a full account, see Pochet 2002a).

The Belgian posture on Europe has had two different dimensions. The political elite has used European integration to force adoption of domestic policies, perhaps more than its counterparts elsewhere. Europe has also been perceived as a relevant context for widening the scope for national action, and Belgium has long seen its own definition of a "social Europe" as a priority.[11] Governments have simultaneously sought tax harmonization, social convergence (particularly social security convergence), and employment at the European level (Dehaene 1998). Competition with Luxembourg has played a major role in raising general awareness concerning taxes.[12] The FGTB/ABVV and CSC/ACV have acted as a driving force on tax matters in the European Trade Union Confederation, which originally hesitated to tackle the subject. On wages, Belgian unions contacted counterparts in neighboring countries after the adoption of the 1996 Competitiveness Act to propose cross-national wage coordination, which led to a more formal request from the DGB (the German trade union umbrella organization) for a meeting in 1997. Agreement to hold an annual meeting led to a second meeting in Doorn in 1999. This attempt to coordinate wage claims at a supranational level indicates a shift in the union position from resisting a wage norm toward trying to find new room for maneuver within an EMU framework (Dølvik, chapter 12 in this volume). Belgium has also displayed particular interest in the coordination of social security systems at the European level.[13] Unlike Sweden's success on employment at Amsterdam, however, Belgian efforts on tax harmonization and social security coordination have not led to a coalition at the European level that could force these issues onto the

[11] The idea of a social charter and of guaranteeing minimum rights at the European level was originally proposed by the Belgian Employment Minister, M. Hansenne (see Jonckheer and Pochet 1990).

[12] The Minister of the Economy has acknowledged that his main political error was the lack of minimum tax harmonization with regard to the liberalization of capital.

[13] An initial study related to the establishment of a special social security system for migrant workers (*The Thirteenth State*, Pieters, Palm, and Vansteenkiste 1993) and was linked with supposed increased mobility due to the single market. The second study related to the establishment of a social "Snake" that would lead to convergence of the social security systems (Dispersyn and Van Der Horst 1992). The third, commissioned by the Minister for Social Security, De Galan, focused on the concept of social convergence within EMU and argued for the creation of a specific stabilization fund (OSE 1997, 1998).

Community agenda.[14] A Belgian proposal to redraft the Social Protocol to allow coordination of national social security policies based on
the model of the Amsterdam Employment chapter was not supported by
other delegations.

At a more technical level, in 1988 the social partners in the CEC
asked "to be systematically involved in the preparation of Belgium's economic positions within the European family. This relates in particular to
the Broad Economic Policy Guidelines of the Member States and the
Community and the economic aspects of the guidelines on employment"
(CEC 1998). It was decided later that members of the employment and
the social protection committees would present the documents and the
main stakes at the CNT (National Labor Council) before each pertinent
meeting of the Commission. By doing so, Belgian social partners have a
better view of the European debate in order to influence it.

## 4    Conclusions

Why has Belgium taken ten to fifteen years to follow the path of the
Netherlands? The answer lies in the distinctive Belgian model and the difficulty of renegotiating the social contract that was established at the end
of the Second World War. A major source of the difficulty has been the
country's increasingly intense linguistic divisions, anchored in regions
that have experienced divergent economic development. The declining
power of the national political parties representing the traditional Christian and Socialist pillars (*verzuilen*), which at least partially cut across
regional divisions, has further aggravated Belgium's structural dualism.
Thus, for the first time on June 13, 1999, when the Liberal and Green
parties won the elections, the two Christian parties became a minority in
the country's three regions.

Union responses to the change in monetary regime in 1982 also slowed
negotiation. While labor made a strategic commitment to stable exchange
rates following the 1982 devaluation, the unions failed to recognize fully
the conditions of the new monetary regime, and a lack of coordination
across bargaining levels (industry, sectoral, and multi-industry) and the
automatic indexing of wages to prices led the government to intervene

---

[14] The Belgian Central Bank stated: "The single currency and economic integration will
also modify the reference framework within which the national authorities operate. This
will have an increasingly European dimension which should not be overlooked, whether
it is a question of setting tax rates, dealing with industrial relations or influencing economic life . . . This process, although sound in itself, could lead to harmful fiscal and
social competition. Co-ordination and harmonization are therefore necessary" (Belgian
National Bank, *Annual Report 1997*: 14).

heavily in wage increases. Attempts at a new Social Pact in 1993 ended up in a governmental plan and at that point only the union leadership was fully convinced of the need for change, while divisions within the socialist union made it impossible to impose change on the membership.

EMU, as defined in the Treaty of Maastricht, constrained Belgian political forces, despite the many pressures they faced, to stay the course, and it also obliged the social partners to find new compromises. As in Italy, "EC level developments and commitments were used by . . . elites to restructure the domestic policy process, thereby revising the balance of power between key actors and opening up new opportunities for policy reform at home" (Dyson and Featherstone 1996). The state thus had a central role in adapting the Belgian model to the elimination of exchange rates as an instrument for economic stabilization, first by linking the Belgian franc to the D-mark and then through membership in EMU. The resulting reconfiguration of both the wage-setting and social security systems led to a strengthening of the Federal level at least temporarily as the political priority given to entering EMU in the first wave put traditional "community problems" on the back burner. Nevertheless, these problems still dominate political decision-making, as the debates on social security reform have shown. In addition to the state's strong intervention, employers have supported the coordination of wage-setting. Belgian employers have never desired a decentralized collective bargaining system, largely because of the legitimacy of unions at the company level and the competition between them.

The course of adaptation has gradually changed the institutional configuration established by the postwar Pact, with its independence of social partners, systematic consultation, and virtual monopoly over social security. The most important changes have taken place in the system of collective bargaining, where the independence of social partners and wage increases linked to productivity have given way to bargaining focused on competitiveness and controlled by government. Wage increases have been gradually dissociated from domestic productivity calculations and are now based on comparison with those in three neighboring countries. The sectoral level, which had traditionally played a central role in setting employment and working conditions, has been given new tasks in job creation and training (Jadot 1999; Van Gyes, De Witte, and van der Hallen 1999). Since the late 1970s, Belgium has thus moved progressively from strongly autonomous dialog between unions and employers to a tripartite system in which the state plays a central role (Ministry of Labour 1998).

Within EMU constraints, coordination across levels of bargaining has become a key imperative, necessitating new organizational relations and balances of power among the constituents of each social partner. To achieve the necessary coordination, the unions have resisted tendencies toward regionalization, choosing instead to maintain a unified structure and sign multi-industry agreements (2001–2002) permitting regions to interpret the federal agreement within their own area of responsibility (e.g. training). EMU and the EU more generally have been used to promote new measures such as employment policy and stimulate interchange among regions. Rather than centralization, the result has meant a dialog among autonomous actors in which the upper level determines the framework in which the other levels can express their preferences. An important dimension of this has been the proliferation of semi-independent expert bodies such as the Higher Employment Council, Higher Finance Council, Planning Bureau, Central Economic Council, and National Employment Council, through which a dense network of reports prepares government action and explores possible options. As discussion has become progressively more technocratic – and, some would claim, more rational– upgraded statistical tools have become available, and the government has decided to give itself the means, through the Higher Employment Council, of short-circuiting the social partners when they cannot agree on measures intended to create employment. This new configuration symbolizes the changes under way. Whereas after 1945 the social partners were members of the Regency Council of the Belgian Central Bank and so able to discuss Belgian monetary policy, the National Bank now directly influences the newly created Higher Employment Council (Van Gyes, De Witte, and van der Hallen 1999).[15] Changes in the Belgian model of industrial relations under the rules of EMU and globalization, however, have occurred within the CEC, the key institution during the 1990s.

These changes have not been free of problems. As Denayer (1996) states: "changes are obviously being imposed from outside and are expressed by the will for increased 'normalisation' following external criteria. Very often the domestic objectives of reforms are hidden, political debates become impoverished and discussions are limited to a technical presentation of the files." Furthermore, state modernization and new social compromise have not been present everywhere. Accelerated reduction of the debt and deficits was achieved at the expense of investment in areas such as justice and the police. At first glance, EMU might appear responsible. But these issues present few external constraints, as they invite no comparison with neighbors and are not subject to EU action. In such matters, change emanates only from the national level, which in

---

[15] The 1999–2000 multi-industry agreement shows the social partners' determination to reappropriate the role of "experts" and to supplant the various centers.

Belgium raises linguistic, cultural, and political differences. The cause of such investment failures is thus not to be found in rapid debt reduction but rather in a lack of consensus about what to do and a risk that increasing resources and redefining tasks will trigger new tensions between the communities.

The final impact of monetary integration on Belgian federalism remains unclear, but conflict continues over the extent to which the welfare state should be federalized. For social security, recent changes have to do more with internal factors than external constraint. Whereas the linguistic debate obliges elites to find at least discreet ways to modify the system, reducing the deficit found support in both linguistic communities, though for different reasons. For the Flemish, reducing the global debt might facilitate an eventual division of the country. For Francophones, reducing or controlling regional debts permits negotiations without asking for more transfer of funds. Recent events, however, have taken a different course. The 1999 political agreement offers new regionalization by areas of competence (development cooperation, agriculture, external trade, "community" legislation) in exchange for additional fund transfers from the Federal government to the regions and communities. Having lost the pretext of EMU, Belgian elites themselves have to redefine the fate of the country. Beneath the surface, things are changing.

# 10 The political dynamics of external empowerment: the emergence of EMU and the challenge to the European social model

*Kevin Featherstone*

Economic and Monetary Union (EMU), on the one hand, and existing models of labor market regulation and welfare provision within the European Union (EU), on the other, have often been assumed to stand in contradiction to one another. The re-appearance of EMU on the European agenda in the late 1980s, following the de-regulation paradigm of the Single European Market (SEM), raised widespread concern that it might serve as a "Trojan horse" for a neo-liberal policy shift across EU states. The "sound money, sound finances" principles underlying the particular design of EMU, strengthened in the Stability and Growth Pact (SGP) of 1997, seemed to threaten traditional social models and the scope for national differentiation. By the time the new Euro currency was launched in 1999, the evidence to confirm or remove such fears was, in reality, limited and varied. As in other spheres, it has been hazardous to judge the relationship between endogenous and exogenous pressures for reform. External pressures are mediated within distinct institutional settings, with different roles and interests on the part of actors. Moreover, pressures of "Europeanization" and of "globalization" may be difficult to distinguish. Indeed, some equate the two (Wylie 2002). Case study investigations, such as those presented in this volume, are needed to assess causation rather than incidental correlation.

The argument of this chapter is that progress may be made by examining the more limited issue of how EMU has been used within different institutional settings: that is, how it has been deployed as a *strategic* lever for reform and as a stimulus to a shift of *norms* and *beliefs* affecting policy in contingent areas. Such an analysis draws on the growing literature on the theme of "Europeanization," which typically examines the domestic impact of EU obligations (Knill and Lehmkuhl 1999; Caporaso *et al.* 2000; Featherstone and Radaelli 2003). Fundamentally, EMU may be seen as a system of regulation that proscribes certain (budget) options ("negative integration"), but which prescribes policy models only in particular "core" aspects of monetary policy ("positive integration").

As such, much discretion remains over domestic policy choices set within the fiscal parameters of EMU and the SGP. To Knill and Lehmkuhl, the question becomes one of how EMU redistributes "powers and resources between domestic actors, and hence challenge [*sic*] existing equilibria" (1999: 5). The strategic position of domestic actors is altered, and the variations in the pattern of national adjustment are a question of the "varying domestic opportunity structures." Consistent with this perspective, the structural power of actors and institutions is reconfigured by the EMU constraint and the setting for the political contestation over labor market regulation and welfare provision gains new forms. Here the reconfiguration is seen as potentially affecting both the *interests* and the *ideas* of actors.

This chapter addresses two empirical questions that derive from this context:

- How has EMU been used by domestic actors and institutions to gain advantage in relation to policy outcomes affecting national social models?
- What explains the variations in the use of EMU in this policy area?

The use of EMU as an external source of domestic empowerment is a further manifestation of part of the original economic rationale advanced in support of the single currency. Economists, like Giavazzi and Pagano, argued the advantages of tying one's hand from a "hard" EMS and the importation of central bank credibility (1988). In an extension of the same logic, Guido Carli – a central banker turned politician – argued that EMU was a *vincolo esterno* (external tie) to engineer otherwise elusive domestic reform in Italy (1993). Further, Dyson and Featherstone (1996, 1999) identified how particular actors in Italy were able to use EMU to gain advantage and secure major policy shifts: a re-structuring of power to the disadvantage of the profligacy associated with the *partitocrazia*.

## 1    The conceptualization of the *vincolo esterno*

The domestic use of external constraints in this fashion can have both a "narrow" and a "broad" interpretation. The former involves a process of differential empowerment resulting from the interests actors pursue and the impact of EU constraints upon how they are defined. In the narrow interpretation, the conceptual framework follows that of rational-choice institutionalism, which has been applied by an increasing number of authors (e.g. Scharpf 1988, 1997a; Tsebelis 1994, 1995; Garrett and Tsebelis 1996). The setting is, however, one in which interests and capabilities might be redefined across a "two-level" bargaining structure (Putnam 1988). The complex interpenetration between the "domestic" and the "European" is important here insofar as it creates strategic opportunities for certain actors to exploit. Whether and how the potential is exploited depends on the will (priorities, interests) and capability (strategies, information, institutional position) of actors competing within the particular domestic setting. The scope ("political opportunity structure") can be seen as circumscribed by domestic *veto points* and by the availability of "politically integrated leadership" (Börzel and Risse 2000; Héritier and Knill 2000).[1] EU policy inputs are "a political resource which may be exploited by some domestic actors in order to improve their relative positions in domestic political conflicts" (Héritier and Knill 2000). Consistent with the logic of the *vincolo esterno*, governments can identify strategic advantages in being bound by EU commitments (Grande 1995). Grande argues that governments can use the need to compromise and the temporal closure of the decision-making process for all but state actors at the EU level in order to gain autonomy with regard to domestic groups. He refers to a "paradox of weakness" in which it is not the strong state, but rather the state that has lost part of its autonomy to a supranational decision-making system which has gained power to pursue its own structural interest against strong pressures from societal actors. Moravcsik (1994) pursued a similar line of argument. Integration redistributes political resources by "shifting control over domestic agendas (initiative), altering decision-making procedures (institutions), magnifying informational asymmetries in their favor (information), and multiplying the potential domestic ideological justifications for policies (ideas)" (1994: 1, parentheses in the original). In addition, binding EU commitments can enable governments to implement unpopular reforms at home while engaging in "blameshift" towards the "EU," even if they themselves had desired such policies.

The broader conception of the *vincolo esterno* places it within the constructivist perspective of the role and circulation of ideas in the domestic policy process, albeit straddled across the domestic and European contexts. By contrast to the rational-choice approach, there have been few attempts to apply this framework to the EU. McNamara's (1998) study of the role of ideas in shaping the EMU agenda is a notable exception. She stressed how capital mobility and a neo-liberal policy consensus had narrowed the options for governments. Indeed, "This policy

---

[1] Formal veto-points may arise from federalist–decentralized political systems; multi-party coalition governments; high ministerial autonomy; an independent constitutional court and an independent central bank. Factual veto-points may result from the form of interest mediation, as in corporatist arrangements. Integrated political leadership can be provided by "formal majoritarian hierarchical government" or by established practices of consensualism.

consensus redefined state interests in cooperation, underpinned stability in the EMS, and induced political leaders to accept the domestic policy adjustments needed to stay within the system" (1998: 3). The consensus was an elite-level phenomenon: governments had "painted" themselves into a corner, but "it is important to remember that they have themselves wielded the brushes that put them there" (1998: 178). More particularly, Checkel (1997) analyzed how international norms reached the domestic arena, with the effect of empowering actors. He distinguished between actors "internalizing" international norms, adopting new values and interests, and actors opting to follow the new norms for purely instrumentalist reasons. One process involves "elite learning," the other "societal pressure." The operationalization of this kind of distinction is problematic, however. Rather more helpful may be Börzel and Risse's notion of *norm entrepreneurs* mobilizing others to "redefine their interests and identities." This logic is reminiscent of that of Kingdon (1984) on policy entrepreneurs exploiting windows of opportunity in the policy process. Interests and ideas are often seen as involving separate processes. But, as Börzel and Risse rightly stress, their two logics are not mutually exclusive: rather, they often occur simultaneously or sequentially. It is only at a theoretical level that they can be easily separated: for actors and institutions, in reality, they are part of a common whole. Evidence of their empirical separation is likely to be elusive.

## 2    The use of EMU as a *vincolo esterno*: pre-Maastricht

EMU offered an unprecedented means within the then EC of utilizing an external economic discipline on domestic policy, potentially privileging distinct institutional interests and policy ideas. In the Italian case already referred to, a small group of technocrats straddling the Tesoro, the Banca d'Italia, the Prime Minister's Office, and the Foreign Affairs Ministry steered the negotiating mandate towards an acceptance of a paradigm that would strengthen the power of monetary officials over policy, as both institutional actors and as norm entrepreneurs (Dyson and Featherstone: 1996, 1999). The IGC coordinators had a clear conception of their role in this regard: sharing values of foreign and monetary policy, and a common interest in their independence from political manipulation. The losers were intended to be the leaders of the *partitocrazia*, who placed political self-interest and patronage above the depoliticized management of "sound money, sound finances." Symbolically, the Maastricht Treaty was signed just months before the old party system collapsed in the elections of April 1992: Andreotti's pre-election fiscal laxity contrasted like the "old" and the "new" with the straitjacket of EMU's convergence criteria.

In reality, the technocratic group was going with the grain of both globalization and earlier domestic reforms. EMU exposed the Italian sensitivity about staying at the core of Europe. Each of these factors provided the window of opportunity. The room for maneuver available to the technocratic actors was limited, however: EMU, like the wider global financial shifts, seemed unstoppable and largely uncontrollable by Italy. The task was to keep Italy on track with European and international trends. Prior domestic reforms had helped. Entry into the EMS in 1979 had already represented a shift away from competitive devaluation of the lira to a stable currency and price regime. This shift had been prompted by policy learning after the failures of the 1970s, a decade marked by low priority being given to inflation and weak external constraints following the breakdown of the Bretton Woods system. The shift would be consolidated by participation in EMU. The placing of EMU on the agenda after 1988 fostered two further critical shifts, however: the completion of central bank independence and domestic financial market liberalization. Moreover, the combined effect of these reforms was to strengthen the structural power of the Banca d'Italia over domestic monetary policy and to heighten the role of technocratic expertise over its management. The Italian state had undergone a process of "hollowing out" (Della Sala, 1997).

The Italian case displays exceptional features. The search for a *vincolo esterno* exposed her domestic economic weakness and her concomitant credibility problem in EU negotiations. These latter features seem to have parallels elsewhere in southern Europe, however. Pérez (chapter 7 in this volume) shows how the perception of domestic policy failure in the 1980s in Spain prompted attention to the advantages of external discipline. EMU fitted the domestic need for a *vincolo esterno* to secure disinflation after the breakdown in 1987 of the incomes policy agreements with the unions. Monetary integration became an indispensable weapon for the González government to circumvent union vetoes, as evident in the decision to bring forward the entry of the peseta into the ERM by one year to July 1989. More particularly, entry met the long-term preferences of the monetary policy establishment for greater discipline. The latter had opposed Franco's *dirigisme* and had emerged like "norm entrepreneurs" to spread and nurture their shared orthodoxy amongst influential younger economists. In consequence, the voice of the central bank became stronger and more assertive over economic and monetary policy. There are clear parallels here with the convergent attitudes of monetary economists and officials in Italy in the 1980s and 1990s.

EMU also provided the means by which key actors in Greece could realize their domestic self-interest and restructure the policy discourse (Featherstone, Kazamias, and Papadimitriou 2000). The Bank of Greece saw EMU as a vehicle for its own independence: a status not established until just before Greece entered the eurozone. The two relevant ministries – of National Economy and of Finance – found an opportunity for their own empowerment in upholding fiscal discipline over the manipulations and clientelism of party leaders elsewhere in the government structure. Greece had entered the EMU negotiations in a critically weak state: a letter from Delors in March 1990 to the Greek government emphasized the gravity of its fiscal position, as did the emergency EC loan the following January. The Ministry of National Economy and its Council of Economic Advisers (SOE) grew in institutional importance, however, as the struggle for entry into Stage Three progressed to EU acceptance in 1999. Efthimnios Christodoulou and, more emphatically, Yannos Papantoniou, became exceptionally strong ministerial figures by virtue of the EMU constraint. The scope for strong policy leadership was provided by the external imperative, and individual actors rose to the challenge, confronting the inertia and inefficiencies of the archipelago state machine.[2] EMU led to a critical juncture in subsequent domestic policy: a stimulus to continued discipline and associated reforms.

The common theme among these cases is of domestic economic weakness prompting support for externally imposed discipline. The form of domestic policy leadership on EMU shows some variation across different institutional settings. The precise composition and balance of ministerial and technocratic leadership is not consistent: between ministries and central banks, state actors and wider policy communities. While the reform "coalition" took a varied form, it had a common domestic enemy, however: the profligacy and clientelism of those interests hiding behind protectionism and political favor. As Boyer put it, for the South "monetary integration means economic modernization and political democratization" (Boyer 2000: 86).

The policy style was in all cases elitist and relatively enclosed. A particular feature is the role of entrepreneurs isolated within a disparate and insular bureaucracy. The specific opaque and distant nature of the monetary policy sector found in most states is a contributory factor here, of course. But insofar as there are shared traits of the domestic state tradition in southern/Latin Europe – in essence, the difficulties of coordination across an archipelago state structure – the scope may be created

---

[2] The term "archipelago" is taken from Guiliano Amato's description of the Italian state machine, quoted in Ginsborg (1990: 423).

for entrepreneurial leadership, by default, to compensate for the systemic weakness. A qualified parallel may be drawn with Schmidt's observation about France and the difficulty of implementing reform (Schmidt 2002). The French state, she notes, is ideal-typically strong and societal groups weak. The effect is that a small, restricted governmental–technocratic elite often sets policy in an "heroic" fashion, vulnerable to subsequent pressures of implementation. The ideal-model highlights an important condition of policy-making relevant to southern Europe, though its precise relevance will vary between cases. The attempts at pension reform may exemplify this pattern in several southern states (see below).

The common need for external discipline does not, by itself, provide a basis for constructing a cross-national coalition within the EU. In the EMU negotiations in 1991, Greece sought to coordinate the negotiating position and strategy of its southern European partners, plus Ireland: the "periphery" (Featherstone, Kazamias, and Papadimitriou 2000). In reality, the coalition "dare not speak its name": their interests proved too diverse and several delegations were uncomfortable with the shared identity. Italy, in particular, was embarrassed by participation in such a bloc, as she was struggling to sustain her credibility as a serious EMU partner with the other big EU states. The rest were unable to approximate their positions on anything other than the demand for a new Cohesion Fund. Even on the latter, success was limited. It came, not as a result of a new coalition of the periphery pressing the case, but as a result of a rather more traditional-style veto threat against the Treaty by the González government in Spain. The structure of the EMU negotiations had imposed limits on this type of coalition: all sought the status of core EU membership, all needed special help and aid, and all were dependent on the EU's core to grant them both. The latter could divide and rule.

The use of EMU as a *vincolo esterno* prior to Maastricht is not only found in states exhibiting the need for external economic help. EMU offered other political and institutional advantages to bureaucratic actors seeking to defend their interests within the state machine. Thus, the espousal of the "sound money" principles of EMU could mask interests of gaining power and influence. Most EC central banks lacked autonomy and EMU promised Bundesbank status to their personnel, wrapped within the ESCB/ECB. Central bank governors were provided with much scope to shape, and at times determine, the content of the EMU agreement (Dyson and Featherstone, 1999: 12–58 *passim*). The Maastricht stipulations required a shift to central bank independence in a majority of EU states, and for many (e.g. France) independence represented a severe contradiction of the entrenched state tradition. As already suggested, EMU also significantly upgraded the relative position of many finance ministries within their domestic governmental systems. Finance ministers and their officials positively sought the gain, as they also endeavored to steer EMU down institutional routes at the EC level over which they held sway such as ECOFIN and the EC Monetary Committee. Pierre Bérégovoy, in France, for example, set the assertion of the primacy of domestic control over the EMU agenda by his finance ministry as one of his key objectives in 1990–1991 (Dyson and Featherstone 1999: 209). Bérégovoy and his German counterpart, Theo Waigel, agreed to work very closely together, seeking to keep Mitterrand and Kohl and both foreign ministries removed from the problem-solving process. For similar reasons, the respective finance ministries and central banks agreed to hold regular secret bilateral meetings from March onwards (Dyson and Featherstone 1999: 412–417).

Moreover, officials in the French Trésor saw EMU as a means of empowering not only their institutional interests, but also their policy norms (Dyson and Featherstone 1999: 82). EMU would entrench the norms underpinning the Trésor's cherished policy of the *franc stable* and the associated domestic "rigor," with which it had long struggled, binding successor governments (Dyson and Featherstone 1999: 203). To the Bundesbank and the German Finance Ministry, EMU was a matter of the rest of Europe adopting their model and putting their own house in order, consistent with the precepts of ordo-liberalism. Ordo-liberal attitudes meant that German (and Dutch) leaders and officials were deeply skeptical of the will and capability of south European governments such as Italy and Greece to meet the obligations of EMU. Notably, in 1995–1997, Waigel and his officials repeatedly questioned the preparedness of the Italians – Greece was put aside as a near-lost cause – to meet the convergence criteria. Indeed, persuading the German public to accept the single currency seemed to require that they be reassured that the Italians would not be involved.

By contrast the British and Danish governments resisted the binding commitments being advanced in the EMU negotiations. Both were sensitive on the question of preserving their sovereignty and both sought an "opt-out" to be available to all governments. The Thatcher and Major governments shared much of the monetary and market-related philosophy promoted by their Dutch and German counterparts. Indeed, the proximity of their core values gave scope for a tri-partite coalition on EMU (Dyson and Featherstone 1999: 766). What prevented this from occurring was the British stance on not ceding sovereignty and not giving a binding commitment to participation. The British were sympathetic to ordo-liberalism, they believed in good "house-keeping" at home, but were opposed to it being imposed from abroad. The dominant attitude in Denmark was similar: greater discipline in monetary policy had been achieved since the 1970s, the kroner was part of the hardening ERM in the 1980s, but public opinion opposed supranationalism. Political leadership on "Europe" was tightly constrained electorally, whilst policy-makers had to manage the economic dependency of a small state and limit the costs of marginalization (Haahr 2000). The dilemma was represented by the 50.7 percent majority against the Maastricht Treaty in the June 1992 referendum and the attempts of the Rasmussen government to secure ratification of a compromise treaty package in a second referendum the following year.

Issues of sovereignty and democracy have traditionally cast a shadow over the domestic debate in Sweden. Yet, at the start of the 1990s the Swedish Social Democrat government broke with the past and moved closer to the EC. Prior to accession, the Social Democrat government decided in 1989 to complete the process of capital liberalization, in parallel with the EC's adoption of the same policy. The government "had, in effect, given up on the trade unions' ability to restrain wage formation in a tight, inflationary labor market, and now looked instead for an external anchor for the price system" (Aylott 2000). The announcement the following year that Sweden would be applying for EC accession and ERM entry was seen by some Social Democrat leaders as "sending a clear signal to the parties in the domestic labor market" that they would not be bailed out by devaluation (Aylott 2000). Instead, the private sector would feel the pressure and be more likely to tackle its flagging productivity growth. Both episodes indicate a transition in policy thinking from the traditional neo-Keynesian emphasis on full employment to one of prioritizing price stability. Specifically, its implementation involved a rejection of national solutions to one of seeking an external anchor. This represented a momentous paradigm shift for Sweden. Fiscal discipline was also justified by reference to "Europe." The strongly pro-European ("bourgeois") government of Carl Bildt (1991–1994) sought to curtail the soaring budget deficit in readiness for the EC and EMU entry it advocated. However, the September 1992 ERM crisis hit the Swedish krone hard, and made the ERM seem unsustainable as an external anchor. By the end of 1992, Bildt's coalition and the Social Democrats agreed to rule out entry into the first wave of EMU. There was little alternative if they were to secure support for EU membership in the impending referendum, which was held in 1994. The ERM crisis and the benefits of a looser exchange rate policy had shifted opinion away from EMU. Once inside the EU, the domestic political constraint had hardened and the government postponed its entry into the single currency indefinitely (see below).

The cases surveyed here suggest that the relevance of the *vincolo esterno* in Italy at the time of the negotiations on EMU was exceptional, but not unique. There are parallels evident in Greece, Spain, and France, though the precise context varies. What was distinctive was the attempt of technocratic leaders in each state to impose discipline on errant politicians exerting weak policy leadership. However, those seeking a *vincolo esterno* were neither free agents nor in effective control. For Italy, Spain, and Greece, the strategic opportunity arose from additional factors: the fear of exclusion from a major new step in European integration; a recognition that EMU was consistent with the demands of the wider global economy, to which adjustment was also necessary; and, a calculation that reform of the EMS and then EMU itself was unstoppable. For France, a state that had from the start seen itself as *the* leader of the integration process, the additional fear was one of irretrievably falling behind its powerful neighbor, Germany, and of suffering the economic and monetary costs of its hegemony.

The choice of EMU as a *vincolo esterno* stemmed not only from strategic calculations, but also from a set of policy beliefs, both cognitive and normative. These determined the causal value placed on EMU as a form of external economic discipline to bring about the necessary domestic adjustment. Here, German ordo-liberal values contrasted with the search for credibility and stability on the part of some of her weaker partners and the unique sensitivity of the British and the Danes over sovereignty. France and Italy had made difficult shifts in domestic policy, but the sustainability of these shifts remained uncertain. The critical turn of policy in France amid the currency crisis of March 1983 – when Mitterrand finally chose to keep the franc in the ERM rather than pursue the radical unilateralist option of *"une autre politique"* – came to represent the domestic victory of a set of monetary policy beliefs, identified with the Finance Ministry and the Banque de France. The victory placed France within a wider international policy community upholding "sound money" and its associated disciplines. But, French policy suffered lesser credibility that of Germany. Thus, EMU would overcome this deficit, while also securing the domestic shift. A similar logic was evident in Italy, as the Amato Paper on ERM reform in 1988 made plain. Outside the EC, the shift of policy in Sweden at the start of the 1990s – to seek an external anchor for price stability – also reflected a paradigm shift.

3    **The use of EMU as a *vincolo esterno*: post-Maastricht social models**

The strategic purpose of empowerment from EMU has been exhibited by governments using it as a constraint to promote reforms over the domestic opposition of actors wielding a potential veto. EMU possessed crucial features in this regard: a temporal constraint, as states sought to qualify within a set time-scale; a set of rational benchmarks, with the convergence criteria defining policy targets; pressure to comply, from "peer" governments in ECOFIN and from domestic publics concerned with national pride and "catch-up" with EU partners; a technocratic asymmetry, as state institutions possessed greater information on current trends and, in most cases, a greater expertise on how to manage and interpret policy; a normative foundation, with EMU as the central condition for states being at the core of a "Europe" which often had large residues of public support; and a distinctive type of policy process, as monetary policy was traditionally handled in a relatively closed policy community, seemingly opaque and rarefied to the wider public.

This latter aspect is in striking contrast to the politics of bargaining between government and sectional interests that conventionally marks the policy process when dealing with labor and welfare reform (Bonoli 1997a: 113). In principle, EMU offered state actors a strategic tool the like of which had rarely been provided by an international body. But, as EMU entered the domestic politics of labor and welfare reform, the particular characteristics of the institutional setting and the effectiveness of political leadership would determine its potency as a stimulus to reform. In other words, both structure and agency have to be part of the explanation. The former involves the institutional design of particular provision: for example, Bonoli cites evidence to suggest that Bismarckian pension schemes (constituting the main source of income for their recipients) may encounter greater resistance to reform (as evident in France and Germany) than the reform of state pensions in systems where occupational pensions play a greater role (Britain, Switzerland) (Bonoli 1997a: 114).

As already suggested, simple statements of cause and effect are elusive here. Where time-consistency exists, then the association will be strengthened with evidence of a clear strategy to gain empowerment from EMU in this regard and to use it to provide a justificatory discourse for domestic reform. It may still, however, not be the *prime* lever or rationale: the role of EMU has to be weighed against other impacts.

A brief survey is useful, covering different state types, policy models and EU membership experiences:

### Italy

Given the origins of the term *"vincolo esterno,"* it is appropriate to note that the importance of the EU as a stimulus to domestic reform is often cited. Indeed, Ferrera and Gualmini (1999: 42) have claimed that:

Through an impressive sequence of reforms, this country has been able to put in order its battered public finances, to start an incisive modernization of its backward bureaucratic apparatus, its rigid labor market and its unbalanced welfare state, without jeopardizing social peace nor the overall competitiveness of its economy in the global context. The dynamics of internationalization and, especially of European integration, have been crucial in promoting this qualitative jump in terms of institutional capabilities: indeed, the Italian experience shows that internationalization may well be a solution, instead of a problem.

With respect to pension reform, a series of measures were introduced after 1983, but radical shifts occurred in 1992 (the Amato reform) and in 1995 (the Dini reform), in parallel to the concern about participation in the EMU project. Exogenous pressures, Ferrera and Gualmini argue, have contributed to a "hardening" of the Italian state, in terms of the strengthening of its capabilities (see also Della Sala 1997). This represents a notable shift from the position in the 1980s (Walsh 1994). As elsewhere, concertation with the social partners has been reinforced. More generally, a crucial part of the domestic adaptation has been at the level of learning, both cognitive and sociopolitical, flowing from technocratic and political circles to some sector-specific policy networks and to the social partners. EMU has been a key exogenous pressure stimulating such changes, albeit indirectly and in combination with other indigenous factors (Giuliani 2001), and technocratic communities have been a major conduit in this regard. The Onofri Committee, for example, established by Prodi in 1996, to examine how social spending could support macroeconomic objectives, assigned special importance in its report to the power of EMU to challenge the "protected" interests of the social state (Della Sala, chapter 6 in this volume).

As Della Sala argues, EMU was seen in Italy as a means to political modernization and democratization. Even the Left could embrace the reform momentum of EMU: privatization and pension funds became a means of democratizing the economy and taking power away from closed private interests and political oligarchies. EMU was a crucial trigger to reform of the Italian social state. Moreover, it created opportunities and incentives to political actors across the system, such that few were left to defend the status quo.

### Spain

The relevance of EMU as a *vincolo esterno* is also shown in other southern European states. In Spain, changes to the contributory pension system began in 1985, but reform was started in earnest only in the runup to EMU (the so-called "Toledo Pact" of 1995 signed by the social partners and the PSOE government, and the move to its implementation agreed under the successor conservative government in 1996). In establishing an agreement to limit the cost of the system, the government used EMU as a justification for restricting nonwage labor costs in order to maintain competitiveness in the eurozone. The acceptance of this constraint by all sides meant that a striking consensus was achieved, unlike in France and Italy.

Soon afterwards, a decisive shift towards labor market reform was achieved in Spain by a three-year social pact signed by the UGT (socialist) and CCOO (communist) unions with the CEOE (employers' federation) and CEPYME (small businesses) in 1997.[3] The main thrust of the reform was to reduce the cost of workers on permanent contracts being dismissed, and it was intended to tackle the dualism in the labor market between those on permanent and those on fixed-term contracts. Again, the acceptance of the EMU constraint on labor costs played a major role in easing the reform.

### Greece

In Greece, the connection between EU constraints and domestic adaptation has often been made (Diamandouros 1994; Pagoulatos 1996; Lavdas 1997; Featherstone 1998; Ioakimidis 1998). Moreover, public support for Greek participation in a deepening process of European integration is among the highest to be found in the EU. Against this background, much political capital was invested by Premier Costas Simitis and the Minister of National Economy, Yannos Papantoniou, to have Greece qualify for the single currency by 2001. With the huge fiscal imbalances sustained by the Greek state, the stimulus of EMU to pension reform was evident in the explicit statements of the government. Yet, the stimulus was dissipated by the entrenched opposition of sectoral interests and the strategic weakness of key actors, not least a supportive technocratic community or advocacy coalition (Featherstone, Kazamias, and Papadimitriou 2001). Pension reform has been comparatively slow and modest.

The need for reform has been apparent to many, however. The severe weakness of the Greek economy at the start of the 1990s represented a critical juncture for the Greek state. The clientelistic profligacy of the "party-state" – at new heights under Andreas Papandreou – was confronted by the EMU prospectus, with its tight fiscal policy requirements. The fragmented state pension funds were caught within these conflicting

---

[3] The Pact, entitled "Interconfederal Agreement for Stability of Employment," was agreed in April 1997.

pressures, but also threatened by a demographic "time bomb," as elsewhere. Early reform of the pensions system was limited: a small-scale reform (the Souflias Law) in 1990 was passed as an emergency measure, and a more substantial reform in 1992 was greatly watered-down in the face of stiff union opposition and internal party dissension. The pension problem remained: it sustained gross inequalities of provision and bureaucratic inefficiency, which conflicted with the "modernization" program of the new Socialist Premier, Costas Simitis. The latter soon ordered a report from a technocratic committee, headed by Yiannis Spraos. The need for reform in the context of the EMU entry objective was stressed. Its 1997 report was fiercely opposed by those with vested interests in the status quo. Crucially, government leaders quickly distanced themselves from it and there was little support from relevant policy experts. The gestation of the Spraos Report was closeted, corporatist-type negotiation was absent, no effective advocacy coalition was available to offer support, and union opposition was intense. Reform was postponed. The external empowerment of EMU had been blocked by domestic veto-players and by the political weakness of the technocratic community.

### Belgium

In Belgium – another state with parlous finances during and after the EMU negotiations – EMU has been used as a stimulus to domestic reform. As Pochet (chapter 9 in this volume) notes, political elites in Belgium – perhaps more than their counterparts elsewhere – have long used "Europe" as a pretext to force the adoption of domestic solutions. Already in the 1980s, the discipline of the "hard" ERM had encouraged domestic policy shifts. Pochet argues that EMU was a catalyst for the attempt at signing a new Social Pact after 1990. When these attempts failed, a new Competitiveness Act was adopted, which strictly limited wage increases and, in the name of EMU, imposed controls on collective bargaining. The government also used EMU to justify budget reductions and the reform of the social security system.

### France

In France, shifts in social policy began well before EMU. Pension reform seemed more intractable, however. Between 1985 and 1993, at least seven official reports on the subject were produced making roughly the same recommendations (Bonoli 1997a: 115). The main parties accepted the need for pension reform, but little was done. The Balladur package of 1993 reformed the largest pension scheme, the *régime général*, which covers private sector workers in industry and commerce (Bonoli 1997a: 112). The politics of cohabitation had encouraged a consensual approach. With most recognizing that wider reform was needed, the Juppé Plan of October 1995 was perhaps the most significant proposal for the reform of welfare provision since 1981. The package covered health insurance and healthcare, pensions, and control over spending. The package was hatched from a small technocratic group and presented effectively as a *fait accompli* to interested groups. While not alien to the French state tradition, this approach contrasted with the 1993 reforms and ignored the potential veto-power of major sectional interests. EMU was a crucial stimulus to its origination and timing – given the entry constraint on budget deficits – as both Juppé and Chirac made clear. Indeed, the plan signaled that Chirac was intent on keeping to the EMU timetable (Ross, chapter 4 in this volume; Howarth 2000). The closeted manner of the plan's origination meant that it would have to be sold carefully ("communicative discourse," in Schmidt 2002). However, the normative foundation was weak: Chirac had previously indicated a soft transition to EMU and had seemingly equivocated over the timetable commitment. The public reaction was fierce, with Juppé politically defeated. In sum, EMU had not served as an easy off-the-peg justification and Juppé had proved politically inept. His successor, Jospin, soon sought to change the discourse, by enveloping EMU in a wider agenda of protecting employment.

### Germany

The German case was destined to be the least likely to provide evidence of EMU serving as a lever to domestic social reform. EMU provided opportunities to the social partners: the Deutsche Gewerkschaftsbund (DGB) sought EMU as a means of weakening the Bundesbank, the business community as an opportunity for labor market flexibility and a means of getting rid of an overvalued D-mark. But, the German labor regime was shaped by institutionalized monetarism long before EMU re-appeared, as Siegel argues (chapter 5 in this volume). While the Kohl Government had seen EMU as exporting discipline, these attitudes were turned upside down, of course, when the strains of adjusting to domestic unification led Germany to veer away from meeting the tough convergence criteria it had largely defined earlier. EMU was used after 1996 to justify welfare reforms and cuts. Now ordo-liberals, like Otmar Issing of the Bundesbank in 1996, called for the disciplinary effect of EMU to be preserved, as did Wolfgang Schäuble, the CDU parliamentary leader, the following year. The key point is that unification initiated the reform pressure, while EMU amplified the stress emanating from unification by defining a budget constraint.

### The Netherlands

The link between EMU and social reform is even more distant in the case of the Netherlands. Here, welfare state reform and economic liberalization were under way well in advance of EMU (de Beus, chapter 8 in this volume). "Europe" has seldom been seen as a prime stimulus to domestic reform and EMU has played no significant part in the justificatory discourse for recent social reform. The consociationalism associated with the "*Polder* model" (of social and economic liberalism) has been strengthened independent of EMU.

### Denmark

The scope for domestic leverage from supranational commitments has been minimal in Denmark, given public opposition to supranationalism. This opposition has prevented Denmark from adopting the single currency thus far, though policy-makers have had little difficulty in following the disciplines associated with the SGP for sound finances. A long-term concern in Denmark has been the narrowness of the EMU project: sustaining employment should be of equal importance to price stability and a sub-committee of ECOFIN was suggested with a remit to secure this. Of more relevance than EMU as a stimulus to domestic retrenchment of welfare benefits has been the Danish concern about a more general EU threat to her existing high levels of provision. Thus, despite wider concerns on sovereignty, the Social Democrats pressed for majority decision-making in the Council of Ministers on "social conditions," as well as environmental protection and health, with a view to "leveling-up" standards (Haahr 2000).

### Sweden

Further contrasts may be sought from the Nordic states that joined the EU *after* the EMU agreement had been reached. Again, the domestic context is different here with respect to the development and support for distinctive national models of labor and welfare policy.

In Sweden, at the start of the 1990s, the decision to seek EC entry (allied to capital liberalization and ERM participation) had been used as an external anchor to better secure price stability and revive labor productivity. After accession, however, domestic political conditions had changed and this ruled out the option of using EMU entry as a pretext for further policy shifts. Divisions within the ruling Social Democrat party (SAP), a change in the latter's relations within the party system, and opposition from the grass-roots provided a clear party political obstacle to any direct attempt at external leverage via EMU (Aylott 2000). The Persson government postponed a decision on participation in the single currency, fearing the domestic political cost. The decision also goes with the grain, however, of the belief in sovereignty and democracy, so deep-rooted in the Swedish social democratic project of "welfare nationalism" (Elvander 1994, noted in Pekkarinen 2000). In particular, the traditional belief in *folkstyre* ("popular steering") is the polar opposite of the *vincolo esterno* logic.

### Finland

There is an interesting contrast here with the case of Finland, a country that has often seemed to follow the lead of Sweden but which decided to diverge from it and join the first wave of states to adopt the Euro. Finland had followed Sweden in applying for EU membership in March 1992 and the level of public support for EMU was very similar in both countries. Yet domestic conditions in Finland soon diverged from those of Sweden: the party system constraint was more conducive to EMU entry; in particular, the Social Democrat leadership was firm and consistent in its pro-European line; public opinion was more tolerant of elite leadership; and, significantly, the Markka remained outside the ERM until just before Finland's first European elections in October 1996. The political discourse more readily accepted that EMU membership meant that Finland would be at the EU's "core," a condition felt to be very much in her security interest (Pekkarinen 2000). Paavo Lipponen, the Prime Minister, also warned that necessary economic reforms, including those to domestic labor markets, would have to be more severe if made outside EMU.

Moreover, economic conditions in Finland were markedly different: the Finnish model of social corporatism had traditionally prioritized supply-side economics to maintain export competitiveness (over and above Keynesian demand management); this had not overcome high levels of cyclical volatility (historically, a consequence of the undiversified structure of the economy); indeed, the experience of the economic depression of the early 1990s – the deepest of the twentieth century for Finland, prompting some of the deepest cuts in public spending found anywhere in Western Europe (Pakaslahti 1997) – had questioned the value of monetary policy autonomy; and, added to this, the recognition of the instability that existed with speculative capital flows in a deregulated financial market led to the conclusion that Finland needed to be tied to a large currency area and single currency, in order for it to sustain monetary stability (Pekkarinen 2000). Consistent with this logic, EMU was seen as offering, *inter alia*, a stable anchor for "responsible" wage bargaining. By contrast to Sweden, the logic was to see EMU as part of a necessary process of wider external adaptation, rather than as a block to *folkstyre*.

The cases briefly surveyed here provide contrasted evidence with respect to the use of EMU (after Maastricht) as a stimulus to the reform of domestic social models. There is some consistency in the timing of the EMU entry constraint and reform initiatives in the cases of Italy, Spain, Greece, Belgium, and France. However, in Germany, the EMU constraint became relevant rather late and reinforced that stemming from German unification. In Sweden, early reforms were linked to EU entry but then public sensitivities and changing conditions in the party system led to a postponement of EMU participation and it thus became less relevant as a lever. In Finland, EU and EMU entry were seen as tied together; both received support, but there is little evidence of EMU being exploited as a separate stimulus to reform. In the Dutch case, social reform and EMU appear as independent processes with little time-consistency between them. In Denmark, public sensitivity on national sovereignty greatly limited the scope for stimulating domestic reforms in the name of "Europe." A loose geographical division between the national cases may exist, rooted in setting and perhaps fiscal condition.

In Italy, Spain, Greece, Belgium, and France political leaders made an explicit link between social reform and EMU. Clear attempts at blame-shifting were evident, in order to overcome likely domestic opposition. However, in the cases of Greece and France the implementation of reform faced severe domestic opposition. In Greece, pension reform was thwarted in 1997 by the strength of union protests and the alarm of those with vested interests in the status quo, the caution of a government facing new elections, and the weakness of anything akin to a technocratic advocacy coalition or policy community to support reform. Pension reform was shelved, and the government relied on other means to EMU entry. Yet, all knew that wide-ranging pension reform had to come soon. In France, the public protests against pension and welfare reform in 1995 were even stronger. Chirac was humbled, Juppé soon brought down. Paradoxically, however, much of the original Juppé package was implemented, despite the political protests. The difference of outcome between France and Greece may be explained by reference to a "strong" state/"weak" state contrast. In France, however, technocratic policy innovators in different networks were rather more prominent in the reform process than in Greece, making it stronger. In Greece, such innovators were swamped by the clientelistic "party-state" culture and lacked sufficient profile and autonomy.

Pochet (chapter 9 in this volume) identifies two main effects of EMU: elite empowerment and "technocratization." First, EMU facilitated a new type of political leadership, based on the prime minister, the central bank and the leader of the Christian trade union acting in concert to steer adaptation and weaken domestic opposition. Secondly, EMU became a smokescreen, shifting the discourse in a more technocratic direction. Pochet cites Denayer's (1996) observation that changes were being imposed from outside, with the domestic objectives of reform being hidden, and debate being depoliticized. A "benchmarking" system was established by which decisions on wages and welfare were to be made by reference to an external standard: defined in terms of the performance of the Dutch, French, and German economies. The policy style has thus changed: a new kind of technocratic rationality has entered the space previously dominated by the pillars of the party system and regional communities.[4] The Belgian case suggests a further effect of EMU as a domestic lever: that on the pattern of relations existing between the social partners. In Belgium, according to Pochet, EMU gave an additional and significant stimulus to the state's role in a developing tri-partite management of the labor market. The Federal level enjoyed a rare boost. This has not been a process of centralization so much as one of the development of a structured dialog respecting a hierarchy of tasks. An important aspect of this structure is the proliferation of semi-independent expert bodies. A network of reports makes the debate more technocratic and rational.

In the Spanish case, EMU has been linked to a re-centralization of the wage-bargaining process with the social pact of April 1997 (Pérez, chapter 7 in this volume). This included a re-structuring of the collective bargaining system, expanding the role of national–sectoral bargains, while leaving lesser issues to be settled by lower bargaining units. The shift to centralization contrasted with a 1994 law, which had given an impetus to decentralized bargaining. National bargaining was seen as a crucial adjustment mechanism for EMU, to maintain competitiveness. EMU has thus strengthened "corporatist" tendencies, though its effect was to reinforce a wider transformation already evident domestically.

The re-centralization of bargaining is not unique to Spain. The Spanish agreement of 1997 closely resembled the 1993 agreement on collective bargaining reform reached between government, employers and unions

---

[4] I am grateful for comments on this point from Philippe Pochet.

in Italy (Pérez, chapter 7 in this volume; Pérez 2000a). Both agreements attributed distinct roles to different levels of bargaining, with the purpose of achieving greater national coordination, though in the Spanish case such changes were not mandated, given the confederal nature of the employers' organization. The philosophy behind the agreement showed some consistency with the Belgian shift to a more structured dialog.

It would be misleading to suggest that the adjustment to EMU has deepened conflict between social actors and led to more adversarial policy styles. The case of the Juppé Plan of 1995 elicited severe reactions and mass protests. Yet, in Spain the Toledo Pact of 1995 and the 1996 agreement on pension reform were reached without any of the bitter confrontations that accompanied similar efforts in Italy and France, and a strong consensus marked the changes made in labor regulation and collective bargaining (Pérez, chapter 7 in this volume). Moreover, in existing consociational systems, such as in the Netherlands, EMU-related changes have not disturbed the domestic tradition of social bargaining, rather they have been enveloped by it. In short, there is no simple relationship here between consensus-formation in small states in the face of external challenge (as Lijphart 1973 suggested) – the Greek and Spanish cases are polar opposites here – nor one of a core–periphery contrast, given the protests in both France and Italy.

## 4     Conclusions

This brief survey can be seen as a study of "Europeanization," linking EMU obligations to domestic politics, as both a strategic tool and a cognitive resource (Featherstone and Radaelli 2003). The *vincolo esterno* may be deployed as a ("narrow") instrumental means to overcome vetopoints and to create a different political "opportunity structure" (Knill and Lehmkuhl 1999). A broader usage involves domestic elites "internalizing" the norms and values of EU policies. Both usages are to be seen in their institutional context: circumscribed by the existing policy regimes (regulatory and institutional conditions), prevailing policy beliefs, patterns of interest mediation (such as neo-corporatist concertation), party competition and interests, and public attitudes to reform. Though analytically useful, in practice the distinction between "strategic usage" and "norm shift" can be blurred (Checkel 1997, 1999).

The instrumental use of EMU as a *vincolo esterno* is a more likely strategy in those states that have not fully "internalized" the norms and values associated with the "sound money, sound finances" paradigm of EMU. Moreover, the need for such usage is greater in those states that are most divergent from the convergence criteria (and the later SGP), but in which key actors are committed to fulfilling European obligations. Such conditions create an opportunity structure for actors to exploit EMU as a *vincolo esterno*. Moreover, institutional structures and routines with strong domestic roots prevent easy adaptation to exogenous pressures (March and Olsen 1989; Di Maggio and Powell 1991b). In Denmark and Sweden there was a further resistance – in the form of a sensitivity about sovereignty and the defence of existing policy models – to the use of EMU as a domestic lever.

The strength of the *vincolo esterno* for domestic actors is affected by the form the European policy takes: EMU was an indirect pressure on social models, allowing much discretion to be determined by political competition. Thus, EMU encouraged a reform *direction*: it did not determine the choice or content. Moreover, the relative importance of EMU as a stimulus to reform has clearly varied between states.

The utility of EMU as a *vincolo esterno* for domestic reform is circumscribed by both structure and agency, which are mutually defining. The relevance of the institutional setting, and in particular the number of veto-points, is a clear structural constraint on "reform-capacity" (Héritier and Knill 2000). Yet, reform momentum also needs leadership: either as agents pursuing strategic interests with a view to re-structuring domestic power, and/or as "norm entrepreneurs" helping to shift the prevailing beliefs in a particular direction (Börzel and Risse 2000). Advocacy coalitions or policy networks may strengthen political leadership and establish reform-capacity (Sabatier 1998). It was the relative absence of such phenomena that helped to explain why the attempt at pension reform failed in Greece, but succeeded in Italy. But an "integrated political leadership" (Héritier and Knill 2000) may also be provided by the form of social mediation – for example, a corporatist consensus helped to deliver pension and labor reform in Spain – and by consociational party systems that share consociational characteristics – as in the Nordic states, albeit with different outcomes on the EU and EMU.

A long-term contrast is evident in the domestic usage of EMU between two groups of states. The first is composed of Italy, Greece, Spain, Belgium, and France; the second by Germany, the Netherlands, Denmark, Sweden, and Finland. The contrast is broadly a north–south one, and the political opportunity structure to exploit EMU as a *vincolo esterno* appears linked to the pattern of domestic political development. To southern states, EMU was perceived as a stimulus to "modernization". In the early phase of EMU, technocratic leadership in Italy, Greece, Spain, and France sought to use it as a lever to domestic reform, curtailing the indiscipline and clientelism of party politicians. The strength of EMU as a *vincolo esterno* in southern states is reinforced by a self-imposed political constraint: the fear of exclusion from the EU's "core," in the context of a rapidly deepening and widening integration process. Mass publics seek that their states remain full EU members: political leaders are expected to deliver this objective. Yet, EMU had the potential to reinforce cleavages in these states based on contested notions of "modernization" (Diamandouros 1994; Featherstone 1998), with traditional "internal protectionism" confronting modern "external liberalism." EMU was a critical juncture in the political development of the south. In some states, such as Italy, the response to EMU reflected the existence of the "institutional stabilizers" of a new macroeconomic regime underscored by technocratic elites, accelerated policy learning, and new styles of policy-making (Ferrera and Gualmini 1999: 43). In Greece and Portugal, the shift of policy regime seemed less secure.

The general impact of EMU on domestic social models across the EU remains unclear. The opportunity to use EMU to secure strategic interests and/or promote shifts of policy ideas is clearly linked to the type of conditions prevailing within domestic settings. EMU as a *vincolo esterno* is tied to the pattern of political development and state tradition; the compatibility of appropriate policy beliefs; support for "Europe"; the record of economic discipline; and the will and capability of actors to engineer compliance. These conditions are distinct and are most closely associated with "Latin" and southern Europe. The enlargement of the EU in 2004 will provide a new test for the *vincolo esterno*. Moreover, the nature of EU policy commitments is becoming more differentiated – from conventional EU directives to the shared learning and policy pressures of the Open Method of Coordination (OMC) – and these are likely to strengthen asymmetries across states and sectors, differentiating the game of EU politics.

# 11 Welfare reform in the shadow of EMU

*Anton Hemerijck and Maurizio Ferrera*

## 1 A welfare state world of path-dependent, but not predetermined, solutions

Since the 1980s European monetary integration has been a driving force behind domestic welfare reform across the European Union (EU). Triggered by the failure of Keynesianism in the 1970s and by macroeconomic instability in the 1980s and early 1990s, monetary integration to EMU marks a sea-change in macroeconomic policy. It has indirect effects on labor market institutions (Franzese, Jr., and Hall 2000) as well as direct effects on domestic budgetary and fiscal policy that have major implications for social policy. It means that macroeconomic policy can no longer shield labor market institutions and social protection arrangements from the need to adjust to international competition. With nominal exchange rate adjustments ruled out and fiscal stimulation greatly constrained by the Stability and Growth Pact (SGP), policy-makers must seek national solutions within the heart of European social models. Monetary integration is not the only driving force behind welfare state reform, however. Internal dynamics like aging populations, de-industrialization, changing gender roles in labor markets and households, and new technologies place severe strains on welfare state programs designed for a previous era (Daly 2000; Pierson 2001a). Such endogenous social and economic challenges are all aspects of post-industrial change (Esping-Andersen *et al.* 2001).

Recent comparative research shows convincingly the extent to which most EU welfare states have recast the policy mix of the national systems of industrial relations and social protection built after 1945 (Scharpf and Schmidt 2000). In the 1970s, stagflation stimulated adjustment in macroeconomic management, wage-bargaining to mitigate distributive conflict, and limits to spiraling cost-push inflation and demand-gap increases in unemployment. Since the early 1980s, movement to harder currencies refocused attention on competitiveness, bringing a decisive shift towards supply-side measures, especially in employment policy. Along with deregulating labor markets, many mature welfare states tried to contain open unemployment by reducing labor supply, mainly through early retirement and disability pensions (Ebbinghaus 2000). The destabilizing consequences of large-scale early retirement and other forms of paid inactivity then became major policy problems in the 1990s, when transition to EMU limited deficit and debt financing. In the wake of the Maastricht Treaty, policy-makers became more willing to adopt cost-containment measures, often connected to a shift from passive compensation of social risks to the active promotion of employability. The institutional makeup of social insurance administrations also became a reform target. Strong interdependencies among the different policy areas of macroeconomic management, employment regulation, and social protection that make up mature welfare states thus unleashed a process of sequential policy adjustment and created a chain of unintended consequences as changes in one policy area spilled over to others (Hemerijck and Schludi 2000). Ultimately, substantive adjustments in macroeconomic policy produced ground-breaking changes in social and economic policy.

Critics have often portrayed EMU as a "Trojan horse" for a full-fledged neo-liberal policy shift that will erode the underpinnings of the European social model (McNamara 1998). Many believe that EMU, given its restrictive mandate, will reinforce low growth and high unemployment and thus increase pressures on welfare financing. Some even argue that EMU could undermine Europe's growth potential by triggering a vicious cycle of deflationary "beggar-thy-neighbor" strategies of internal devaluation through social dumping and competitive wage moderation. In these perspectives, EMU, like the single market, will greatly constrain the viability of Europe's mature welfare states. Applying the basic tenets of political institutionalism, we take issue with such unilinear conjectures, however. The European social model is built around a solidaristic commitment that society should not abandon those who fail (Schmidt 2000). Institutionally, the model is marked by high degrees of interest organization and comprehensive negotiation between governments and social partners over conflicts of interests. Patterns of social partnership based on trust encourage concerted problem-solving and give collective actors the necessary social capital to overcome particularistic interests (Swank 2001). Based on the recognition that social justice can contribute to economic efficiency and progress, the European social model is further marked by "beneficial constraints" (Streeck 1992) through which social policy can reduce uncertainty, mitigate social conflict, and enhance adjustment capacity and readiness to accept change, bear more risks, acquire more specialized skills, and pursue investment opportunities. This line of reasoning refuses contradictions and large trade-offs among economic competitiveness, social cohesion, and political stability (Streeck 1992). In general, a world of path-dependent solutions practically rules out radical change in Europe's welfare states (Pierson 1996, 2001a).

It is thus no easy task to destroy the normative, institutional, and cognitive underpinnings of the European social model. In the neo-liberal 1980s it was extremely difficult to launch successful attacks on the mature welfare states of Western Europe (Pierson 2001a), and in the 1990s citizen disenchantment with neo-liberal recipes fueled political reversals and a resurgence of social democracy in which voter reaction against the social costs of widening wage disparity and rising poverty revealed deep popular commitment to the European social model. The effects of monetary integration – intended or unintended – are thus unlikely to establish a fully-fledged neo-liberal model of completely deregulated labor markets with low standards of poverty protection. Europeans have recognized that social protection is more than expensive charity and that it need not undermine long-term competitiveness.

The chapters in this volume show that the social and employment policy reforms since the 1980s have rarely followed textbook neo-liberal outlines. The impact of EMU on social and employment policy is a case in point. Those architects of EMU and the Single Act (SEA) who believed that the new economic environment would trigger massive structural reforms in product markets, labor markets, collective bargaining systems, social protection programs, and welfare financing, therefore eliminating supply-side rigidities, have been greatly disappointed. To be sure, center-left parties, in office during the runup to Stage Three of EMU, could no longer aspire to social justice and full employment through expansionary demand-side policies and were instead forced in more painful policy directions. As Dølvik (chapter 12 in this volume) shows, governments forged novel agreements with the social partners, reminiscent of corporatist exchanges between the trade unions and employers' organizations in the 1970s (see also Fajertag and Pochet 2000; Rhodes 2001).

Until the launch of the SEM and EMU, European integration was largely shaped by business interests. A narrow understanding of the principle of subsidiarity left labor interests to individual member states. "Negative," market-making integration thus prevailed over "positive," market-correcting integration, challenging the viability of the welfare state (Scharpf 1999). Paradoxically, EMU has changed all this. The ultimate goal of Europe's internationally oriented business class, EMU had to be endorsed by national parliaments, and by the 1990s social and employment policy issues had begun to find their ways onto the European agenda. Moreover, despite welfare reforms in member states, persistently high levels of unemployment opened a debate on common European strategies to promote employment and social inclusion. Finally, with a shift to the center-left in the balance of political power across the EU, a number of important breakthroughs contributed to a building and deepening of social Europe.

Acknowledging domestic welfare reform and European social policy innovation is not to claim that Europe, prodded by monetary integration, has achieved a novel effective policy mix for sustainable economic growth, price stability, high levels of employment, and generous standards of social protection and income redistribution. The current mix of a fully European monetary policy and national fiscal policy, subject to the constraints of the SGP, is far from optimal. With employment and social policy commitments firmly anchored in diverse national traditions and institutions, minimally bolstered by light institutional procedures of open coordination, a unified interest rate is likely to create different effects, including divergent inflationary and deflationary pressures, to which the ECB can respond only on the basis of average conditions. Recessions are therefore likely to produce political tensions between national governments and the ECB, especially after the enlargement of the EU to Central and Eastern European (CEE) countries. The SGP could also in the long run be wholly inappropriate for managing long-term shifts in public finances to address the needs of an aging population.

The profound social policy changes made to national welfare states and the European-level initiatives in employment and social policy do, however, have a distinctly "European" character. Arguments that the welfare state has retreated in the shadow of EMU do not stand up under available evidence. Instead, ongoing reform remains deeply seated in normative notions of equity and solidarity, cognitive understandings of the efficiency-enhancing effects of social policy, and institutional preferences for negotiated policy change rather than hierarchical imposition. The result has been a highly dynamic process of "self-transformation of the European social model(s)" (Hemerijck 2002), marked not by retrenchment but by more comprehensive trajectories of "recalibration" (Ferrera, Hemerijck, and Rhodes 2000). In addition, by the end of this story it could be that there are three rather than the two streams of politics that chapter 1 in this volume maintains. Beyond intergovernmental dealings (Dyson and Featherstone 1999) and domestic reconfiguring of welfare state programs and industrial relations arrangements (Scharpf and Schmidt 2000), a supranational, EU-level, stream may be emerging that seeks to establish social and employment policy commitments, procedures, and institutions (Ferrera, Hemerijck, and Rhodes 2000). Indeed, it may be that, social policy is no longer the stepchild of European integration (Lange 1993).

## 2    The fine structures of the European social model

The European social model is too often seen as a homogeneous entity transcending national boundaries. The welfare states of the EU share features that set them apart from those in other geo-political regions, such as North America, but they also display substantial differences in development, policy design, and institutional makeup along the following dimensions (Esping-Andersen 1990; Ferrera 1998; Ferrera, Hemerijck, and Rhodes 2000; Ferrera and Rhodes 2000; Scharpf and Schmidt 2000):

- *Eligibility and risk coverage*    Access to provisions of social protection can be based on citizenship, need, work-related contributions, or private contracts.
- *Benefit structure and generosity*    Benefits can be generous or minimal, means-tested, flat-rate, earnings-related, or contribution-related. Benefit structure is also related to country-specific objectives of social protection: income maintenance, poverty alleviation, or equality.
- *Methods of financing*    Financing can encompass general taxation, payroll contributions, and user charges, or some combination thereof.
- *Service intensity*    Social services can be provided through professional (public) services, through the market, or informally by the (extended) family.
- *Family policy*    Family policy can be passive, with an emphasis on cash transfers in support of traditional, single-breadwinner family patterns, or very active, with support for gender equality within and outside households and an emphasis on service through public daycare and generous parental leave.
- *Logic of governance*    Management of welfare and employment policy does not necessarily fall within the jurisdiction of national public administration. Of special importance is local administration and the degree of extra-parliamentary institutional integration of the social partners (representatives of employers and employees) and private or third-sector parties in management and delivery.

The rich literature on welfare models has shown that these variables are systematically related to one another, producing distinctive, but not exclusive, clusters of nations in "social Europes" (Ferrera, Hemerijck, and Rhodes 2000; Ferrera and Hemerijck 2002) including a Scandinavian model, continental regimes, Southern European regimes and the Anglo-Saxon model.

In the comprehensive Scandinavian welfare states, including the EU member states of Denmark, Finland, and Sweden, social protection is a citizen's right, coverage is fully universal, and everyone is entitled to the same basic guarantees. Besides generous replacement rates, the Nordic systems offer a wide array of public social services beyond health and education, together with active labor market programs that encourage and sustain gender egalitarianism and high levels of female participation in the labor market. Public employment is also extensive. General taxation plays a dominant, though not exclusive, role in financing the welfare state, making taxing and spending levels high by international standards, especially in Sweden. Public assistance plays a circumscribed, residual, and supplementary role. The various functions of social protection are highly integrated, and the provision of benefits and services is mainly the responsibility of central and local public authorities. In fiscal and monetary policy, Scandinavian welfare states originally featured a strong commitment to full employment.

The continental European model includes Austria, Germany, France, and the Benelux countries. Here the Bismarckian tradition, based on a tight link between work position (and/or family status) and social entitlements, is characterized by occupationally distinct, employment-related social insurance, normatively supported by traditional (single-breadwinner) family values (Kersbergen 1995).[1] Benefit formulae proportional to earnings and financing through social security contributions largely reflect the logic of insurance, though not in a strict actuarial sense, with different rules for different professional groups. Replacement rates are generous, benefit duration is very long, and coverage is highly inclusive, if fragmented. Spending and taxing levels are therefore high as well. The institutional structure of Bismarckian welfare states reflects their occupational basis: trade unions, employer associations, and "third sectors" actively participate in governing the insurance schemes. Most of the population is covered through individual or derived rights. Insurance obligations are triggered automatically at the beginning of a gainful job, although Germany and Austria require a minimum earning threshold, and those who fail to meet it can fall back on fairly substantial social assistance. The Bismarckian design is congruent with modest public social services beyond health and education. Except perhaps for France, the continental welfare states have been more committed to a hard-currency macroeconomic policy.

The Southern European model, comprising Italy, Spain, Portugal, and Greece, resembles the continental model, with a number of common

---

[1] Only the Netherlands has modified this tradition by providing a basic public pension.

institutional traits that set them somewhat apart (Ferrera 1996). Their coverage reflects a mixed orientation, Bismarckian in income transfers, with especially generous pension formulas, but Beveridgean in health-care, with fully universal national health services only in Italy and Spain. The safety net beneath social insurance is not well developed. Occupational funds and the social partners play a prominent role in income maintenance policy. Social charges are widely used (causing some of the "traps" typical of continental Europe), but general taxation is gradually replacing them in financing social services. The family is still highly important in Southern Europe and acts largely as a welfare "broker" for its members, with particularly adverse implications for women's position (Esping-Andersen 1999). Inadequate administrative capacities reinforce poor social policy implementation and patterns of clientelism. Macroeconomic policy reveals strong preferences for a soft currency, especially in Italy and less so in Spain.

The Anglo-Saxon model, found in the UK and Ireland, is guided by utilitarian market principles, with social protection that is highly inclusive though not fully universal, except for healthcare. Benefits – which are flat rate – are modest, with social protection reflecting an emphasis on targeted, needs-based, means-tested entitlements with low replacement rates. Healthcare and social services are financed through general taxation, but contributions play an important role in financing cash benefits, especially pensions. Both public social services and family services are underdeveloped. The UK and Ireland lack active labor market policies and vocational training and education. As in Scandinavia, however, the organizational framework of the welfare state (including unemployment insurance) is highly integrated and entirely managed by public administration, with the social partners only marginally involved in policy-making and management. In the UK in particular, macroeconomic policy has historically shown a tendency toward "stop–go" decision-making.

Tables 11.1 and 11.2 suggest that differences in policy design are closely related to variations in economic development and employment performance, service intensity, levels of income inequality, and structures of taxation (Ferrera, Hemerijck, and Rhodes 2000; Hemerijck and Schludi 2000; Hemerijck 2002). European welfare regimes vary widely in their levels of social protection expenditure and total taxation, with the Nordic and continental countries ranking high and the Anglo-Saxon and Southern European countries low. The Nordic countries are by far the most generous welfare states in Europe, paid for by high taxation. The continental countries hold an intermediate position, closely followed by Southern Europe, and then by Anglo-Saxon countries, which have the lowest overall levels of taxation. The Scandinavian welfare state is also

Table 11.1 *Levels of social security, active labor market policy, and collective bargaining coverage in the EU*

| | Social expenditures as percentage of GDP[a] | Total taxation[b] | Old-age and survivors' as percentage of GDP[a] | Family/children as percentage of GDP[a] | Social exclusion[c] 1995 | Active labor market policy[d] | Labor market training[e] | Coverage collective wage bargain[f] |
|---|---|---|---|---|---|---|---|---|
| Denmark | 30.0 | 52.2 | 11.49 | 3.90 | 1.1 | 2.01 | 0.48 | 0.52 |
| Finland | 27.2 | 47.3 | 9.38 | 3.48 | 0.4 | 1.66 | 0.21 | 0.67 |
| Sweden | 33.3 | 53.3 | 13.12 | 3.60 | 0.1 | 0.87 | 0.28 | 0.72 |
| Austria | 28.4 | 44.4 | 13.69 | 2.84 | 1.5 | 1.89 | 1.07 | 0.97 |
| Belgium | 27.5 | 46.5 | 11.77 | 2.34 | 0.7 | 1.23 | 0.41 | 0.82 |
| France | 30.5 | 46.1 | 13.42 | 2.99 | 0.3 | 0.42 | 0.09 | 0.75 |
| Germany | 29.3 | 37.5[c] | 12.69 | 3.03 | 0.3 | 0.44 | 0.15 | 0.80 |
| Greece | 24.5 | 40.6 | 12.89 | 1.98 | 0.7 | 1.29 | 0.29 | – |
| Italy | 25.2 | 45.0 | 16.13 | 0.91 | 0.6 | 1.27 | 0.34 | – |
| Luxembourg | 24.1 | – | 10.65 | 3.40 | 0.4 | 0.30 | 0.01 | – |
| Netherlands | 28.5 | 43.3 | 11.71 | 1.28 | 0.7 | 1.76 | 0.22 | 0.79 |
| Portugal | 23.4 | 34.5 | 9.99 | 1.24 | – | 0.35 | 0.06 | 0.80 |
| Spain | 21.6 | 35.3 | 9.96 | 0.45 | 0.0 | 1.08 | 0.01 | 0.67 |
| Ireland | 16.1 | 34.8 | 4.01 | 2.04 | 0.5 | 1.37 | 0.35 | – |
| United Kingdom | 26.8 | 35.3 | 11.77 | 2.30 | 0.1 | 0.72 | 0.21 | 0.35 |
| Average | 27.7 | 42.6 | 12.66 | 2.30 | 0.5 | 1.1 | 0.27 | |

*Notes:*
[a] 1998.
[b] 1997.
[c] 1996.
[d] 1995, workers covered, figures not including Greece, Italy, Luxembourg, and Ireland.
[e] 1995 data, or latest year available.

*Sources:* [a] "Statistics in Focus: Social Protection in Europe," Theme 3-15/2000 (European Commission 2000b).
[b] OECD (1999), own calculations.
[c] EC (there may be some overlap with other categories of expenditure).
[f] Ebbinghaus and Visser (2000).

Table 11.2 *Employment performance in the EU, 2000*

| | Employment rate[a] | Unemployment rate[b] | Long-term unemployment[c] | Female employment rate | Youth unemployment rate[e] | Activity rate, men aged 55–64 | Public employment ratios[d] |
|---|---|---|---|---|---|---|---|
| Denmark | 76.3 | 4.7 | 1.0 | 71.6 | 5.3 | 55.7 | 22.7 |
| Finland | 67.5 | 9.8 | 2.8 | 64.4 | 11.2 | 42.0 | 14.6 |
| Sweden | 73.0 | 5.9 | 1.3 | 71.0 | 5.5 | 64.4 | 21.9 |
| Austria | 68.3 | 3.7 | 1.0 | 59.4 | 2.9 | 28.8 | 10.0 |
| Belgium | 60.5 | 7.0 | 3.8 | 51.5 | 6.5 | 26.3 | 10.3 |
| France | 62.2[f] | 9.5 | 3.8 | 55.3[f] | 7.1 | 30.3 | 14.5 |
| Germany | 65.4[f] | 7.9 | 4.0 | 57.9[f] | 4.6 | 37.5 | 9.3 |
| Greece | 55.6[f] | 11.1 | – | 40.9[f] | – | 38.6 | 6.9 |
| Italy | 53.5 | 10.5 | 6.4 | 39.6 | 11.8 | 27.7 | 8.9 |
| Luxembourg | 62.9[f] | 2.4 | 0.6 | 50.3[f] | 2.5 | 26.7 | – |
| Netherlands | 73.2[f] | 2.7 | 0.8 | 63.7[f] | 3.6 | 38.2 | 6.8 |
| Portugal | 68.3 | 4.2 | 1.7 | 60.3 | 4.2 | 51.0 | 12.0 |
| Spain | 55.0 | 14.1 | 5.9 | 40.3 | 11.4 | 36.8 | 7.5 |
| Ireland | 65.1 | 4.2 | 1.7 | 54.0 | 3.3 | 45.3 | 9.3 |
| UK | 71.2 | 5.5 | 1.5 | 64.6 | 8.3 | 61.7 | 9.5 |
| EU-15 | 63.3 | 8.2 | 3.6 | 54.0[f] | 7.8 | 37.8[f] | 11.7 |

*Notes:*

[a] Total employment/population 15–64 years.

[b] Standardized ratio.

[c] Long-term unemployed (twelve months and over) as percentage of labor force.

[d] Percentage of population 15–24, 1998.

[e] Unemployed as percentage of population aged 15–24.

[f] Eurostat estimation.

*Source: Employment in Europe* (2000), European Commission (2000a); OECD (1999a) (public employment figures).

a large employer, especially for women in the social services sector. The Nordic countries thus spend almost twice as much on family services as the average among continental and Anglo-Saxon countries and three times as much as some Southern European countries. Scandinavian welfare states devote large financial resources to active labor market policies and training programs, with Sweden and Denmark again in the leading positions. The continental welfare states, however, are catching up, and Ireland is now far more enthusiastic about active labor market policies than Great Britain. The Southern countries again trail the continental welfare states, except in providing pensions. Social security systems in Mediterranean countries are "pension heavy," with Italy spending 16.1 percent of its GDP, about two-thirds of total social expenditures, on pensions, and other Southern European countries spending about half their social budgets on pension provision.

In overall levels of employment, female employment, public employment, and unemployment, the Nordic countries outperform the Anglo-Saxon and continental models of welfare (see table 11.2). The Anglo-Saxon countries have favorable levels of employment with relatively low rates of public employment, with exceptionally low rates of female employment in Ireland. The continental countries take the middle ground, while low levels of employment are evident in Southern Europe, especially among women and elderly workers (Portugal is the exception).

## 3    Regime-specific problems and pressures

A combination of fiscal constraints largely derived from monetary integration, liberalized capital markets, and post-industrial challenges confronts mature welfare states with thorny policy dilemmas. Some argue that with full monetary integration tax competition will intensify, leading to an underprovision of welfare protection and services (Ganghoff 2000; Genschel 2001). To attract and preserve capital, some countries will then be pressed to provide advantageous taxation and/or regulation for internationally mobile firms (Steinmo 1996; Le Cacheux 2000). Others will follow, lowering levels of taxation and jeopardizing current standards of social protection. At the same time, international competition and rapid technological change will drive up productivity and skill requirements in exposed sectors, so that employment growth will favor medium- and high-skilled jobs, while low-skilled employment will shrink (Wood 1994; Drèze and Sneessens 1997). Job loss in exposed sectors can be offset by employment gains in sheltered service sectors, but public employment will remain stagnant largely because of fiscal constraints associated with monetary integration and EMU. Job opportunities in private social services are on the rise, but their growth will be constrained by welfare state regulation of private provision. Employment opportunities for the less skilled are thus doubly constrained. Growth in well-paid public sector jobs will be stagnant while growth in private services is limited by prevailing levels of social protection, high minimum wages, and the high tax wedge derived from heavy payroll contributions or general taxation (Scharpf 1997b, 2000; Iversen and Wren 1998).

Evidence suggests that tax competition has so far been limited. Europe has seen no decrease in total taxation levels and little indication of a tax shift from mobile to immobile factors. Data show that while property and consumption taxes have declined, corporate taxes have gone up, leading some to conclude that there is no significant pressure on taxation (Garrett 1998; Swank 2001). This may be misleading, however, because increasing unemployment, rising poverty, expanding pensions and healthcare costs could be expected to increase taxes while during the 1980s most welfare states turned instead to deficit spending, suggesting that tax competition led instead to deficit financing. Total tax revenues as well as tax ratios appear "frozen" since the mid-1970s, suggesting downward pressure on taxation. The evidence does not indicate a "race to the bottom," however, nor does it show that immobile tax bases are immune from tax base erosion. Higher taxes on labor increase wage costs for employers and decrease labor demand, especially in an open, competitive economy. In addition, high taxes on labor generate incentives to engage in the underground economy (Genschel 2001).

Common pressures on macroeconomic policy and labor markets generate distinctive problems in different welfare systems. Scandinavian welfare states have expensive revenue requirements but are demonstrably better adapted to the exigencies of post-industrial change, largely because of service-intensive, women- and children-friendly public policies which seek to avoid poverty and long-term unemployment. As early as the 1960s and 1970s Denmark and Sweden both embarked on a road to high public employment based on effective Keynesian strategies of fiscal stimulation and monetary reflation. The result was a self-reinforcing mechanism whereby the expansion of welfare state jobs encouraged women and single parents to enter the labor market. As the welfare state "defamilialized" many caring functions it fostered demand for more social services which in turn led to near-maximum labor participation among both men and women, less early retirement, and relatively high birth rates, all helping reduce the long-term financial strains on pension systems (Esping-Andersen 1999). The main difficulty confronting the Scandinavian model is that financing the welfare state is made more difficult by high capital mobility, the fiscal and budgetary constraints that European monetary integration imposes, and increased tax resistance (Scharpf 1999; Hemerijck and Schludi 2000). Since the 1980s tax revenues as a share of GDP have been stagnant, along with public employment (indeed, with falling tax revenues during the 1990s, public employment fell markedly in Sweden). With the need to expand private sector jobs to compensate for losses in public employment, the Nordic countries face a hard choice between liberalizing private services, entailing more wage inequality, or continuing wage equality, which, under conditions of budget constraint, implies more unemployment.

Continental countries suffer from low employment rates, especially among youth, women, and older men, and are under pressure to transform their inclusive pay-as-you-go pension systems. The vulnerability of most Continental welfare states lies in their chronic inability to stimulate employment growth. Job stagnation is directly related to payroll-based social insurance financing (Esping-Andersen 1996; Scharpf 1997b), which breeds complicated interactions among investments, productivity, labor supply, and wage costs. The strategy of boosting international competitiveness by early retirement and high-quality training and education may have placed a premium on high productivity, but the indirect effect has been a substantial increase in the tax on labor as ever-fewer workers must support ever-more people outside the active labor market. Maximizing worker productivity may have thus resulted in an "inactivity trap," whereby productivity growth brings a vicious cycle of rising wage costs and the exit of less productive workers requiring further productivity increases and eliciting another round of workforce reductions through subsidized early exit (Hemerijck and Manow 2001).

The same "inactivity trap" is operative in Southern European welfare states, where it reinforces existing "insider–outsider" cleavages and social exclusion. The primary victims have been the young and women, especially women with children, with the effects evident in fertility and labor supply patterns. In Southern Europe birth rates are low, first because of difficulties among youth to gain a firm foothold in labor and housing markets, and second because of a lack of affordable childcare. Women especially are thus forced to choose between participating in the workforce or forming families (Saraceno 1994; Trifiletti 1999), and youth experience protracted dependence on their parents. Although with rising education, women's preferences have changed dramatically, the institutional environment continues to support the traditional male-breadwinner model. With overall job stagnation worsened by the severe incompatibilities that women face when they opt for careers (Esping-Andersen et al. 2001), far higher female employment rates are needed to counteract population aging and reduce household poverty risks.

Recent Anglo-Saxon experience with both Conservative and New Labour governments sacrificed egalitarian goals for jobs and monetary and fiscal prudence. Although Anglo-Saxon welfare states no longer face problems of financial sustainability, the conservative adjustment strategy in the UK has encouraged wage inequalities and an expansion of low-pay, low-skill jobs (Rhodes 2000). The result has been a significant polarization of incomes and increasingly unequal access to social insurance. Although wage subsidies now supplement the incomes of low-paid workers and their families, those who can afford private insurance are well covered while those who cannot are at risk of poverty. Moreover, rising female employment is not accompanied by efforts to diminish gender inequities and the lack of quality daycare compels women to accept low-quality part-time work (Esping-Andersen *et al.* 2001). Furthermore, labor market deregulation has rendered the British system of industrial relations unable to engage in cooperative relations between management and trade unions, exacerbating Britain's long-standing inability to produce a well-trained labor force. Skill shortages, low wages, and poverty have produced cumulative cycles of social disadvantage and exclusion of vulnerable groups.

### Reform agendas in EMU

Welfare state futures are not predetermined. Path-dependency is about historical contingency and welfare states are not the immovable objects that many observers assert (Pierson 2000a). Ground-breaking social policy changes have been implemented in most member states of the EU. More surprising is that policy reforms in core distributive areas of the welfare state received such late attention during economic adjustment. The reason is largely political: the more reform embraces core distributive areas of social protection, the more political conflict is likely. Moreover, if, as economists argue, wages are sticky then social protection enshrined in law is probably even stickier. Because social rights are usually attached to strong interest groups political opposition is likely to render the reform process unpredictable (Pierson 1994), particularly for pension benefits, regarded as sacrosanct rights (Hinrichs 2001; Myles and Pierson 2001).

The Maastricht convergence criteria clearly operated as a trigger helping to overcome political resistance to welfare reform. The need to qualify strengthened the relative position of finance ministers and central bankers at the expense of other national actors, but has not provided windows of opportunity to launch labor market deregulation and welfare retrenchment. The fiscal strain brought by the Maastricht criteria, the promise to meet standing commitments, and the need to address new social risks curtailed the immanent danger of regime competition. The EMU criteria concurrently fostered a search for new economically viable, politically feasible, and socially acceptable reform options. Policy reforms are conditioned by at least three distinct sets of causal factors: (1) the relevant economic and social policy challenges facing European welfare states, (2) variation in policy design, and (3) differences in institutional conditions, including structures of political decision-making and systems of interest mediation (see Ferrera, Hemerijck, and Rhodes, 2000; Scharpf and Schmidt 2000a).

*Scandinavian joint problem-solving*   Nordic systems, thanks to institutional solidity and coherence, have long been regarded as quasi-ideal-type welfare states whose architecture is well matched to a policy repertoire addressing new risks and needs associated with aging societies, gender equality, and transition to the new economy. Basic income guarantees are a safeguard against poverty and exclusion and also against penalties from out-of-work spells and broken or changing career trajectories. A wide array of services allows Nordic welfare systems to respond more effectively to the needs of families and to socialize costs of care, including for children. High rates of labor market participation attenuate financial strains on pension systems.

Monetary integration and post-industrial challenges nonetheless generate cost and job problems. Resistance to extremely high tax rates has been growing across the Scandinavian countries and the need for fiscal retrenchment has intensified. Throughout the 1990s, the Nordic countries grappled with pressures to contain high and increasing costs and reorganize labor markets to generate more demand for private employment. As stringent budgetary requirements constrain Swedish-style public sector job growth and active labor policies, Sweden and Denmark have begun to reduce public sector employment with a reform agenda shaped by pragmatic problem-solving centered on cost containment and without "grand controversy" over alternative views and scenarios (Eitrheim and Kuhnle 2000; Kuhnle 2000). Principles of universalism remain largely unquestioned even while across-the-board cuts in replacement rates (e.g. sickness benefits) or basic guarantees (e.g. family allowances) have taken place.

Important steps have been taken toward the Bismarckian tradition in pensions, in particular by strengthening links between contributions and benefits in Sweden and Finland to maintain the relative weight of pensions within overall social protection in years to come. Cost containment was the motive in 1999 when Sweden switched from a defined-benefit to a defined-contribution scheme in which each insured employee's contributions are recorded in an interest-earning individual account, typically at a rate tied to wage growth either in average or total wages. At retirement, the balance in the account is converted to a life annuity (Schludi 2001). Because Sweden continues to finance pensions on pay-as-you-go principles, its defined-contribution scheme is "notional" because contribution credits (rather than financial assets) are accumulated in these individual accounts. When a worker retires, the balance of the individual account is converted into a stream of monthly payments using a transformation coefficient that depends on the worker's age at retirement and cohort-specific life expectancy (OECD 2001). The Swedish reform also introduced a small privately funded defined-contribution component. Because shifting from defined-benefits to a notional defined-contribution system involved the unknown, Swedish policy-makers carefully forged consensus, first between the social democrat and bourgeois parties and then among the social partners. The deep recession in the first half of the 1990s strengthened agreement across the political spectrum about the need for fiscal sustainability of the Swedish welfare state, including the pension system.

The second important leitmotif in the Scandinavian reform agenda has been "activation," the modification of programs to give actual and potential beneficiaries incentives to find and maintain gainful employment. Denmark has gone farthest (Kautto *et al.* 1999; Goul Andersen 2000) with reforms that have significantly changed the institutional profile and logic of labor market policy. Eligibility for cash benefits, especially duration, were tightened and the total period gradually reduced from nine to four years between 1994 and 1999. There have also been individual action plans to ease occupational reintegration, especially for unemployed youth. Denmark has deployed a wide array of "activating" instruments including information and counseling, subsidized employment in public and private sectors, training and educational initiatives, and job rotation combined with an expansion of leave possibilities for employed workers. This effort has arguably contributed to a fall in unemployment from 8.1 percent in 1994 to 5.6 percent in 1999 and an increase in the employment rate from 72.4 percent to 76.5 percent over the same period. Despite workforce activation and pension reforms, however, unresolved problems remain. Many observers of the Nordic labor markets (especially Sweden and Finland) see lack of growth in private sector employment and a wage structure reflecting the overarching importance of egalitarian principles as major problems (Iversen and Wren 1998).

*Confronting the continental syndrome of welfare without work*    The continental syndrome of "welfare without work" has generated a complex reform agenda aimed at containing the expansionary dynamics of social insurance, rationalizing spending by curtailing pension commitments and "passive" benefits, improving family policy, introducing "active" incentives into short-term cash benefits, reforming labor markets to overcome insider–outsider cleavages, and reducing the incidence of social charges through broad financial restructuring. As early as the 1970s most continental welfare states had embarked on a strategy of using the social security system for shedding older and less productive workers, mainly through disability pensions, early retirement, and long-term unemployment schemes.[2] By the end of the 1970s dealing with rising unemployment, increasing deficits, and declining competitiveness became priorities.

After the second oil price shock, the Netherlands experienced the most severe recession in Western Europe. The depth of its crisis in 1981–1982 catalyzed policy change, beginning with a deflationary macroeconomic policy program, pegging the guilder to the D-mark, suspending wage indexation, squeezing the minimum wage, and lowering social benefits. By the late 1980s organized wage restraint and incremental cuts had proved insufficient for economic recovery and emphasis shifted to reducing the number of recipients (Visser and Hemerijck 1997). A new conditional indexation procedure encouraged social partners to internalize the employment and social policy effects of wage-bargaining. From 1994 onwards, the government, committed to a "jobs, jobs, and more jobs" strategy, sought greater efficiencies in social security, including partial re-privatization of social risks, managed liberalization of administration, reducing social partner involvement, and the introduction and intensification of activation obligations for the long-term unemployed.

Throughout the 1980s Belgian governments sought wage concessions to fight inflation and rising wage costs without touching automatic stabilizers. In 1982, after devaluation, monetary authorities pegged the franc to the D-mark. The subsequent fight against inflation was successful, but at the price of high real interest rates that worsened Belgian competitiveness. Wage restraint was traded for improvements in social security and early retirement, causing the Belgian welfare state to expand throughout the 1980s. Since unions refused wage restraint and higher profits, however, restraint had to be imposed by a state weakened by a truncated process of federalization and inability to reverse the "welfare without work" caused by a highly incoherent policy mix of macroeconomic management, wage bargaining, and social policies. Notwithstanding formidable

---

[2] Germany was the exception. Its strong commitment to a hard-currency policy, together with a tighter fiscal policy, had already brought some incremental cuts in German social benefits in the second half of the 1970s.

barriers to modernization, signs of policy change have been evident since the second half of the 1990s. In the runup to EMU, a new consensus promoted expanding employment levels among women (and perhaps older workers) as a *sine qua non* for long-term sustainability. The same consensus has substantially increased spending on active labor market policy in recent years, thereby emphasizing activation rather than passive transfers in social insurance (Cantillon and De Lathouwer 2001).

French governments responded to change in the 1970s with an inflationary growth strategy based on a soft-currency policy, with problematic results. The shift toward competitive deflation in 1983 led to gradual abandonment of *dirigiste* principles – heavy industrial subsidies were reversed, credit, price, and capital controls lifted, and restrictions on layoffs and temporary and part-time employment relaxed (Levy 2000). As described in chapter 4 in this volume, the *franc fort* policy came to be central to the new strategy. By pegging the franc to the D-mark in the second half of the 1980s, policy-makers hoped to bring inflation down to German levels and lower interest rates. To avoid popular resistance, however, governments expanded the welfare state, in particular by early retirement programs and, after 1988, introduced a major new anti-poverty program, the RMI (*Revenu Minimum d'Insertion*) plus novel means to finance it through a flat-rate tax, the CSG (*Contribution Sociale Generalisée*). The post-German reunification recession was a huge setback, however. The French, with others, were under the gun to meet the EMU convergence criteria.

As Levy (2000) points out, the end of *dirigiste* economic policy has not ended French state activism. Jospin was elected in 1997 on the promise of a more equitable approach to welfare retrenchment and eliminated allowances for more well-to-do families and abandoned means testing. In 1998, corporate taxes were slightly increased. Most healthcare expenditures and the RMI have been shifted from payroll contributions to general taxation through the CSG. A constitutional amendment allowed parliament to vote on the social security budget and a change in the administration of the social security funds also permitted state officials to gain influence at the cost of the social partners.[3] This change in governance structure and policy signals a gradual transformation from a largely Bismarckian to a more Beveridgean, tax-financed, state-run system of social security (Bonoli 1997). France's large question mark remained pension reform, however.

Germany was the monetary benchmark through the EMS and pre-EMU years, making it relatively free from many of the strains experienced

---

[3] Rather than negotiate interventions with the social partners, Members of Parliament are now able to plan adaptation measures, especially for cost containment (Palier 2000).

by other continental welfare states, at least until the difficulties around reunification. The economic turmoil created by the 1990 currency reform and the difficult integration of the former GDR changed this, however, and placed reform on the German agenda. The central weakness in the German social model has been the limited capacity of political actors to link policy problems and solutions in industrial relations and social security. In 1996, the Kohl government called both unions and business associations to the bargaining table to talk about a moderate wage settlement in the west and delayed adjustment of eastern wages to the western levels and to enhance investments in the new *Länder*. Yet the talks over the Alliance for Jobs failed because of the government's sick pay reform package, and the unions walked out of the talks (Manow and Seils 2000). Under Schröder, the Alliance for Jobs, Training and Competitiveness of 1999 remained fragile but alive. Broader reform, and resistance to it, came back onto the scene after the Schröder coalition was – barely – re-elected in 2002.

The general macroeconomic environment was relatively favorable in the later 1980s and in most countries inflation and deficits could be controlled, while economic growth picked up. The reunification of Germany however, prevented a soft landing for European economies. *Bundesbank* fear that monetary unification and sharply rising budget deficits might endanger price stability led it to an excessively restrictive monetary policy in 1991–1992. Other European economies followed into deep recession in the early 1990s, with a sharp rise in unemployment and ballooning public debt.[4] The pressures of international tax competition greatly restricted possibilities for raising taxes and constrained the scope for expenditure-based social and employment policies. Rising costs associated with aging populations and rising healthcare spending made the situation worse. Policy attention and reform efforts increasingly gravitated to the core areas of the welfare state, social policy and labor market regulation.

The reform of public pensions, which absorbed large parts of budgets, thus came onto the political agenda, often with intense political conflict. Most continental welfare states considered reducing the number of early beneficiaries by changing labor market rules, tightening administrative controls, or reducing benefit replacement rates in social insurance programs. In the Netherlands, sickness and disability were made more costly. Germany tried to encourage returning to work with targeted training and employment policies, including subsidized jobs for older workers. The

---

[4] To reduce debt and the debt service in line with EMU convergence criteria, some countries, especially Belgium and Italy, would have had to run a primary budget surplus of over 5 percent for several years.

result has been a general trend toward later withdrawal from the labor market (OECD 2001).

Pension reform in continental welfare states has been especially cumbersome. Ground-breaking pension reforms, as in Italy in 1995 and Sweden in 1999, have thus far proved difficult to pursue. It has been common to raise contribution rates, especially in Germany and the Netherlands. In Austria, the reference period has been extended as part of a larger package of reforms. Changes to indexation rules have also been enacted across the board. Germany has moved from gross to net wage indexation and France has shifted from wage to price indexation. Some continental welfare states, notably the Netherlands, France, and more recently Belgium, have also started building reserve funds to maintain adequate pension provision when the baby-boom generation retires (Esping-Andersen *et al.* 2001). Germany has gone furthest, with direct transfers and tax advantages to encourage savings in private pensions. German policy-makers are also planning to use state subsidies to support supplementary pension schemes for low-income earners. Wage-earners are encouraged to contribute up to 4 percent of their income, but German policy-makers failed to make private old-age provision compulsory, as it is in the Netherlands (Schludi 2001). Another weakness is that German reforms involved no efforts to harmonize civil servants' pensions with the general scheme.

In France, unions blocked proposals for system integration, and in 1993 Balladur extended the number of years for calculating the reference salary in the private sector to the best twenty-five career years and the minimum required years to forty. Then in 1995, when Juppé proposed to extend the Balladur reforms to the public sector, the response was a six-week strike that paralyzed the country, caused substantial economic loss and forced the Prime Minister to abandon his reform proposal. The absence of cooperation and consensus among mainstream parties and social partners in France is a major cause for the lack of progress in reforming the French pension system (Bonoli 1997; Levy 2000). A largely majoritarian electoral system creates fierce bi-polar competition between the Left and Center-Right. Because France lacks the institutions for close cooperation between government and the social partners, unions can mobilize large-scale opposition to reform but are incapable of organizing consent among the rank and file. Notwithstanding lack of progress, there is growing consensus among French pension policy makers for prefunded pension plans. The Jospin government also supported the creation of private pension funds, to be managed collectively by employer and union organizations, to complement the pay-as-you-go system. Electoral timetables have so far prevented serious change, however, and when the

Raffarin government began, once again, to promote an alignment of public sector pensions on the private sector model, street protests and strikes escalated.

Fighting social exclusion has also become a priority, with added stimulus from the new EU Open Method of Coordination (OMC) inclusion process launched in 2001. All EU members are taking an integrated approach to social exclusion though specific mechanisms of policy coordination and issue linkage across relevant policy areas. Most continental welfare states continue their half-hearted efforts to introduce women- and child-friendly policies that promote affordable access to daycare, paid maternity and parental leave, a more equal division of household tasks between men and women, and more generous provisions for absence from work when children are ill. Across continental Europe, however, most policy-makers recognize that caring services, especially for small children and for the aged, are becoming an urgent matter.

Most continental welfare states have developed policies to increase demand for low-skilled workers, typically by exempting employers from social contributions. For Belgium, France, and the Netherlands, with high minimum wages and labor costs, regressive employment subsidies are creating a low-wage job-intensive service sector with potential for expanding in wholesale and retail trade, personal services, personal and public safety, house improvement, environmental protection, tourism, and cultural recreation. Targeted wage subsidies could lead to labor cheapening and job growth without an American-style surge in poverty and inequality and open a range of additional, economically viable employment opportunities at the lower end of the labor market. In-work benefits for low-income households have now also begun to play a role in the Netherlands and Belgium, and with employment subsidies likely to increase labor demand, Scharpf (1997b) believes that subsidies could pay for themselves in reduced outlays for full-time unemployment compensation. The overall advantage is that job creation and hiring decisions remain in the hands of private firms in the regular economy. Employment subsidies can also create problems, however. Many programs are targeted on the long-term unemployed, for example, giving employers incentives to substitute them for the short-term unemployed or even to delay hiring at all. Reducing social security contributions for employers hiring low-skilled workers can also reduce incentives to upgrade skills. Graduated schemes, modeled after a negative income tax, provide clear incentives to seek better education and better jobs, but the danger is that employment subsidies lock low-skilled workers in a secondary, low-wage economy from which they cannot escape. A "skill trap" then replaces the "inactivity trap."

Pressure on the unemployed to accept suitable job offers or participate in education programs has generally strengthened activation initiatives (Lødemel and Trickey 2000). All continental welfare states have promoted activation programs based on individual guidance and training opportunities, with youth and low-skill groups as primary targets. Many recent reforms have triggered institutional changes (Ferrera, Hemerijck, and Rhodes 2000), including reconfiguration of the social partners and the division of labor between public and private actors and levels of governance. In Belgium, for example, the proliferation of supply-side approaches to labor market policy, providing for one-to-one mediation services, has developed in tandem with the a de-monopolization and regionalization of public employment services (Cantillion and de Lathouwer 2001). In the Netherlands, the privatization of public employment services and liberalization of regulations governing private temporary agencies has encouraged market mechanisms, such as contracting-out, and organizational reform, including separating purchasers and providers. Private reintegration and health and safety at work services exist in a fair number of continental welfare states and represent a shift away from centrally legislated, rule-governed labor market regulation and employment policy to decentralized coordination that includes social partners, private actors, and third-party groups.

*Modernizing southern welfare states under hard fiscal constraints*
Modernizing southern welfare states has been difficult because of EMU, globalization, and adverse demography. South European populations, especially in Italy and Spain, are aging faster than most others (Castles 2001). These welfare states have thus been forced to carry out politically perilous internal restructuring to catch up with other EU member states. To lower deficits and debts, and – to the extent budgetary constraints have allowed – to finance benefits and services for outsiders, new policies have meant less generous benefits for insiders (Ferrera, Hemerijck, and Rhodes 2000). Yet despite this southern European states have an ambitious agenda, including attenuating generous guarantees for historically privileged occupational groups accompanied by improved minimum benefits, introducing and consolidating the safety net, especially through means-tested minimum income schemes, expanding and improving family benefits and social services, with explicit attention to gender equality and equity issues, taking measures against the underground economy and tax evasion, reforming labor markets with attention to de-segmenting labor and markets, and modifying unemployment insurance benefits. Another distinctive element of South European reforms has been politico-institutional. More oversight has been assigned to regional and local

governments, especially health and social services in Spain and Italy, and innovative concertational approaches (e.g. territorial pacts) have been tried at national and sub-national levels to promote actors' involvement in policy-making and mixed partnerships for policy implementation. Strikingly, across Southern Europe in the 1990s there was renewed interest in social pacts, with an agenda beyond wage policy, including welfare issues and labor market reform (Ebbinghaus and Hassel 1999). In countries that were relative latecomers to welfare state reform, most notably Italy and Spain, these pacts proved very important in enhancing national budgets.

Italy in the 1970s was marked by very rapid growth of expenditures on public pensions, mainly from generous social security reforms. Without a corresponding increase in revenues, deficits soared and by the early 1980s, large deficits and escalating inflation made reorientation of macroeconomic policy inevitable.[5] In fact, by the late 1980s, rather than becoming a modern welfare state Italy was becoming a pension state. Proposals to rationalize the pension system and restore financial balance led to incremental cuts and little progress. The growth of debt led to speculative attacks on the lira until in 1992 Italy had to leave the EMS.

The Maastricht criteria made fiscal restraint indispensable, however, and a devaluation of 30 percent spurred recovery and policy reforms in industrial relations, social security, and labor market regulation. Thus only in the 1990s, pressed by impending EMU entry, did Italian policymakers turn a vicious cycle of industrial decline, budgetary crises, welfare without work for some and poverty for many into a virtuous cycle of economic change and welfare state reform. A quick succession of reforms between 1992 and 1998 included abolishing wage indexation mechanisms (agreed by the social partners), reorganizing collective bargaining, deregulating and decentralizing labor market policy from state to regions and private intermediaries, privatizing state-owned industries and banks, and – most important – reforming the pension system. Together the reforms were a "qualitative leap" in Italian history coinciding with the shift in the Italian political system from the "First" to "Second" Republic (Ferrera and Gualmini 2000). Political transformation allowed autonomy for governments to encourage responsive policy concertation among the state, unions, and employers' associations.

---

[5] In 1981 a so-called "divorce" between the government and the central bank implied that the Banca d'Italia was no longer obliged to finance residual government debt. The bank's restrictive policy pushed the government to adopt budgetary restraint, which proved insufficient for reducing the dramatic budget deficits as rising real interest rates required higher spending on public debt service.

The reforms of the 1990s worked to level off social rights and obligations (e.g. contributory rates) across various occupational groups.[6] Beyond pensions, some traditional gaps in social coverage were filled. The introduction of means-tested maternity benefits for noninsured mothers, for example, was accompanied by thoroughgoing reform of parental leaves, and new schemes were created for poor households (e.g. a means-tested allowance for families with three or more children as well as experimentation with the RMI). The reforms have sculptured a new organizational profile for the Italian welfare state, especially in healthcare, active labor market policies, social services, and assistance. Between 1997 and 2001, substantial powers were transferred from central government to the regions and from these to municipalities. While creating numerous new problems, this quasi-federalization of Italy's social protection constitutes a far-reaching experiment in institutional change. Despite the efforts of the *Ulivo* governments (1996–2001), little progress was made in de-segmenting the Italian labor market, however: rigid norms protecting the employed were only marginally relaxed and the baroque system of "social shock absorbers" (i.e. the panoply of wage guarantee and unemployment compensation schemes) was not reformed.

European monetary integration played a prominent role in prompting welfare reform in the Iberian countries (Guillén, Alvarez, and Adao e Silva 2001). In Spain, immediately after the first democratic elections in 1977 the new centrist government gave the Spanish central bank substantial powers in economic policy and put the country on a course of economic orthodoxy, intensified after 1982 when the PSOE government imposed an unprecedented austerity program. Spain joined the EC in 1986 just as the SEM was launched, at which point the Spanish welfare state contained a highly codified system of labor market regulation that offered substantial protection but limited collective bargaining, plus a rudimentary system of social provision falling short of European standards yet regarded as overly generous. PSOE orthodoxy curtailed the expansion of the welfare state, and by the end of the 1980s it had also provoked a serious deterioration of relations between the government and the labor unions. When in 1992 the EMS entered intense crisis, the Spanish government did not follow its Italian counterpart out, but instead maintained the peseta through intense interest rate hikes and three quick devaluations. These measures plunged the economy into an unprecedented recession that led unemployment to

---

[6] Within the pension system, for example, the privilege enjoyed by civil servants to retire after only twenty years of service regardless of age (that had created a mass of "baby pensioners" since the 1960s) was phased out. Yet pension rights were accorded to "atypical" workers, and lower pensions were repeatedly upgraded, eventually through the budget law for 2002 passed by the new Berlusconi government.

almost 25 percent in 1994. and a sharp increase in unemployment outlays which caused a severe deterioration of Spanish public finances.

Despite unfavorable economic circumstances, the Spanish government maintained its determination to implement convergence programs to participate in EMU from the start. In 1995, the government and the social partners agreed to the Toledo Pact which included drastic pension reform, including gradual change in the formula for calculating the basis of pensions and a three-part agreement on labor market reform. Financing sources for social security were strictly segregated: contribution-based schemes would be financed only through contributions while noncontributory pensions were financed though general taxes (Pérez 2000a). With trade union consent, cuts in pension benefits for the "better off" were traded for improving the positions of lower-income earners. Like Italy, in the 1990s Spain also engineered thoroughgoing decentralization in social services from central government to the regions. The major challenge for Spanish policy-makers, however, was labor market reform to reduce the remarkably high levels of unemployment. The PSOE government introduced several measures until it lost power in 1996 and thereafter the conservatives continued the effort. Reforms included flexible contract forms, rationalization of unemployment benefits, new programs and incentives to reconcile family and work (and thus gender equality), activation measures, and broad changes in employment services (Moreno 2000). Unlike Italy, Spain has also progressed toward labor market desegmentation: in 1997 and again in 2001, labor laws were changed, relaxing protection for core employees and improving the social security rights of irregular and temporary workers and their opportunities to access the primary labor market. This, along with sharp easing of monetary policy, may have contributed to Spain's improved employment performance. Unemployment, however, is still the highest in the EU, although it fell from 24 percent in 1994 to 13 percent in 2001.

In Portugal, pension reform was part of an encompassing packages in the runup to EMU and unions had an important say over areas of social protection that were wider than in Spain and many other European countries. Although the superior employment performance of the Portuguese labor market is a result of economic structure and expansionary policy, its low unemployment rates during the 1990s are also linked to specific policy choices, especially those of the new Socialist government in 1995. The modernization of social protection was a prime objective of the new government, which emphasized active labor market measures and, more generally, social inclusion (Cabral Villaverde 1999; Guillén, Alvarez, and Adao e Silva 2001). Unemployment insurance was broadly reformed, occupational training and insertion programs were expanded, and specific incentives were deployed to promote a "social market for employment" based on local initiatives that targeted the most vulnerable workers. In 1996, the government and associations of municipalities, charities, and mutualities signed an innovative "social pact for solidarity" designed to mobilize local enterprise and create employment. Both Spain and Portugal improved minimum benefits: pensions, family allowances, and a basic safety net. In Spain, all the regions introduced RMI schemes, on a path originally opened by the Basques in 1989, and in 1996 Portugal piloted a national minimum income scheme.

*Anglo-Saxon "third ways"*    Welfare state financing and private sector service employment do not appear problematic in the Anglo-Saxon countries. In the UK, reforms under the Conservative governments of the 1980s and 1990s deregulated labor markets and encouraged income polarization between households through a hard-budget/hard-currency macroeconomic policy. Westminster parliamentarism allowed Conservative governments to speed up social security retrenchment and benefits eroded in real value while the middle classes were encouraged to opt out toward nonpublic forms of insurance (e.g. in pensions). As the costs of targeted, means-tested benefits started to soar despite tightening of eligibility rules inspired by the new "workfare" philosophy a stricter benefit regime contained costs by reducing the number of claimants. These developments have had significant consequences. The erosion of universal provision has helped restore public finances, radical labor market deregulation has fostered an expansion of private employment, and inequality and poverty have markedly increased, partly because of the perverse effects of means-testing (Rhodes 2000).

Strong dualistic tendencies in economy and society inherited from the Conservatives posed serious ideological and normative problems for New Labour. The Blair government embarked upon a broad strategy of reform, fine-tuning benefit rules to neutralize "traps" created by welfare-to-work schemes, fighting poverty and social exclusion by increasing minimum wage and income guarantees, reforming the tax code, and introducing new targeted programs (Clasen 2001; Glyn and Wood 2001). The most distinctive feature in New Labour's strategy of welfare reform, however, is reliance on work and employability in addressing poverty, disadvantage, and social exclusion. Labour's "welfare-to-work" strategy combines prescriptive job search enhancement with in-work benefits to help "make work pay." In 1997, the Blair government introduced the New Deal for skill enhancement and compulsory job searching aimed especially at moving youth from public benefit to employment (Clasen 2001). New Deal activation programs rely heavily on tax credits, which have gained in importance, particularly since the introduction of the Working Families Tax Credit (WFTC) in 1998, aimed at guaranteeing any family with a full-time worker a relatively generous minimum income. The WFTC avoids the stigma of applying for benefits, while the direct link with wages clearly reveals the advantage of work over welfare (Glyn and Wood 2001). Institutionally, the Blair government has deliberately avoided corporatist exchanges (Crouch 2001). Instead, New Labour's approach is to minimize intervention and regulatory burdens on a well-functioning deregulated labor market. It also stresses individual responsibility for training and favors business as a vehicle for education and human resource management in the "knowledge-based economy."

Clasen (2001) concludes that the overall scope of New Labor's strategy of "welfare-to-work," including special programs for single parents and disabled workers, is much wider than Conservative workfare policies. Moreover, New Labour's policy repertoire is far more coherent in its fit between employability measures and more passive wage subsidies to support the goal of "making work pay." More critically, Clasen finds that temporary jobs, which play a large role in activation strategies in Scandinavian countries, remain underdeveloped and that "Third Way" welfare-to-work strategies lack the generous income transfers of many mature continental welfare states. In sharp contrast to "Third Way" rhetoric about "learning and education as the key to prosperity," vocational training, skill enhancement, and upward mobility are rather limited. The emphasis is on sticks rather than carrots, and implies that for those who remain outside the workforce, poverty remains an immanent threat (Clasen 2001).

Ireland has followed a different path toward welfare state modernization, closer to that observed in continental Europe and Scandinavia. In the late 1970s and early 1980s, the Irish mimicked British decentralization of wage bargaining and radical labor market deregulation. These measures failed to bring down unemployment, however, which reached 18 percent in 1987, and the Irish abandoned a decentralized, market-led approach in favor of a more coordinated approach that led to qualification for EMU. Beginning with the National Recovery accord, in effect between 1987 and 1991 (Hardiman 2000), the Irish strategy of competitive corporatism combined with massive flows of foreign direct investment (FDI) and EU Structural Funds to turn Ireland into one of Europe's success stories, with the highest rates of output and employment growth in the EU and structurally healthy fiscal balance. Since the mid-1990s, however, poverty measured by relative incomes has not decreased, principally because transfers per recipient, although rising significantly in real terms, have lagged behind the exceptionally large

increases in average incomes. Therefore, while numbers relying on transfers have fallen as unemployment has declined, more of those remaining
reliant on them are poorer. However, measures combining both relative
income lines and other deprivation indicators show a marked decline in
poverty from 1994 (Nolan, O'Connell, and Whelan 2000; Atkinson *et al.*
2001). Such progress induced Irish policy-makers to make their original
poverty-reduction targets more ambitious, reflecting strong commitment
to the European social model. Irish policy-makers have also experimented with new forms of cooperation and partnership, some of which
have involved the socially excluded, together with the traditional social
partners.

## 4    The European social policy agenda

National welfare reforms throughout the 1990s mark distinctive and often
successful responses to European monetary integration and the momentum will likely intensify in the first decade of the twenty-first century. Far
from sclerotic or disintegrating, the European social model thus remains
dynamic, with distinctly European reform processes deeply embedded
in normative notions of equity and solidarity, shared understanding of
the efficiency-enhancing effects of social policy, and institutional preferences for negotiated change rather than top-down imposition. Country-
specific trajectories of welfare reform have hinged on many contingencies:
major recessions, multiple policy failures, regime-specific pathologies,
severe coordination deficits between national and European tiers of governance, and changes in the balance of political and economic power.
Reform has required hard-won changes, interrupted policy experiments,
and learning processes, both fast and slow (Hemerijck and Schludi
2001).

Successes in domestic policy innovation also shaped the employment
and social policy agenda of the EU. Persistently high levels of unemployment in the runup to EMU, despite national reform efforts, raised the
stakes for common European employment and social inclusion strategies.
In the wake of the neo-liberal 1980s, after a period of "Eurosclerosis"
marked by domestic redistributive conflict, European integration took a
new direction and gained speed in the 1990s. With the Single Market
Program, initiated in 1985, social policy became a secondary concern.
Moving to EMU foreclosed the use of monetary policy by member states
as a tool against unemployment (Hall 2001: 223), however, and with
the 1997 Dutch Presidency, employment relations and social protection
resurfaced on the EU agenda. In the deepening of "social Europe," the
"social democratic moment" of the 1990s defined social protection as a

productive factor. Today, virtually all European governments agree that comprehensive welfare policy is an asset and not a liability. Social policy is deemed a "productive factor" in the competitive knowledge-based society. Institutionally, a consensus accepts a productive balance between economic and social policy, best achieved through dialog with multiple actors, including the social partners, and the EU. The institutionalization of a social space at EU level will inevitably render the ECB unable to lead opposition to the deepening of "social Europe" under conditions of high unemployment (Forder 2001).

A first breakthrough was the insertion of an Employment Chapter in the Amsterdam Treaty (1997). The European Employment Strategy has its roots in the Delors White Paper on Growth, Competitiveness and Employment (1993), which propagated closer coordination of national efforts to fight unemployment and enhanced intra-Union communication on best practices. Pressed by representatives of the European Parliament (EP), heads of state and governments agreed, at the 1997 Intergovernmental Conference (IGC), to introduce an employment title into the Amsterdam Treaty, officially raising employment to the status of a "common concern" for European policy (Goetschy 1999). The employment chapter (Title VIII, Articles 125–130) stipulates an obligation for member states to participate in policy coordination around a common strategy defined by the Council in accordance with objectives laid out in the Treaty. Second, the chapter does not confer competencies on the part of the Community to regulate or interfere in domestic labor markets. Third, the employment chapter formally accords public status to the social partners, both at the level of the EU in formulating guidelines and at the level of individual nation states in drafting national action plans (NAPs) (Article 138 (ex-Article 118a)). The goal is to foster and deepen the social dialog.

Agreement over the employment title, its specific procedures, and institutional format was politically enhanced by changed political circumstances. Unacceptably high levels of unemployment in the mid-1990s sealed the fates of many conservative governments. The rise of center-left governments in the EU, particularly in large countries like France, Italy, the UK, and Germany, triggered a search for a new European approach to employment and social policy. After the victory of New Labour in the British general election of May 1997, Blair instantly supported the European employment strategy. Shortly thereafter, even before Jospin's victory, France endorsed it. Meanwhile, social unrest in Belgium, Germany, Italy, and France in 1995–1997 fueled fears of competitive social dumping in the shadow of EMU. Although French proposals for a centralized – demand-led – macroeconomic response to mass unemployment were rejected, European leaders began to show willingness to move toward EMU with a European employment strategy, capable of bolstering domestic reform initiatives and capacities while acknowledging a responsibility for employment (Larsson 1998).

The Lisbon summit in March 2000 marked another watershed in the "Europeanization" of employment and social policy. Governments agreed to concrete commitments to increase overall employment in the EU to 70 percent and to over 60 percent for women by 2010. Employment guidelines were amended to include "lifelong learning" and "increasing employment in services." The Lisbon summit also launched a new mode of European governance, broadly applicable to all European policy-making, coined the Open Method of Coordination (OMC). OMC delineates a procedure for fostering a "learning-friendly" environment for employment and social policy innovation and experimentation (Hemerijck and Visser 2001), and it may provide a way to cope with the problems and constraints resulting from European economic and monetary integration in areas where national differences in interests and policy legacies still limit common European solutions (Scharpf 2000b). The core advantage of the OMC is its potential for reconciling national diversity and democratic accountability at the level of the nation state with common policy ambitions and measures of effectiveness through benchmarking and monitoring (Zeitlin 2001).

At the heart of OMC lies an explicit recognition that national welfare states are profoundly different from one another (de la Porte, Pochet, and Room 2001). The Lisbon Council thus proposed to extend OMC to policy initiatives for fighting poverty, combating social exclusion, and modernizing systems of social protection. The Portuguese Presidency agreed to draft European guidelines for social protection, to be implemented like the employment guidelines: setting common objectives that are ambitious and realistic, using clear indicators whenever possible; ensuring necessary flexibility for member states to implement policy; and promoting closer cooperation among member states (European Commission 2000b). At the Nice Council in December 2000, European leaders agreed to an ambitious social agenda, and common objectives integrated into the treaty formally established the Social Protection Committee (Article 144). The Belgian Presidency forged an agreement on quantitative indicators for monitoring progress toward social inclusion across member states and reached an agreement at the Laken Council in December 2001 on common objectives for pension systems, including a consensus over a new procedure of open coordination. With these innovations, the fight against unemployment and social exclusion became part of the EU constitution.

The proliferation of "management by objectives" in European social and employment policy may well unleash a process of differentiated policy convergence, or "hybridization," in welfare and labor market policy. These areas have thus far tended to cluster in different regimes, characterized by high degrees of "lock-in" and path-dependency. A new convergence could lead to promising new configurations of policies, mixes already apparent in small countries such as Denmark, Ireland, the Netherlands, and Portugal.

# 12 Industrial relations in EMU: are renationalization and Europeanization two sides of the same coin?

## Jon Erik Dølvik

Recent decades have strained the national systems of industrial relations and collective bargaining that were a cornerstone of the postwar European social model. EMU is widely expected to intensify this strain and change European industrial relations profoundly. The supranationalization of monetary policy and economic governance implies relative decentralization of collective bargaining systems, as national systems become regions of the eurozone economy. Improved transparency of prices and wages and elimination of currency risk will intensify competition among producers and nation states. Without the option of adjusting national exchange rates (and interest rates) and with fiscal policies constrained by the Stability and Growth Pact (SGP), labor market actors will increasingly bear the burden of fluctuating economic circumstances and preventing new unemployment. All this poses a dual challenge of increasing labor market adaptability and enhancing policy coordination both within and across national systems.

The implications of EMU for industrial relations are ambiguous, however. With fiercer regime competition and contradictory pressures for adaptation of national systems, the responses of social actors and governments will depend largely on EMU's effects on growth and employment and hence on the macroeconomic policies adopted by EU authorities, and the ECB in particular. At the same time, however, differences in national systems and responses will produce as much potential for diversity as convergence. Three broad scenarios emerge:

• First, a *status quo scenario* assumes that the economies and industrial relations systems in the major eurozone countries have already become accustomed to operating under the conditions of fierce competition, strict monetary policies, and high unemployment and that most of the constraints of the Euro-regime have already been absorbed. The emerging path will thus codify trends observable during the 1990s. The central issue for this path will be the long-run influence of present trends on national systems.

- The second, *vicious-circle, scenario* assumes that restrictive ECB policies and the inability of countries to pursue effective stabilization policies will lock most of the Euro-economy into sluggish growth and high
unemployment (Martin, chapter 2 in this volume, Noé 1998). As a
result, micropressures for restructuring will further diminish the space
for national collective bargaining, eroding current patterns of industrial relations. The outlook for substantial Europeanization of collective bargaining is bleak, as unions seek to preserve whatever is left at
the national level and cannot generate the clout to be a credible force
at European level. Because unemployment and fiercer competition for
market shares will restrain wages, governments and employers will have
few incentives to engage in European coordination.
- The third, *virtuous-circle, scenario* assumes higher growth and lower
unemployment stimulated by more expansionary macroeconomic policy, increasing room for maneuver in collective bargaining, labor markets, and welfare reform. The outlook for trade unions would be
brighter. Higher growth and declining unemployment could trigger a
catch-up process in wage-setting, however, posing difficult questions
for the ECB, governments, and the peak associations of labor and capital. To prevent inflation and avoid an undesired tightening of monetary
policies, governments, employers' associations, and possibly the ECB
may see advantages in Euro-level coordinated wage restraint. Unions
could gain bargaining capital for incomes policy exchanges at European
level, but national unions might resist a European coordination that
implies forgone wages at home, while single employers might prefer
using wages to compete. The question for this scenario is whether collective actors can muster internal support for participating in European
coordination of wage and economic policies that would require them
to cede autonomy and comply with higher-order commitments.

Recent responses to monetary integration together with the continuing
challenges posed by the operation of EMU nevertheless suggest a direction. EMU, as such, seems unlikely to lead either to "Americanization"
or to strong "Europeanization." Instead, it will more likely encourage
stronger coordination among actors in existing national industrial relations systems, a process implied by "renationalization" and exemplified
by the recent proliferation of social pacts. Yet because of collective action
problems, the renationalization scenario is not an alternative to looser
forms of coordination at cross-national European level but is rather a
prerequisite for it. Such a dual-level structure of coordinated wage bargaining could contribute to creating conditions for the sustained economic growth needed to lower unemployment and maintain institutionalized systems of industrial relations under EMU. Whether unions, facing

domestic decline, are capable of developing such a structure, however, remains a central question for the future viability of EMU.

## 1    Implications of EMU for national industrial relations systems

How does EMU alter the environment of national trade unions and their role in the governance of terms of employment? What are the principal challenges facing unions in the new EMU environment? The single currency and monetary policy can help with common problems of economic instability and symmetric shocks, and act as a buffer against the volatility of global financial markets. The design of EMU and the application of its rules so far, however, suggest that the ECB is more inclined to use interest rates to dampen than stimulate eurozone growth and employment, seen as a supply-side issue – to secure price stability. Moreover, the rules of the SGP and structural budget deficits in many countries limit possibilities for stimulating employment by any coordinated fiscal policy.

The variation in national economies in the eurozone implies that countries and regions will face disparate economic developments calling for different macroeconomic policies (Eichengreen 1993). This presents serious dilemmas for a single monetary policy. For example, should the ECB be most concerned with cooling down strong-growing economies in the periphery or with stimulating stagnant regions in the Euro-core? Diverse policy needs can aggravate nation-specific problems if a common monetary policy functions pro-cyclically in countries in cyclical positions deviating from the eurozone average. The EMU regime, however, leaves countries no choice but to compensate for the loss of macroeconomic instruments by strengthening their domestic ability to cope with fluctuating economic circumstances. National governments can no longer respond to problems of competitiveness or economic shocks by adjusting exchange or interest rates and the SGP limits the use of fiscal policies. Thus the brunt of macroeconomic adjustment will increasingly have to be shouldered by labor market actors. With limited cross-border labor mobility and virtually no eurozone fiscal stabilizers, labor market organization and collective bargaining will become key means for economic adaptation at the national level (Boyer 2000). In general, under EMU, maintaining competitiveness and employment requires that overall wage growth largely reflect productivity growth.[1] EMU does not require larger wage flexibility in normal times (Calmfors 2000: 2), but the alternative

---

[1]  As Boyer (1994) argues, unless wage-bargainers internalize the low-inflation requirement of the EMU regime and take account of the need for company competitiveness by adopting moderate and flexible wage policies, "variations in unemployment levels may well replace those in exchange rates as the key variable in economic adjustment" (1994: 116).

for preventing higher unemployment resulting from demand shocks is to replace exchange rate flexibility with increased flexibility of labor costs, in effect turning wage-setting systems into "functional equivalents to devaluation" (Crouch 2000).

The effect of EMU on the average level of real wages and unemployment over the cycle depends on the effects of enhanced product market integration (trade competition and foreign direct investment (FDI) flows) and on the interaction between monetary policy-makers and wage-bargainers. Whereas disappearance of the "deterrent effect" of national central bank policy on national wage increases promotes stronger wage growth, product market integration works in the opposite direction. Elimination of exchange rate risk and the enhanced comparability of prices and wages across boundaries are expected to reinforce capital mobility, price competition, and pressures on firms to keep profits and labor costs down (Rose 2000). Enhanced macroeconomic stability and increased predictability of FDI will influence investment patterns, probably strengthening the attractiveness of the low-cost countries in the EU periphery, including new Central and Eastern European (CEE) members, which have previously been regarded as risky. EMU thus augments pressures for restructuring and rationalization of production across Europe. Generally, because nominal wage differences largely reflect variations in productivity, national unit labor costs are assumed to be approximately the same in the eurozone (Schubert 1997; CEC 1998a). Enhanced capital mobility is then likely to speed up the protracted historical trend of labor cost convergence (Sisson et al. 1998). Employers (especially in low-cost countries) are thus concerned that improved comparability might trigger undue upward convergence of wages (Norman 1998), whereas most trade unions fear downward pressures (EMF 1998).

These changes will affect the entire range of institutions that determine labor costs and the attractiveness of countries to investment – taxation, pensions, infrastructure, education and training, and regulations of all sorts. The microdynamics of international competition are thereby expected to interact with the macrodynamics of "regime competition," suggesting that national states and organizations will engage in tougher competition to attract investment and jobs by offering the most favorable conditions for companies. Besides the constraints of the SGP, the impact of regime and tax competition probably means that fiscal rigor and curbing of indirect labor costs (payroll taxes and the like) will become more important under EMU – so-called "internal devaluations" – and presumably more so in countries with uncoordinated bargaining systems and low aggregate wage flexibility. As the national case-studies show, most European countries are still struggling to consolidate their budgets and face increasing strains on social security systems, making the reduction of social security costs and reform of the welfare state/labor market nexus burning issues. At the same time, the central role of the social partners as financial contributors and sometimes co-managers of social security systems means that comprehensive reform is hard to accomplish without their consent. Governments, and perhaps employers, thus have incentives to find consensus and legitimacy through concerted reform strategies (Ebbinghaus and Hassel 1999). Beyond the increased need for wage moderation, this might provide trade unions with bargaining capital in tri-partite political exchange (Dølvik 1993).

Calmfors (2000) and Crouch (2000) similarly suggest that wage-setting compatible with EMU is more likely to be achieved through centralized coordination, whereas the ECB and scholars closer to business argue that greater need for flexibility calls for decentralization of bargaining and deregulation of labor markets (Issing 1999). European unions also seem to acknowledge the need for improved labor market adaptability – as recommended by the European employment strategy – but in their view this objective is more efficiently achieved through negotiated adjustment and centralized concertation.

According to the official EU view, EMU will "inevitably modify the structural parameters of national economic systems and, hence, the differences across countries" (CEC 1998a). That is, market-driven harmonization or convergence of social outcomes is foreseen. Their effects on different national systems of industrial relations, however, will depend on the macroeffects of EMU. If the vicious-circle deflationary scenario proves correct, a situation of virtually zero-sum competition will evolve, amplifying the microdynamics and conflicts of interests between regions and posing severe pressures on national industrial relations systems. If, by contrast the virtuous-circle scenario takes hold, it will alleviate pressures, smooth restructuring and reform, and reduce destructive competition based on social standards between countries and regions. Moreover, the quest for economic "shock absorbers" and safeguards of macroeconomic stability, on the one hand, and for labor market flexibility on the other, points to EMU's contradictory implications for national industrial relations. So far, the impact remains ambiguous. Examining actual changes in European industrial relations during the period of monetary integration reveals more insights.

### General trends in Western Europe

Initially, the single market and EMU were expected to strengthen tendencies to deregulation, decentralization, and the demise of national industrial relations systems. However, even in the absence of a strong social dimension of European integration, national systems of industrial relations have shown greater resilience than anticipated (Ferner and Hyman 1998). Some commonalities – such as wage moderation and more decentralized collective bargaining – are observable, but trends in union density, collective bargaining coverage and levels (Figure 12.1), and the role of the state, show diversity and ambiguity (Ferner and Hyman 1998; Fajertag and Pochet 2000; Traxler, Blaschke, and Kittel 2001). While the overall rate of organization among the employers has remained high in most EU countries (Traxler 1998), union membership has, with some exceptions, been declining.[2] Contrary to the expectation of a decline in collective bargaining, levels and coverage have been relatively stable, although they have fallen sharply in countries with decentralized bargaining systems, the UK in particular. Despite more company-level bargaining, excepting the UK, EU countries have not dismantled centralized wage negotiations (OECD 1997; Traxler, Blaschke, and Kittel 2001). Although sectoral bargaining has replaced confederal negotiations in Sweden and Denmark, centralized, nation-wide agreements still prevail, and in Italy, Ireland, Spain, Portugal, and Finland there has even been recentralization as part of tri-partite strategies to adjust to external pressures, EMU in particular (Regini 1997; Fajertag and Pochet 2000). The dominant tendency has been toward more multi-tiered, articulated bargaining systems.[3]

Probably the most important reason for persisting with centralized bargaining has been employer propensity to organize and apply collective agreements to the entire workforce. In addition, legal and institutional mechanisms for mediation and dispute management in Scandinavian countries and extension of collective agreements to nonunionized companies in continental countries have underpinned coordinated solutions (Stokke 1999). These factors highlight the key role of the state in facilitating centralized coordination (Traxler 1998). In contrast, where no such institutional framework exists and wages become a key parameter in interfirm competition, employers have incentives to avoid collective bargaining and union recognition, illustrated by the dramatic drop in coverage rates in the UK since the 1980s.

One significant feature of the 1990s was convergence of outcomes in reduced nominal wage growth, reflecting, among other things, falling inflation and shifting bargaining power between capital and labor. The overall picture in the eurozone has been one of sustained wage moderation

---

[2] Union density in accession countries varies from around 10 percent in Lithuania and Estonia to 30–40 percent in Poland, the Czech Republic, and Slovakia (Kohl, Lecher, and Platzer 2000).

[3] The accession of ten new member states with fragmented industrial relations may contribute to changing this picture, according to Meardi (2002) introducing stronger dynamics of Anglo-American-style labor market disorganization.

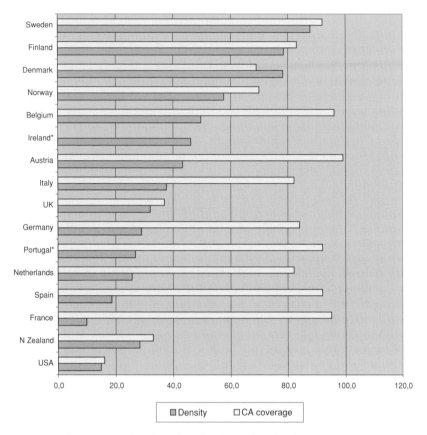

Figure 12.1    Trade union density and collective agreement coverage,
1995
*Notes*:
CA = Collective agreement.
*Sources*: OECD 1997; Traxler *et al.* 2001.

(*EIRO Online* 2003a) and rising labor productivity (40+ percent between
1980 and 2000 in EU-15 member states while real wage compensation
rose just over 20 percent) (CEC 1998a; Mermet 2000). Unit labor costs
have decreased and profitability increased in virtually all EU countries.
With some important exceptions, however, this has not triggered a virtuous circle of investment-driven employment growth, leading defenders of conventional economic thought to blame alleged labor market
rigidities and many unions to question the wisdom of continued wage
moderation.

Despite the relative stability of industrial relations in most West European countries, fiercer external competition and domestic labor market restructuring have caused national strains and declining trade union power, prompting initiatives to modernize union structures, organization, and recruitment. These efforts have thus far been insufficient to turn the tide (Waddington and Hoffmann 2000). The impact of European integration has, in this respect, been ambiguous – pressuring national unions and undermining some sources of their power, on the one hand, and promoting European social partnership and minimum labor standards, on the other. The latter has provided unions with certain opportunities and resources that have improved their political credibility and protected against unfettered market competition (Dølvik and Visser 2001). But the modesty of such steps toward Europeanization has tended to encourage national actors to continue investing most of their resources in what remains of their national systems (Dølvik 1997; Streeck 1998; Martin and Ross 1999). The EU has thereby both restrained and facilitated the role of trade unions in adjusting European labor markets in a direction compatible with international competitiveness and the requirements of the EMU regime.

### Adjusting to EMU: cross-national distinctions and commonalities

Pre-EMU, national wage-setting institutions varied in their capacity to calibrate wage growth with macroeconomic stability, depending on what Traxler refers to as their *structural responsiveness* (1998: 2).[4] Traxler, Blaschke, and Kittel (2001) take this further by investigating the conditions under which wage-bargainers can affect wage behavior to avert macroeconomic imbalances and/or restrictive monetary policies, concluding that structural responsiveness depends critically on the *governability* of wage-bargaining – that is, local compliance with increases agreed at higher levels. They add that governability is strongly influenced by the legal and institutional frameworks provided by the state, especially as regards strike rights and peace duties. Horizontal coordination has a tendency to break down, especially during booms, because of defection by union rank-and-file. Its effectiveness, through which economy-wide external effects are internalized by wage bargainers, depends on

---

[4] An OECD analysis (1997) finds little evidence that any specific bargaining system generates better or worse performance. Another approach concludes that such studies are inconclusive because variations in performance are due not only to wage-bargaining structures but also to the way they interact with monetary policy and monetary regimes (Hall and Franzese, Jr., 1998; Holden 1999; Iversen 1999). In this view, institutionalized interaction and anticipatory signaling between a central bank credibly committed to price stability and wage-bargainers are central.

vertical coordination – the ability of higher levels of wage-setting institutions to secure compliance at the lowest levels at which wages are determined. Centralized coordination performs best if governability is high, but worst if lack of compliance allows decentralized wage increases to augment centrally agreed pay rises. Unless appropriate legal and institutional frameworks provide for such compliance, decentralized uncoordinated bargaining is the second-best solution.[5]

Traxler (1998) groups the structural responsiveness of bargaining systems of the current EU member states in the pre-EMU period in three clusters. There has been *high responsiveness* in Austria, Germany, Finland, the Netherlands, Sweden, and Denmark (with variants of pattern bargaining, peak-level concertation, and high governability). Responsiveness has been *intermediary* in the UK (with uncoordinated bargaining) and France (state-imposed coordination). *Low responsiveness* has been the case for Belgium, Spain, Ireland, Italy, Portugal, and Greece (with voluntary peak-level coordination and low governability).[6] Although wage-setting behavior has provided moderation during the transition to EMU, this may reflect high unemployment and the imperative of qualifying for EMU entry. Awareness that wage-bargainers cannot now be bailed out by exchange rate policy may have induced more lasting changes in strategies, but the elimination of links between national monetary policy and wage-setting could work in the opposite direction, reducing national responsiveness, especially in smaller countries.

EMU raises three questions about these national systems. First, will particular national systems provide sufficient responsiveness to prevent more restrictive monetary policies and rising unemployment? Next, how might the transfer of monetary policy to the ECB influence the responsiveness of national systems? Finally, is European coordination of wage policies required to construct viable means of communication and interaction between monetary authorities and wage-bargainers in the euro-zone? A look at the changes that have taken place during the transition to EMU and since suggests that any simple projection of variation in responsiveness in the pre-EMU period into the EMU era may be misleading.

[5] One reason why decentralized, market-based bargaining systems perform worse than governable, coordinated, systems is that monetary policies have little direct impact on bargaining behavior in decentralized systems, as illustrated in the UK in the 1980s, thus requiring stronger doses of deflation and unemployment to curb excessive wage pressures (Crouch 2000: 208–209).

[6] That most countries belonging to the former D-mark zone have had high responsiveness indicates a causal connection between monetary regime and wage behavior (Iversen 1999). For example, Visser and Hemerijck (1997) suggest that the shift to coordinated wage restraint in the Netherlands in the early 1980s was triggered by the introduction of a hard guilder regime, and similar tendencies have been witnessed in Ireland, Italy, Spain, and the Nordic countries.

*The inflationary periphery: re-centralization and social pacts*   In the least responsive countries, transition to EMU has been accompanied by notable changes in industrial relation. In the 1990s Italy, Spain, Portugal, Greece, and Ireland saw re-centralization of wage negotiations and social pacts to internalize EMU constraints, to develop clearer definitions of the roles of decentralized actors, and to reach agreement on reforms in the labor market–welfare state nexus (Regini 1997). In several cases, the revival of tri-partite concertation in the 1990s occurred in response to failed attempts to curb inflation through tough monetary policies in fragmented bargaining systems. While the transformation of the Italian system in the 1990s successfully curbed wage–price inflation, economic and employment growth has remained sluggish. By contrast, Spain experienced a downturn followed by a strong recovery and employment growth from the late 1990s, combined with sustained wage moderation.

Beyond the cases explored in this volume, Portugal, despite a rigid system of labor market regulation and collective bargaining, strong union rivalry, and a shallow tradition of social pacts, showed much better economic and employment performance than Spain (*EIRO Online* 2000), but has recently run into a deep crisis. Fragile institutions of wage-bargaining and coordination, plus the stance of the most influential union, Intersindical (CGTP), raise concern that soaring wages could put jobs in the less productive sectors in jeopardy if growth again accelerates. Thus far, however, wage moderation has prevailed. In Greece, now in EMU, doubts about the viability of the industrial relations system and the stop–go pattern of state-led social concertation have been widespread (Ioannou 2000). The 1997 Confidence Pact between the government and the social partners led to some adjustments in the regulation of industrial relations aimed at decentralization of bargaining and flexibilization of the labor market (Christofi 2000), but the measures were partial and ineffective (Ioannou 2000). Nevertheless, the transition to EMU has been accompanied by wage moderation, bringing pay rises in line with the European average. In view of the inconsistent pattern of social concertation and collective bargaining, however, how actors will tackle pressures for further reform now that EMU membership has been achieved, remains to be seen. In Ireland, deep crisis in the 1980s prompted wide-ranging national tri-partite pacts centered on improving competitiveness and modernization anchored in consensus about wage restraint (Wallace *et al.* 1998). Although the Irish economy is in the sterling zone, actors have been committed to entering EMU, with the latest social partnership agreements tailor-made for doing so. Irish economic transformation and incorporation into the EMU regime has brought remarkable growth in investment, production, and employment (in 1995–2002 increasing by 6–8 percent per year). Inflation has surged as well, however, and the looming question is whether centralized wage restraint is sustainable in a context of labor scarcity and without the legal frameworks usually associated with high bargaining governability.[7]

In many of the new member states, the fragmented organizations and shallow institutions for collective bargaining (Kohl, Lecher, and Platzer 2000) might suggest that shifting to the Euro is a risky undertaking.

*Small corporatist states: seeking more articulated and flexible coordination*    Changes in the supposedly better-prepared countries of the former D-mark zone have been less pronounced. Still, within frameworks of centralized coordination, moves toward "organized decentralization" – more industry- and company-based negotiations have been widespread (Traxler 1998; Crouch 2000). The Austrian industrial relations system has been exceptionally stable and has ensured moderate labor cost increases and unemployment while allowing significant wage differentiation in accordance with local and sectoral productivity developments. This has persisted unchanged despite political unrest, economic growth, and shrinking unemployment in recent years (Blaschke *et al.* 2000). In the Netherlands, which after the "Dutch disease" in the early 1980s introduced a hard guilder regime and fiscal austerity, the Wassenaar Accord of 1982 initiated persistent, centrally concerted wage restraint that, combined with tax relief and decentralization of wage-setting, led to significant employment growth, especially in part-time female employment (Visser and Hemerijck 1997). Because of the consistent drop in relative unit labor costs (34 percent from 1982 to 1993), the Netherlands has been accused of beggar-thy-neighbor policies, and according to Bispinck and Schulten (2000), the Dutch case is a prototype of competitive corporatism and the risk of deflationary wage policies and collective irrationality under EMU. With tighter labor markets, wages and prices rose sharply from the late 1990s, but the trade unions swiftly returned to moderation and even offered a wage freeze in 2003–2004 as part of a tri-partite deal aimed at preventing cuts in social benefits and overcoming economic recession.

---

[7] March 2000 saw signing of the fifth national social pact since 1987, the Program for Prosperity and Fairness (PPF), providing pay increases of at least 15 percent over thirty-three months. With inflation surpassing 6 percent in October 2000, an additional pay increase of 3 percent in 2001–2002 was implemented, and unions consented to a (voluntary) reinforced industrial peace clause, underpinned by income tax relief and reduced VAT rates. The expansionary effects of these measures triggered a harsh reaction from the ECOFIN Council, stating that the budget represented a breach with the EU Economic Policy Guidelines and calling for fiscal tightening.

Although the Belgian system of industrial relations, in a context of public indebtedness and deteriorating competitiveness, has gone through periods of forceful state intervention, wage laws, and tension between rival unions and regions, shared determination to enter into EMU catalyzed controversial change in industrial relations in the late 1990s. According to the law on competitiveness, wage increases in Belgium must align with the weighted average in Germany, France, and the Netherlands. If the social partners are unable to agree on a two-year wage norm, the government can decide alone. Belgium thus provides a prototype for state-imposed coordination. Since the late 1990s, the situation has normalized, and bargaining rounds have been pursued without state intervention.

In Finland, the only Nordic EMU country thus far, commitment to monetary union stimulated innovative adjustments of labor market institutions (Bolt 1999; Pekkarinen 2001) that reflected deviation of Finnish economic cycles and production structures from the Euro-core and the asymmetric shocks that frequently hit the Finnish economy. After Finland experienced severe depression in the early 1990s,[8] the government in 1995 invited the social partners to negotiate a long-term program of wage moderation, labor market reforms, and cuts in taxes and public debt. This initiated rising, noninflationary growth and falling unemployment and helped Finland meet the EMU convergence criteria a brief few years after the deepest depression in Europe since the Second World War. Tri-partite talks also led to the creation of domestic "shock absorbers" assigned to substitute for currency devaluations (Bolt 1999; Kauppinen 1998). Emphasizing the need for centralized concertation and flexible, productivity-based wage-setting, the social partners in 1997 agreed to set up two national *buffer funds* to make the negotiation of pro-cyclical nominal wage cuts unnecessary during downturns. Linked to the system of pension and unemployment insurance and financed through extra employer contributions and reduced union wage demands over three–five years, the buffer funds permit adjustment of the employers' indirect labor costs to the economic cycle. In contrast to devaluations or nominal wage cuts, explicitly linking employer contributions and wage growth to the cycle builds an extra countercyclical element into the system while remaining competition neutral over the cycle (avoiding beggar-thy-neighbor shifts). Although doubts still prevail over the utility of buffer

---

[8] Because of the crisis caused by domestic overheating after deregulation of credit markets and collapse of trade with the Soviet Union, production and employment dropped by 12 percent and unemployment soared toward 20 percent between 1990 and 1994. The crisis was aggravated by a nonaccommodative monetary policy stance based on a fixed exchange rate with the ECU, which because of speculative pressures led to soaring interest rates (Bolt 1999; Pekkarinen 2001).

funds in a real crisis, the process has heightened awareness of the changing role of wage-setting under EMU. While corporatist crisis management in Finland often has been followed by inflation and labor disaffection (Lilja 1992), in the most recent recovery the main actors have persisted in efforts to bring down unemployment and continued social partnership with new moderate agreements for income policy.

In the 1950s and 1960s Sweden and Denmark, which have so far chosen to stay out of EMU, developed a centrally coordinated pattern of wage-setting based on the leading role of competition-exposed manufacturing. This model has largely persisted, despite adjustments to changing conditions (Kjellberg 1998). In Denmark, following a period of tough adjustment, state-imposed crisis deals, and the linking of the Danish currency to the D-mark/ECU in the early 1980s, the interplay between macroeconomic policies and wage formation became well attuned to EMU requirements during the ERM years (Iversen 1999). As one of the few EU countries with no problems meeting the EMU convergence criteria and with the krona now pegged to the Euro, Denmark has retained a generous welfare state, egalitarian wage structure, and high and growing employment, while wage-formation has become more decentralized and flexible within centralized coordination (Due *et al.* 2000). To prepare for EMU, the main parties in private industry signed a path-breaking four-year Stability Pact in 2000. Although the Danish central bank first shadowed Bundesbank monetary policy and now shadows the ECB, and dominant forces on both sides of industry campaigned in favor, the September 2000 referendum again rejected Danish EMU membership. Political winds, however, indicate that public opinion may be changing and a new referendum is foreseen in coming years.

In Sweden, the 1980s brought increasing interunion rivalry, economic crisis, and eventually a breakdown of cross-sectoral bargaining, due to tension over the role of sheltered sectors and employer disaffection (Kjellberg 1998). To curb inflation, the Swedish krona was briefly pegged to the ECU, but after mounting speculation in 1992 it was allowed to float, and a nonaccommodating, anti-inflationary monetary policy regime was installed. Following failed state initiatives to restore coordination, the Calmfors Commission (SOU 1996: 158) suggested that insufficient capacity for wage coordination would make EMU membership risky. After recession and soaring unemployment in the early 1990s, Sweden surprisingly re-balanced public budgets, squeezed out inflation, and embarked on significant growth and employment creation while maintaining the most elaborate welfare state in the world. This transition has been accompanied by notable changes in wage-setting. Alongside new patterns of coordination at sectoral level, major unions have committed to keep wage growth in line with "European norms" of inflation plus productivity (Kjellberg 1998). Pay rounds in the late 1990s largely stuck to this formula (Dølvik and Vartiainen 2002). In analyzing the conditions for EMU membership, the Calmfors Commission-II (SOU 2002: 17) found that the wage-setting system had made preparations for EMU. The main union confederation (LO) had made the establishment of buffer funds a condition for Swedish entry, but in view of the connotations of the controversial wage earner funds of the 1980s the proposal was rejected by the government, which instead proposed a larger fiscal margin (2.5 percent surplus over the cycle). Despite strong support for Swedish entry into EMU among the leaderships of the main social partners, a solid popular majority rejected EMU membership in the referendum held in September 2003.

*The UK: the dark horse?*   Although the UK did not join EMU in the first round and polls show a majority opposed to joining, Prime Minister Blair's pro-membership approach has had strong support from the union confederation (TUC) and employers' association (CBI). If the exchange rate of sterling can be reduced before entering, the British decentralized, market-based, wage-setting system is well attuned to the need for wage and labor market flexibility under EMU. If Britain joins, however, will decentralized wage flexibility be sufficient to substitute for the loss of monetary policy, which in recent years has played an essential role in macroeconomic adjustment? Throughout the 1980s and 1990s, high interest rates have been used repeatedly to cool down the economy (Crouch 2000), while UK wage growth has not been particularly responsive to cyclical shifts. As the British cycle is sometimes out of sync with the Euro-core, the ECB cannot be expected to stabilize the British economy. This might accentuate the need for crisis management through social concertation, if the British relinquish the pound.

*The critical factor: the larger countries of the Euro-core*   In the 1990s the dominant economies in the eurozone – Germany and France – faced political gridlock, sluggish growth, and inability to agree on means for adjusting social security and industrial relations systems. Because Germany alone accounts for one-third of production in the eurozone and together with France around half of Euro-GDP, developments in these two countries will presumably constitute the most important references for the monetary policies of the ECB.

France has had a state-dominated bargaining system with weak and fragmented social actors. Successive legislation on working-time reduction and virtual de-unionization of the private sector has induced considerable flexibility and decentralization of industrial relations (Dufour 2000). Combined with high unemployment, "*franc fort*" policies introduced in the 1980s have been accompanied by moderate wage growth. Still, the faction-ridden French labor movement commands considerable capacity for political mobilization, and questions remain as to systemic compatibility with EMU requirements (Boyer 2000). Curbing soaring indirect labor costs, particularly pensions, through the tri-partite social security system may become the critical test of the French industrial relations system's ability to adjust to the new circumstances.

The crucial question, however, is what happens in Germany, long a stronghold of monetary stability, responsive social partnership, and economic success, although the double pressures of reunification and internationalization have severely taxed actors' abilities to find solutions (Streeck 1997). The shift to the Euro has reversed the appreciation of the D-mark, reduced interest rates, and improved German competitiveness and exports, but the economy has not recovered and proposals for more far-reaching reforms – including American-style deregulation of the labor market – have been voiced in business circles. In 1998, the incoming SPD government, inspired by the Dutch example, revived the idea of a tri-partite Alliance for Employment, to forge solutions to welfare and labor market issues. While employers pushed for adoption of "employment-oriented" moderate wage policies, unions remained reluctant to accept wage restraint and defended *Tarifautonomie* and industrial pattern bargaining. Key unions have even called for an "end to modesty," arguing that recent wage moderation had aggravated unemployment by restraining domestic demand (Bispinck and Schulten 2000). *IG Metall* leaders, in particular, have expressed skepticism about national social pacts based on wage moderation, which in their view engender competitive and potentially deflationary wage underbidding, and have repeatedly called for a more offensive, coordinated wage policy among European trade unions.

In response to a deepening crisis, the besieged Chancellor Schröder in the spring of 2003 launched a reform agenda that included calls for more local "opening clauses" in collective agreements, cuts in taxes, unemployment and social security schemes, and easing of job protection in smaller companies – fueling rage among the trade unions. After the main parts of the cuts in taxes and social benefits had been adopted in late 2003 a slow economic recovery seemed under way. But with the decline in collective bargaining coverage, high unemployment, sluggish growth, the strong Euro, and severe problems in complying with the SGP, uncertainty about the German model of *Sozialpartnerschaft* as an "anchor" in EMU still looms large.

*Summary: changing industrial relations during the transition to EMU*   The coincidence of transition to EMU and the German post-unification crisis contributed to economic stagnation and rising unemployment in core economies in the EMS. Although labor markets recovered in the late 1990s, especially in the EU periphery, wage growth has been moderate, even if with tight labor markets and rising inflation there has been some wage growth in a few countries. Contrary to predictions, the transition to EMU did not bring the dismantling or convergence of national institutions of industrial relations toward the deregulated and decentralized Anglo-American model and the British case remains an outlier. With persistent institutional diversity, the shift to a low-inflation monetary regime paradoxically brought the resurgence of centralized concertation, social pacts, and state intervention in labor market governance, especially in previously inflation-ridden countries in the Euro-periphery. Wage-setting became more decentralized, but nation-wide, multi-employer collective agreements still determine the wage-setting framework. Widespread "social dumping" and a "race to the bottom" have not materialized (Teague 2000). Faced with the alternative of unilateral state-led convergence programs and flexibilization, many unions chose to participate in "credibility bargaining" (Teague 2000), offering wage restraint as a functional alternative to labor market deregulation (Calmfors 2000). In Germany and France, however, retrenchment, unemployment, and union decline caused conflict and stalemate over the adjustment of national regimes, contributing to ambiguity and uncertainty about the future trajectory of European industrial relations.

The new wave of renationalized "competitive corporatism" is markedly different from the neo-corporatism of the 1970s, more oriented to supply-side issues and less associated with redistribution brokered by state financial concessions (Dølvik 1993). A common feature has nevertheless been the coupling of supply-side factors with overall wage formation for the credibility and stability of macroeconomic policies – a linkage accentuated by the monetary integration process in Europe (Teague 2000). As Ferner and Hyman (1998) point out, the resurgent importance of the "social wage" – still under the influence of organized labor – seemingly strengthened governments' and employers' interest in social concertation and brought national unions some political leverage and bargaining capital. Consistent with Katzenstein's (1985) analysis that flexible corporatism tends to flourish in small, open economies, and contrary to the view that internationalization and monetary integration would render corporatism obsolete (Schmitter and Streeck 1992), fiercer external constraints and market competition were the preconditions for new concertation in the 1990s (Visser and Hemerijck 1997). These things were particularly salient in countries where economic decline and/or severe political crisis coincided with the imperatives of reaching the EMU deadline, generating a climate of emergency conducive to reform. In contrast with the gridlock over welfare and labor reform in some of the larger Euro-countries, the transition to EMU passed surprisingly smoothly in several of the countries considered least prepared for the Euro.

Why no "Americanization" so far? One reason is that, in contrast to the US, the decentralized territorial entities of the multi-tiered European industrial relations framework are still embedded in fairly coherent national polities where social institutions, legislation, and state support facilitate multi-employer bargaining and cross-sectoral coordination, while limiting cross-national labor market competition and mobility. However, because recent developments have occurred during a period of economic crisis in which social actors have recognized cross-class interests for national entry into the EMU, there are reasons to be less sanguine about the viability of national social pacts after this point. Whether they represent the last gasps of the social corporatist model (Teague 2000) or a new European formula of "competitive solidarity" (Streeck 1999) remains to be seen. Thus Boeri *et al.* (2001) and Calmfors (2000) suggest that even though social pacts are better suited than decentralized systems to cope with globalization and monetary integration and are likely to predominate in the medium term, they may in the longer run be overrun by structural forces (e.g. changing technology, management policies, and workforce differentiation) promoting decentralization. Similar forecasts were made in the 1980s, however, and their failure enjoins caution about such determinist predictions.

*National social pacts and EMU?*    In assessing whether national social pacts are a viable mode of adjustment under EMU, it is important to bear in mind the fragile nature of recent social pacts and the uneven responsiveness of national wage-setting systems in the eurozone. Union discussion has centered on whether social pacts entail a form of competitive corporatism incompatible with broader labor interests and whether they are simply a defensive form of crisis management that will evaporate in better times.[9] But to the extent that solidaristic wage policies and

---

[9] This controversy has been associated with claims that excessive national wage moderation, supply-side reforms, and tax relief have boosted employment and competitiveness to the detriment of jobs and labor standards in other countries, amounting to a zero- or minus-sum game in the European economy as a whole (Bispinck and Schulten 2000;

social reform help eliminate obstacles to work, get more people into paid employment, and boost profitability and investment, they appear, other things being equal, to increase disposable income, consumer demand, imports and GDP growth. In the 1990s in the Netherlands, Denmark, and Ireland, wage restraint, in a context of growing labor supply and investment, apparently made room for some fiscal stimulus and higher growth than would otherwise have occurred. Thus the impact of wage moderation on jobs in other countries depends not only on labor cost effects in exposed sectors but also on macroeconomic policies, investment, GDP growth rates, and the effects on imports (affecting employment in other countries' export sectors).

Because social models vary, it is hard to determine objective criteria for national policies that promote national growth and competitiveness. Some guidelines are nevertheless desirable, especially about the impact of measures for winning international market shares on growth and social justice in the eurozone. One principle is to disallow national policies that, if simultaneously applied by other countries facing the same problem or situation, would generate detrimental collective effects. The need would remain, however, to find shared understandings of the circumstances under which national deviations from such norms might be acceptable. Searching for common norms places the idea of European wage coordination on the same plane as the quest for common minimum standards in company taxation and labor protection to prevent rational individual behavior from causing collective irrationality and a "race to the bottom" (Dølvik 1993).

Whether social pacts will be sustainable in more prosperous times, plausible assumptions are that fiercer competition, the shift in monetary regime, and awareness that wage-bargainers can no longer rely on bail-outs by governments or central banks have influenced strategic considerations for many national union federations (Teague 2000). Doubts remain, however, over the ability of national union leaderships to ensure rank-and-file compliance with centrally determined policies once labor markets become tighter. Especially in catch-up countries on the European periphery, it may be hard to keep members, not least in multinational companies, from demanding equal pay with colleagues doing similar jobs in high-wage/high-productivity countries (Streeck 1998).

Martin 2000). Despite its plausibility, this view is overly general and simplistic. National economic and employment growth is not exogenously given or determined solely by macroeconomic policies but is affected by a variety of endogenous factors, among them the role of wages and supply-side factors in the labor market–welfare state nexus, as indicated by the immense differences in employment levels and the effects of growth on job creation in the EU countries (Padalino and Vivarelli 1997).

This is a challenge not only for the Euro-periphery, however. Ongoing changes in the composition of labor may weaken the coordinating capacity of unions as well as employers (Dølvik 2001), and the shift to EMU could complicate the pursuit of solidaristic wage policies in the Euro-core. Without the disciplining role of national central banks and financial markets, union bargainers may be encouraged to adopt tougher approaches and their leaderships will have difficulties mustering support for coordinated moderation – the problem that led to breakdown of incomes policies in the 1970s. After a long period of wage restraint and widening income inequality, tension and frustrated demands can easily explode. Employers' efforts to compete for and retain labor in tight labor markets work in the same direction. Such dynamics might interact with the fact that unions in domestic and exposed sectors are differently affected. While ceding national monetary policy reinforces the disciplinary effect of product market competition in export-oriented sectors, it removes the pressures of financial markets on wages in the domestic service sectors formerly caused by awareness that excessive wage growth would raise interest rates. As wage growth in these domestic sectors spills over to costs in export sectors, shrinking manufacturing unions will probably have an even stronger interest in economy-wide coordination, whereas unions in growing service sectors could turn to more forceful pursuit of particularistic interests, which, other things being equal, will hamper employment growth.[10]

Social pacts have recently enabled unions to ensure a shift to employment-oriented, responsible wage policies in a context of sluggish labor markets, but the task will become more arduous if EMU, as promised, brings about growing prosperity – as indicated by Dutch and Irish developments. The more economically successful EMU becomes, the more important it becomes for industrial relations systems to resist labor cost inflation and maximize job creation, bring down unemployment, and retain a sense of solidarity in wage-setting. Growth can be expected to vary significantly across the eurozone, along with the governability of bargaining. Inflationary and deflationary wage impulses will therefore likely operate simultaneously in different regions. Although these tendencies might function as adjustment mechanisms and buffers against cumulative dynamics in the entire eurozone, they imply that ECB monetary policy may function pro-cyclically in certain regions, as it has in Ireland. The apparently contradictory concerns with deflationary and

---

[10] *HBV* and *IG Medien*, the service sector unions, withdrew from the German Alliance for Jobs precisely because of its disciplining effect on pay policies. Similar defection tendencies have occurred in Ireland, Finland, and Norway.

inflationary wage spirals under EMU thus reflect two sides of the same coin, namely that the reduced macroeconomic stabilization capacity at the national level, combined with the quest for increased wage flexibility, can readily trigger pro-cyclically oscillating wage policies. As national unions face stronger incentives to accept real wage cuts during economic slumps, they will, absent some sort of buffer funds, aim at making wages equally flexible upward during economic boom – possibly triggering penalizing countermoves by the ECB.[11] The risk is that without institutionalized patterns of communication between (coordinated) wage-bargainers and the ECB, given the lack of stabilization capacity at the national level, a counterproductive dynamic of mutual overshooting could evolve between the ECB and uncoordinated national wage-bargainers, harming growth and employment. Assuming that national policy coordination alone will prove sufficient to ensure optimal interplay between macroeconomic policies and aggregate wage-setting in the eurozone thus seems optimistic.

To sum up, although EMU makes national concertation more essential, the contradictory pressures on national systems suggest that it will be harder to sustain. The more economic policies develop in an expansionary direction, the stronger becomes the need for a common framework of European guidelines that ensure that wage growth does not get out of control and prompt retaliation by the ECB and macroeconomic policy-makers. If the aim is to maximize employment growth in the eurozone without copying the Anglo-American model, the revival of national concertation represents an indispensable but insufficient precondition. National social pacts as such do not undermine the quest for Europeanization of collective bargaining and economic policy coordination. The broader functioning of social pacts should not be assessed only on form alone, however, but also on their content and ways of interacting. If social actors cannot maintain policy coordination to help weaker parts of the labor force back into paid work at the national level, it is hard to see how these goals can be accomplished on a European scale, where social identification is weaker, the structure of interests much more complex, and mechanisms for ensuring compliance virtually absent. If labor interests are to be accommodated on a European scale, working national systems of interest intermediation (upstream) and implementation (downstream) must be in place. Effectuation of a European wage norm hinges

---

[11] These considerations suggest that coordinated wage-setting at the national level should aim at smoothing wage developments over the cycle (synchronically) and not be narrowly targeted at short-term economic fluctuations. Such an understanding should preferably also shape the way the ECB (and European trade unions) judge the impact of national wage-setting on inflation (and competition).

on the comprehensiveness and efficiency of the national systems assigned to implement it.

## 2     From national to European concertation?

*National flexibility and European coordination: an irresolvable contradiction?*

If the implications of EMU for national industrial relations systems are contradictory and hard to predict, the aggregate effects and conditions for developing a viable European model of labor market governance are even harder to disentangle. For the social actors the challenge is to transcend the gap between microrationality and macrorationality and to reconcile the seemingly incompatible quest for national flexibility and European coordination.

The basic rationale for European-level coordination of pay bargaining stems from the asymmetric relationship among the three main determinants of macroeconomic policy under EMU: monetary, fiscal, and wage policies. These three policy levers were formerly determined at national level, but under EMU they are distributed over multiple levels where actors are assumed to operate independently of each other, making for significant collective action problems (Dyson 2000). With the ECB governing monetary policy, nations conducting fiscal policies within the SGP, and decentralized national actors determining wage policies, the risks are both free-riding and policies that pull in different, if not contradictory, directions leading to sub-optimal outcomes (Boyer 2000). Unlike various institutionalized and informal patterns of communication that usually help facilitate policy congruence at the national level, the original EMU design, with ECB as the focal point, provides no mechanism for interaction or coordination among the main actors, who carry very different preferences and interests.[12] The problem, however, "is that none of these actors is able to adequately satisfy its preferences without the cooperation of the others, whether implicit or explicit" (Dyson 2000: 46). Besides the trade unions' aspiration to make wage policies a lever to gain influence on EU policies, the main purpose of coordinating wage policies on a European scale is to enhance predictability and means of communication among wage-bargainers, the ECB, and fiscal policy-makers. European wage coordination might thus substitute for the loss of national

---

[12] On the contrary, the ECB cannot receive political instruction or develop ties with external actors, precluding it from any overt European policy concertation. ECB actors have also actively opposed *ex ante* coordination, which in their view would blur responsibilities and risk destabilizing short-term activism (Issing 1999, quoted in Dyson 2000: 30).

monetary policy as a reference point for national wage-setting and facilitate national actors' consideration of ECB policies when designing their own wage policies. The process might provide scope for more expansionary monetary policies, a better attuned interplay among the different pillars of economic policy, and higher employment growth than would otherwise be the case.[13]

The hurdles are considerable. What formulae or criteria are needed for coordination? How can it be designed and implemented? Most European employers' associations and their European representatives have opposed any move toward European collective bargaining, preferring to keep wages and working conditions decentralized.[14] National governments have also been cautious. The Maastricht Social Agreement (MSA) explicitly stated that the EU has no mandate in issues of pay and industrial conflict, even if the EU's role has gradually expanded in labor market regulation, social dialog, and the negotiation of European framework agreements on parental leave, part-time work, and temporary work. The crisis after the German reunification recession led, moreover, to the European employment strategy, emphasizing benchmarking and coordination of national labor market policies in dialog with the social partners. (Goetschy 1999). The leap into EMU did prompt EU governments to establish a macroeconomic dialog (among the ECB, finance ministers, the Commission, and the social partners) at the 1999 Cologne Summit. The launch of the Euro and the European employment strategy has thus generated some political and institutional spillover effects.

Although these developments have certainly contributed to the European trade unions' domestically contentious "yes, but" support for EMU, its restrictive design has not matched trade union expectations (Foden 1998). The ETUC has therefore constantly called for a more expansionist interpretation of the Maastricht Treaty and coordination of monetary,

---

[13] Two different arguments can support the case for European coordination. First, coordination can serve as a functional equivalent to nonaccommodating monetary policies (Holden 1999). Second, in the zone where ECB policy is nonaccommodating, national experience indicates that results are better in coordinated than in uncoordinated bargaining systems (Iversen 1999), where decentralized actors usually do not respond directly to signals from a distant central bank (Crouch 2000), and more draconian monetary policies may be required to curb inflationary pressures (Hall 1994).

[14] The Union of Industrial and Employers' Confederations of Europe (UNICE) is clear: "It is sometimes argued that wage bargaining at European level is the logical consequence of EMU and a necessary part of a European strategy for employment. According to UNICE, this is wrong. Wage negotiations are based on many factors such as competitiveness, productivity, taxation, cost of living, etc. They must therefore remain the responsibility of national industrial relations systems" (UNICE 1999: 14). This view is basically shared by CEEP, mainly organizing (semi-)public enterprises, UEAPME (organizing SMB firms), EURO-COMMERCE, and the main European industry associations on the employer side (FEBIs).

fiscal, and wage policies on a European scale. With less than 10 percent of the total GDP in the EU stemming from imports, the ETUC has made a strong case for a Keynesian revival at the European level (Coldrick 1998; ETUC 1999). From the early 1990s, the prospect of EMU and the negotiating option enshrined in the MSA gave impetus to deepened trade union cooperation in the ETUC and its associated European Industry Federations (Dølvik 1999; Martin and Ross 1999).[15] Their declared ambition to develop transnational coordination of collective bargaining, however, came to naught (Keller 1996). With EMU, this debate gained renewed momentum, fueled by concern that unions would be played off against each other in an intensified competition over jobs and income.

### Different pathways to the Europeanization of collective bargaining

At European level centralized wage bargaining between employers and unions is out of the question, and there is also employer association opposition to European coordination of pay policies. The issue is therefore whether the unions are capable of developing a workable form of coordination among themselves, and whether their efforts might create a feasible mode of interaction with the EU macroeconomic authorities. In principle, Euro-wide trade union coordination of collective bargaining might occur at three different levels: (1) the multinational company level, possibly related to European Works Councils (EWCs); (2) the sectoral/industrial level organized by the European Industry Federations (EIFs); and (3) the cross-sectoral, confederal level organized by the ETUC.

At company level, EMU enhances management opportunities to pursue coercive comparison of labor performance. Together with establishment of EWCs, this development might stimulate cooperation between unions in different national branches of transnational European companies, and might, in certain cases, provide the basis for eventual framework agreements on labor standards and "arm's length" bargaining relations (Marginson and Sisson 1998). There are also indications that company negotiations on fringe benefits, bonuses, and performance benefits (i.e. on pay-related issues) are emerging within certain EWCs. With only a small minority of European workers employed in transnationals and with cross-border company bargaining potentially in conflict with coordination at the national and European industry levels, such a path would poorly serve economy-wide coordination, however, and unless properly anchored in industrial coordination might even impede such an objective.

---

[15] ETUC membership consists of sixty-eight national confederations from all over Europe and twelve European Industry Federations (EIFs), together representing more than 60 million members. The overall density was 32 percent in the EU in 2000, down from some 36 percent in the mid-1980s (Ebbinghaus and Visser 2000).

At industrial level, the German *IG Metall,* seeking European pattern bargaining, has been pivotal in regional initiatives to coordinate national collective bargaining with unions in neighboring countries. This has included not only the Benelux countries, where the Doorn Agreement of 1998 brought together both industry unions and the national confederations, but also counterparts on Germany's eastern, southern, and northern borders. Coordination gravitating around Germany, however, has caused concern among some unions outside the Euro-core (Pochet 1999), and attempts to extend these initiatives through the European Metalworkers Federation (EMF) and other EIFs are crucial to prevent new regional and national divisions among European unions.

A common feature of all these initiatives has been adoption of a tentative European norm for development of labor costs, based on the formula of anticipated *inflation + productivity growth,* leaving national actors to determine priorities among wage increases, working-time reduction, training, and other social purposes (e.g. jobs). Apart from whether productivity growth is to be calculated at the national, regional, sectoral, or company level (Mermet 2000), the EMF compromise formula (a "balanced share of productivity growth") reflects discrepant views among European unions on wage moderation as a means to spur employment.[16] While *IG Metall* adheres to a neo-Keynesian interpretation of the employment crisis and tends to see wage restraint mainly as a zero-sum game, unions in many southern and northern countries are concerned not to price national members out of work. Despite the lukewarm response by some unions outside the former D-mark zone, the creation of common arenas for discussion of such essential issues – exchange of information and demands, mutual representation, conflict support, and increased synchronization of pay rounds across national boundaries – is a significant expression of new dynamics in transnational union cooperation in response to EMU. As envisaged in the EMF strategy (Schulten 2000), such dynamics are most likely to gain headway through clusters of national unions operating under comparable economic and social conditions, implying that the most feasible model of European coordination is through interlinked, regional bargaining networks.

At confederal level, transition to EMU has triggered new developments in macroeconomic dialog to promote information exchange and confidence among actors involved in monetary, fiscal, and wage policy. Although the talks have been secretive and nonbinding and none of the actors has a mandate to engage in anything more, past national experience shows that such tri-partite institutions of signal exchange stimulate

---

[16] A more elaborate formula, based on the idea of a sectoral European wage "Snake" with broader corridors for adjustment over the cycle, has been developed by the EIF of textile unions.

trust-building, learning, and sometimes tacit forms of concertation. So far, however, the process has appeared fairly ritualistic.[17]

At the 1999 Congress, the ETUC decided to become a key actor in developing union wage coordination, followed by adoption of common guidelines in December 2000 that were very much like the EMF approach (ETUC 2000). Representatives of national confederations and the sectoral EIFs take part in the ETUC collective bargaining committee and on the ETUC side in macroeconomic dialog meetings. Without autonomous coordination of wage policies at the industrial level, the ETUC representatives in macroeconomic dialog would have no leverage, and, conversely, without the ETUC role in the macrodialogue, industrial actors could not exchange direct signals with the ECB. However, the belated and timid ECB interest rate drop in 2001 associated with US downturn and the slowdown in Euro-core countries demonstrates that the ECB has not shifted toward the bolder expansionary policies called for by the ETUC.

### A two-level model of soft European wage coordination in the making?

Prospects for coherent trade union coordination of collective bargaining under EMU seem dim, therefore. There are different approaches inside the European trade union movement – at the national, sectoral, regional, and European confederal levels – and the EIFs and the ETUC are marked by internal heterogeneity, incongruent structures around sectoral/industrial boundaries, fragile mandates, and weak capacity to ensure compliance with agreed-upon policies (Ebbinghaus and Visser 2000).[18] The hurdles are significant, therefore, but one should not overestimate the problems. Social learning processes, based on the emergent pattern

---

[17] Despite the ECB-centric nature of the network of interdependent eurozone institutions, Dyson (2000: 63) suggests that the "the European Employment Pact, the employment guidelines, and the macroeconomic dialog, alongside the Economic Policy Committee and the Employment and Labor Market Committee, formed another potential focal point in Euro-zone negotiations. Potentially they could evolve to counterbalance the role of the ECB." By identifying policy strategies and exploiting "arenas without rules" states have in this view sought to bring new ideas to bear on eurozone policy by stimulating broader learning processes and implicit coordination (Dyson 2000: 63). So far, however, these initiatives have been defined by their consistency with the dominant economic policy paradigm of "sound money." To Dyson, it would be desirable to promote anticipatory reforms centered on establishment of some modest fiscal transfer mechanism and development of macroeconomic dialog to devise procedures for "demand management" in case of severe economic slump and ensure that wage bargaining is coordinated with monetary policy (Dyson 2000: 267–269).

[18] Ebbinghaus and Visser (2000) suggest that the recent mergers and tendency to establish conglomerate mega-unions – especially in Germany – might cause even less compatible (idiosyncratic) structures, undermine the confederations, and as a result further complicate the development of cross-national coordination.

of what Teague (2000: 430) has coined multi-tiered "credibility bargaining" with the Euro-regime as "focal point", might point toward a two-level model of soft European coordination, or "shadow" pattern bargaining. With the potential to link national and transnational coordination of wage policies and help accommodate the need for national flexibility and European coherence, such a model would combine two components. First would be *European cross-national coordination of wage policy on the sectoral level*, perhaps led by *IG Metall* and the EMF process, defining the general pace and margins for collective bargaining in the eurozone. Next would be *National cross-sectoral coordination of wage policy*, through either centralized concertation or industrial pattern bargaining, conditioning (upstream) national union participation in European coordination and transposing (downstream) European margins and parameters into national systems in accordance with different national and sectoral conditions.

In such a model, industrial pattern bargaining or social pacts within the nation state would be the precondition for a "soft" mode of cross-national coordination that would not impede social cohesion and employment growth nationally. Conversely, the development of cross-national sector coordination could provide a framework that helped prevent national concertation from turning toward "beggar-thy-neighbor" policies. One condition is that European coordination aims mainly at defining normative criteria, guidelines, and corridors for wage increases over the cycle and allows ample leeway for adjustment to national and sectoral differences in productivity, resembling the "Open Method of Coordination" (OMC). By ensuring that trend-setting actors in chosen European front industries, notably the metal sectors, are embedded in ties and commitments to their fellow unions in less productive sectors at the national levels, actors would thus face strong incentives to consider the externalities of their policies when operationalizing strategy and criteria for wage claims.

Moreover, by constituting a visible referent for the ECB and making clear that the union front runners are assigned a pace-setting role for other unions in the eurozone, such a model can contribute to a credible signaling system and interaction among the key unions, the ECB, and the EU authorities. Besides creating stakes and incentives for the development of a more binding mode of interest accommodation among national and sectoral union actors inside the ETUC, this process provides the trade unions, represented by the ETUC, a platform for acting on the basis of a certain strength and autonomy when entering into macroeconomic dialog at EU level. European sector coordination is thus not an alternative to but a prerequisite for the evolution of "arm's length" soft concertation at the European level.

Such a two-level model of bargaining coordination may look fine in theory but turn out to be utopian in practice. Its operation does presuppose that national unions are prepared and capable of complying with commonly agreed norms and objectives and, at this point, this is far from the case. Indeed, indications suggest that many national unions, despite their official consent at meetings in the ETUC, EMF, or other EIFs, prefer to pursue national goals or, alternatively, are not strong enough to meet the objectives they themselves have proposed in European union meetings. Despite loud language against competitive restraint, wage growth in German manufacturing, for example, has been among the most modest in the eurozone, showing that even the Doorn process of the Euro-core unions is still in its infancy.[19] The Dutch wage freeze in 2003–2004 adds to this picture. And with employers pushing for decentralization and individualized performance-related pay, only time can tell whether unions can maintain economy-wide national coordination, a precondition for European coordination. If unions prove willing and capable of acting in concert on a European scale, the viability of the two-level model of cross-national and cross-sectoral coordination also hinges on whether the ECB is prepared to provide the growth-inducing policies required to entice the unions to sustain their efforts.

A related question is whether such a model can work when key unions cover only a limited share of the workers in relevant European industries, and when only the core unions in, for example, the EMF seem committed to such a venture. First, it is important to recognize that the prime function of European wage norms is to define economically viable criteria for national wage growth over the cycle, not to regulate relative wage differentials. Second, even in countries where economy-wide coordination has remained strong, the pioneer unions in the exposed sectors represent only a limited share of employment, but agreements struck by the wage-leading unions are generalized throughout the economy, partly by legal statute, partly through imitation by other unions and firms. If most companies in the leading sectors comply, full coverage is unnecessary for coordination to be effective. Theoretically, in situations with many dispersed and interdependent actors, effective coordination can be achieved if a small critical mass of key actors commit themselves to act in concert (Traxler 1998). In practical terms, it would probably suffice to curb detrimental wage spirals (upward and downward) and provide a credible referent for the ECB if unions in the Euro-core managed to construct an adequate degree of responsiveness and coordination among

---

[19] A friendlier interpretation would be that such deviations are perfectly sensible if motivated by specific national circumstances and if they are compensated for over the cycle.

Table 12.1 *Multi-tiered European coordination network of bargaining and industrial relations*

| Level | European | National |
|---|---|---|
| Cross-sectoral | Macroeconomic dialog | Social pacts on incomes policies Labor/welfare reform |
|  | Social dialog on European framework agreements | Negotiated implementation of European agreements |
|  | Employment strategy | National action plans |
| Sectoral/industrial | Wage coordination (e.g. EMF and Doorn process) | Industry and sector (pattern) bargaining |
|  | Social dialog, framework agreements | Negotiated implementation |
| Company | Framework agreements, codes of conduct | Company bargaining, "arm's length coordination" |
|  | European Works Councils (EWCs) | Information and consultation |

*Sources*: Author's version of Jacobi (1998) and Schulten (1998).

themselves – for example through the EMF/Doorn process. Moreover, with divergent economic developments in different regions of the euro-zone, coordination without the whole range of peripheral unions would probably enhance consistency in the core and flexibility in the periphery.[20]

In general, the leap into EMU has heightened awareness of the essential role of labor market organizations in mastering economic change and given impetus to Europeanization of trade union strategies. Together with negotiated EU framework regulations within social dialog and the European employment strategy, these changes have stimulated the development of frameworks for what might be considered a nascent European system of industrial relations (see table 12.1).

If the main actors are capable of acting in accordance with their declared intentions, evolving multi-tiered and multi-speed cross-national coordination in key sectors – combined with cross-sectoral concertation at national and, possibly, peak European levels – fits reasonably well with the functional requirements of EMU. If so, EMU will require neither far-reaching centralization of collective bargaining at European level nor anything resembling a European replica of former national models of

---

[20] Such an all-encompassing form of coordination would probably be ineffective, lack credibility, and rob the unions in the catching-up countries of an indispensable means of adjustment, notably the relative autonomy to revert to "free-rider" strategies until their economies become better attuned to the EMU regime.

macrocorporatism. Collective bargaining will remain at the national level, but the actors will be embedded in an increasingly dense web of European commitments, guidelines, and framework understandings, together pointing toward an uneven, articulated, and predominantly horizontal Europeanization of collective bargaining and trade unionism. In such a trajectory, outcomes may converge across states, but institutional diversity and national distinctions are likely to persist. This does not preclude that "arm's length" coordination or virtual European collective bargaining in some sectors and companies, under certain conditions, might be transcended by a more profound trans-nationalization of collective bargaining. The history of industrial relations suggests that path-breaking institutional change has emerged in response to major crisis and conflicts (Sisson 1987). If the main unions in the Euro-core succeed in synchronizing their bargaining rhythm and demands, eventually causing industrial conflict to spread across borders, such a situation might occur.

## 3    Conclusions

EMU presents daunting challenges to industrial relations in Europe. With monetary policies governed by the ECB, limited space for fiscal policies, intensified regime competition, and fiercer struggle for market shares, the adaptability and responsiveness of the national industrial relations systems is ever more crucial for European growth, employment, and social cohesion. EMU has contradictory implications for industrial relations. Microdynamics indicate needs for greater labor market adaptability. Macrodynamics indicate a need for more flexibility and coherence in aggregate wage developments. Both leave actors with complicated strategic choices. Thus far, some convergence of outcomes is evident between countries, alongside increased differentiation within countries, but significant diversity in employment institutions and performance prevails. Despite strain and stagnant labor markets, most national regimes of collective bargaining and trade unionism have shown greater resilience than expected. The deregulated Anglo-American model remains an outlier, centralized institutions of collective bargaining prevail, and in several of the countries considered least fit for the EMU adjustment has been accompanied by revitalization of centralized concertation and modernization of labor market governance. If the crisis of the German model leads to reform rather than abolition of existing frameworks, the prevailing mode of national industrial relations may become reasonably well attuned to requirements for EMU.

In contrast to the many predictions that EMU would prompt sweeping transformations of national social models, a more likely scenario is that recent trends in European industrial relations will persist and underlie continuing institutional variation. Although transition to EMU has brought a reinvigoration of existing labor market institutions, the changing conditions under which these institutions operate have implied significant changes in their function and content, as enshrined in the notion of "credibility bargaining" (Teague 2000). In this sense, many European social models have gone through an ambiguous process of institutional stabilization and qualitative transformation. The contours of a leaner, more flexible, streamlined version of the European social model are visible, suggesting that EMU in itself will not abolish the European social model in industrial relations but will pressure further for adjustment and renewal. Enlargement is likely to strengthen such pressures. Although in several countries EMU has catalyzed change, usually through the *vincolo esterno* effect, these trends may have more to do with international restructuring of markets and domestic social change. Whether such developments point toward a viable peace formula between capital and labor in Europe, replacing broken postwar settlements, is too early to say (Streeck 1999). Nonetheless, uncertainty remains about actors' capacities and commitments to sustain concertation after the race for EMU qualification is over. In several countries organizational fragmentation and union decline, due to structural changes in production and the composition of labor and social interests, cast doubts about actors' ability to muster legitimacy and domestic support for continued participation in concerted reform processes. A critical factor will be whether the unions can stem membership decline and reshape their organizations in response to the changing aspirations of the postindustrial workforce (Dølvik 2001).

EMU might aggravate or alleviate these strains, depending upon its macroeconomic effects. Unions in particular need positive reasons to participate in burdensome adjustment processes. An essential prerequisite of the US "employment miracle" of the 1990s was the Federal Reserve's accommodating policy. Can something like the expansionary monetary policy of the American recovery in this period be replicated under EMU? Given labor's much stronger position in Europe, such a trajectory would be contingent on fiscal prudence and the coordinating capacity of collective bargaining systems to prevent inflationary pressures from strangling the upswing and to remove structural obstacles to labor market expansion. If, by contrast, the trajectory of sluggish growth and restrictive economic policies of the EMU transition period prevails – or, as the most pessimistic observers fear, is aggravated – the risk is that struggle for market shares will unleash a spiral of competitive wage-bidding, with decreasing scope for national bargaining, downward pressures on social standards, and (in the longer term) erosion of national industrial relations.

To forestall such destabilizing dynamics, it would seem desirable that soft cross-national coordination of wage and economic policies complement national concertation. Such a venture cannot be expected to gain much headway under the "vicious-circle" scenario. However, in a more virtuous trajectory of higher growth and accommodating economic policies it could become more important and also more attractive to the ECB and to unions' political and social counterparts. In this light, it seems pertinent to conclude with Sisson (1998: 1) that "the pressure EMU brings for further economic and political union will add greater urgency to the debate over the reconstruction of European industrial relations."

# 13    Conclusions

*Andrew Martin and George Ross*

Monetary integration and EMU have fundamentally transformed the European political economy. EMU transfers monetary policy, the key instrument of macroeconomic policy and a core function of the modern state, to the exceptionally independent European Central Bank (ECB). At the same time, it strictly limits the member states' discretion in using fiscal policy, the main macroeconomic policy instrument remaining in their hands. Power has been more centralized and supranationalized in EMU than in any other European-level policy domain.

Member states have retained the power to shape the social policy and employment relations institutions at the core of the European social model, however. These institutions lie at the heart of domestic politics because of the central roles they play in the distribution of burdens and benefits among citizens. They help define voter expectations around which contenders for political power mobilize support and the normative basis of political legitimacy. With such basic issues at stake, national governments have consistently resisted transferring authority over core social model issues to the EU. EMU has not changed this.

The allocation of powers between the EU center and its constitutive units creates a European polity whose effects and even sustainability are problematical. Tensions between centralized macroeconomic policy and decentralized control over national social models are inherent in the interdependence of the two policy domains. Macroeconomic policy significantly affects the burdens on social policy and capacities to meet them. It also changes the distribution of bargaining power among actors in the labor market and politics. In turn, the national institutions that jointly structure labor markets condition the impact and effectiveness of macroeconomic policy measures.

This is not simply a theoretical matter. While prioritizing price stability, the EMU policy regime assigns responsibility for employment to the national institutions structuring labor markets. Moreover, the ECB repeatedly insists that reducing unemployment is contingent on reforming these institutions and eliminating the "rigidities" it attributes to them.

In contrast to those who see the deregulatory thrust of such reforms and continued high unemployment as threats, the European social model's survival depends on transforming the EMU regime to accept as much responsibility for employment as for price stability. Tensions between the EMU policy regime and the European social model are thus manifest in the EU political arena.

The preceding chapters sought to understand these tensions and their trajectories. EMU has been in existence for too short a time to draw more than tentative conclusions about its effects, however. We have tried to gain further insight by tracing interactions between the Europeanization of monetary policy and the politics of change in national social models over the two decades of monetary integration. Monetary restrictiveness characterizes all phases of European monetary integration. While each phase embodied efforts to shield intra-European transactions from exchange rate volatility, the "island of currency stability" they were designed to create was predicated on policies that limited variation of inflation rates among the participating countries. Germany, the first to make the shift to a price stability macroeconomic regime that all OECD countries eventually made, and with the strongest commitment to price stability, could make its own low inflation rate the EMS standard because of the Bundesbank's ability to influence economic conditions across Europe. Germany was thus able to impose the largest adjustment burdens on others and give monetary integration a restrictive bias. The desire to escape Bundesbank dominance was a driving force in the move to EMU, but German bargaining power succeeded instead in transferring the Bundesbank model to the European level. The thread of restrictive monetary policy was thus woven tightly into the fabric of EMU, continuing to frame member states' policy options.

Over time, successive forms of monetary integration have differed, however, while national social models have also evolved. Although monetary restrictiveness has pervaded successive phases of monetary integration, the general course was shaped by the complex dynamics of international economic forces and intergovernmental bargaining. At the same time, national variants of the European social model, however diverse, have continued the high levels of protection against economic insecurity, inequality, and unilateral employer power that distinguish them from the American model. The evolution of national social models has reflected the separate dynamics of domestic institutions and political competition confronting problems shaped by specific national welfare states and employment relations systems.

Policy problems raised by common challenges such as population aging, sectoral shifts in economic structure, changing gender roles, and diversification of job characteristics were framed, therefore, by possibilities that were facilitated or inhibited by national social models and national distributions of political power (chapter 11 in this volume). It would be a mistake to conclude that all the social model change occurring concurrently with monetary integration was caused by it. Many issues would have been salient without monetary integration. At the same time, the zealous devotion of monetary policy to price stability built into the successive forms of monetary integration inevitably affected the range of possible policy responses. Indirectly this happened as a result of recurrent periods of slow output and employment growth that weighed heavily on national budgets and fiscal capacities. It also came directly through rules and arrangements limiting national economic policy options and explicit pressures for "structural reforms" exerted by the ECB and other EU actors. Finally, the impacts of monetary integration have also influenced the distribution of political resources among domestic actors (chapter 10 in this volume).

To answer the question of how tensions between monetary integration and the European social model have worked out, we had first to analyze interactions between monetary integration and the politics of social model change in individual national contexts. Section 1 of this concluding chapter begins with a summary and comparison of the six country cases. This summary suggests tentative conclusions about timing, variation, and common trends (also taking into account European countries not included in our case studies). In section 2 we then consider changes in the nature of interaction between Euro-level moves to monetary integration and national systems. We then end in section 3 with observations about the simultaneous resiliency and vulnerability of the European social model in the context of EMU.

## 1 Responding to monetary integration

Monetary integration has produced pressures for change on national variants of the European social model. These have come first of all from restrictive macroeconomic policy, primarily monetary policy, from the German Bundesbank within EMS and more recently from the ECB. They have also come from budgetary squeezes caused by recessions and slower growth resulting from disinflationary monetary policies. There have been direct fiscal pressures from the convergence criteria and the Stability and Growth Pact (SGP). Another source has been promotion of "reforms" to eliminate labor market "rigidities," more recently assuming subtler forms as actors internalize "structural reform" discourses about employment.

These pressures have varied over time, particularly in two main stages, the EMS period until Maastricht (roughly the 1980s), and the transition/EMU years (from 1992 on). There has been variation within these periods as well. The EMS period was difficult for everyone, excepting Germany, until the economic upturn in the later 1980s. When the transition to EMU began after Maastricht most aspiring members could look forward to a period of austerity to meet the convergence criteria. But what actually happened was much worse than this. When the Bundesbank clamped down on post-unification inflation in 1992, pursuing its domestic mission, with EMU far in the background (although possibly to prevent EMU), convergence turned into a very tough process. This may have enhanced desires to deprive the Bundesbank of powers that could produce such unpleasant results. The product, however, was an EMU as fixated on low inflation and price stability as the Bundesbank had been.[1] Initially, though, convergence to the relatively low interest rates set by the ECB for the start of EMU in 1999 brought a sharp easing of monetary policy which supported a brief rapid recovery and a lessening of fiscal pressures. Rate-tightening returned quickly, however, contributing to new budgetary squeezes that have created a crisis in the SGP.

## Timing

When a country committed to monetary integration, and its situation at that point, made a great difference for trajectories of response. In this respect there are two sub-groups. Germany, the Netherlands, and Belgium embraced hard-currency, low-inflation policy orientations early on. France, Italy, and Spain signed on later. Timing, in turn, played an important role in the ways in which national elites used monetary integration in domestic politics, in particular their resort to *vincolo esterno* strategies.

The Germans had a long-standing commitment to price stability, enshrined in the statutes of the Bundesbank. EMS was built around the German price stability regime; others had to adjust. Germany could thus carry on its export-oriented growth strategy, which its "institutionalized monetarism" was designed to serve. The German social model could get through most of monetary integration with little reform, but only with an accretion of problems arising from efforts to cope with a changing situation. The Germans used their social model – particularly early retirement – to bear the financial costs of cushioning an industrial production regime that systematically shed (older) labor and a macroeconomic policy

---

[1] Things may then have turned out even worse for Germany, given the effects of the ECB's restrictive one-size-fits-all policy.

regime that kept employment growth too low to absorb the labor thereby shed, eroding the longer-run viability of the social model. In consequence, Germany began to feel EMU pressures only in the second half of the 1990s and then primarily because the immense costs of unification put the social model under high tension (chapter 5 in this volume). Endogenous pressures on the social model built up through the vaunted German "variety of capitalism" are now running up against the realities of EMU.[2] The Germans have had problems meeting the SGP 3 percent deficit limit (which was, ironically, their own creation) and have of late begun timid welfare state and labor market reforms. Germany's EMU problems lie in the near future, therefore, and they could well be large ones.

Some smaller European countries (the Netherlands and Belgium among our cases, plus Denmark, Luxembourg, and Austria) were so deeply engaged in trade with Germany that they had to sign on to a *de facto* D-mark zone in the early 1980s, well before the trajectory to European monetary union was clear. They thus began domestic adjustments early on. The Dutch, who aligned with the D-mark when key national actors were forced to recognize that "Golden Age" arrangements no longer worked, embarked on a steady and thorough course of reform that culminated in the *Polder* model in the 1990s (chapter 8 in this volume). The Dutch also became one of Germany's staunchest supporters throughout monetary integration.

The Belgians aligned themselves with the D-mark at the same time as the Dutch. Given precarious Belgian national unity, however, consensus for major social reform was impossible to build and adjustment proved painful (chapter 9 in this volume). Belgian social partners, whose situation was complicated by regional, linguistic, economic, and political fissures, were unwilling to internalize the costs of big changes. Instead, they delegated the allocation of adjustment costs to bureaucrats and experts, using competitiveness criteria that constrained social policy budgets and wage deals by law. This was a particularly Belgian version of the use of monetary integration by domestic elites as an external imperative to promote national changes. In the Belgian case, the results are unclear, however, because of the decentralized nature of actions taken in response to the competitiveness criteria.

Turning to the second group of countries, the French made the key choice for monetary integration in 1983 and then pushed hardest to make

---

[2] The German system relied on early retirement to cope with the side-effects of the combination of high productivity inherent in the German production regime. Restrictive macropolicy then meant increasing the burden on social insurance while diminishing its economic base (people in employment on whose payroll taxes financing depended). This built up pressures for change by reversing the early-retirement tendency, but this presupposed increasing employment.

it happen, in the process inflicting adjustment costs on themselves. As a result, throughout the 1980s long-held political beliefs were shattered, inequality and poverty increased, while unemployment and welfare state expenses shot up. The French wanted to establish conditions for a new situation in which German monetary rigidity no longer foreclosed their own options. In France an elite-orchestrated drive to monetary integration was therefore a major cause of domestic social model change. In the 1980s electorally precarious governments tried to limit the pain of rising unemployment by promoting lower labor force participation, using early retirement and youth programs, for the most part. In the 1990s these choices made confrontation with the convergence criteria even more difficult, but growing union weakness and the unanticipated effects of labor law reforms helped create greater flexibility. Governments began to reform first through the means-tested RMI, to confront poverty and social exclusion and then, on the revenue side, by creating the CSG to ease the tensions on social insurance funds. The Euro-level plans stimulating dramatic domestic policy changes rarely entered domestic political debate, however, because European integration tended to split both Left and Right coalitions. External tie effects only appeared late in the game, during the tough convergence years when the pace of welfare state and labor market reforms picked up. One of the reasons why such a risky political course was possible was the unusual power of the French Fifth Republic President, particularly in foreign affairs. The unusual political gifts of François Mitterrand were also central.

Italy and Spain were "takers" of monetary integration. At the beginning of EMS each was at a different developmental stage than most of Northern Europe. Elite technocrats and central bankers tried to push Italy toward ERM in the 1980s but did not get far, *de facto* giving the Italians more monetary space and allowing endogenous pressures for social model change to accumulate. It took the coincidence of massive regime crisis in the early 1990s with the EMU convergence period to change things. At this point it became possible for center-left parties, financial and other technocrats, and willing social partners to formulate far-reaching programs for domestic reform that used the *vincolo esterno* pretext that entry into EMU was a necessary step for Italian modernization. They promoted pension and healthcare reform, privatized unresponsive public agencies, and tried to flexibilize the labor market in limited ways. This external tie strategy was feasible, however, only because these new leaders and social partners, given the pro-European state of Italian public opinion, saw domestic political opportunities in doing so. Governmental change to the Right in 2001 made it difficult to predict how long this strategy would be available, however.

Spain took the external tie approach in different directions. The master narrative of Spanish politics after Franco was "democratization," with key democratization years coinciding with the Spanish drive to join the EU and the European mainstream. Internal pressure for widespread reform in social model and other areas was very strong. The external tie provided by this drive to Europeanization reinforced early elite commitment to monetary stringency and marketization. These commitments seriously limited Spain's simultaneous drive to build its own catch-up variant of the European social model, however. The constraints of monetary integration helped to structure economic and social policy targets for reforms that the PSOE elites desired in the 1980s, leading at points to the highest unemployment levels in Western Europe. The results, along with efforts to soften Francoist labor market rigidities through shorter-term contracts, contributed to the breakdown of earlier pactist cooperation by Spanish unions. Massive unemployment was one reason why PSOE was voted out of power in the early 1990s. Then, paradoxically, because Spain's interest rate had to converge downward to EMU's common starting rate, EMU subsequently helped the Aznar conservatives to stay in power. In general, "becoming European" was the basic strategic goal of Spanish elites and the particular context of monetary integration during the critical period of Spanish rapprochement with the EU provided many of the resources for their action.

### Common patterns?

There are many common patterns in our cases, despite timing differences. To take but one important example, EU-wide public spending on social protection, which grew at rates well above GDP from the 1970s into the mid-1990s, slowed thereafter. Behind earlier growth were trends such as maturing welfare state programs, aging populations, skyrocketing health-care costs and rising dependency ratios, plus expanding unemployment.

The key question for us is the degree to which slowdown in public social spending in the 1990s can be attributed to monetary integration. There are two interacting mechanisms through which monetary integration may have done this. One is the incorporation of the shift to a price stability macroeconomic policy regime, forcing convergence on Germany's low inflation rate. The resulting slow economic growth retarded expansion in the tax base required to meet the rising costs of old commitments – including benefits for the resulting rise in the number of unemployed – and meet new needs without rising budget deficits. The other is restricted budget deficits built into transition to EMU by the convergence criteria and the SGP. Even the growth and job creation at the end of the 1990s was not enough to restore the tax base enough to bring deficits down. As the European Commission puts it:

> Firstly, *rising employment* reduced the need to support the unemployed and their families. However, slowdown in expenditure growth is not confined to unemployment benefits but extends into other areas. This reflects Member States' efforts to *consolidate public finances* in the light of the Maastricht Treaty. (European Commission 2000: 6, emphasis in the original)

*Welfare state reforms*    Pension reforms would have been on national agendas without monetary integration. Aging populations and rising dependency ratios are serious problems everywhere and welfare state specialists usually attribute European pension changes exclusively to them. In reality, however, demographic trends and the constraints of monetary integration have crossed paths. The budgetary and fiscal squeezes necessitated by convergence and the SGP narrowed governmental choices. The issue became even more urgent because of revenue losses due to rising unemployment caused by lowered growth, in part tied to the constraints of monetary integration. Monetary integration also ruled out certain options, in particular incurring significant new debt.

The design of pension reform has been partially contingent on which groups were best placed when reform came on to the table in the 1990s. One recent observer notes that "in the last decade there has been an influx of new institutional actors into most European policy communities," in particular from the banking and insurance sectors, along with new media involvement, challenging "the cognitive monopoly of conventional pension knowledge" (Ney 2003: 91–92). Many in these groups bore proposals for "paradigmatic reform" from the existing system of high-cost, high-replacement rate public pensions based on social insurance topped up by smaller contributory supplementary systems, towards the three-tier Anglo-American model of much lower public pensions, larger second-tier private systems (often collectively bargained), and third-tier individual retirement accounts favored by tax incentives and the financial services sector. The EMU logic of opening European financial markets and the new claims that key actors in these markets will make will enhance the clout of these new voices, whose prosperity depends upon success.

In our country cases we see movement in this "paradigmatic" direction in the Netherlands, although in France and Germany first-tier replacement rates have been lowered slightly and limited individual third-tier accounts proposed.[3] Nonetheless, the nature of pension reform debate

---

[3] The terms "paradigmatic" and "parametric" come from Holzmann, Orenstein, and Rutkowski (2003: 9). To them, paradigmatic reform comes from conclusions that "individual accounts embody desirable work and compliance incentives; funding can increase a nation's savings and investment under the right fiscal conditions; and funding

has changed. Prior to the 1990s "paradigmatic" reform proposals were marginal. Since then they are everywhere. This is important, because, as the European Commission noted about national cases, "the measures taken since 1999 . . . have in most countries been relatively modest in scale given the scale of the demographic challenge ahead" (European Commission 2002: 36).

If countries don't proceed to neo-liberal "paradigmatic" change, the tool box of "parametric" reforms to pay-as-you-go pension schemes is limited. One can eliminate system anomalies, cut benefits, increase contributions, or raise the retirement age, and some combination of all these is found in our cases. Pension systems that originally came in multiple formats for different occupational groups, often with separate regimes for public and private sector workers, are being simplified toward one general model. Typically, contribution periods have been lengthened, along with methods for calculating benefits (particular "reference periods") that lower replacement rates. The taboo on raising the retirement age has also been broken. Changing benefit indexing methods has also been common. Germany and the Netherlands (and, outside our cases, Sweden and Denmark) have added "capitalized" pension arrangements that could be precedents.[4] Shifting from defined benefits to defined contributions, like the Italians and the Swedes (in their own social democratic ways), is also likely to spread. Monetary integration may also help to make some of these recently chosen options unworkable in the future. Raising the retirement age, even when couched in the trendy language of labor market "activation," can help only if there are jobs for older workers who are obliged to work longer. Those jobs will not be available if, as we argue, the EMU policy regime is likely to restrict rather than expand the creation of new jobs.

The European model in healthcare, based upon public commitment to universality and equality of access to high-quality care, may be unchallenged, but it is also ever-more expensive. Population aging, costly technology, and increasing demand for service have placed great strain on healthcare systems, and healthcare costs as a percentage of GDP are rising everywhere. There would have been problems without monetary integration. As with pensions, however, EMU convergence has increased reform pressures on healthcare systems to slow cost increases and contain deficits. And the negative employment effects of EMU convergence,

accounts can accelerate the development of a nation's capital market institutions and its efficiency in capital allocation and, therefore, its economic growth rate (2003: 9)."

[4] What is "paradigmatic" is not always easy to spot at first sight. The Swedish reform included strong public regulation to minimize risks and information asymmetries and aimed generally to preserve as much of the Swedish welfare state's universality as possible (Palmer 2002). There are choices in how capitalization can be introduced, therefore. Pensions need not be thrown totally to the market wolves.

by feeding new poverty, have played an important indirect role. Chronically unemployed citizens cannot contribute to social insurance funds for healthcare, and this has created a growing insider–outsider problem. Since it would be unthinkable to allow these citizens to go uninsured or be unequally insured, acute safety-net issues have arisen. It has thus become necessary to fund more and more healthcare out of general taxation. This has helped stimulate shifts from Bismarckian toward Beveridgean systems in Italy, Spain, and France which are fraught with implications. To the degree to which they replace contributory payroll insurance with general taxation and corporatist structures by governmental management the strategies and resource bases of different actors will change.

The repertory of available reform measures is limited. Virtually everyone now tries to control demand through selective co-payments for prescription drugs, visits to specialists, and hospitalization. Extensive work has been done to pinpoint the real costs of different treatments better to control them. Limiting healthcare "luxuries" (spas and the like) is in the works. Devolving responsibility for cost controls (and sometimes costs themselves) to regional and local levels, and promoting new "internal markets" are common. Approaches differ from country to country, however. The Dutch specialize in decentralization and promoting internal markets. The Belgian competitiveness criteria place strict legal limits on cost growth. The Italians and Spaniards have been moving to Beveridgean approaches on the revenue side, regionalizing and federalizing. The French have developed sophisticated cost-control contracts with providers, squeezed hospital budgets, done some devolution and begun shifting revenue sources to general taxation. The Germans, blessed with a venerable, and very expensive, Bismarckian system, were slow to do much of anything but reinforce it. In 1994 they even added a "fifth pillar of social protection" with long-term care insurance. The 2003 German reforms were a major shift, in contrast, increasing co-payment and other costs while lightening the burden on employers.

Thus there has been a lot of change in "big-ticket" welfare state areas, partly attributable to indirect pressure from the transition to EMU. But there is little evidence, except perhaps in the Netherlands, of changes away from the basic blueprint of the European social model. There may be a hidden dimension in this, however. Esping-Andersen (1999, 2002) develops powerful arguments about the difficulties of continental welfare regimes – including our country cases – in confronting new problems. In his view, because of commitment to male-breadwinner social insurance models and familialism, these regimes are ill-equipped to respond to rising poverty, female labor force participation, dual-earner households, and family change in general. Esping-Andersen reads the challenges through the lens of childcare (as do Jenson and Sineau 2001). Other things being equal, social insurance programs and high wage rates (tied to high minimum wages) allegedly tend to price private childcare out of reach (along with many other private services).[5] The costs of overcommitted mature welfare state programs then often crowd out needed new public childcare programs. Female labor force participation is critical to economic success, yet poor childcare provision has a measurable effect in limiting it and/or on fertility rates (when women are obliged by the structures of social programs to choose between work and childbearing).[6] If Esping-Andersen's analyses are accurate, it may be that monetary integration, by restricting funding for all welfare state programs, has accentuated this "crowding out" phenomenon.

Analogous things could be said about anti-poverty programs. High unemployment, partly attributable to Europe's new price stability regime, has accentuated insider–outsider differences and significant poverty has emerged almost everywhere, a "welfare without work" trap (Esping-Andersen *et al.* 2002: 17). In response, most continental countries have created new means-tested anti-poverty programs, usually decentralized and with explicit "activation" goals (often connected with changes in unemployment insurance programs, the development of shorter-term labor contracts, and all manner of experimentation with training and skill enhancement). France provides good examples, introducing the RMI in 1988 along with the vocabulary of "social exclusion," then following with means-tested targeted support for the elderly without official pensions and for those without supplementary insurance to cover ambulatory care (chapter 4 in this volume). These programs, although consistent with the European social model, are worrisome. They shift an important part of the welfare state away from traditional principles of social insurance to means-testing. Transfers from "insiders" to targeted "outsiders" establish a different logic of solidarity that could make such programs vulnerable to future neo-liberal political thrusts. In the present context of high unemployment, particularly among the lower skilled, the absence of job opportunities undermines "social inclusion" ambitions.[7]

---

[5] The notion that childcare has to be low-valued, low-skilled, and low-paid work despite the enormous formative importance of a child's early years surely reflects a fundamental irrationality in today's capitalist market societies.

[6] Among continental welfare states Esping-Andersen cites France, with its extensive public childcare programs tied to natalism, as an exception and also allows that the Dutch "*Polder* model" provides a solution, albeit one that devalues certain kinds of female labor force participation. In other areas Esping-Andersen and Jenson and Sineau recognize that Sweden provides a lot of quality childcare that employs a lot of women and facilitates other employment by women (accounting for its very high participation rate of women) despite high bargained minimum wage rates.

[7] To be fair, the discussion of social inclusion has gone well beyond employment into other areas of social life – housing, education, social services, and the like. Job availability remains the key problem, however (European Commission 2002, part II).

It is hard to "include" the chronically unemployed without being able to find them jobs. Finally, despite "activation" and skill upgrading, a significant part of the "new poor" will be unable to acquire sufficient new human capital to escape from their difficult situations. Here the Anglo-American social model is quite different in accepting, even promoting, a low-wage population of "working poor." There is as yet no substitute for fuller employment for preventing poverty in the European social model, however, and monetary integration has so far worked against this.

*Employment relations*   There have been significant employment relations changes, many of which are connected to monetary integration. High unemployment is the most significant issue. Wage-earners' willingness to take risks has declined with rising job insecurity. Unions continue to lose members and strike levels are much lower. There is also continuing decentralization of bargaining while in many countries unions are much weaker at firm and workplace level and less able to resist employer moves to promote flexibility in unilateral ways. Collective bargaining coverage remains high, however, and the extension of collective agreements is now routine, demonstrating the relative stability of basic labor market legal institutions.[8] There have also been longer-term trends that are independent of (or very loosely coupled to) monetary integration that have contributed to flexibilization and union weakening, Shifts in the structures of labor forces – more women, more services, more highly skilled and educated workers – are in this category.

On the other hand, largely because of monetary integration, trade unions in many places have gained new importance through a form of "renationalization" of employment relations matters. Wage restraint is important for open economies to help sustain national competitiveness, even in ordinary circumstances. From the 1990s to the present incentives to coordinate wage growth have intensified, however. With the convergence criteria and the SGP, EMU candidates and members, losing control over interest and exchange rates, have had to produce wage moderation. The most effective way, where institutional structures allowed, was to seek support from national union movements. There has thus been a resurrection of a peak-level neo-corporatism, or "social pactism," best documented in our cases in the Netherlands, Italy, and Spain.[9] No such resurrection was needed until recently in Germany, of course, because the existing bargaining system usually did the job. And there was little to

---

[8] See ILO (1998: 235–240).
[9] For broader discussion see Fajertag and Pochet (2000).

resurrect in France, where complicated state-led improvisation was used to get wage restraint. In Belgium, where pactism was part of the historical repertory, there was no new neo-corporatism, with the competitiveness criteria binding social partners to needed discipline. In general, as Dølvik underlines (chapter 12 in this volume), in the 1990s wage moderation led to reduced wage growth and declining unit labor costs in the eurozone. Alas, although the post-1997 three-year-long growth spurt was relatively rich in new job creations, there was little sign of any accompanying investment boom, and the spurt ended with the help of the ECB.

These developments are paradoxical. Monetary integration has made life more difficult for unions while national wage and social protection levels are now the most significant factors for adjustment to variations in competitiveness. At the same time, new "pactism" has given unions a lift in legitimacy and visibility, running against a medium-term trend to devalue unions as "social partners." This has given some union movements new leverage to advocate favorable changes in labor law and social policy. Finally, the need to engage unions has made it more necessary for governments to negotiate rather than impose changes, giving unions opportunities to influence their direction.

There is also increased labor market flexibility across the EU (OECD 1999: 141–159). The European postwar settlement was built around the mass-production worker. A new employment model is being built around workers who accept more flexible hours, cooperate more in the workplace, engage in periodic retraining, work occasionally on temporary contracts and/or part-time, and live with greater job insecurity. Bosses in most places now have a somewhat easier time hiring and firing. Government-subsidized, below-minimum-wage entry-level employment, particularly of young people, is widespread in the name of "activation." Different kinds of "atypical" work have been institutionalized: part-time, temporary and short-term contracts now flourish. Despite this, workers remain protected by strong labor law, relatively high minimum wages, and strong, often updated, social protection systems. The largest and most obvious remaining labor market problem, however, is that too many people fall outside the labor market altogether.

## 2   EU social policy: promises and practices

Euro-level social model action has been peripheral to our national stories. The most important reason for this is that there has not been that much Euro-level social policy. Changing the Treaties on social matters to permit an extensive new Euro-level harmonization effort has seemed out of the question. Yet national adaptation to monetary integration calls for new trans-national coordination. In recent years there have been signs of important "second order" EU-level responses to monetary integration emerging to face this problem.

The Treaty of Rome left most social policy in national hands. The SEA proposed qualified majority voting (QMV) on health and safety, justified on the grounds that it could help prevent "social dumping" and support the relatively high regulatory standards of Northern member states. The SEA also included clauses encouraging "social dialog," largely because Jacques Delors was a firm believer in corporatist coordination. Initial social dialog quickly reached a dead end, however, mainly because employers had no interest in such corporatism.

In 1989 the Delors Commission proposed a "Community Charter on the Fundamental Social Rights of Workers," aimed at adding a "social dimension" to the single market. The non-binding Social Charter was followed by an "Action Program" proposing EU-level regulation in those (few) social policy and labor market matters where the Commission could act legally. "Social dialog" was also relaunched and produced results after the Maastricht Treaty's "Social Protocol" made possible new "negotiated legislation" between Euro-level social partners.[10]

New social policy and labor market powers at EU level then became a moot point after member states made clear in the mid-1990s that new Euro-level legislation on social model matters was not to happen. The Delors Commission's last efforts came in a 1993 White Paper on *Growth, Competiveness, and Employment* (European Commission 1993). The document urged pro-active social and economic policies to move Europe into high-technology areas, from energy conservation through the "information society." Higher employment levels could be reached, in particular, by lowering payroll tax levels – implying that there had to be alternative financial sources for social programs. Greater labor flexibility could be achieved by regulatory relaxation, but mainly through new active labor market policies with enhanced stress on more active approaches. The White Paper also suggested general European guidelines for member state labor market changes, providing incentives through different EU-level programs and regularly monitoring and coordinating member state activities. Finally, the White Paper advocated substantial borrowing to

---

[10] The Commission would announce its intention of legislating, after which the "social partners" could choose to negotiate an agreement which, if negotiation succeeded, would become Community law after Council approval. There were agreements about legal constraints on "atypical" (part-time, short-term contract) work and rights to parental leave. The procedures did not spawn the active Euro-level collective bargaining for which some had hoped, however.

finance "Trans-European Networks," continent-wide infrastructure programs in transport, energy, and telecommunications.

The Council of Ministers did not like Delors' spending proposals. The White Paper's other ideas lingered on, however. By the Amsterdam Treaty (signed in 1997) unacceptably high levels of unemployment had fed public rejection of hard neo-liberalism, leading to center-left governments in France, Italy, Portugal, and the UK, soon followed by Germany. This facilitated the inclusion of an "Employment title" and employment policy clauses in the Amsterdam Treaty, giving the EU legal prerogatives and duties to "contribute to a high level of employment by encouraging cooperation between member states," and create a new "European employment strategy" (EES). The EU did not gain new legislative authority, however. Its new role was to promote action at national level and then to coordinate such action at euro level.

The employment strategy, which began in 1997, was designed to promote coordination among member states, each working through its own approaches and institutions toward common general goals. It starts when the European Council announces annual Employment Guidelines (benchmarks) for member states derived from four central concerns – promoting employability (skills and labor market participation), entrepreneurship (encouraging business startups), adaptability (new flexibility), and equal opportunities (creating conditions for greater female labor market participation).[11] Each member state then draws up a national action plan (NAP) projecting how they will put these guidelines into practice. The Commission and the Council then review these NAPs and present a Joint Employment Report to the European Council. The Commission also submits a proposal for revising the guidelines for the year to come. The Council of Ministers, by qualified majority, can issue country-specific recommendations.

The EES process, now six years old, was the first experiment with what was later named the "Open Method of Coordination" (OMC) now sweeping European policy circles. It takes a broad range of European economic policy goals and social policy instruments into consideration, in particular the European Social Fund (ESF), and uses "management by objectives" (MBO) techniques, using new statistical bases, setting targets,

---

[11] The EES was evaluated after its first five years (2002). As a result the Commission proposed restructuring it around three objectives, achieving full employment, raising quality and productivity at work, and promoting cohesion and inclusive labor markets. Procedural changes were suggested that would tie the timetable of EES more closely to the Broad Economic Policy Guidelines (BEPGs) (Pakaslahti and Pochet 2003: 109–132).

benchmarking best practices, and then reviewing achievements comparatively (including "naming and shaming" by the Commission). It recognizes that national social models differ and encourages actors in each model to design their own paths toward common targets. Finally, the EES enjoins national social partners to work together to produce and implement the NAPs. No clearer encouragement to national social pactism could be imagined, and, in this respect, the EES is working reasonably well.[12]

The EES, on its own, is unlikely to produce far-reaching changes, however. Its central objective is to increase the EU employment rate, but it has few ways of actually doing so. Its mandate excludes issues about the demand for labor, a factor at least as important for employment levels as the supply-side matters to which the EES is largely confined. All of the activation, training, energetic job prospecting, and efforts to engage women and older workers in the workforce are unlikely to make much difference without many more jobs. Addressing the demand side would involve making demands on monetary policy, a forbidden encroachment into the ECB's domain. Indeed, it may be that EES has an additional underlying agenda. If it cannot deliver on its employment-creation promises, it could nonetheless be a useful tool to give key national actors lessons in "EMU-speak" through iterative exercises that communicate the idea, however illusory, that monetary policy is job-creation neutral and that only supply-side changes can create jobs.

There is another side to the story, however. The EES gives actors a new arena to voice their own conceptions of the kind of changes needed in labor market institutions. In the words of the Belgian Minister for Social Affairs:

an effective Open Method of Co-ordination is more than an intelligently managed learning process and a defensive instrument. If we handle it judiciously, open-co-ordination is an offensive method that allows us to concretely define a "social Europe" and to firmly anchor it into the European co-operation process as a common good. (Pakaslahti and Pochet 2003: 133)

In this sense the employment strategy is also a venue for articulating the positions of those who disagree with a macroeconomic policy regime that abdicates responsibility for employment and places it entirely on supply-side measures. For such reasons the EES – and, more broadly, OMC – as a new way of promoting social Europeanization out of national diversity, has elicited enthusiasm among progressive social policy experts, who see it as a useful tool for positive reform and a forum that provides

---

[12] For a useful commentary see Goetschy and Pochet (2000).

new legitimacy for national "social partners," particularly unions and civil society groups. EES and OMC have also become an enthusiasm of Habermasian advocates of "deliberative democracy," who see it as a way to re-create democratic participation (Zeitlin and Trubek 2003). The codification of EES' general practices into OMC by the Lisbon Summit in 1990 has spread to broader social policy areas (Lundvall and Joao-Pires 2002). In 2000, OMC began in the two new areas of pensions and social inclusion. Unlike EES, neither of these areas is embedded in the Treaty.[13]

Nothing comparable to the EES exists in industrial relations, however. Dølvik (chapter 12 in this volume) explores the different avenues that might be followed to innovate in this area, but is concerned that they will not be followed. There is an obvious danger that in the absence of transnational wage coordination, existing national "pactism" for wage restraint will tilt toward "beggar-thy-neighbor" strategies.[14] Neither euro-level peak and sectoral collective coordination nor efforts by powerhouse German unions like *IG Metall* to influence trans-national wage setting have gotten very far. There is also a danger that competitive wage compression may happen in countries where peak-level national coordination is weak. If OMC involves some movement toward trans-national European coordination in employment policy matters, we do not find anything analogous yet in the area of wage determination.

## 3    Resilience, resistance, adaptation?

Our story details the multiple and complex reasons why European monetary integration has taken on the forms now consecrated in EMU. One of the most important results has been that monetary integration has served as an all-purpose tool for shifting macroeconomic policy away from the postwar goal of full employment to the new price stability regime. What has this meant for the European social model?

EMU is just beginning. The two transitional decades we review have nonetheless brought higher unemployment and lower growth, both implying social policy and employment relations changes. EU member states have had difficulty in coping. Some advocates of European monetary integration argue that this is needed to correct destructive habits

[13] This brief narrative of the EU's hesitant and "soft" efforts in social model areas contrasts with the determined and tough efforts made to keep national economic policies in line with the SEP carried out in the BEPGs exercise. Recommendations after the five-year review of EES suggest that EES should be tied more tightly to the BEPGs exercise. It is difficult at this point to know what this will entail, however.

[14] de Beus (chapter 8 in this volume) notes that recent Dutch practices may have approximated such competitive wage restraint.

from the postwar boom. They add that the shift will eventually create the conditions for healthy new growth. These arguments may or may not turn out to be correct. What we do know is that the change has so far produced few positive results in terms of job creation and growth.

It is important to underline that the basic structures of the European social model are still standing. European publics remain committed to extensive social protection, labor market regulation, and negotiation between social partners. Social models are a complex of institutions and interconnected social contracts that morally engage actors. However much they may disagree on specific issues, a critical mass of these actors will normally act to preserve the broader engagements of the contract. The institutions are interconnected, or clustered, such that actors often perceive threats to particular arrangements as threats to others, even if the functional relationships may be different. Everything considered, Europeans continue to believe that the European social model is essential (Boeri *et al.* 2001; Svallfors 2003). As Portugal's Secretary of State for European Affairs, Francesco Seixas da Costa (2000), put it, "we are not sure that the American model, which is a radical model, one of deep injustices, one which has introduced factors of great social injustice and of great marginalization and exclusion, is the model for the future. We do not want this model for Europe." The effectiveness of the European model may need to be enhanced, but most Europeans do not see it as an albatross portending European decline.

The survival of the European social model does not mean that it has gone unchallenged by monetary integration, however. The fundamental issue for the future concerns the medium-term logic of changes now under way. Change has characterized the European social model from the outset. European welfare states and employment relations systems constantly evolved during the three decades of postwar boom, in part because prevailing views on macroeconomic policy created new space for such change. Pension systems were elaborated, healthcare systems built, unemployment compensation expanded, collective bargaining systems and labor law consolidated, and forms of collective representation, often parastatal or "paritary," were elaborated. The logic at work in this period was nothing less than the unfolding of postwar European social models.

It should not be surprising, therefore, that the national variants of the European social model have also changed in the context of monetary integration. The most important question about these changes concerns their medium-term meanings: is the postwar social model being eroded by retrenchment and dismantling? Problems of unemployment and low labor force participation are now chronic. Confronting them, given commitment to the European social model, is a fundamental issue. The

Delors' White Paper on *Growth, Competitiveness, and Employment* (1993) was the first general effort to understand this, beginning a long process that has not always been pursued with great energy. More recently, the 2000 Lisbon European Council set out a detailed program to make the EU the most advanced "knowledge economy" in the world, with full employment by 2010. Time will tell whether Lisbon will achieve its goals – and, quite as important, whether the OMC that it promoted will help achieve its employment growth and technological progress targets.

*Enlargement?*

There will be many obstacles in the way, not least the inevitable difficulties of enlarging the EU from fifteen to twenty-seven members. Accurate projections about the effects of enlargement on the European social model are not possible, but reflection about prospects is nonetheless necessary. The European social model is a Western European phenomenon. The Central and Eastern European countries (CEECs) have very different histories. Any weak impulses toward founding a European model in the CEECs were eroded by decades of Communism in which extensive welfare state and employment relations commitments were made and then discredited by hyper-bureaucratic administration, undemocratic politics, and low living standards. Market-building and democratization since 1989 has succeeded, but in this emulating the European model of society has had low priority. The old order collapsed in disrepute. The new order, which varies from country to country, is characterized by social policy improvisation, weak and divided employer and union organizations, and an absence of the kinds of social forces that built the European social model in the West (Pakaslahti and Pochet 2003: chapter 1).

The CEECs live in a different era from the one that fostered the building of the European model of society. European and global economic openness, relatively weak national states, lowered expectations of growth, the need to devise catch-up strategies, and the EU institutional context, among a multitude of factors, dictate higher priorities to CEEC elites than constructing a European model, even were they to want it. It is not surprising that social policy has been much less important than market, monetary, legal, and administrative matters in the accession dealings around the *acquis communautaire*. This simultaneously reflected what really mattered and replicated the EU's existing division of labor, leaving social model issues to member states.

What might this mean? A dozen new EU members with considerably less commitment to the European social model than core continental countries might enhance the Euro-level power of advocates of more neo-liberal approaches to social matters. Given unwieldy EU institutions, it seems unlikely that new direct (i.e. legislative) Euro-level initiatives in social model matters will occur in the next period. Concerns about "social dumping" from lower-wage, lower-regulation CEEC economies are being voiced, but without the urgency that one heard about the single market program. The CEECs are by and large small economic places that will be held to high standards of EU behavior in the near future. There are larger concerns about population migration and CEEC political futures than about social policies.

What can be concluded? The accession of the CEECs will complicate already ponderous and creaky EU decision-making across the board, almost no matter the results of the 2003 convention proposals. If influence over the construction of new CEEC social models is to be exercised at EU level, it is most likely to come from "soft" procedures of the OMC type. This does not seem immediately promising, given uncertainty about the effectiveness of these procedures. Changing normative commitments about things as profound and complicated as social models takes long persuasion, however. The most significant shorter-term issue for the CEECs in this respect will be their own accession to EMU. How and when this happens will be of huge importance for the shape of whatever social model emerges among new EU members.

*Whither the European model of society?*

The unfolding trajectories of change to the European social model are uncertain, but nonetheless essential to explore. In a positive scenario, the two decades that we have observed could be but a difficult transition to future growth encouraged by EMU. This would be most likely to happen in new institutional circumstances where a Euro-level political structure would be empowered to determine macroeconomic policy for the euro area as a whole. Because growth and employment depends on investor expectations of demand and perceptions of the monetary and fiscal policy commitments of governments, Euro area macroeconomic policy would have to create those expectations. This would not be easy, since it would involve solving the chronic puzzle of reconciling low unemployment and low inflation. In this scenario, however, the ECB could manage EU macroeconomic policy to encourage, rather than discourage, potential growth. In turn, this would allow the Lisbon OMC process to facilitate higher labor force participation and new "quality" job creation. Higher employment and participation would ease national revenue and budget squeezes and the effects of demographic pressures on welfare state programs, particularly pensions and healthcare, making pension reforms and healthcare cost controls less difficult to implement. Resources would also become available to underwrite new social programs, particularly in "caring" areas (childcare, reconciling family and work, elder care). With fuller employment and refined "pactism," social partners could agree on greater labor market flexibility and wage restraint without compromising the institutions and mores underlying the European model. At the end of this happy story, the European model would emerge reconfigured without compromise to its basic integrity.

A negative scenario in which two decades of low growth and high unemployment turn out to be the norm is as conceivable, however. The ECB could facilitate this by continuing to focus exclusively and overcautiously on price stability, whatever the cost in growth and jobs. Beyond this, the EU might well be unable to find the institutional solution needed for an optimal "mix" between monetary, fiscal, and wage policy goals to reconcile low unemployment and low inflation. At present there is little effective economic governance to provide adequate signals and authoritative goals to the ECB. Perhaps most important, a negative scenario could develop if European elites, including ECB leaders, came to believe more widely that their most important job was to maximize "structural reform."

If the European social model is indeed based upon widespread normative commitment to a complex of interconnected institutional arrangements, this would amount to a war of attrition. The effectiveness of different institutions might decline, bringing with it new public skepticism, declining normative support for the European model, and resistance to further initiatives in European integration. In these circumstances reforms already begun could turn against the European model, rather than working to reconfigure it. Pressure on pensions, for example, could precipitate more "capitalization" and individualization at the expense of intergenerational solidarity. Analogous pressures could work toward the privatization and eventual "de-universalization" of health insurance programs. Finally, low growth and high unemployment would continue to change the balance in labor markets further in favor of employers. Workers and unions would both suffer from this, but the greater danger for the European model would be new incentives to employer unilateralism. Pieces of the European model's systems of labor market regulation could, in time, fall by the wayside.

Recent developments do not presage this negative trajectory. Throughout much of the monetary integration period, Europe's trouble provided an important resource for renascent neo-liberalism. Indeed, the most difficult moments in the 1980s and early 1990s looked like a major and irrevocable shift toward neo-liberal commitments, even where the Left was in power. The mid-1990s brought political rejection of any such shift, however, as election after election returned social democrats to power with a clear mandate to protect the European social model. The next round of elections, after the turn of the twenty-first century, brought an equally sweeping second shift back to the center-right, however. But with the exception of Berlusconi in Italy, none of these new governments advocated strong neo-liberal positions.

These events can be read as a sign that most Europeans are determined to stand by the social models that they built earlier. This is all the more remarkable because Europe is under constant rhetorical and conceptual siege from sources, including the ECB, insisting that the European social model prevents Europe from thriving economically. There are also trends in current European political life that might undermine commitment to the European social model. In certain circumstances New Right anti-immigrant politics could prove disruptive. The stresses and strains of enlarging the EU may also create new difficulties. But the central threats remain continuing low growth and high unemployment, however. It therefore cannot be ruled out that these will create conditions for a war of attrition that would sap the European models by stealth.

# References

*ABC* (Madrid), 1997, September 4

Åberg, Rune, 2001, "Equilibrium Unemployment, Search Behaviour and Unemployment Persistency," *Cambridge Journal of Economics*, 25: 131–147

2003, "Unemployment Persistency, Overeducation and Employment Chances of the Less Educated," *European Sociological Review*, 19: 131–147

Akerlof, George A., Dickens, William T., and Perry, George L., 2000, "Near Rational Wage and Price Setting and the Long Run Phillips Curve," *Brookings Papers on Economic Activity*, 1: 1–59

Albert, Michel, 1991, *Capitalisme contre capitalisme*, Paris: Editions du Seuil

Anderson, Jeffrey, 1999, *German Unification and the Union of Europe: The Domestic Politics of Integration Policy*, Cambridge: Cambridge University Press

Année Social, 1997, *Revue de l'Institut de Sociologie*, Free University of Brussels (ULB)

1998, *Revue de l'Institut de Sociologie*, Free University of Brussels (ULB)

Antoons, J. and Pochet, Philippe, 1998, "L'impact de l'Union européenne sur la pauvreté et l'exclusion sociale à Bruxelles," in J. Vranken, B. Vanhercke, and L. Carton (eds.), *2.ans CPAS, vers une actualisation du Project de Société*, Leuven: ACCO

Arcq, E., 1991, "La concertation sur la compétitivité," *Courrier hebdomadaire du Crisp*, 1326, Brussels: Centre de recherche et d'information socio-politiques

1993, "Du pacte social au plan global," *Courrier hebdomadaire du Crisp*, 1420–1421, Brussels: Centre de recherche et d'information socio-politiques

Arcq, E. and Chatelain, E., 1994, *Pour un nouveau pacte social, emploi, compétitivité, sécurité sociale*, Brussels: Editions Vie ouvrière

Arcq, E. and Pochet, Philippe, 2000, "Toward a New Social Pact in Belgium?," in G. Fajertag and Philippe Pochet (eds.), *Social Pacts in Europe – New Dynamics*, Brussels: ETUI

Armstrong, Keith and Bulmer, Simon, 1998, *The Governance of the Single European Market*, Manchester: Manchester University Press

Ashenfelter, Orley and Card, David, 1999, *Handbook of Labor Economics*, 3, Amsterdam: North-Holland

Astudillo, Ruiz J., 1998, *Los recursos del socialismo: las cambiantes relaciones entre el PSOE ya la UGT (1982–1993)*, Madrid: Centro de Estudios Avanzados en Ciencias Sociales, Instituto Juan March de Estudios e Investigaciones

Atkinson, A., Cantillon, B., Marlier, E. and Nolan, B., 2001, *Indicators for Social Inclusion in the European Union*, Oxford: Oxford University Press

Aylott, N., 2000, "The Swedish Social Democratic Party," in Ton Notermans (ed.), *Social Democrats and Monetary Union*, Oxford: Berghahn Books

Baglioni, Guido, 1998, "Il sistema delle relazioni industrali in Italia: caratteri edevoluzione storica," in Primo Celli and Tiziano Treu (eds.), *Le nuove relazioni industriali: l'esperienza italiana nella prospettiva europea*, Bologna: Il Mulino

Baker, Dean, Glyn, Andrew, Howell, David, and Schmitt, John, 2002, "Labor Market Institutions and Unemployment: A Critical Assessment of the Cross-Country Evidence," Center for European Studies Working Paper Series, 98, Harvard University

Baker, Dean and John Schmitt, 1999, "The Macroeconomic Roots of High European Unemployment," *WSI Mitteilungen*, Fall

Bakker, Age, 1996, *Met gelijke munt*, Amsterdam: Contact

Ball, Laurence, 1997, "Disinflation and the NAIRU," in Christina Romer and David N. Romer (eds.), *Reducing Inflation: Motivation and Strategy*, Chicago: University of Chicago Press

1999, "Aggregate Demand and Long-Run Unemployment," *Brookings Papers on Economic Activity*, 2: 189–251

Balling, Morten *et al.* (eds.), 1998, *Corporate Governance, Financial Markets and Global Convergence*, Dordecht: Kluwer

Banca d'Italia, 1995, *Bolletino Economica*, 25, October

Bank of Spain, 1988, *Informe Anua*, Madrid: Banco de España

Barca, Fabrizio, Ferri, Giovanni, and Pesarei, Nicola, 1998, "Banks and Corporate Governance in Italy: A Two-Tier Model," in Morten Balling *et al.* (eds.), *Corporate Governance, Financial Markets and Global Convergence*, Dordrecht: Kluwer

Bartocci, Enzo (ed.), 1997, *Lo stato sociale in Italia*, Rome: Donizelli

Bauchard, Philippe, 1986, *La guerre des deux roses*, Paris: Grasset

Bean, C., 1998, "Discussion: What is Labour-Market Flexibility?," in *1997 Lectures and Memoirs: Proceedings of the British Academy*, Oxford: Oxford University Press

Becker, Jean-Jacques, 1998, *Crises et alternaces, 1974–1995*, Paris: Editions du Seuil

Becker, Uwe, 1999, "The Dutch 'Miracle'," SPRC Discussion Paper, 99, Sydney: Social Policy Research Centre

2001, "A Dutch Model: Employment Growth by Corporatist Consensus and Wage Restraint? A Critical Account of an Idyllic View," *New Political Economy*, 6: 19–43

Beer, Paul de, 2001, *Over werken in de postindustriële samenleving*, The Hague: SCP

Begg, David, Fabio Canova, Paul De Grauwe, Antonio Fatas, and Philip R. Lane, 2002a, *Surviving the Slowdown*, Monitoring the European Central Bank, 4, London: CEPR

2000b, "MECB Update," London: CEPR, December

Begg, Iain, 2003, "Soft Economic Policy Co-Ordination under EMU: Problems, Paradoxes and Prospects," Center for European Studies, Working Paper Series, 103

Bemporad, Simone and Giannino, Oscar, 1998, "Storia di un'illusione italiana: Come e perché banche e aziende rimangono di Stato," *Liberal*, July 16: 11–15

Benner, M. and Bundgaard, Vad, T., 2000, "Sweden and Denmark: Defending the Welfare State," in F. W. Scharpf and V. A. Schmidt (eds.), *Welfare and Work in the Open Economy*, I and II, Oxford: Oxford University Press

Bermeo, N. (ed.), 1999, *Unemployment in Southern Europe – Coping with the Consequences*, Special Issue of *Southern European Politics and Society*, 4(3)

2000, *Unemployment in the New Europe*, Cambridge: Cambridge University Press

Berthold, Norbert, Fehn, Reiner, and Thode, Eric, 1999, "Falling Labor Share and Rising Unemployment: Long-Run Consequences of Institutional Shocks?," *Wirtschaftswissenschaftliche Beiträge des Lehrstuhls für Volkswirtschaftslehre, Wirtschaftsordnung und Sozialpolitik*, 30

Bertola, Giuseppe, Blau, Francine D., and Kahn, Lawrence M., 2001, "Comparative Analysis of Labor-Market Outcomes: Lessons for the United States from International Long-Run Evidence," in Alan B. Krueger and Robert M. Solow (eds.), *The Roaring Nineties: Can Full Employment Be Sustained?*, New York: The Russell Sage Foundation and The Century Foundation Press

De Beus, Jos and Kersbergen, Kees van, 1994, "Employment Policy Legacy and Political Party Strategy in the Netherlands," Paper prepared for the Conference of Europeanists, Chicago, March 31–April 2

2001a, "Een primaat van politiek," Inaugural Lecture, Amsterdam: Amsterdam University Press

2001b, "Dutch Social Democracy and EMU," in Ton Notermans (ed.), *Social Democrats and Monetary Union*, Oxford: Berghahn Books

Beyme, Klaus von, 1994, "Verfehlte Vereinigung – Verpaßte Reformen? Zur Problematik der Evaluation der Vereinigungspolitik in Deutschland seit 1989," *Journal für Sozialforschung*, 34: 249–270

Beyme, Klaus von and Schmidt, Manfred G. (eds.), 1990, *Politik in der Bundesrepublik Deutschland*, Opladen: Westdeutscher Verlag

Bispinck, Lothar, 2000, "The Chequered History of the Alliance for Jobs," in G. Fajertag and Philippe Pochet (eds.), *Social Pacts in Europe – New Dynamics*, Brussels: ETUI

Bispinck, R. and Schulten, T. 2000, "Alliance for Jobs – Is Germany Following the Pattern of 'Competitive Corporatism'?," in G. Fajertag and Philippe Pochet (eds.), *Social Pacts in Europe – New Dynamics*, Brussels: ETUI

Blaise, P., 1986, "L'accord interprofessionnel du 7 novembre 1986," *Courrier hebdomadaire du Crisp*, 1137, Brussels: Centre de recherche et d'information socio-politiques

Blaise, P. and Beaupain, T. 1995, "La concertation sociale 1993–1995 II. L'accord interprofessionnel du 7 décembre 1994," *Courrier hebdomadaire du Crisp*, 1498, Brussels: Centre de recherche et d'information socio-politiques

Blanchard, Olivier, 1997, "Comment," in Christina Romer and David N. Romer (eds.), *Reducing Inflation: Motivation and Strategy*, Chicago: University of Chicago Press

2000, "Comment and Discussion," *Brookings Papers on Economic Activity*, 1

Blanchard, Olivier and Lawrence H. Summers, 1986, "Hysteresis and the European Unemployment Problem," *NBER Macroeconomics Annual 1986*, Cambridge, MA: NBER

Blanchard, Olivier and Wolfers, Justin, 2000, "The Role of Shocks and Institutions in the Rise of European Unemployment: The Aggregate Evidence," *Economic Journal*, 110: C1–C33

Blanchard, Olivier *et al.*, 1995, *Spanish Unemployment: Is there a Solution?*, London: Clarendon Press

Blinder, Alan and Yellin, Janet L., 2001, "The Fabulous Decade: Macroeconomic Lessons from the 1990s," in Alan B. Krueger and Robert Solow (eds.), *The Roaring Nineties: Can Full Employment be Sustained?*, New York: The Russell Sage Foundation and The Century Foundation Press

Blitz, James, 2002, "Tremonti Calls for Overhaul of EU Stability Pact," *Financial Times*, June 25: 4

Boeri, Tito, 1997, "Le istituzioni del mercato del lavoro: un confronto internazionale," in S. de Nardis and G. Galli (eds.), *La disoccupazione italiana*, Bologna: Il Mulino

Boeri, Tito, Axel Börsch-Supan, and Guido Tabellini, 2001, "Welfare State Reform: A Survey of What Europeans Want," *Economic Policy*, April: 8–50

Boix, Carles, 1998, *Political Parties, Growth and Equality: Conservative and Social Democratic Economic Strategies in the World Economy*, Cambridge: Cambridge University Press

Boldrin, Michele, Jimenez-Martin, Sergi, and Peracchi, Franco, 1997, "Social Security and Retirement in Spain," NBER Working Paper, 6136

Bolkestein, Frits, 1999, "The Dutch Model," *The Economist*, May 22

Bolt, P., 1999, EMU and the Labour Market, the Finnish Case, SAK Reports, Helsinki

Bonoli, Giuliano, 1997a, 'Pension Politics in France," *West European Politics*, 20(4): 160–181

   1997b, "Classifying Welfare States: A Two Dimensional Approach," *Journal of Social Policy*, 26(3): 351–372

   1997c, "Reclaiming Welfare: The Politics of French Social Protection Reform," in Martin Rhodes (ed.), *Southern European Welfare States*, London: Frank Cass

   2000, *The Politics of Pension Reform: Institutions and Policy Change in Western Europe*, Cambridge: Cambridge University Press

Boonstra, Wim W. and Eijffinger, Sylvester C. W. (eds.), 1997, *Banks, Financial Markets and Monetary Policy*, Amsterdam: NIBE

Bordogna, Lorenzo and Provasi, Gian Carlo, 1998, "La conflittualita," in Primo Celli and Tiziano Treu (eds.), *Le nuove relazioni industriali: l'esperienza italiana nella prospettiva europea*, Bologna: Il Mulino

Börzel, Tanja A. and Hosli, Madeleine O., 2002, "Brussels between Bern and Berlin: Comparative Federalism Meets the European Union," *Constitutionalism Web-Papers*, ConWEB No. 2/2002: http://les1.man.ac.uk/conweb.

Börzel, Tanja A. and Risse, T., 2000, "When Europe Hits Home: Europeanization and Domestic Change," Paper presented to the Annual Convention of the American Political Science Association, August 31–September 3, Washington, DC

Bossier, F., Hendrickx, K., Herveldt, B., Lebrun, I., Masure, L., Streel, C., and Verlinden, J., 1998, "Les déterminants macro-économiques de l'emploi, contribution aux rapports 1997 du CSE et CCE," Working Paper, 05.98, Brussels: Federal Planning Bureau

Boulding, K. E. (ed.), 1984, *The Economics of Human Betterment*, London: Macmillan

Bout, J. K. et al., 1999, *A Dutch Approach for Creating Growth and Employment: The Polder Model in the French Landscape*, The Hague: SMO

Boyer, Robert, 2000, "The Unanticipated Fallout of European Monetary Union: The Political and Institutional Deficits of the Euro," in Colin Crouch (ed.), *After the Euro: Shaping Institutions for Governance in the Wake of the European Monetary Union*, Oxford: Oxford University Press

Boyer, Robert and Drache, Daniel (eds.), 1996, *States against Markets*, London: Routledge

Braun, Dieter, 1988, *Die Niederländische Weg in die Massenarbeitslosigkeit 1971– 1981*, PhD. dissertation, Amsterdam University

Broertjes, Pieter (ed.), 1989, *Gettos in Holland*, Amsterdam: Van Gennep

Brunetta, Renato and Turatto, Renzo, 1996, "The Italian Labour Market and European Convergence," *Review of Economic Conditions in Italy*, July– December: 199–213

Brunila, Anne, Buti, Marco, and Franco, Daniele (eds.), 2001, "Introduction," *The Stability and Growth Pact: The Architecture of Fiscal Policy in EMU*, London: Palgrave: 1–22

Budge, Ian and McKay, David H. (eds.), 1994, *Developing Democracy: Comparative Research in Honour of J. F. P. Blondel*, London: Sage

Bull, Martin and Rhodes, Martin (eds.), 1997, *Crisis and Transition in Italian Politics*, London: Frank Cass

Bundesministerium für Arbeit und Sozialordnung (BMAS), 1999, *Statistische Übersichten zur Geschichte der Sozialpolitik in Deutschland seit 1945 Band West*, Bonn: Verfasser Hermann Brié

Busch, Andreas, 1995, *Preisstabilitätspolitik*, Opladen: Leske & Budrich

Buti, M., Eijffinger, S., and Franco, D., 2003, "Revisiting the Stability and Growth Pact: Grand Design or Internal Adjustment?," *European Commission Economic Papers*, 180, January

Buti, Marco, Lucio R. Pench, and Paolo Sestito, 1998, *European Unemployment: Contending Theories and Institutional Complexities*, Florence: European University Institute, Robert Schuman Centre, Policy Papers, RSC 98/1

Cabral Villaverde, M., 1999, "Unemployment and the Political Economy of the Portuguese Labour Market," in N. Bermeo (ed.), *Unemployment in Southern Europe – Coping with the Consequences*, Special Issue of *Southern European Politics and Society*, 4(3): 222–238

Calmfors, L. and Driffill, J., 1988, "Bargaining Structure, Corporatism and Macroeconomic Performance," *Economic Policy*, 6: 13–61

Camera Dei Deputati, 1994, *XII Legislatura, Atti Parlamentari: Discusioni*, 1, Rome, June 2

1996, *Atti Parlamentari. XI Commissione: Lavoro*, Rome, July 19

1997, *Atti Parlamentari, Documento de programmazione e finanziaria, 1998–2000*, 2, Rome, May 31

1998a, *Atti Parlamentari, Documento di programmazione economico e finanziaria, 1999–2001*, Rome: Doc. LVII, n. 3, April 18

1998b, *Atti Parlamentari, Commissione XII – Affari Sociali*, Rome: September 23

1999, *Atti Parlamentari, Indagini Conoscitivi, V Commissione*, Rome: February 24

Cameron, David R., 1995, "Transnational Relations and the Development of European Economic and Monetary Union," in Thomas Risse-Kappen (ed.), *Bringing Transnational Relations Back In: Non-State Actors, Domestic Structures and International Institutions*, Cambridge: Cambridge University Press: 37–78

1996, "Exchange Rate Politics in France, 1981–1983: The Regime-Defining Choices of the Mitterrand Presidency," in Anthony Daley (ed.), *The Mitterrand Era*, New York: St. Martin's Press

1998, "Creating Supranational Authority in Monetary and Exchange Rate Policy: The Sources and Effects of EMU," in Wayne Sandholtz and Alec Stone Sweet (eds.), *European Integration and Supranational Governance*, Oxford: Oxford University Press

2000, "Unemployment, Job Creation and EMU," in N. Bermeo, *Unemployment in Southern Europe – Coping with the Consequences*, Special Issue of *Southern European Politics and Society*, 4(3)

Cantillon, B. and Lathouwer, L. de, 2001, "Report for Belgium," Paper presented at the Conference on "Welfare Systems and the Management of the Economic Risk of Unemployment," Florence: European University Institute, December 10–11

Caporaso, James, Cowles, Maria Green, and Risse, Thomas, 2000, "Europeanization and Domestic Change," unpublished manuscript

Carini, Alessandra, 1999, "Flessibilità, il Veneto fa l'americano," *La Repubblica – Affari e Finanza*, March 8: 1

Carli, G., 1993, *Cinquant'anni di vita Italiana*, Rome: Editori Laterza

Carlin, Wendy and Soskice, David, 1997, "Shocks to the System: The German Political Economy under Stress," *National Institute Economic Review*, 159: 57–76

Cassese, Sabino, 1994, "Deregulation and Privatization in Italy," in M. Moran and T. Prosser (eds.), *Privatisation and Regulatory Change in Europe*, Buckingham: Open University Press

Cassiers, I. (ed.), 2000, "Que nous est-il arrivé? Un demi-siècle d'évolution de l'économie belge," *Reflets & Perspectives de la vie économique*, 39(1), Brussels: De Boeck Université

Cassiers, I, De Villé, P., and Sollar, P. M., 1994, "Economic Growth in Post-War Belgium," Discussion Paper, 986, London: Centre for Economic Policy Research

Castles, F., 2001, "The Future of the Welfare State: Crisis Myths and Crisis Realities," Paper presented at the RC19 Annual Conference, Oviedo University, September 6–9

Cazzola, Giuliano, 1995, *Le nuove pensioni degli italiani*, Bologna: Il Mulino

Commission of European Communities (CEC), 1993, *Growth, Competitiveness, Employment: The Challenges and Ways forward into the 21st Century,*

White Paper, Luxembourg: Office for Official Publications of the European Communities

(ed.) 1996, *Negotiated Economic and Social Governance and European Integration*, Proceedings of Cost A7 Workshop, Dublin, May 24–25

1998a, Commission Recommendation for the Broad Guidelines of the Economic Policies of the Member States and the Community, DG II, COM (98) 279 final

1998b, *Social Protection in Europe 1997*, Collection Employment and Social Affairs, Luxembourg: Office for Official Publications of the European Communities

1998c, "Opinion on the Impact of Economic and Monetary Union on the Implementation of Belgian Policies," October 22

2002, *Lettre mensuelle socio-économique*, 77, December: 8

Celli, Primo and Treu, Tiziano (eds.), 1998, *Le nuove relazioni industriali: l'esperienza italiana nella prospettiva europea*, Bologna: Il Mulino

Central Planning Bureau (CPB), 1992, *Scanning the Future*, The Hague: SDU

CEOE 1997, *Acuerdos para la estabilidad del empleo y la negociación colectiva*, Madrid: Confederación de Organizaciones Empresariales

1999, "Balance de la encuesta sobre negociación colectiva en 1998," *Informes y Estudios de CEOE*, 81

CERC (Conseil Emploi Revenus Cohésion Sociale), 2002, *La Longue Route vers l'Euro, Rapport No. 2*, Paris: La Documentation Française

CES 1998, *Economía, trabajo y sociedad: memoria sobre la situación socioeconomica y laboral, 1997*, Madrid: Consejo Económico y Social

1999, *Economía, trabajo y sociedad: memoria sobre la situación socioeconomica y laboral, 1997*, Madrid: Consejo Económico y Social

Charpin, Jean-Marie, 1999, *L'Avenir de nos retraites, rapport au Premier ministre*, Paris: La Documentation Française

Checkel, J., 1997, "International Norms and Domestic Politics: Bridging the Rationalist–Constructivist Divide," *European Journal of International Relations*, 3: 473–495

1999, "Social Construction and Integration," *Journal of European Public Policy*, 6/4: 545–560

Clarida, Richard and Mark Gertler, 1997, "How the Bundesbank Conducts Monetary Policy," in Christina D. Romer and David N. Romer, *Reducing Inflation: Motivation and Strategy*, Chicago: University of Chicago Press

Clarida, Richard, Galí, Jordi, and Gertler, Mark, 1998, "Monetary Rules in Practice: Some International Evidence," *European Economic Review*, 42

Clark, G. L. and Whiteside, N. (eds.), 2003, *Pension Security in the 21st Century – Redrawing the Public–Private Debate*, Oxford: Oxford University Press

Clasen, J., 2001, "Managing the Economic Risk of Unemployment in the UK," Paper presented at the Conference "Welfare Systems and the Management of the Economic Risk of Unemployment," Florence: European University Institute, December 10–11

Closa, Carlos, 2001, *The Domestic Basis of Spanish European Policy and the 2002 Presidency*, Notre Europe, *Groupement d'études et de recherches, European Studies*, 16, December

CNNItalia.it, 2002, "Scioperi: sette volte piu dell'anno scorso," June 28

Cofferati, Sergio, 1999, "Il capitalismo e i fondi pensioni," *La Repubblica*, February 28

Coffineau, Michel, 1993, *Les Lois Auroux, dix ans après*, Paris: La Documentation Française

Coldrick, P., 1998, "The ETUC's Role in the EU's New Economy and Monetary Architecture," *Transfer*, 4(1): 21–35

Collicelli, Carla, 1998, *Benessere e tutela*, Milan: Feltrinelli

Collignon, Stefan, 1998, "Does the Central Bank Set the Natural Rate of Unemployment?," AUME Working Paper, 30, October: http://www.stefancollignon.de

   2001, "Economic Policy Coordination in EMU: Institutional and Political Requirements," Center for European Studies, Program for the Study of Germany and Europe Working Paper, 01.5D Cambridge, MA: Harvard University

   2002, *Monetary Stability in Europe*, London: Routledge

   2004, "The End of the Stability and Growth Pact?," *International Economics and Economic Policy*, 1(1): 1–5

Commissione per l'Analisi delle Compatibilità Macroeconomiche della Spesa Sociale (Commissione Onofri), 1997, *Relazione finale*, Rome, 27 February

Conant, Lisa, 2002, *Justice Contained*, Ithaca, NY: Cornell University Press

Concialdi, Pierre, 2000, "Débat et enjeux autour des retraites: un état des lieux," in *Année de la Régulation*, Paris: La Découverte

Connolly, Bernard, 1995, *The Rotten Heart of Europe*, London: Faber & Faber

Corcione, Annabella, 1997, "Riorganizzazione sanitaria e nuovo ruolo delle Regioni," in Euro Bartocci (ed.), *Lo stato sociale in Italia*, Rome: Donizelli

Coser, Lewis, 1977, *Masters of Sociological Thought: Ideas in Historical and Social Context*, Stamford, CT: International Thomson Publishing

Council of the European Union, 2002a, *Council Recommendation of 18 February 2002 on the Implementation of Member States' Employment Policies*, 2002/178/EC L60/76

   2002b, *Council Recommendation of 21 June 2002 on the Broad Guidelines of the Economic Policies of the Member States and the Community*, Seville, June 21, 10093/02

Cowles, Maria Green, Caporaso, James, and Risse, Thomas (eds.), 2001, *Transforming Europe: Europeanization and Domestic Change*, Ithaca NY: Cornell University Press

Crawford, Leslie, 2002, "Unions Ready to Strike Over Benefit Reform," *Financial Times*, May 2

Crouch, Colin, 1993, *Industrial Relations and European State Traditions*, Oxford: Clarendon Press

   1996, "Revised Diversity: From the Neo-liberal Decade to Beyond Maastricht," in J. van Ruysseveldt and Jelle Visser (eds.), *Industrial Relations in Europe*, London: Sage

   (ed.) 2000, *After the Euro: Shaping Institutions for Governance in the Wake of European Monetary Union*, Oxford: Oxford University Press

   2001, "Welfare State Regimes and Industrial Relations Systems: The Questionable Role of Path-Dependency Theory," in B. Ebbinghaus and P. Manow (eds.), *Comparing Welfare Capitalism: Social Policy and Political Economy in Europe, Japan, and the USA*, London: Routledge

2002, "The Euro and Labour Market and Wage Policies," in Kenneth Dyson (ed.), *European States and the Euro: Europeanization, Variation, and Convergence*, Oxford: Oxford University Press: 278–305

Crouch, Colin and Alessandro Pizzorno (eds.), 1978, *The Resurgence of Class Conflict in Western Europe Since 1968*, London: Macmillan

Crouch, C. and Streeck, W. (eds.), 1997, *Political Economy of Modern Capitalism: Mapping Convergence & Diversity*, London: Sage

Custers, Jos and Gils, Monique van, 1997, "The Netherlands: A Demonstration of Dedication," in Wim W. Boonstra and Sylvester C. W. Eijffinger (eds.), *Banks, Financial Markets and Monetary Policy*, Amsterdam: NIBE

Czada, Roland, 1998, "Vereinigungskrise und Standortdebatte," *Leviathan*, 26: 4–59

Czada, Roland and Wollmann, Hellmut (eds.), 2000, *Von der Bonner zur Berliner Republik*, Opladen: Westdeutscher Verlag

Daley, Anthony (ed.), 1996, *The Mitterrand Era*, New York: St. Martin's Press

Daly, M., 2000, "A Fine Balance: Women's Labour Market Participation in International Comparison," in F. W. Scharpf and V. A. Schmidt (eds.), *Welfare and Work in an Open Economy*, I and II, Oxford: Oxford University Press: 467–509

De Grauwe, Paul, 1994, *The Economics of Monetary Integration*, 2nd edn., New York: Oxford University Press

1998, "The Risk of Deflation in the Future EMU: Lessons of the 1990s," CEPR Discussion Paper, 1834

2002, "Challenges for Monetary Policy in Euroland," *Journal of Common Market Studies*, 40: 693–718

2003a, "The Pact Should be Replaced and not Mourned," *Financial Times*, March 27

2003b, "Undue Pessimism is Driving the Eurozone's Recession," *Financial Times*, August 8

Degryse, C. and Pochet, Philippe (eds.), 2002, *Social Developments in the European Union 2001*, Brussels: ETUI, Observatoire social européen, and SALTSA

Dehaene, J. L., 1998, "La portée de l'Union monétaire pour les marchés financiers et les citoyens européens," *Reflets & Perspectives de la vie économique*, 37(1): 5–10

Della Sala, Vincent, 1997, "Hollowing Out and Hardening the State: European Integration and the Italian Economy," *West European Politics*, 20(1): 14–33

DeLong, J. Bradford, 1997, "America's Peacetime Inflation: The 1970s," in Christina Romer and David N. Romer (eds.), *Reducing Inflation: Motivation and Strategy*, Chicago: University of Chicago Press

Delsen, Lei, 2000, *Exit poldermodel?*, Assen: Van Gorcum

Delvaux, Y., 1996, "La préparation de la Belgique à l'union économique et monétaire," *Courrier hebdomadaire du Crisp*, 1536–37, Brussels: Centre de recherche et d'information socio-politiques

Denayer, L., 1996, "Brief Account of Belgian National Project," in CEC (ed.), *Negotiated Economic and Social Governance and European Integration*, Proceedings of Cost A7 Workshop, Dublin, May 24–25

Denayer, L. and Tollet, R., 2002, "Institutional Mechanisms of Wage-Setting in Belgium," in Philippe Pochet (ed.), *Wage Policy in the Eurozone*, Brussels. PIE – Peter Lang: 177–194

Department of Social Affairs and Employment, 1997a, *Social Policy and Economic Performance*, Report and Summary, Amsterdam, January 23–25

Deutsche Bundesbank, 1990, *Stellungnahme der Deutschen Bundesbank zur Errichtung einer Wirtschafts- und Währungsunion in Europa*, Frankfurt/M., September 19

1991a, *Ein Jahr deutsche Wirtschafts-, Währungs- und Sozialunion. Monatsberichte der Deutschen Bundesbank*, 43/7: 18–30

1991b, *Die deutsche Wirtschaft unter dem Einfluß der Vereinigung Deutschlands*, Monatsberichte der Deutschen Bundesbank, 43/10: 15–21

1996, "Zur Diskussion über die öffentlichen Transfers im Gefolge der Wiedervereinigung," *Monatsberichte der Deutschen Bundesbank*, 48(10): 17–31

Deutscher Gewerkschaftsbund (DGB), Bundesvorstand 1995, *Zur Europäischen Wirtschafts- und Währungsunion (EWWU)*, Düsseldorf

Deutsches Institut für Wirtschaft (DIW), 1997, "Vereinigungsfolgen belasten Sozialversicherung," *DIW-Wochenbericht*, 40/97: 725–729

Diamandouros, N., 1994, "Cultural Dualism and Political Change in Post-Authoritarian Greece," Estudios – Working Papers, 50, Madrid: Centro de Estudios Avanzados en Ciencias Sociales

Di Maggio, P. J. and Powell, W. W. (eds.), 1991a, *The New Institutionalism in Organizational Analysis*, Chicago: University of Chicago Press

1991b, "The Iron Cage Revisited: Institutional Isophormism and Collective Rationality in Organizational Fields," in P. J. Di Maggio and W. W. Powell (eds.), *The New Institutionalism in Organizational Analysis*, Chicago: University of Chicago Press

(eds.), 1991, *The New Institutionalism in Organizational Analysis*, Chicago: University of Chicago Press

Dispersyn, M. and Van Der Horst, P., 1992, *The Construction of a European "Social Snake,"* Feasibility Study, Brussels: Ministère de la Prévoyance sociale

Dock, T., 1996, "Vers de nouvelles formes de concertation sociale en Belgique comme préparation à l'Union économique et monétaire," Brussels, mimeo

Documentation Française, 1997, *La protection sociale en France*, Paris: La Documentation Française

Dolado, Juan J., Maria-Dolores, Ramón, and Naveira, Manuel, 2000, "Asymmetries in Monetary Policy Rules: Evidence for Four Central Banks," CEPR Discussion Paper, 2441

Dølvik, Jon Erik (ed.), 2001, *At Your Service?*, Brussels: PIE–Peter Lang

Dølvik, Jon Erik and Vartianen, J., 2002, *Globalisering og europeisk integrasjon – utfordringer for lønnsdannelsen og kollektivavtalene i de nordiske land*, Stockholm: Saltsa/Fafo

Dølvik, Jon Erik and Waddington, J., 2004, "Organizing Marketized Services: Are Unions up to the Job?," *Economic and Industrial Democracy*, 25(1): 9–41

Dornbusch, Rudi *et al.*, 1998, "Immediate Challenges for the European Central Bank," *Economic Policy*, 26, April

Drèze, J. H. and Sneesseens, H., 1997, "Technological Development, Competition from Low-Wage Economies and Low-Skilled Unemployment," in D. Snower and G. de la Dehesa (eds.), *Unemployment Policy: Government Options for the Labour Market*, Cambridge: Cambridge University Press: 250–282

Due, J., Madsen, J. S., and Lubanski, N., 2000, "Nordic Labour Relations: Between Autonomy and EU Integration," in R. Hoffmann, O. Jacobi, B. Keller and M. Weiss (eds.), *Transnational Industrial Relations in Europe*, Düsseldorf: Hans-Böckler-Stiftung

Dufour, C., 2000, "France," in G. Fajertag (ed.), *Collective Bargaining in Europe 1998–99*, Brussels: ETU 1: 165–192

Duisenberg, Wim, 1997, "Monetary Policy in Europe – Quo Vadis?," London, November 27

Dyson, Kenneth, 1994, *Elusive Union: The Process of Economic and Monetary Union in Europe*, London: Longman

1998, "Chancellor Kohl as Strategic Leader: The Case of Economic and Monetary Union," *German Politics*, 7(1): 37–63

2000, "EMU as Europeanization: Convergence, Diversity and Contingency," *Journal of Common Market Studies*, 38(4): 645–666

2002, "Germany and the Euro: Redefining EMU, Handling Paradox, and Managing Uncertainty and Contingency," in Kenneth Dyson (ed.) *European States and the Euro: Europeanization, Variation, and Convergence*, Oxford: Oxford University Press: 173–211

(ed.) 2002, *European States and the Euro: Europeanization, Variation, and Convergence*, Oxford: Oxford University Press

Dyson, Kenneth and Featherstone, Kevin, 1996, "Italy and EMU as a '*Vincolo esterno*': Empowering Technocrats, Transforming the State," *South European Society and Politics*, 1(2): 270–292

1999, *The Road to Maastricht: Negotiating Economic and Monetary Union*, Oxford: Oxford University Press

Ebbinghaus, Bernhard, 2002, "Dinosaurier der Dienstleistungsgesellschaft? Der Mitgliederschwund deutscher Gewerkschaften im historischen und internationalen Vergleich," Working Paper, 2002/3, Cologne: Max Planck Insitute for the Study of Societies

Ebbinghaus, Bernhard and Hassel, Anke, 1999, "Striking Deals: Concertation in the Reform of Continental European Welfare States," MPIfG Discussion Paper, 99/3, Cologne: Max Planck Institute for the Study of Societies

Ebbinghaus, Bernhard and Manow, Philip (eds.), 2001, *Comparing Welfare Capitalism: Social Policy and Political Economy in Europe, Japan, and the USA*, London: Routledge

Ebbinghaus, B. and J. Visser (2000), *Trade Unions in Western Europe since 1945*, London: Macmillan

Economic Policy Committee, 2002, *Annual Report on Structural Reforms 2002*, Brussels, March 5, ECFIN/EPC/117/02-EN

*Economist*, 2002, "The Model Makers: A Survey of the Netherlands," May 4

Egan, Michelle P., 2001, *Constructing a European Market: Standards, Regulation, and Governance*, Oxford: Oxford University Press

Egle, Christoph and Henkes, Christian, 2003, "Später Sieg der Modernisierer über die Traditionalisten," in Christoph Egle, Tobias Ostheim, and Zohlnhöfer, Reimut, *Das rot-grüne Projekt*, Wiesbaden: Westdeutscher Verlag: 67–92

Egle, Christoph, Ostheim, Tobias, and Zohlnhöfer, Reimut (eds.), 2003, *Das rot-grüne Projekt*, Wiesbaden: Westdeutscher Verlag

Egurbide, P., 2002, "Seguridad frente al terror y reforma de las economias," *El Pais*, January 2

Eichengreen, Barry, 1996, *European Monetary Integration: Theory, Practice and Analysis* Cambridge, MA: MIT Press

*EIRO Online*, 1998, "Spain: Dispute between Unions and Government over National Minimum Wage," European Industrial Relations Observatory Online, January 28, www.eiro.eurofound.ie

1999a, "Spain: New Agreement in Chemicals Extends Union Rights," European Industrial Relations Observatory Online, May 28, www.eiro.eurofound.ie

1999b, "Spain: Debate on Minimum Pensions Intensifies," European Industrial Relations Observatory Online, September 28, www.eiro.eurofound.ie

1999c, "The 'Europeanisation' of Collective Bargaining," July

2000, "Transnational: Pay Developments: Annual Update 1999," European Industrial Relations Observatory Online, February 28, www.eiro.eurofound.ie

2001, "Spain: Pensions Agreement Signed," European Industrial Relations Observatory Online, June 28, www.eiro.eurofound.ie

2003a, "Pay Developments 2002," www.eiro.eurofound.ie

2003b, "Spain: Renewal of Pension Agreement," November 12, www.eiro.eurofound.ie

*EIRR*, 1997, *European Industrial Relations Review*, December

1998a, *European Industrial Relations Review*, February

1998b, *European Industrial Relations Review*, May

Eitrheim, P. and Kuhnle, S., 2000, "Nordic Welfare States in the 1990s: Institutional Stability, Signs of Divergence," in S. Kuhnle, *Survival of the European Welfare State*, London: Routledge

*El Pais*, 1998, August 4

2000, July 5

Ellman, Michael, 1984a, *Collectivisation, Convergence, and Capitalism*, London: Academic Press

1984b, "Natural Gas, Restructuring and Re-Industrialisation: The Dutch Experience of Industrial Policy," in Michael Ellman, *Collectivisation, Convergence, and Capitalism*, London: Academic Press

1984c, "The Crisis of the Welfare State – The Dutch Experience," in K. E. Boulding (ed.), *The Economics of Human Betterment*, London: Macmillan

1986, "Recent Dutch Macroeconomic Experience," in J. Sargent (ed.), *Foreign Macro-Economic Experience*, Toronto: Toronto University Press

Emerson, Michael, 1998, *Redrawing the Map of Europe*, London: Macmillan

Englert, M. *et al.*, 2002, "Perspectives financières de la sécurité sociale 2000–2050: le vieillissement et la viabilité du système légal des pensions," Planning Paper, 91, Brussels: Federal Planning Bureau

Epstein, Gerald and Schor, Juliet, 1989, "The Divorce of the Banca d'Italia and the Italian Treasury: A Case Study of Central Bank Independence," in Peter Lange and Marino Regini (eds.), *State, Market and Social Regulation: New Perspectives on Italy*, Cambridge: Cambridge University Press

Espina, Alvaro, 1996, "Reform of Pension Schemes in the OECD Countries," *International Labour Review*, 135(2): 181–206

Esping-Andersen, G., 1990, *The Three Worlds of Welfare Capitalism*, Cambridge: Polity Press

1994, "Budgets and Democracy: Towards a Welfare State in Spain and Portugal, 1960–1986," in Ian Budge and David H. McKay (eds.), *Developing Democracy: Comparative Research in Honour of J. F. P. Blondel*, London: Sage

(ed.) 1996, *Welfare States in Transition*, London: Sage

1999, *Social Foundations of Post-Industrial Economies*, Oxford: Oxford University Press

Esping-Andersen, G., Gallie, D., Hemerijck, A., and Myles, J., 2001, *A New Welfare Architecture for Europe*, Report submitted to the Belgian Presidency of the EU

2002, *Why We Need a New Welfare State*, Oxford: Oxford University Press

European Central Bank (ECB), 1999a, *Annual Report 1998*, Frankfurt: ECB

1999b, "The Stability-Oriented Monetary Policy Strategy of the Eurosystem," *ECB Monthly Bulletin*, January: 39–50

2000a, *Annual Report 1999*, Frankfurt: ECB

2000b, *Monthly Bulletin*, May

2000c, *Monthly Bulletin*, August

2000d, *Monthly Bulletin*, October

2001a, *Monthly Bulletin*, April

2001b, *Monthly Bulletin*, May

2001c, *Monthly Bulletin*, June

2001d, *Monthly Bulletin*, July

2001e, *The Monetary Policy of the ECB*, Frankfurt: ECB

2002, *Labor Market Mismatches in Euro Area Countries*, Frankfurt, March

2003, *Monthly Bulletin*, May

European Commission, 1993, *White Paper on Growth, Competitiveness, and Employment*, COM 93/700

1995, The *European Councils: Conclusions of the Presidency 1992–1994*, Brussels

1999, *Employment in Europe*, Brussels

2000a, *Public Finances in EMU – 2000*, Report of the Directorate General of Economic and Financial Affairs, May 24, Ecfin/339/00

2000b, *Presidency Conclusions*, Lisbon European Council

2002, *Communication from the Commission to Council and the European Parliament: Strengthening the Co-Ordination of Budgetary Policies*, COM (2002) 668

*European Economy* 2001, no. 72

European Parliament, 2000, Committee on Economic and Monetary Affairs, Hearing, September 27

European Union, 1997, *Treaty of Amsterdam*, Luxembourg: EU

Ewijk, Casper van 1980a, "Monetaire ontwikkeling, inflatie en het beleid van De Nederlandsch Bank," in Casper van Ewijk *et al.* (eds.), *Economisch beleid uit de klem*, Amsterdam: Sua

*et al.* (eds.), 1980b, *Economisch beleid uit de klem*, Amsterdam: Sua.

Fabbrini, Sergio, 1994, *Quale democrazia: l'Italia e gli altri*, Bari: Laterza

Fajertag, Ginseppe and Pochet Philippe (eds.), 2000, *Social Pacts in Europe – New Dynamics*, Brussels: ETUI

Fase, M. M. G. and Tieman, A. F., 2001, "Wage Moderation, Innovation and Labour Productivity," *De Economist*, 149(1): 115–127

Favier, Pierre and Martin-Roland, Michel, 1990, *La Décennie Mitterrand 1. Les Ruptures*, Paris: Seuil

Featherstone, Kevin, 1998, "'Europeanization' and the Centre Periphery: The Case of Greece in the 1990s," *South European Society and Politics* 3(1): 23–39

Featherstone, Kevin and Kazamias, G. (eds.), 2001, *Europeanization: Asymmetrical Responses in the EU's Southern Periphery*, London: Frank Cass

Featherstone, Kevin, Kazamias, G., and Papadimitriou, D., 2000, "Greece and the Negotiation of Economic and Monetary Union: Preferences, Strategies, and Institutions," *Journal of Modern Greek Studies*, 18: 393–414

2001, "The Limits of External Empowerment: Greece, EMU and Pension Reform," *Political Studies*, 49(3): 262–280

Featherstone, K. and C. Radaelli, 2003, *The Politics of Europeanization*, Oxford: Oxford University Press

Feldstein, Martin and Horst Siebert (eds.), 2002, *Social Security Pension Reform in Europe*, Chicago: University of Chicago Press

Ferner, Anthony and Hyman, Richard (eds.), 1998, *Changing Industrial Relations in Europe*, 2nd edn., Oxford: Blackwell

Ferrera, Maurizio, 1995, "The Rise and Fall of Democratic Universalism: Health Care Reform in Italy, 1978–1994," *Journal of Health Politics, Policy and Law*, 20(3): 275–302

1996, "The Southern Model of Welfare in Social Europe," *Journal of European Social Policy*, 6(1): 17–37

1998, "The Four Social Europes: Between Universalism and Selectivity," in Martin Rhodes and Yves Mény (eds.), *The Future of European Welfare: A New Social Contract?*, London: Macmillan

2000, "Reconstructing the Welfare State in Southern Europe," in S. Kuhnle (ed.), *Survival of the European Welfare State*, London: Routledge

Ferrera, Maurizio and Gualmini, Elisabetta 1999a, *Salvati dall'Europa?*, Bologna: Il Mulino

1999b, "Italy: Rescue from Without?," Cologne: Max Planck Institut für Gesellschaftsforschung, unpublished paper

2000, "Italy: Rescue from Without?," in F. W. Scharpf and V. A. Schmidt (eds.), *Welfare and Work in the Open Economy*, I and II, Oxford: Oxford University Press: 351–397

2003, *Rescued by Europe?: Italy's Social Reforms from Maastricht to Berlusconi*, Amsterdam: Amsterdam University Press

Ferrera, Maurizio and Hemerijck, Anton, 2003, "Recalibrating Europe's Welfare Regimes," in J. Zeitlin and D. Trubek (eds.), *Governing Work and Welfare in a New Economy: European and American Experiments*, Oxford: Oxford University Press

Ferrera, Maurizio, Hemerijck, Anton, and Rhodes, Martin, 2000, *The Future of Social Europe*, Oeiras: Celta editora

Ferrera, Maurizio and Rhodes, Martin (eds.), 2000, *Recasting European Welfare States*, London: Frank Cass

Festjens, M. J., 1997, "La réforme des pensions," *Planning Paper*, Brussels: Bureau fédéral du plan

*Financial Times*, 1996, October 21
  2001a, March 24
  2001b, "The ECB's Siege Mentality," Editorial, April 27
  2001c, "Germany's Ifo Calls on ECB to Cut Rate," July 26
  2001d, "Inflation is key to ECB thinking," August 3
  2003, "Ending the Blame Game," Editorial, July 12–13

Fine, Sidney, 1956, *Laissez Faire and the General-Welfare State*, Ann Arbor: University of Michigan Press

Fitoussi, Jean-Paul, 1995, *Le Débat Interdit: Monnaie, Europe, Pauvreté*, Paris: Arléa

Fitoussi, Jean-Paul, Jestaz, David, Phelps, Edmund S., and Zoega, Gylfi, 2000, "Roots of the Recent Recoveries: Labor Reforms or Private Sector Forces?," *Brookings Papers on Economic Activity*, 1

Fitoussi, Jean-Paul and Olivier Passet, 2000, "Réformes structurelles et politiques macroéconomiques: les enseignements des 'modeles' de pays," in *Réduction du chomage: les réussites en Europe*, Conseil d'analyse économique, 21, Paris: La Documentation française

Follain, John, 2002, "Italy Offers Britain Skeptical Alliance," *Sunday Times*, London, February 10

Forder, J., 2001, "Image and Illusion in the Design of EMU," in A. Menon and V. Richt (eds.), *From the Nation State to Europe: Essays in Honour of Jack Hayward*, Oxford: Oxford University Press

Fraile, L., 1999, "Tightrope: Spanish Unions and Labour Market Segmentation," in Andrew Martin and George Ross (eds.), *The Brave New World of European Labor*, New York: Berghahn Books

France, 1997, Commissariat Général du Plan, *Chômage: le cas français*, Paris: La Documentation Française

Franzese, Jr., Robert J. and Hall, Peter, 2000, "Institutional Dimensions of Coordinating Wage Bargaining and Monetary Policy," in Torben Iversen, Jonas Pontusson, and David Soskice (eds.), *Unions, Employers, and Central Banks: Macroeconomic Coordination and Institutional Change in Social Market Economics*, Cambridge: Cambridge University Press

Freeman, Richard B., 1998, "War of the Models," *Labour Economics*, 5

Freeman, Richard and Rodgers, William M., III, 1999, "Area Economic Conditions and the Labor Market Outcomes of Young Men in the 1990s Expansion," NBER Working Paper, WP7073

Freyssinet, Jacques, 2000, "La réduction du taux de chômage: les enseignements des expériences européennes," in *Réduction du chômage: les réussites en Europe*, Conseil d'analyse économique, 21, Paris: La Documentation française

Friedman, Benjamin M. (ed.), 1999a, *Inflation, Unemployment, and Monetary Policy*, Cambridge, MA: MIT Press

1999b, "Comments," in Benjamin M. Friedman (ed.), *Inflation, Unemployment, and Monetary Policy*, Cambridge, MA: MIT Press

Fröhlich, Hans-Peter, 1991, "Die Europäische Währungsunion aus Sicht der Unternehmen," in Manfred Weber (ed.), *Europa auf dem Weg zur Währungs union*, Darmstadt: Wissenschaftliche Buchgesellschaft: 276–295

Galbraith, James K., 1997, "Time to Ditch the NAIRU," *Journal of Economic Perspectives*, 11: 93–108

Gambier, Dominique and Vernières, Michel, 1995, *L'emploi en France*, Paris: La Découverte

Ganghof, S., 2000, "Adjusting National Tax Policy to Economic Internationalization: Strategies and Outcomes," in F. W. Scharpf and V. A. Schmidt (eds.), *Work and Welfare in the Open Economy*, I and II, Oxford: Oxford University Press

Garrett, G., 1998, *Partisan Politics in the Global Economy*, Cambridge: Cambridge University Press

Garrett, G. and Tsebelis, G., 1996, "An Institutional Critique of Intergovernmentalism," *International Organization*, 50: 269–300

Gautié, Jérome and Nauze-Fichet, Emmanuelle, 2000, "Déclassement sur le marché du travail et retour au plein employ," in Complement E, *Plein Emploi: Rapport Jean Pisani-Ferr.*, Conseil d'analyse économique, 30, Paris: La Documentation française

Gauvin, André, 1993, "Les contraintes de la politique d'emploi, de 1986 à 1992," in INSEE, *La Société Française: Données Sociales 1993*, Paris: INSEE

Geelhoed, L. A., 1991a, "1991: meer dan een tussenbalans," *Economisch Statistische Berichten*, 76

1991b, "EMU dwingt ons tot verlagen arbeidskosten," *De Volkskrant*, December 16

1992, "1992, en verder," *Economisch Statistische Berichten*, 77

1993, "1993: meer dynamiek gevraagd," *Economisch Statistische Berichten*, 78

1994, "1994: uitdagingen voor het sociaal-economisch bestel," *Economisch Statistische Berichten*, 79

Genschel, P., 2001, "Globalization, Tax Competition and the Fiscal Viability of the Welfare State," MPIfG Working Paper, Cologne: Max Planck Institut für Gesellschaftsforschung

German Council of Economic Experts, 1998, *Annual Report 1998/99: Vor Weitreichenden Entscheidungen*

Giavazzi, F. and Pagano, M., 1988, "The Advantage of Tying One's Hands: EMS Discipline and Central Bank Credibility," *European Economic Review*, 24: 1055–1082

Giddens, Anthony, 1998, *The Third Way*, Cambridge: Polity Press

2000, *The Third Way and Its Critics*, Cambridge: Polity Press

Giesen, Bernd and Leggewie, Claus (eds.), 1991, *Experiment Vereinigung: ein sozialer Großversuch*, Berlin: Rotbuch-Verlag

Gillespie, Richard, 1990, "The Break-up of the 'Socialist Family': Party–Union Relations in Spain, 1982–1989," *West European Politics*, 16: 78–96

Ginsborg, P., 1990, *A History of Contemporary Italy*, London: Penguin

Giuliani, M., 2001, "Europeanization and Italy: A Bottom-Up Process?," in Kevin Featherstone and G. Kazamias (eds.), *Europeanization: Asymmetrical Responses in the EU's Southern Periphery*, London: Frank Cass

Glyn, A. (ed.), 2001, *Social Democracy in Neoliberal Times: The Left and Economic Policy since 1980*, Oxford: Oxford University Press

Glyn, A. and Wood, S., 2001, "New Labour's Economic Policy," in A. Glyn (ed.), *Social Democracy in Neoliberal Times: The Left and Economic Policy since 1980*, Oxford: Oxford University Press

Goetschy, J., 1999, "The European Employment Strategy: Genesis and Development," *European Journal of Industrial Relations*, 6(2): 117–137

Goetschy, Janine and Pochet, Philippe, 2000, "Regards croisés sur la stratégie européenne de l'emploi," in Paul Magnette and Eric Remacle (eds.), *Le Nouveau modèle Européen*, 2, Brussels: Editions de l'Université Libre de Bruxelles

Golden, Miriam, 1988, *Labor Divided: Austerity and Working-Class Politics in Contemporary Italy*, Ithaca, NY: Cornell University Press

Goodin, Robert E. *et al.*, 1999, *The Real Worlds of Welfare Capitalism*, Cambridge: Cambridge University Press

Goodrich, Carter, 1950, "The Revulsion against Internal Improvements," *Journal of Economic History*, 10: 145–169

Goul Andersen, J., 2000, "Welfare Crisis and Beyond: Danish Welfare Policies in the 1980s and 1990s," in S. Kuhnle (ed.), *Survival of the Welfare State*, London: Routledge

Gramlich, Edward M., 2001, "Asset Prices and Monetary Policy," *New Technologies and Monetary Policy International Symposium*, Bank of France, November 30

Grande, E., 1995, "Das Paradox der Schache, Forschungspolitik und die Einfluss-slogik europäischer Politikverflechtung," in M. Jachtenfuchs and B. Kohler-Koch (eds.), *Europäische Integration*, Opladen: Leske & Budrich

Grant, Charles, 1994, *Inside the House that Jack Built*, London: Nicholas Brealey

Griffiths, Richard T. (ed.), 1980, *The Economy and Politics of the Netherlands since 1945*, The Hague: Martinus Nijhoff

Gros, Daniel and Thygesen, Niels, 1998, *European Monetary Integration*, 2nd edn., London: Longman

Grosser, Dieter, 1998, *Das Wagnis der Wirtschafts- und Währungsunion: Geschichte der deutschen Einheit, Band 2*, Stuttgart: Deutsche Verlags-Anstalt

Guillén, A. M., Alvarez, S., and Adao e Silva, P., 2001, "Redesigning the Spanish and Portuguese Welfare States: The Impact of Accession into the European Union," Center for European Studies Working Paper, Harvard University

Haahr, J.-H., 2000, "The Danish Social Democrats," in Ton Notermans (ed.), *Social Democrats and Monetary Union*, Cambridge: Cambridge University Press

Hall, Peter, 1987, "The Evolution of Economic Policy under Mitterrand," reprinted in George Ross, Stanley Hoffmann, and Sylvia Malzacher (eds.), *The Mitterrand Experiment*, Cambridge: Polity Press

1989, *The Political Power of Economic Ideas*, Princeton: Princeton University Press

1999, "The Political Economy of Europe in an Era of Interdependence," in Herbert Kitschelt, Peter Lange, Gary Marks, and John D. Stephens (eds.), *Continuity and Change in Contemporary Capitalism*, Cambridge: Cambridge University Press: 135–163

2001, "The Evolution of Economic Policy-Making in the European Union," in A. Menon and V. Richt (eds.), *From the Nation State to Europe: Essays in Honour of Jack Heyward*, Oxford: Oxford University Press

Hall, Peter and Franzese, Robert J., Jr., 1998, "Mixed Signals: Central Bank Independence, Coordinated Wage Bargaining, and European Monetary Union," *International Organization*, 52(3): 505–535

Hall, Peter and David Soskice (eds.), 2001, *Varieties of Capitalism*, Oxford: Oxford University Press

Hallerberg, Mark, 2002, "Introduction: Fiscal Policy in the European Union," *European Union Politics*, 3(2): 139–150

Hardiman, N., 2000, *The Political Economy of Growth: Economic Governance and Political Innovation in Ireland*, Society for the Advancement of Socio-Economics (SASE), London, July 7–9

Hartwich, Hans-Hermann, 1998, *Die Europäisierung des deutschen Wirtschaftssystems*, Opladen: Leske & Budrich

Hartz, Louis, 1948, *Economic Policy and Democratic Thought: Pennsylvania, 1776–1860*, Cambridge, MA: Harvard University Press

Hassel, Anke and Thorsten Schulten, 1998, "Globalisation and the Future of Central Collective Bargaining: The Example of the German Metal Industry," *Economy & Society* 27(4): 241–577

Hassenteufel, Patrick, 1997, *Les médecins face à l'état*, Paris: Presses de Sciences Po

Heisenberg, Dorothee, 1999, *The Mark of the Bundesbank: Germany's Role in European Monetary Cooperation*, Boulder, CO: Lynne Rienner

Heller, J.-L., 1987, "Les retraites anticipées," in INSEE, *La Société Française: Données Sociales 1987*, Paris: INSEE

Helms, Ludger (ed.), 2000, *Institutions and Institutional Change in the Federal Republic of Germany*, London: Macmillan

Hemerijck, Anton, 1992, "The Historical Contingencies of Dutch Corporatism," PhD thesis, Balliol College, Oxford University

2002, "The Self-Transformation of the European Social Model(s)," in G. Esping-Andersen, D. Gallie, A. Hemerijck, and J. Myles (eds.), *Why We Need a New Welfare State*, Oxford: Oxford University Press: 173–213

Hemerijck, Anton and Manow, Philip, 2001, "The Experience of Negotiated Reforms in the Dutch and German Welfare States," in Bernhard Ebbinghaus and Philip Manow (eds.), *Comparing Welfare Capitalism: Social Policy and Political Economy in Europe, Japan, and the USA*, London: Routledge: 217–239

Hemerijck, Anton, Manow, Philip, and Kersbergen, Kees van, 1999, "Welfare without Work?: Divergent Experiences of Reform in Germany and the Netherlands," in S. Kuhnle (ed.), *Survival of the Welfare State*, London: Routledge

Hemerijck, Anton, Meer, M. van der, and Visser, Jelle, 2000, "Innovation through Coordination – Two Decades of Social Pacts in the Netherlands," in

G. Fajertag and Philippe Pochet (eds.), *Social Pacts in Europe – New Dynamics*, Brussels: ETUI: 257–278

Hemerijck, A. and Schludi, M., 2000, "Sequences of Policy Failures and Effective Policy Responses," in F. W. Scharpf and V. A. Schmidt (eds.), *Welfare and Work in the Open Economy*, I, Oxford: Oxford University Press

Hemerijck, Anton, Unger, Brigitte, and Visser, Jelle, 2000, "How Small Countries Negotiate Change," in F. W. Scharpf and V. A. Schmidt (eds.), *Welfare and Work in the Open Economy*, II, Oxford: Oxford University Press

Hemerijck, Anton and Visser, Jelle, 2001, *Learning and Mimicking: How European Welfare States Reform*, unpublished manuscript

Henning, Randall C., 1994, *Currencies and Politics in the United States, Germany, and Japan*, Washington, DC, Institute for International Economics

1998, "Systemic Conflict and Regional Monetary Integration: The Case of Europe," *International Organization*, 52(3): 537–573

Héritier, Adrienne, 1999, *Policy-Making and Diversity in Europe: Escape from Deadlock*, Cambridge: Cambridge University Press

Héritier, Adrienne and Knill, C., 2000, "Differential Responses to European Policies: A Comparison," Paper presented to the International Workshop "Europeanization: Concept and Reality," University of Bradford, May 5–6

Hine, David and Finocchi, R., 1991, "The Italian Prime Minister," *West European Politics*, 14(2): 79–86

Hinrichs, K., 2001, "Elephants on the Move. Patterns of Public Pension Reform in OECD Countries," in S. Leibfried (ed.), *Welfare State Futures*, Cambridge: Cambridge University Press

Hodson, Dermot and Maher, Imelda, 2001, "The Open Method as a New Mode of Governance," *Journal of Common Market Studies*, 39(4): 719–746

Hoffmann, R. and Waddington, J. (eds.), 1999, *Trade Unions in Europe: Facing Challenges and Searching for Solutions*, Brussels: ETUI

Holden, Steinar, 1999, *Wage Setting under Different Monetary Regimes*, Oslo: Bank of Norway and University of Oslo

Holzmann, Robert, Orenstein, Mitchell, and Rutkowski, Michal, 2003, *Pension Reform in Europe: Process and Progress*, Washington, DC: World Bank

Hombach, Bodo, 1998, *Aufbruch*, Munich: Econ

Hooghe, Lisbet and Marks, Gary, 1999, "The Making of a Polity: The Struggle over European Integration," in Herbert Kitschelt, Peter Lange, Gary Marks, and John D. Stephens (eds.), *Continuity and Change in Contemporary Capitalism*, Cambridge: Cambridge University Press: 70–97

2001, *Multi-Level Governance and European Integration*, Lanham, MD: Rowman & Littlefield

Houben, A. C. F. J., 1997, "Het stabiliteitspact en de begrotingsdiscipline in de EMU," *Economisch Statistische Berichten*, 82

Howarth, D., 2000, "The French State in the Euro-Zone: 'Modernization' and Legitimizing *dirigisme* in the 'Semi-Sovereignty' Game," Paper presented to the British Academy Conference on "European States and the Euro," London, September 14–15

Hoynes, Hilary, 1999, "The Employment, Earnings, and Income of Less Skilled Workers Over the Business Cycle," NBER Working Paper, 7188

ILO, 1998, *International Labor Report*, Geneva: ILO

IMF, 2001, *International Monetary Fund Press Conference on the World Economic Situation*, Washington, DC

INSEE, 1987, *La Société Française: Données Sociales 1987*, Paris: INSEE

1993, *La Société Française: Données Sociales 1993*, Paris: INSEE

1995, *Tableaux de l'Economie Française 1994–1995*, Paris: INSEE

Ioakimides, P., 1998, *The European Union and the Greek State*, Athens: Themelio

Iaonnou, C. A., 2000, "Social Pacts in Hellenic Industrial Relations: Odysseys or Sisyphus?," in G. Fajertag and P. Pochet (eds.), *Social Pacts in Europe – New Dynamics*, Brussels: ETUI/OSE

Issing, Otmar, 2000, "How to Promote Growth in the Euro Area: The Contribution of Monetary Policy," Conference of the National Bank of Belgium, May 12

2001a, quoted in the *Financial Times*, March 24

2001b, quoted in the *Financial Times*, August 3

2002, "On Macroeconomic Policy Coordination in EMU," *Journal of Common Market Studies*, 40(2): 345–358

Gaspar, Vítor, Angeloni, Ignazio, and Tristani, Oreste, 2001, *Monetary Policy in the Euro Area: Strategy and Decision-Making at the European Central Bank*, Cambridge: Cambridge University Press

Iversen, Torben, 1998a, "Wage Bargaining, Central Bank Independence and the Real Effects of Money," *International Organization*, 52: 469–504

1998b, "The End of Solidarity? Decentralization, Monetarism, and the Social-Democratic Welfare State," Cambridge, MA mimeo

2001, "The Dynamics of Welfare State Expansion: Trade Openness, De-Industrialization, and Partisan Politics," in Paul Pierson (ed.), *The New Politics of the Welfare State*, Oxford: Oxford University Press

Pontusson, Jonas, and Soskice, David, 2000, *Unions, Employers, and Central Banks: Macroeconomic Coordination and Institutional Change in Social Market Economies*, Cambridge: Cambridge University Press.

Iversen, Torben and Wren, Anne, 1998, "Equality, Employment and Budgetary Restraint: The Trilemma of the Service Economy," *World Politics* 50: 196–205

Jabko, Nicolas, 2001, "Expertise et politique à l'âge de l'euro: La Banque Centrale Européenne sur le terrain de la démocratie," *Revue française de science politique*, 51(6): 903–930

Jachtenfuchs, M. and Kohler-Koch, B. (eds.), 1995, *Europäische Integration*, Opladen: Leske & Budrich

Jacobi, Otto, 1998, "Contours of a European Collective Bargaining System," Paper prepared for the IIRA 11th World Congress, Bologna, September 22–25

Jacobi, Otto, Keller, Berndt, and Müller-Jentsch, Walther, 1998, "Germany: Facing New Challenges," in Anthony Ferner and Richard Hyman (eds.), *Changing Industrial Relations in Europe*, Oxford: Blackwell: 190–238

Jadot, M., 1999, "Présentation des lignes de forces du rapport," La politique fédérale de l'emploi, Rapport d'évaluation 1998, Brussels: Ministère Fédéral de l'Emploi

2000, "La concertation sociale," in I. Cassiers (ed.), "Que nous ent-il arrivé? Un demi-siècle d'évolution de l'économie belge," *Reflets & Perspectives de la vie: économique*, 39(1), Brussels: De Boeck Université

Jaffré, Jérôme, 2003, "La droite sans complexe," *Le Monde*, July 11

Jenson, Jane and Pochet, Philippe, 2002, "Employment and Social Policy since Maastricht: Standing up to the European Monetary Union," Document prepared for the Conference of the Nanovic Institute for European Studies "The Year of the Euro," University of Notre Dame, December 6–8

Jenson, Jane and Sineau, Mariette, 2001, *Who Cares: Women's Work, Childcare and Welfare State Redesign*, Toronto, University of Toronto Press

Jochem, Sven, 2001, "Reformpolitik im deutschen Sozialversicherungsstaat," in Manfred G. Schmidt (ed.), *Wohlfahrtsstaatliche Politik: Institutionen, Prozess und Leistungsprofil*, Opladen: Leske & Budrich: 193–226

Jochem, Sven and Siegel, Nico A., 2000, "Wohlfahrtskapitalismen und Beschäftigungsperformanz – Das 'Modell Deutschland' im Vergleich," *Zeitschrift für Sozialreform* 46(1): 38–64

(eds.), 2003, *Verhandlungsdemokratie, Konzertierung und wohlfahrtsstaatliche Reformpolitik*, Opladen: Leske & Budrich

Join-Lambert, Marie-Thérèse *et al.*, 1997, *Politiques Sociales*, 2nd edn., Paris: Presses de la FNSP and Dalloz

Jonckheer, P. and Pochet, Philippe 1990, "La Charte sociale et le programme d'action," *Courrier hebdomadaire du Crisp*, 1273/74, Brussels: Centre de recherche et d'information socio-politiques

Jones, Erik, 2003, *The Politics of Monetary Integration: Integration and Idiosyncrasy*, Lanham, MD: Rowman & Littlefield

Kaltenthaler, Karl, 1998, *Germany and the Politics of Europe's Money*, London: Duke University Press

Kam, C. A. de, 1998, "Belastingen," in *Koninklijke Vereniging voor de Staathuishoudkunde*

Kam, Flip de *et al.*, 1998, *Draagkracht onder druk*, Amsterdam: Wiardi Beckman Stichting: *Belastingherziening in het fin de siècle*, Utrecht: Lemma

Kapner, Fred, 2002, "Rome Pressure on Stability Pact," *Financial Times*, July 8: 2

Kapner, Fred and Parker, George, 2002, "Budget Deficit Dispute: Angry Italy Agrees to EU Guideline on Accounts," *Financial Times*, July 5: 2

Katzenstein, Peter J., 1985, *Small States in World Markets*, Ithaca, NY: Cornell University Press

(ed.) 1989, *Industry and Politics in West Germany: Toward the Third Republic*, Ithaca, NY: Cornell University Press

Kauppinen, T. (ed.), 1998, *The Impact of EMU on Industrial Relations in the European Union*, no. 9, Helsinki: Finnish Industrial Relations Association

Kautto, M. *et al.*, 1999, *Nordic Social Policy: Changing Welfare States*, London, Routledge

Keeler, John and Schain, Martin (eds.), 1996, *Chirac's Challenge*, New York: St. Martin's Press

Kersbergen, K. van, 1995, *Social Capitalism: A Study of Christian Democracy and the Welfare State*, London: Routledge

King, Desmond and Wood, Stewart, 1999, "The Political Economy of Neoliberalism: Britain and the United States in the 1980s," in Herbert Kitschelt, Peter Lange, Gary Marks, and John D. Stephens (eds.), *Continuity and Change in Contemporary Capitalism*, Cambridge: Cambridge University Press: 371–397

Kingdon, J., 1984, *Agendas, Alternatives and Public Policy*, Boston: Little, Brown

Kitschelt, Herbert *et al.*, 1999, "Convergence and Divergence in Advanced Capitalist Democracies," in Herbert Kitschelt, Peter Lange, Gary Marks, and John D. Stephens (eds.), *Continuity and Change in Contemporary Capitalism*, Cambridge: Cambridge University Press

Kitschelt, Herbert, Lange, Peter, Marks, Gary, and Stephens, John D. (eds.), 1999, *Continuity and Change in Contemporary Capitalism*, Cambridge: Cambridge University Press

Kjellberg, A., 1998, "Sweden: Restoring the Model?," in A. Ferner and R. Hyman (eds.), *Changing Industrial Relations in Europe*, Oxford: Blackwell

Kloosterman, R. C. and Elfring, T., 1991, *Werken in Nederland*, Schoonhoven: Academic Service

Knill, C. and Lehmkuhl, D., 1999, "How Europe Matters: Different Mechanisms of Europeanization," *European Integration Online Papers (EIOP)*, 3(7)

Knoester, A., 1989, *Economische politiek in Nederland*, Leiden: Stenfert Kroese

Koene, J.-C., 1997, "Quelles politiques macro-économiques pour réussir l'intégration de la Belgique à l'UEL," *Reflets & Perspectives de la vie économique*, 36(1): 43–69

Kohl, H. *et al.*, 2000, "Transformation, EU Membership and Labour Relations in Central and Eastern Europe: Poland–Czech Republic–Hungary, Slovenia," *Transfer* 6(3): 399–415

Kohl, H, Lecher, W., and Platzer, H. W., 2000, *Arbeitsbeziehungen in Ost-Mitteleuropa zwischen Transformation und EU Beitritt*, Bonn: Friedrich Ebert Stiftung

Kremers, J. J. M., 1993, *Inspelen op Europa*, Schoonhaven Academic Service

Krueger, Alan B. and Solow, Robert (eds.), 2001, *The Roaring Nineties: Can Full Employment Be Sustained?*, New York: The Russell Sage Foundation and The Century Foundation Press

Krugman, Paul, 2004, "The Maestro of Chutzpah" *The New York Times*, March 3
2000, "The Scandinavian Welfare State in the 1990s: Challenged, but Viable," in M. Ferrera and M. Rhodes (eds.), *Recasting European Welfare States*, London: Frank Cass: 209–227

Kuhnle, S. (ed.), 2000, *Survival of the European Welfare State*, London: Routledge

Kurzer, P., 1997, "Decline or Preservation of Executive Capacity? Political and Economic Integration Revisited," *Journal of Common Market Studies*, 35(1): 31–56

Labbé, Dominique, 1996, *Syndicats et Syndiqués en France depuis 1945*, Paris: l'Harmattan

Labohm, Hans and Wijnker, Charles (eds.), 2000, *The Netherlands' Polder Model: Does it Offer any Clues to the Solution of Europe's Socioeconomic Flaws?*, Amsterdam: De Nederlandsche Bank

La Découverte, 2002, *L'état de la France 2002*, Paris: La Découverte

Lamas, R., 1997, "La loi de sauvegarde préventive de la compétitivité: un nouvel encadrement des négociations salariales," *Année sociale de l'ULB 1997*, Brussels: ULB: 87–98

Lange, Peter, 1993, "Maastricht and the Social Protocol: Why Did They Do It?," *Politics and Society*, 21(1): 5–36

Lange, Peter and Regini, Marino (eds.), 1989, *State, Market and Social Regulation: New Perspectives on Italy*, Cambridge: Cambridge University Press

Larsson, A., 1998, "The European Employment Strategy and EMU: You Must Invest to Save," The 1998 Meidner Lecture, "Economic and Industrial Democracy," 19: 391–415

Lavdas, K. A., 1997, *The Europeanization of Greece: Interest Politics and the Crises of Integration*, London: Macmillan

Layard, Richard, 1999, *Tackling Unemployment*, London: Macmillan

Layard, Richard, Basevi, Giorgio, Blanchard, Olivier, Buiter, Willem, and Dornbusch, Rudiger, 1984, "Europe in 1984: The Case for Unsustainable Growth," in Richard Layard, *Tackling Unemployment*, London: Macmillan (1999)

Layard, Richard, Nickell, Stephen, and Jackman, Richard, 1991, *Unemployment: Macroeconomic Performance and the Labour Market*, Oxford: Oxford University Press

Le Cacheux, 2000, "Labor Markets, Social Protection, Tax and Social Competition in the European Monetary Union," Preliminary paper prepared for the conference on "Europe One Labour Market, Challenge for Workers and Employers," Brussels: SALTSA

Leering, Raoul, 1998, "Concurrentie binnen de EMU," in Geert Reuten *et al.* (eds.), *De prijs van de Euro*, Amsterdam: Van Gennep

Lehmbruch, Gerhard, 1991, "Die deutsche Vereinigung: Strukturen und Strategien," *Politische Vierteljahresschrift*, 32(4): 585–604

1996, "Die korporative Verhandlungsdemokratie in Westmitteleuropa," *Schweizerische Zeitschrift für Politische Wissenschaft*, 2: 19–41

*Le Monde*, 2003, July 11

Leibfried, Stephan (ed.), 2001, *Welfare State Futures*, Cambridge: Cambridge University Press

Leibfreid, Stephan and Pierson, Paul., 2000, "Social Policy," in H. Wallace and W. Wallace (eds.), *Policy Making in the European Union*, 4th edn., Oxford: Oxford University Press: 267–291

(eds.), 1995, *European Social Policy: Between Fragmentation and Integration*, Washington, DC: Brookings

Lerner, Gad, 1997, "Elogio del consenso sociale," *La Stampa*, November 6: 1

Lescohier, Don D. and Brandeis, Elizabeth, 1935, *Working Conditions and Labor Legislation: History of Labor in the United States 1896–1932, III*; reprinted, New York: Augustus M. Kelley, 1966

Levy, Jonah, 2000, "France: Directing Adjustment," in F. W. Scharpf and V. A. Schmidt (eds.), *Welfare and Work in the Open Economy*, I and II, Oxford: Oxford University Press

Lijphart, Arend, 1973, *The Politics of Accommodation*, Berkeley: University of California Press

1999, *Patterns of Democracy*, New Haven: Yale University Press

Lilja, K., 1998, "Finland: No Longer the Nordic Exception," in A. Ferner and R. Hyman (eds.), *Changing Industrial Relations in Europe*, Oxford: Blackwell

Lipset, Seymour Martin and Marks, Gary, 2000, *It Didn't Happen Here: Why Socialism Failed in the United States*, New York: W. W. Norton

Locke, Richard and Baccaro, Lucio, 1996, "Learning from Past Mistakes? Recent Reforms in Italian Industrial Relations," *Industrial Relations Journal*, 27: 289–303

Lødel, Peter Henning, 1999, *Deutsche Mark Politics*, Boulder, CO: Lynne Rienner

Lødemel, I. and Trickey, H. (eds.), 2000, *"An Offer You Can't Refuse": Workfare in International Perspective*, Bristol: The Policy Press

Löwenthal, P., 1994, "Compétitivité: enjeux et politiques," *Reflets & Perspectives de la vie économique*, 38(5): 417–423

Ludlow, Peter, 1982, *The Making of the European Monetary System*, Oxford: Oxford University Press

Lundvall, Bengt-Åke and Joao-Pires, Maria (eds.), 2002, *The New Knowledge Economy in Europe: A Strategy for International Competitiveness and Social Cohesion*, Cheltenham: Edward Elgar

Lutz, Burkart, 1984, *Der kurze Traum immerwährender Prosperität*, Frankfurt M.: Campus

Luyten, D., 1995, *Sociaal-economisch overleg in België sedert 1918*, Brussels: Editions de la VUB

Luzi, Gianluca, 1999, "'Cambiamo le pensioni'," *La Repubblica*, July 15: 4

Lynch, Brendan, 2003, "Stability Pact, the Only Game in Town," *Irish Independent – Online*, June 19

Machin, Stephen and Manning, Alan, 1999, "The Causes and Consequences of Long-Term Unemployment in Europe," in Orley Ashenfelter and David Card (eds.), *Handbook of Labor Economics*, 3, Amsterdam: North-Holland

Mackie, David and Pepino, Silvia, 2003a, "Widening Growth Dispersion within the EU Area," JPMorgan Chase Bank, Economic Research Note, February 14

2003b, "Germany's Stagnation is Beyond its Control," *Financial Times*, February 27

MacManus, Susan, 1983, "State Government: The Overseer of Municipal Finance," in A. Sbragia (ed.), *The Municipal Money Chase: The Politics of Local Government Finance*, Boulder, CO: Westview Press: 145–184

Maddison, Angus, 1991, *Dynamic Forces in Capitalist Development*, Oxford: Oxford University Press

Maestri, Ezio, 1987, "La regolazione dei conflitti redistributivi in Italia: il caso della politica pensionistica (1948–1983)," *Stato e mercato*, 20: 249–279

Magnette, Paul and Remacle, Eric (eds.), 2000, *Le Nouveau modèle Européen*, 2, Brussels: Editions de l'Université Libre de Bruxelles

Magnusson, Lars and Stråth, Bo, 2001, *From the Werner Plan to the EMU: In Search of a Political Economy for Europe*, Brussels and New York, PIE–Peter Lang

Mankiw, N. Gregory, 1999, "Comments and Discussion," *Brookings Papers on Economic Activity*, 2: 237–241

Manow, Philip, 2001, "Comparative Institutional Advantages of Welfare State Regimes and New Coalitions in Welfare State Reforms," in Paul Pierson (ed.), *The New Politics of the Welfare State*, Oxford: Oxford University Press

Manow, Philip and Seils, Eric, 2000, "Adjusting Badly: The German Welfare State, Structural Change, and the Open Economy," in F. W. Scharpf and V. A. Schmidt (eds.), *Welfare and Work in the Open Economy*, II, Oxford: Oxford University Press: 264–307

Maravall, José Maria, 1993, "Politics and Policy: Economic Reforms in Southern Europe," in José Maria Maravell, *Economic Reforms in New Democracies*, New York: Cambridge University Press

March, J. and Olsen, J. P., 1989, *Rediscovering Institutions: The Organizational Basis of Politics*, New York: Free Press

Marginson, P. and Sisson, K., 1998, "European Collective Bargaining: A Virtual Prospect?," *Journal of Common Market Studies*, 36

Marglin, Steven and Schor, Juliet (eds.), 1990, *The Golden Age of Capitalism*, New York: Oxford University Press

Markovits, Andrei S., 1982, *The Political Economy of West Germany: Modell Deutschland*, New York: Praeger

Marsh, David, 1992, *The Bundesbank: The Bank That Rules Europe*, London: Heinemann

Martin, Andrew, 1997, "Social Pacts: A Means for Distributing Unemployment or Achieving Full Employment," in Giuseppe Fajertag and Philippe Pochet (eds.), *Social Pacts in Europe – New Dynamics*, Brussels: ETUI
   1999, *Wage Bargaining under EMU: Europeanization, Re-Nationalization or Americanization?*, Brussels: ETUI Discussion Paper
   2000, "Social Pacts, Unemployment and EMU Macroeconomic Policies," in G. Fajertag and Philippe Pochet (eds.), *Social Pacts in Europe – New Dynamics*, Brussels: ETUI: 365–400

Martin, Andrew and Ross, George, 1999a, "In the Line of Fire: The Europeanization of Labor Representation," in Andrew Martin and George Ross, *The Brave New World of European Labor*, New York: Berghahn Books: 312–368
   1999b, *The Brave New World of European Labor*, New York: Berghahn Books

Matsaganis, M., Capucha, L., Ferrera, M, and Moreno, L., 2003, *Mending Nets in the South, in Social Policy and Administration*, forthcoming

McKay, David, 2001, *Designing Europe: Comparative Lessons from the Federal Experience*, Oxford: Oxford University Press
   2002, "The Political Economy of Fiscal Policy under Monetary Union," in Kenneth Dyson (ed.), *European States and the Euro: Europeanization, Variation, and Convergence*, Oxford: Oxford University Press: 78–96

McNamara, K., 1998, *The Currency of Ideas: Monetary Politics in the European Union*, Ithaca, NY: Cornell University Press
   2002, "Rational Fictions: Central Bank Independence and the Social Logic of Delegation," *West European Politics*, 25(1): 47–76

Meardi, G., 2002, "The Trojan Horse for the Americanization of Europe? Polish Industrial Relations Toward the EU," *European Journal of Industrial Relations*, 8(1): 77–99

Meltzer, Allan H., 2000, "Lessons from the Early History of the Federal Reserve," Presidential Address to the International Atlantic Economic Society, Munich, March 17

Menon, A. and Richt, V. (eds.), 2001, *From the Nation State to Europe: Essays in Honour of Jack Hayward*, Oxford: Oxford University Press

Mermet, E., 2000, *Wage Formation in the European Union: A Comparative Study*, Brussels: ETUI

Metze, Marcel, 1999, *Let's Talk Dutch Now*, Amsterdam: Arbeiderspers

Meulders, D., 1994, "Union monétaire et protection sociale: le cas de la Belgique," in OSE, *Union économique et monétaire et protection sociale*, Working Paper, II, Brussels: Observatoire social européen

Michel, E., 1994, "La loi sur la compétitivité: évaluation et proposition," *Reflets & Perspectives de la vie économique*, 38(5): 395–417

Michel, E. and Denayer, L., 1997, "Marché du travail et compromis social: rétrospective et prospective," *Revue politique du CEPSS*, 2: 45–52

Middlemas, Keith, 1995, *Orchestrating Europe*, London: Fontana

Milner, Mark, 2002, "EC Rules Damage Job Creation," *Guardian Unlimited*, June 21

Milward, Alan, 1992, *The European Rescue of the Nation-State*, Berkeley: University of California Press

Ministerio de Trabajo, 1999, *Estadística de Convenios Colectivos de Trabajo, 1997–1998*, Madrid: AVANCE

    2003, *Estadística de Convenios Colectivos de Trabajo 2000–2001*, Avance, Madrid: Ministerio de Trabajo

Ministero del Tesoro, 1998a, "Rapporto sugli aspetti economico-finanziario ed attuativiinerenti alla riforma previdenziale introdotta dalla legge 8 agosto 1995, n.335," Camera dei Deputati, *Atti Parlamentari, Doc. CXXXVII, n.1*, June 2: 14–15

    1998b, *Documento de Programmazione Economica-Finanziaria, 1999–2002*, Rome

Ministry of Labour, 1998, *La politique de l'emploi en Belgique*, Brussels

Mommen, A., 1994, *The Belgian Economy in the Twentieth Century*, London: Routledge

Moran, M. and Prosser, T. (eds.), 1994, *Privatization and Regulatory Change in Europe*, Buckingham: Open University Press

Moravcsik, A., 1994, "Why the European Community Strengthens the State: Domestic Politics and International Cooperation," Center for European Studies Working Paper, 52, Cambridge, MA.: Harvard University

    1998, *The Choice for Europe*, Ithaca, NY: Cornell University Press

Moreno, L., 2000, "The Spanish Developments of the Southern Welfare State," in S. Kuhnle (ed.), *Survival of the European Welfare State*, London: Routledge: 146–165

Mouriaux, René, 1996, *Crises du Syndicalisme*, Paris: Montchrestien

Muet, Pierre-Alain and Fontaneau, Alain, 1990, *Reflation and Austerity: Economic Policy Under Mitterrand*, New York: Berg

Munchau, Wolfgang, 1998, "ECB Squares up to Finance Ministers," *Financial Times*, 10 July: 2

Myles, J. and Pierson, P., 2001, "The Comparative Political Economy of Pension Reform," in P. Pierson (ed.), *The New Politics of the Welfare State*, Oxford: Oxford University Press

Nardis, S. de and Galli, G. (eds.), 1997, *La disoccupazione italiana*, Bologna: Il Mulino

Negrelli, Stefano, 1997, "Social Pacts and Flexibility: Towards a New Balance between Macro and Micro Industrial Relations – The Italian Experience," in Giuseppe Fajertag and Philippe Pochet (eds.), *Social Pacts in Europe – New Dynamics*, Brussels: ETUI

*Newsweek*, 1976, "Germany: The Model Nation?," European edn., September 27

Newton, Kenneth (ed.), 1981, *Urban Political Economy*, London: Frances Pinter

*New York Times*, 1999a, August 13

  1999b, March 13

  1999c, November 15

  2000, March 26

Ney, Steven, 2003, "The Rediscovery of Politics: Democracy and Structural Pension Reform in Continental Europe," in Robert Holzmann, Mitchell Orenstein, and Michal Rutkowski (eds.), *Pension Reform in Europe: Process and Progress*, Washington, DC: World Bank

Nicolaidis, Kalypso and Howse, Robert (eds.), 2001, *The Federal Vision: Legitimacy and Levels of Governance in the United States and the European Union*, Oxford: Oxford University Press

Noé, C., 1998, "The Euro – Wages – Employment," *Transfer*, 4(2): 38–48

Nolan, B., O'Connell, P. J., and Whelan, C. T., 2000, *Bust to Boom: The Irish Experience of Growth and Inequality*, Dublin: Institute of Public Administration

Norman, P., 1998, "Productivity Study Shows Dangers of Euro Wage Claims," *Financial Times*, July 7

Notermans, Ton, 2000, *Money, Markets, and the State*, Cambridge University Press

  2001a, "The German Social Democrats and Monetary Union," in Ton Notermans (ed.), *Social Democrats and Monetary Union*, Oxford: Oxford University Press

  (ed.), 2001b, *Social Democrats and Monetary Union*, Oxford: Berghahn Books

*NRC Handelsblad*, 1994, February 5

  1996, June 18

  1997, February 11

OECD, 1988, *Economic Surveys: Spain*, Paris: OECD

  1992, *Economic Surveys: Spain*, Paris: OECD

  1994a, *The OECD Jobs Study: Facts, Analyses, Strategies*, Paris: OECD

  1994b, *Economic Surveys: Spain*, Paris: OECD

  1994c, "Collective Bargaining: Levels and Coverage," *Employment Outlook*, Paris: OECD

  1996, "L'expérience de l'assainissement des finances publiques dans les pays de l'OCDE," *Perspectives économiques*, Paris: OECD: 37–46

  1997, "Economic Performance and the Structure of Collective Bargaining," *Employment Outlook*, Paris: OECD

  1998, *Employment Outlook 1998*, Paris: OECD

  1999, *Employment Outlook 1999*, Paris: OECD

  2000a, "Social Expenditure Statistics of OECD Member Countries," Paris: OECD

  2000b, *Economic Surveys: Spain*, Paris: OECD

2000c, *Economic Outlook 67*, Paris: OECD

2000d, *Economic Outlook 68*, Paris: OECD

2001, "Ageing and Income: Financial Resources and Retirement in 9 OECD Countries," Paris: OECD

2003, *Etudes économiques de l'OCDE 2002–2003 – Belgique*, 2003/1, Paris: OECD

OFCE, 2002, *L'économie française 2002*, Paris: La Découverte

Offe, Claus, 1991, "Smooth Consolidation in the West German Welfare State: Structural Change, Fiscal Policies, and Populist Politics," in Frances Fox Piven (ed.), *Labor Parties in Postindustrial Societies*, Cambridge: Polity Press: 124–146

Onofri, Paolo, 1998, "Nonostante tutto, un altro pezzo di riforma del sistema pensionistico," *Politica Economica*, 14(1)

Orloff, A. S., 2001, "Gender Equality, Welfare and Employment: Cross-National Patterns of Politics and Policy," Paper presented at the RC19 Annual Conference, Oviedo University, September 6–9

OSE, 1994, *Union économique et monétaire et protection sociale*, Working Paper, 11, Brussels: Observatoire social européen

1997, *Union européenne et processus de convergence sociale*, Rapport complémentaire, Observatoire social européen (2 vols.), Brussels, mimeo

1998, "European Union and the Process of Social Convergence," *Belgian Review of Social Security*, Special Issue, Brussels

Ostheim, Tobias, 2003, "Praxis und Rhetorik deutscher Europapolitik," in Christoph Egle, Tobias Ostheim, and Reimut Zohlnhöfer (eds.), *Das rot-grüne Projekt*, Wiesbaden: Westdeutscher Verlag: 351–380

Padalino, S. and Vivarelli, M., 1997, "The Employment Intensity of Growth in the G-7 Countries," *International Labour Review*, 136(2)

Padoa-Schioppa, Tommaso, 1994, *The Road to Monetary Union: The Emperor, The Kings, The Genies*, Oxford: Oxford University Press

2000, *The Road to Monetary Union in Europe: The Emperor, the Kings, and the Genies*, New York: Oxford University Press

Padoa Schioppa Kostoris, Fiorella (ed.), 1996, *Pensioni e risanamento della finanza pubblica*, Bologna: Il Mulino

Pagoulatos, G., 1996, "Deregulation and Privatization of the Greek Banking System," *West European Politics*, 19(4)

Pakaslahti, J., 1997, "Does EMU Threaten European Welfare? Social and Political Implications of its Transitional Stage in EU Member States," Working Paper, 17, Brussels: Observatoire social européen

Pakaslahti, J. and Pochet, Philippe 2003, *The Social Dimension of the Changing European Union*, Brussels: OSE

Palier, B., 2000, "'Defrosting' the French Welfare State," in Maurizio Ferrera and Martin Rhodes (eds.), *Recasting European Welfare States*, London: Frank Cass: 113–135

2002, *Gouverner la sécurité sociale*, Paris: PUF

Palmer, Edward, 2002, "Swedish Pension Reform – How Did It Evolve and What Does It Mean for the Future?," in Martin Feldstein and Horst Siebert (eds.), *Social Security Pension Reform in Europe*, Chicago: University of Chicago Press

Palmerini, Lina, 2002, "Berlusconi: Patto dedicato a Biagi," *Il Sole 24 Ore.com*, July 6

Papitto, Franco, 2002, "Conti pubblici, ancora gelo la UE e Tremonti," *La Repubblica.it*, July 12

Parker, George and Harnischfeger, Uta, 2003, "Berlin Hopes to Share Eurozone Fines with States," *Financial Times*, April 21: 4

Pasture, P., 1993, "The April 1944 'Social Pact' in Belgium and its Significance for the Post-War Welfare State," *Journal of Contemporary History*, 28: 695–714

1996, "Belgium: Pragmatism in Pluralism," in P. Pasture *et al.*, *The Lost Perspective*, 1, Aldershot: Avebury

Pasture, P. *et al.*, 1996, *The Lost Perspective*, 1, Aldershot: Avebury

Pekkarinen, J., 2000, "Finnish Social Democrats and the EMU," in Ton Notermans (ed.), *Social Democrats and Monetary Union*, Oxford: Berghahn Books

Pérez, Sofía A., 1997, *Banking on Privilege: The Politics of Spanish Financial Reform*, Ithaca, NY: Cornell University Press

1998, "Yet the Century?: The Return to National Social Bargaining in Italy and Spain," Paper presented to the Annual Meeting of the American Political Science Association, Boston, September

1999, "From Labor to Finance: Explaining the Failure of Socialist Economic Policies in Spain," *Comparative Political Studies* 32(6)

2000a, "From Decentralization to Reorganization: Explaining the Return to National Social Bargaining in Italy and Spain," *Comparative Politics*, 32(4): 437–458

2000b, "Collective Bargaining under EMU: Lessons from the Italian and Spanish Experiences," Working Paper Series, 72, Harvard Center for European Studies, February

2002, "Monetary Union and Wage Bargaining Institutions in the EU: Extrapolating from Member State Experiences," *Comparative Political Studies*, 35(10): 1198–1227

Pesole, Dino, 1997, "Welfare, un si fra le polemiche," *Il Sole – 24 Ore*, December 18

Phelps, Edmund, 2000, "Europe's Stony Ground for the Seeds of Growth," *Financial Times*, August 9

Pierson, Paul, 1994, *Dismantling the Welfare State? Reagan, Thatcher and the Politics of Retrenchment*, Cambridge: Cambridge University Press

1996, "The New Politics of the Welfare State," *World Politics*, 48(2): 143–179

2001a, "Coping with Permanent Austerity: Welfare State Restructuring in Affluent Democracies," in Paul Pierson (ed.), *The New Politics of the Welfare State*, Oxford: Oxford University Press: 410–456

(ed.), 2001b, *The New Politics of the Welfare State*, Oxford: Oxford University Press

Pierson, Paul and Stephan Leibfried, 1995, "Multitiered Institutions and the Making of Social Policy," in Stephan Leibfried and Paul Pierson (eds.), *European Social Policy: Between Fragmentation and Integration*, Washington, DC: Brookings: 1–40

Pieters, D., Palm, W., and Vansteenkiste, S., 1993, *The Thirteenth State: Towards a European Social Insurance Scheme for Intra-Community Migrants*, Leuven: Acco

Pisani-Ferry, Jean, 2000, "Les Chemins du plein emploi," *Plein Emploi: Rapport Jean Pisani-Ferry*, Conseil d'analyse économique, 30, Paris: La Documentation française

(2002), "Fiscal Discipline and Policy Coordination in the Eurozone: Assessment and Proposals," Paper prepared for the European Commission President's Group of Economic Analysis

Piven, Frances Fox (ed.), 1991, *Labor Parties in Postindustrial Societies*, Cambridge: Polity Press

Pizzorno, Alessandro, 1978, "Political Exchange and Collective Identity in Industrial Conflict," in Colin Crouch and Alessandro Pizzorno (eds.), *The Resurgence of Class Conflict in Western Europe since 1968*, London: Macmillan

Ploeg, Frederick van der, 1998, "The Political Economy of Consensus Society," in *KVS Jaarboek 1997/98*, Rotterdam: Koninklijke Vereniging voor de Staathuishoudkunde/ESB

Pochet, Philippe, 1999a, "Conclusions and Perspectives," in Philippe Pochet (ed.), *EMU and Collective Bargaining*, Brussels: PIE–Peter Lang: 261–281

1999b, *EMU and Collective Bargaining*, Brussels: PIE–Peter Lang

2002a, "Employment, the Last Year before Change," in C. Degryse and Philippe Pochet (eds.), *Social Developments in the European Union, 2001*, Brussels: ETUI, Observatoire social européen, and SALTSA: 57–83

2002b, "Introduction," in Philippe Pochet (ed.), *Wage Policy in the Eurozone*, Brussels: PIE–Peter Lang: 15–39

(ed.), 2002c, *Wage Policy in the Eurozone*, Brussels: PIE–Peter Lang

2003, "Pensions: The European Debate," in G. L. Clark and N. Whiteside (eds.), *Pension Security in the 21st Century – Redrawing the Public–Private Debate*, Oxford: Oxford University Press

Pochet, Philippe and Fajertag, Giuseppe, 2000, "A New Era for Social Pacts in Europe," in Ginsppe Fajertag and Philippe Pochet (eds.), *Social Pacts in Europe – New Dynamics*, Brussels: ETUI: 9–40

Porte, C. de la, Pochet, Philippe, and Room, G., 2001, "Social Benchmarking, Policy-Making and New Governance in the EU," *Journal of European Social Policy*, 11/4

Prast, H. and Stokman, A., 1997, "Kosten en baten van de EMU," *Economisch Statisische Berichten*, 82

Putnam, R., 1988, "Diplomacy and Domestic Politics: The Logic of Two-Level Games," *International Organization*, 42: 427–460

Quatremer, Jean and Klau, Thomas, 1997, *Ces hommes qui ont fait l'euro*, Paris: Plon

Radaelli, C., 2000, "Whither Europeanization? Concept Stretching and Substantive Change," *European Integration Online Papers (EIOP)*: 4, 8, http://eiop.or.at/eiop.texte/2000-008a.htm

2002, "The Italian State and the Euro: Institutions, Discourse, and Policy Regimes," in Kenneth Dyson (ed.), *European States and the Euro: Europeanization, Variation, and Convergence*, Oxford: Oxford University Press: 212–237

Ratchford, B. U., 1941, *American State Debts*, Durham, MD: Duke University Press

Regalia, Ida and Marino Regini, 1996, "Italia Anni '90: Rinasce la Concertazione," *Collana Discussione*, IRES Lombardia, 23, January

1998, "Sindicati, instituzioni, sistema politico," in Gian Primo Celli and Tiziano Treu (eds.), *Le nuove relazioni industriali: l'esperienza italiana nella prospettiva europea*, Bologna: Il Mulino

Regini, Marino, 1984, "I tentativi italiani di patto sociale a cavallo degli anni ottanta," *Il Mulino*: 2

1997, "Still Engaging in Corporatism? Recent Italian Experience in Comparative Perspective," *European Journal of Industrial Relations*, 3(3)

Regini, Marino and Ida Regalia, 1996, "Italia Anni '90: rinasce la concertazione," IRES Lombardia, *Collana Discussione*, 23, January

1997, "Employers, Unions and the State: The Resurgence of Concertation in Italy?," in Martin Bull and Martin Rhodes (eds.), *Crisis and Transition in Italian Politics*, London: Frank Cass

Rehwinkel, Peter and Nekkers, Jan, 1994, *Regerenderwijs*, Amsterdam: Bert Bakker

1998, "Syndicati, istituzioni, sistemo politico," in Primo Celii and Tiziano Treu (eds.), *Le nuove relazioni industriali: l'esperienza italiana nella prospettiva europea*, Bologna: Il Mulino

Rein, Martin and Freeman, Richard, 1989, *The Dutch Choice*, The Hague: HRWB

Reman, P., 1999, "La bonne forme de la concertation sociale," *Revue Nouvelle*, May–June: 67–73

Reviglio, Franco, 1998, *Come siamo entrati in Europa*, Milano: UTET

Rhodes, Martin, 1997a, *Globalisation, Labour Markets and Welfare States: A Future of Competitive Corporatism?*, EUI Working Papers RSC, 97/36, Firenze: European University Institute

(ed.), 1997b, *Southern European Welfare States*, London: Frank Cass

2000, "Desperately Seeking a Solution: Social Democracy, Thatcherism and the 'Third Way' in British Welfare," in Maurizio Ferrera and Martin Rhodes (eds.), *Recasting European Welfare States*, London: Frank Cass: 161–185

2001, "The Political Economy of Social Pacts: 'Competitive Corporatism' and European Welfare Reforms," in Paul Pierson (ed.), *The New Politics of the Welfare State*, Oxford: Oxford University Press: 165–194

Rhodes, Martin and Mény, Yves (eds.), 1998, *The Future of European Welfare: A New Social Contract?*, London, Macmillan

Richardson, Pete, Boone, Laurence, Giorno, Claude, Meacci, Mara, Rae, David, and Turner, David, 2000, "The Concept, Policy Use and Measurement of Structural Unemployment: Estimating a Time Varying NAIRU Across 21 OECD Countries," OECD Economics Department Working Papers, 250

Riché, Pascal and Charles Wyplosz, 1993, *L'Union monétaire l'Europe*, Paris: Seuil

Risse-Kappen, Thomas, 1995, *Bringing Transnational Relations Back In: Non-State Actors, Domestic Structures and International Institutions*, Cambridge: Cambridge University Press

Rodden, Jonathan, 2002, "Strength in Numbers? Representation and Redistribution in the European Union," *European Union Politics* 3(2): 151–176

Roebroek, Joop M., 1993, *The Imprisoned State*, Tilburg: Katholieke Universiteit Brabant

Røed, Knut, 2000, "Arbeitsledighet, stabiliseringspolitikk og lønnsdannelse – Er kollektiv lønnsmoderasjon er farbar vei mot lav arbeidsledighet?," Vedleg 2, Finansdepartementet, NOU 2000: 21

Romano, Sergio, 1997, "I limiti della concertazione," *La Stampa*, November 5: 1

Romer, Christina D. and Romer, David N., 1997, *Reducing Inflation: Motivation and Strategy*, Chicago: University of Chicago Press

Rosamond, Ben, 2000, *Theories of European Integration*, New York, St. Martin's Press

Rose, A., 1999, "One Money, One Market: Estimating the Effect of Common Currencies on Trade," Working Paper, 7432, Chicago: National Bureau of Economic Research, December

Rosenow, Joachim and Naschold, Frieder, 1994, *Die Regulierung von Altersgrenzen: Strategien von Unternehmen und die Politik des Staates*, Berlin: Editions Sigma

Ross, George, 1982, *Workers and Communists in France*, Berkeley: University of California Press

1995, *Jacques Delors and European Integration*, Cambridge: Polity Press

Ross, George, Hoffmann, Stanley, and Malzacher, Sylvia, 1995, *The Mitterrand Experiment*, Cambridge: Polity Press

Rowthorn, Robert, 1995, "Capital Formation and Unemployment," *Oxford Review of Economic Policy*, 11(1): 26–39

Royo, S., 2000, *From Social Democracy to Neoliberalism: The Consequences of Party Hegemony in Spain, 1982–1996*, New York: St. Martin's Press

Ruysseveldt, J. Van and Visser, Jelle (eds.), 1996, *Industrial Relations in Europe: Traditions and Transitions*, London: Sage

Sabatier, P., 1998, "The Advocacy Coalition Framework: Revisions and Relevance for Europe," *Journal of European Public Policy* 5(1): 98–130

Sachverständigenrat zur Begutachtung der gesamtwirtschaftlichen Entwicklung, 1998, *Vor weitreichenden Entscheidungen, Jahresgutachten 1998/99*, Stuttgart: Metzler-Poeschel

Salvati, Michele, 1984, *Economia e politica in Italia dal dopoguerra a oggi*, Milan: Garzanti

1995, "The Crisis of Government in Italy," *New Left Review*, 213

Sandholtz, Wayne and Alec Stone Sweet (eds.), 1998, *European Integration and Supranational Governance*, Oxford: Oxford University Press

Saraceno, Chiara, 1994, "The Ambivalent Familism of the Italian Welfare State," *Social Politics*, Spring: 60–82

Sargent, J. (ed.), 1986, *Foreign Macro-Economic Experience*, Toronto: Toronto University Press

Saris, Willem E., 1997, "The Public Opinion about the EU Can Easily be Swayed in Different Directions," *Acta Politica*, 32

Sassoon, Donald, 1997, *One Hundred Years of Socialism*, London: Tauris

Sbragia, Alberta, 1981, "Cities, Capital, and Banks: The Politics of Debt in the USA, UK, and France," in Kenneth Newton (ed.), *Urban Political Economy*, London: Frances Pinter: 200–220

1983a, "Politics, Local Government, and the Municipal Bond Market," in Alberta Sbragia (ed.), *The Municipal Money Chase: The Politics of Local Government*, Boulder, CO: Westview Press

(ed.), 1983b, *The Municipal Money Chase: The Politics of Local Government Finance*, Boulder, CO: Westview Press

1992a, "Thinking about the European Future: The Uses of Comparison," in Alberta Sbragia (ed.), *Euro-Politics: Institutions and Policymaking in the "New" European Community*, Washington, DC: Brookings: 257–292

(ed.), 1992b, *Euro-Politics: Institutions and Policymaking in the "New" European Community*, Washington, DC: Brookings

1996, *Debt Wish: Entrepreneurial Cities, US Federalism, and Economic Development*, Pittsburgh: University of Pittsburgh Press

2001, "Italy Pays for Europe: Political Leadership, Political Choice, and Institutional Adaptation," in M. Green Cowles, James Caporaso, and Thomas Risse (eds.), *Transforming Europe: Europeanization and Domestic Change*, Ithaca, NY: Cornell University Press: 79–96

2002, "The Dilemma of Governance with Government," Jean Monnet Working Papers, 3/02: www.jeanmonnetprogram.org/papers/02/020301.html

Scharpf, Fritz W., 1987, *Sozialdemokratische Krisenpolitik in Europa*, Frankfurt M.: Campus

1988, "The Joint-Decision Trap: Lessons from German Federalism and European Integration," *Public Administration*, 66(3): 239–278

1997a, *Games Real Actors Play*, Boulder, CO: Westview Press

1997b, "Employment and the Welfare State: A Continental Dilemma," MPIfG Working Paper, 97/7, Cologne: Max Planck Institute for the Study of Societies

1999, *Governing in Europe*, Oxford: Oxford University Press

2001, "Employment and the Welfare State. A Continental Dilemma," in Bernhard Ebbinghaus and Philip Manow (eds.), *Comparing Welfare Capitalism: Social Policy and Political Economy in Europe, Japan, and the USA*, London: Routledge: 270–283

2002a, "Economic Changes, Vulnerabilities and Institutional Capacities," in Fritz W. Scharpf and V. A. Schmidt (eds.), *Welfare and Work in the Open Economy*, I, Oxford: Oxford University Press

2002b, "Notes Towards a Theory of Multilevel Governance in Europe," MPIfG Discussion Paper, 00/5, Cologne: Max Planck Institute for the Study of Societies, Cologne

2002c, "The European Social Model: Coping with the Challenges of Diversity," *Journal of Common Market Studies*, 40(4): 645–70

Scharpf, Fritz W. and Schmidt, Vivian A. (eds.), 2000, *Welfare and Work in the Open Economy*, I and II, Oxford: Oxford University Press

Schludi, M., 2001, "The Politics of Pensions in European Social Insurance Contracts," MPIfG Discussion Paper, 01/11, Cologne: Max Planck Institute for the Study of Societies, Cologne

Schmidt, Manfred G., 1987, "West Germany: The Policy of the Middle Way," *Journal of Public Policy*, 7(2): 139–177

1998, *Sozialpolitik in Deutschland: Historischer und Internationaler Vergleich*, Opladen: Leske & Budrich (ed.), 2001a, *Wohlfahrtsstaatliche Politik: Institutionen, Prozess und Leistungsprofil*, Opladen: Leske & Budrich

2001b, "Still on the Middle Way? Germany's Political Economy at the Beginning of the Twenty-First Century," *German Politics*, 10(3): 1–12

Schmidt, Vivian A., 2002, *The Futures of European Capitalism*, Oxford: Oxford University Press

forthcoming, *European Economies between Integration and Globalization: Policies, Practices, Discourses*, Oxford: Oxford University Press

Schmitter, P. W. and Streeck, W., 1992, "From National Corporatism to Transnational Pluralism: Organized Interests in the Single European Market," in W. Streeck (ed.), *Social Institutions and Economic Performance: Studies of Industrial Relations in Advanced Capitalist Economies*, London: Sage

Schroeder, Wolfgang, 1996, "Industrielle Beziehungen in Ostdeutschland: Zwischen Transformation und Standortdebatte," *Aus Politik und Zeitgeschichte*, B40, 96: 25–34

Schubert, L., 1997, "The 'European Model' for Growth and Competitiveness," Paper prepared for the conference "Creating Employment in Europe," Brussels, January 16–17

Schuit, Margreet, 1999, "Arbeidsvoorwaardenbeleid en de EMU," *White Paper FNV Bondgenoten*, Utrecht, May 12

Schulten, T., 1998, "Collective Bargaining in Metal Industry under the Conditions of European Monetary Union," in T. Kauppinen (ed.), *The Impact of EMU on Industrial Relations in the European Union*, no. 9, Helsinki: Finnish Industrial Relations Association

2000, "The European Metalworkers' Federation on the Way to a Europeanisation of Trade Unions and Industrial Relations," *Transfer*, 1: 93–103

2001, "On the Way toward Downward Competition? Collective Bargaining under the European Monetary Union," in T. Schulten and R. Bispinck (eds.), *Collective Bargaining under the Euro: Experiences from the European Metal Industry*, Brussels: ETUI: 17–37

Schulten, T. and Bispinck, R. (eds.), 2001, *Collective Bargaining under the Euro: Experiences from the European Metal Industry*, Brussels: ETUI

SCP, 1992, *Sociaal en Cultureel Rapport 1992*, The Hague

1994, *Sociaal en Cultureel Rapport 1994*, The Hague

1998, *Sociaal en Cultureel Rapport 1998*, The Hague

1999, *Sociale en Culturele Verkenningen*, The Hague

2000, *Sociaal en Cultureel Rapport 2000*, The Hague

Seixas da Costa, Francisco, 2000, Speech in the European Parliament, Strasbourg, March 15

Sen, Amartya, 1999, *Development as Freedom*, New York: Knopf

Shonfield, Andrew, 1965, *Modern Capitalism*, Oxford: Oxford University Press

Siebert, Horst, 1997, "Labor Market Rigidities: At the Root of Unemployment in Europe," *Journal of Economic Perspectives*, 11(3): 37–54

1998, "Labor Productivities and Labor Costs in Euroland," Kiel Working Paper, 866, Kiel Institute of World Economics

Siegel, Nico A., 2002, *Baustelle Sozialpolitik: Konsolidierung und Rückbau im internationalen Vergleich*, Frankfurt M.: Campus

2003, "Die politische Ökonomie der Makrokonzertierung in Deutschland: Das Beispiel Bündnis für Arbeit," in Sven Jochem and Nico A. Siegel (eds.), *Verhanglungsdemokratie, Konzertierung und wohlfartsstaatliche Reformpolitik*, Opladen: Leske & Budrich

Siegel. Nico A. and Jochen, Sven, 2000, "Der Sozialstaat als Beschäftigungsbremse? Deutschlands steiniger Weg in die Dienstleistungsgesellschaft," in Roland Czada and Hellmut Wollmann (eds.), *Von der Bonner zur Berliner Republik*, Opladen: Westdeutscher Verlag: 539–566

Simonian, Haig, 2003, "German Government to Expand on Reforms," *Financial Times*, June 19: 2

Sinn, Hans-Werner and Reutter, Michael, 2001, "The Minimum Inflation Rate for Euroland," NBER Working Paper, 8085

Sisson, K., Arrowsmith, J., Gilman, M., and Hall, M., 1998, *EMU and the Implications for Industrial Relations: A Select Bibliography*, Industrial Relations Research Unit, Warwick Business School, University of Warwick

Sisto, Alberto, 1998, "Dimenticando Ciampi," *Il Mondo*, December 24: 12

Smith, W. Rand, 1998, *The Left's Dirty Job: The Politics of Industrial Restructuring in France and Spain*, Pittsburgh: University of Pittsburgh Press

Snower, D. J. and Dehesa, G. de la (eds.), 1997, *Unemployment Policy: Government Options for the Labour Market*, Cambridge: Cambridge University Press

Solow, Robert M., 1999, "How Cautious Must the Fed Be?" in Benjamin M. Friedman (ed.), *Inflation, Unemployment, and Monetary Policy*, Cambridge, MA: MIT Press

Soskice, David, 1998, "De uitdaging: Duitse technologie, Nederlandse lonen," *Economisch Statistische Berichten*: 83

1999a, "Divergent Production Regimes: Coordinated and Uncoordinated Market Economies in the 1980s and 1990s," in Herbert Kitschelt, Peter Lange, Gary Marks, and John D. Stephens (eds.), *Continuity and Change in Contemporary Capitalism*, Cambridge: Cambridge University Press: 101–134

1999b, "The Political Economy of EMU: Rethinking the Effects of Monetary Integration in Europe," Discussion Paper, FS I 99–302, Wissenschaftszentrum Berlin für Sozialforschung, Berlin

SOU, 1996, *Sverige och EMU*, SOU, 158, Stockholm: Finansdepartementet

2002, *Stabiliseringspolitik vid svenskt medlemskap i valutaunionen*, www.finans.regeringen.se

Steinmo, S., 1996, "The New Political Economy of Taxation: International Pressures and Domestic Policy Choices," Center for Western European Studies, Working Paper, 19, Berkeley: University of California

Stokke, T. Aa., 1999, "Collective Bargaining and State Intervention in the Scandinavian Countries," *Transfer* 5: 1–2

Streeck, Wolfgang (ed.), 1992, *Social Institutions and Economic Performance: Studies of Industrial Relations in Advanced Capitalist Economies*, London: Sage

1996, "Public Power beyond the Nation-State," in Robert Boyer and Daniel Drache (eds.), *States against Markets*, London: Routledge

1997, "German Capitalism: Does It Exist? Can it Survive?," in Colin Crouch and W. Streeck (eds.), *Political Economy of Modern Capitalism: Mapping Convergence and Diversity*, London: Sage

1998, "The Internationalization of Industrial Relations in Europe: Problems and Prospects," MPI Discussion Paper, 98/2, Cologne

1999, "Competitive Solidarity: Rethinking the European Social Model," MPI Working Paper, 99/8, Cologne

Streeck, Wolfgang and Rolf Heinze, 1999, "Unausgeschöpfte Potentiale. Strategiepapier der Arbeitsgruppe Benchmarking des Bündnisses für Arbeit," *Der Spiegel*, 19, 5 October: 32

Sturm, Roland, 1990, "Die Politik der Deutschen Bundesbank," in Klaus von Beyme and Manfred G. Schmidt (eds.), *Politik in der Bundesrepublik Deutschland*, Opladen: Westdeutscher Verlag: 255–282

Svallfors, Stefan, 2003, "Welfare Regimes and Welfare Opinions: A Comparison of Eight Western Countries," *Social Indicators Research* 64(3): 495–520

Swank, D., 2001, "Political Institutions and Welfare State Restructuring: The Impact of Institutions on Social Policy Change in Developed Democracies," in Paul Pierson (ed.), *The New Politics of the Welfare State*, Oxford: Oxford University Press

Sykes, Robert, Bruno Palier, and Pauline M. Prior (eds.), 2001, *Globalization and European Welfare States*, London: Palgrave

Szász, André, 1988, *Monetaire diplomatie*, Leiden: Stenfert Kroese

1999, *The Road to European Monetary Union*, London: Macmillan

Targetti, Ferdinando, 1998, "Il governo dell'Ulivo e l'evoluzione del capitalismo italiano," *Il Mulino*, 47(380): 1037

Teague, P., 2000, "Macroeconomic Constraints, Social Learning and Pay Bargaining in Europe," *British Journal of Industrial Relations* 38(3): 429–452

Temin, Peter, 1989, *Lessons from the Great Depression*, Cambridge, MA: MIT Press

Teulings, Coen N. and Hartog, J., 1998, *Corporatism or Competition?*, Cambridge: Cambridge University Press

Teulings, Coen N., Veen, Romke van der, and Trommel, Willem, 1997, *Dilemmas van sociale zekerheid*, The Hague: Vuga

Therborn, Göran, 1989, "Nederland en de falende arbeidsmarkt," in Peter Broertjes (ed.), *Gettos in Holland*, Amsterdam: Van Gennap

Thorbecke, Willem, 2000, "A Dual Mandate of the Federal Reserve," Public Policy Brief, 60, The Jerome Levy Economics Institute of Bard College

Traxler, F., 1998, "Wage-Setting Institutions and European Monetary Union," Paper presented at the Symposium on "Institutional Requirements for European Economic Policies," Vienna, September 4–5

1999, "EMU and Wage Policies: Europeanization and Nationalization?," Paper presented at an ARENA Seminar, Oslo, January 26

Traxler, F., Blaschke, S., and Kittel, B., 2001, *National Industrial Relations in Internationalized Markets: A Comparative Study of Institutions, Change, and Performance*, Oxford: Oxford University Press

Trichet, Jean-Claude, 2001, "The Euro after Two Years," *Journal of Common Market Studies*, 39(1): 1–13

Trifiletti, R., 1999, "Southern European Welfare Regimes and the Worsening Position of Women," *Journal of European Social Policy*, 9(1)

Trommel, Willem and Veen, Romke van der, 1999, "Tien jaar sleutelen aan sociale zekerheid," *Beleid & Maatschappij*, 26

Tsebelis, G., 1994, "The Power of the European Parliament as a Conditional Agenda-Setter," *American Political Science Review*, 88: 128–142

1995a, "Conditional Agenda Setting and Decision Making Inside the European Parliament," *Journal of Legislative Studies*, 1: 65–93

1995b, "Decision Making in Political Systems: Veto Players in Presidentialism, Multicameralism and Multipartyism," *British Journal of Political Science*, 25: 289–325

Tsoukalis, Loukas, 1997, *The New European Economy Revisited*, Oxford: Oxford University Press

Twentieth Century Fund, 1974, *The Rating Game: Report of the Twentieth Century Fund Task Force on Municipal Bond Credit Ratings*, New York: Twentieth Century Fund

UNICE, 1999, *Releasing Europe's Employment Potential: Companies' Views on European Social Policy beyond 2000*, Brussels

United Nations Development Programme (UNDP), 2001, *Human Development Report 2001*, Oxford: Oxford University Press

Vandenbroucke, F., 1999, "The Active Welfare State: A European Ambition," Den Uyl Lecture, Amsterdam, December 13

Van Ewijk, Caspar *et al.*, 1980, *Economisch Beleid Uit de Klem*, Amsterdam: Sua

Van Gyes, G., De Witte, H., and van der Hallen, P., 1999, "Belgian Trade Unions in the 1990s: Does Strong Today Mean Strong in the Future?," in R. Hoffmann and J. Waddington (eds.), *Trade Unions in Europe: Facing Challenges and Searching for Solutions*, Brussels: ETUI: 105–141

Veen, Romke van der and Trommel, Willem, 1998, *The Dutch Miracle: Managed Liberalization of the Dutch Welfare State*, London: IPPR

Verdun, Amy, 1990, "Naar een economische en monetaire unie 1970–1990," Master's thesis, University of Amsterdam, Department of Political Science

2000, *European Responses to Globalization and Financial Integration: Perceptions of Economic and Monetary Union in Britain, France and Germany*, New York, St. Martin's Press

(ed.), 2002, *The Euro: European Integration Theory and Economic and Monetary Union*, Lanham, MD: Rowman & Littlefield

Villé, P. de, 1994, "La compétitivité: concepts, mesures, enjeux," *Reflets & Perspectives de la vie économique*, 36(5): 333–347

Vincent, Catherine, 2002a, "La politique contractuelle fonde-t-elle les relations sociales?," in *L'état de la France*, Paris: La Découverte

2002b, "Le coeur de la 'refondation sociale': la réforme de la négotiation collective," in *L'état de la France*, Paris: La Découverte

Viossat, Louis-Carles, 1997, "La sécurité sociale," in *La Documentation Française 1997*, Paris: La Documentation Française

Visser, Jelle, 1999, "Sociologie van het halve werk," Inaugural Lecture, Amsterdam: Amsterdam University Press

2002, "Is the European Employment Strategy the Answer?," Paper prepared for the NIG Workshop, "Governability in Post-Industrial Societies," University of Utrecht, April 26–27

Visser, Jelle and Hemerijck, Anton, 1997, *"A Dutch Miracle": Job Growth, Welfare Reform and Corporatism in the Netherlands*, Amsterdam: Amsterdam University Press

Visser, Jelle, Wessels, Wolfgang, and Wijnhoven, Rien, 1989, *Baanbrekende Politiek*, Kampen: Kok Agora

Vitali, Lucia and Mauro Visaggio, 1996, "Il regime pensionistico a ripartizione in disavanzo," in Fiorella Padoa Schioppa Kostoris (ed.), *Pensioni e risanamento della finanza pubblica*, Bologna: Il Mulino

Vos, Piet, 1991, Interview with *Financieel Dagblad*, December 31
    1998, "A Preliminary Review of the Industrial Relations Implications of Economic and Monetary Union: Executive Summary," *Warwick Papers in Industrial Relations*, University of Warwick

Vranken, J., Vanhercke, B., and Carton, L. (eds.), 1998, *20 ans CPAS, vers une actualisation du projet de société*, Leuven: ACCO

Waddington, J. and Hoffmann, R., 2000, "Trade Unions in Europe: Reform, Organisation and Restructuring," in J. Waddington and R. Hoffmann (eds.), *Trade Unions in Europe: Facing Challenges and Searching for Solutions*, Brussels: ETUI: 27–80

Wagschal, Uwe, 2000, "Maintaining Independence in Times of Fiscal Stress: Monetary Institutions in Germany," in Ludger Helms (ed.), *Institutions and Institutional Change in the Federal Republic of Germany*, London: Macmillan: 143–165

Wallace, H. and Wallace, W. (eds.), 2000, *Policy Making in the European Union*, 4th edn., Oxford: Oxford University Press

Wallace, J., Dinan, D., and O'Sullivan, M., 2001, "The Contribution of the Services Sector to the Irish Employment Miracle," in J. E. Dølvik (ed.), *At Your Service?*, Brussels: PIE–PeterLang: 231–266

Wallace, J., Turner, T., and McCarthy, A., 1998, "EMU and the Impact on Irish Industrial Relations," in T. Kaupinen (ed.), *The Impact of EMU on Industrial Relations in Europe*, Finnish Industrial Relations Association, no. 9, Helsinki

Walsh, J. I., 1994, "International Constraints and Domestic Choices: Economic Convergence and Exchange Rate Policy in France and Italy," *Political Studies*, 45: 677–688

Weber, Manfred (ed.), 1991, *Europa auf dem Weg zur Währungsunion*, Darmstadt: Wissenschaftliche Buchgesellschaft

Weede, E., 1996, *Economic Development, Social Order and World Politics*, Boulder, CO: Lynne Rienner

Wessels, Wolfgang and Linsenmann, Ingo, 2002, "EMU's Impact on National Institutions: Fusion towards a 'Gouvernance Economique' or Fragmentation?," in Kenneth Dyson (ed.), *European States and the Euro: Europeanization, Variation, and Convergence*, Oxford: Oxford University Press: 53–77

Wilensky, Harold L., 2002, *Rich Democracies*, Berkeley: University of California Press

Wilsford, David, 1991, *Doctors and The State: The Politics of Health Care in France and the United States*, Durham, MD: Duke University Press
    1996, "Reforming French Health Care Policy," in John Keeler and Martin Schain (eds.), *Chirac's Challenge*, New York: St. Martin's Press

Windmuller, John P. and de Galan, G., *Arbeidsverhoud ingen in Nederland*, 2nd edn., Utrecht, Het Spectrum

Witteloostuijn, Arjen van, 1999, *De anorexiastrategie*, Amsterdam: Arbeiderspers

Wolff, P. de and Driehuis, W., 1980, "A Description of Post War Economic Developments and Economic Policy in the Netherlands," in Richard T. Griffiths (ed.), *The Economy and Politics of the Netherlands since 1945*, The Hague: Martinus Nijhoff

Wolfson, D. J., 2001, *Theorie en toepassingen van de economische politiek*, Bussum: Coutinho

Wood, A., 1994, *North–South Trade, Employment and Inequality: Changing Fortunes in a Skill-Driven World*, Oxford: Clarendon Press

Wood, Stewart, 2001, "Labor Market Regimes under Threat?: Sources of Continuity in Germany, Britain, and Sweden," in Paul Pierson (ed.), *The New Politics of the Welfare State*, Oxford: Oxford University Press: 368–409

World Health Organization (WHO), 2000, *World Health Report 2000: Health Systems, Improving Performance*, Geneva: WHO

Wylie, Lloy 2002, "EMU: A Neo-Liberal Construction," in Amy Verdun (ed.), *The Euro: European Integration Theory and Economic and Monetary Union*, Lanham, MD: Rowman & Littlefield

Wyplosz, Charles, 2000, "Do We Know How Low Should Inflation Be?," First Central Banking Conference, ECB, November

Zanden, J. L. van and Griffiths, Richard T., 1989, *Economische geschiedenis van Nederland in de 20e eeuw*, Utrecht: Het Spectrum

Van Zanden, Jan Luiten, 1997, *Een klein land in de 20e eeuw*, Utrecht: Het Spectrum

Zaragoza, Angel, 1998, Pactos sociales, sindicatos y patronal en España, Madrid: Siglo XXI

Zeitlin, J., 2001, "Constructing Social Europe: Social Dialogue, Subsidiarity, and Open Coordination," Comment presented to the European Conference "Pour une politique européene des capacités: Un cadre de travail entre chercheurs et acteurs du dialogue social européen," sponsored by Directorate General Employment and Social Affairs, European Commission, Brussels, January 12–13

Zeitlin, J., 2003, "Introduction: Governing Work and Welfare in a New Economy," in J. Zeitlin and D. Trubek (eds.), *Governing Work and Welfare in a New Economy: European and American Experiments*, Oxford: Oxford University Press

Zeitlin, J. and Trubek, D. (eds.), 2003, *Governing Work and Welfare in a New Economy: European and American Experiments*, Oxford: Oxford University Press

Zohlnhöfer, Reimut, 2000, "Der lange Schatten der schönen Illusion: Finanzpolitik nach der deutschen Einheit, 1990–1998," *Leviathan*, 28: 14–38

2001, *Die Wirtschaftspolitik der Ära Kohl*, Opladen: Leske & Budrich

# Index of names

# Index of subjects